Business Essentials

Supporting Pearson BTEC Higher Nationals and Foundation degrees

Human Resource Management

Course Book

In this July 2013 edition:

- Full and comprehensive coverage of the key topics within the subject
- Activities, examples and quizzes
- Practical, up-to-date illustrations and case studies
- Index
- Fully up-to-date as at July 2013
- Coverage mapped to the Pearson Edexcel Guidelines for the Pearson BTEC Higher Nationals in Business

BPP
LEARNING MEDIA

Third edition July 2013
First edition 2007

Published ISBN 9781 4453 6836 8
(previous edition 9780 7517 9045 0)
e-ISBN 9781 4453 6856 6

British Library Cataloguing-in-Publication Data
A catalogue record for this book is available from the
British Library

Published by
BPP Learning Media Ltd
BPP House, Aldine Place
London W12 8AA

www.bpp.com/learningmedia

Printed in the United Kingdom by Polestar Wheatons

Hennock Road
Marsh Barton
Exeter EX2 8RP

Your learning materials, published by BPP
Learning Media Ltd, are printed on paper
obtained from traceable sustainable sources.

We are grateful to Pearson Edexcel for permission to
reproduce the Guidelines for the Pearson BTEC Higher
Nationals in Business.

BPP
LEARNING MEDIA

Contents

Introduction

BPP Learning Media's **Business Essentials** range is the ideal learning solution for all students studying for business-related qualifications and degrees. The range provides concise and comprehensive coverage of the key areas that are essential to the business student.

Qualifications in business are traditionally very demanding. Students therefore need learning resources which go straight to the core of the topics involved, and which build upon students' pre-existing knowledge and experience. The BPP Learning Media Business Essentials range has been designed to meet exactly that need.

Features include:

- In-depth coverage of essential topics within business-related subjects

- Plenty of activities, quizzes and topics for discussion to help retain the interest of students and ensure progress

- Up-to-date practical illustrations and case studies that really bring the material to life

- User-friendly uncomplicated style, of particular benefit to those for whom English is not their first language

- A glossary of terms and full index

In addition, the contents of the chapters are comprehensively mapped to the **Pearson Edexcel Guidelines**, providing full coverage of all topics specified in the Pearson BTEC Higher National qualifications in Business.

Each chapter contains:

- An introduction and a list of specific study objectives

- Summary diagrams and signposts to guide you through the chapter

- A chapter roundup, quick quiz with answers and answers to activities

BPP Learning Media's Business Essentials range is used by colleges and individual students throughout the world. Tried and tested on numerous different courses and for a variety of qualifications, the course books are ideal generic manuals for students and lecturers everywhere.

BPP Learning Media values your opinion. If you have any comments about this book, or suggestions as to how we could improve it, please e-mail the Publishing Manager, Pippa Riley, at pippariley@bpp.com.

Other titles in this series:

Mandatory core units for the Pearson BTEC Higher Nationals in Business

Unit 1	Business Environment
Unit 2	Managing Finance
Unit 3	Organisations and Behaviour
Unit 4	Marketing Principles
Unit 5	Business Law
Unit 6	Business Decision Making
Unit 7	Business Strategy
Unit 8	Research Project

Pathways for the Pearson BTEC Higher Nationals in Business (specialist units)

Units 9 and 10	Finance: Management Accounting and Financial Reporting
Units 11 and 12	Finance: Auditing and Financial Systems and Taxation
Units 13 and 14	Management: Leading People and Professional Development
Units 15 and 16	Management: Communications and Achieving Results
Units 17 and 18	Marketing Intelligence and Planning
Units 19 and 20	Marketing and Sales Strategy
Units 21 and 22	Human Resource Management
Units 23 and 24	Human Resource Development and Employee Relations
Units 25 – 28	Company and Commercial Law

Generic titles

Economics

Accounts

Business Maths

Interactive CD ROMs are also available for separate sale in support of the three generic titles.

For more information, or to place an order, please call 0845 0751 100 (for orders within the UK) or +44(0)20 8740 2211 (from overseas), e-mail learningmedia@bpp.com, or visit our website at www.bpp.com/learningmedia.

BPP
LEARNING MEDIA

Study guide

This Course Book includes features designed specifically to make learning effective and efficient.

- Each chapter begins with a summary diagram which maps out the areas covered by the chapter. There are detailed summary diagrams at the start of each main section of the chapter. You can use the diagrams during revision as a basis for your notes.

- After the main summary diagram there is an introduction, which sets the chapter in context. This is followed by learning objectives, which show you what you will learn as you work through the chapter.

- Throughout the Course Book, there are special aids to learning. These are indicated by symbols in the margin:

 Signposts guide you through the book, showing how each section connects with the next.

 Definitions give the meanings of key terms. The *glossary* at the end of the book summarises these.

 Activities help you to test how much you have learned. An indication of the time you should take on each is given. Answers are given at the end of each chapter.

 Topics for discussion are for use in seminars. They give you a chance to share your views with your fellow students. They allow you to highlight gaps in your knowledge and to see how others understand concepts. If you have time, try 'teaching' someone the concepts you have learned in a session. This helps you to remember key points and answering their questions will consolidate your own knowledge.

 Examples relate what you have learned to the outside world. Try to think up your own examples as you work through the Course Book.

 Chapter roundups present the key information from the chapter in a concise summary. Useful for revision and to consolidate knowledge.

 Quick quizzes are designed to help you revise and consolidate your knowledge. They test what you have learned (the answers often refer you back to the chapter so you can look over subjects again).

- The wide **margin** on each page is for your notes. You will get the best out of this book if you interact with it. Write down your thoughts and ideas. Record examples, question theories, add references to other pages in the Course Book and rephrase key points in your own words.

- At the end of the book, there is a glossary of definitions, a bibliography where appropriate and an index.

Part A

Human resource management

Chapter 01

The development of HRM

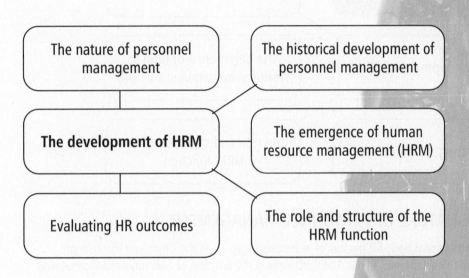

- The nature of personnel management
- The historical development of personnel management
- **The development of HRM**
- The emergence of human resource management (HRM)
- Evaluating HR outcomes
- The role and structure of the HRM function

Introduction

It can be argued that people are an organisation's most important resource: after all, organisations are made up of people, and the way money, technology, information and other resources are used depends on human decisions. So it is generally recognised that the success of any business is greatly influenced by the calibre and attitude of the people who work for it.

It is, therefore, also commonly recognised that *someone* in every organisation will need to be responsible for the many matters that arise in connection with the recruitment, selection, training, motivation, payment and movement of staff through the organisation, as well as compliance with the various laws relating to employment. This is traditionally the role of the personnel function.

However, as the pace of social and technological change has quickened, there has been a growing recognition that thought must be given to managing the vital human resource at an earlier stage and at a higher level of organisational planning than has previously been the case. This has encouraged a longer-term, more proactive and strategic approach to people management, known as 'Human Resource Management' or HRM. In this chapter, we trace the development of this approach, while in Chapter 8, we explore its implications further, as an introduction to some key issues in HRM.

Your objectives

In this chapter you will learn about the following.

- The historical development of personnel management
- The shift towards 'human resource management' as an alternative approach
- The role and tasks of the human resource management (HRM) function
- The involvement of line managers in human resource practices

1 THE NATURE OF PERSONNEL MANAGEMENT

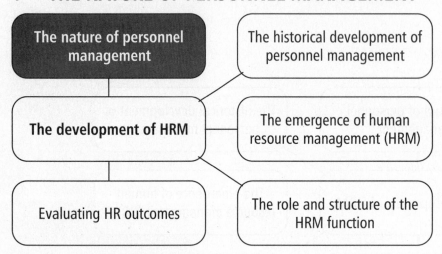

1.1 THE NATURE OF PERSONNEL MANAGEMENT

The main professional body for personnel managers in the UK is the Chartered Institute of Personnel and Development (CIPD). The CIPD defines the function of personnel management as follows.

DEFINITION

'Personnel management' is that part of management concerned with people at work and with their relationships within an enterprise...'

'[Personnel management's] aim is to bring together, and develop into an effective organisation, the men and women who make up an enterprise, having regard for the well-being of the individual and of working groups, to enable them to make their best contribution to its success.

'In particular, personnel management is concerned with the development and application of policies governing:

- Human resources planning, recruitment, selection, placement and termination
- Education and training; career development
- Terms of employment, methods and standards of remuneration
- Working conditions and employee services
- Formal and informal communication and consultation both through the representatives of employers and employees and at all levels throughout the enterprise

- Negotiation and application of agreement on wages and working conditions; procedures for the avoidance and settlement of disputes.

'Personnel management must also be concerned with the human and social implication of change in internal organisation and methods of working, and of economic and social changes in the community.'

This statement highlights a number of useful – and potentially controversial – ideas about personnel management.

(a) It is centrally concerned with **people and relationships**. It is founded on attempts to understand and manage human behaviour: we will encounter some of these attempts – in the form of theories of learning, motivation and so on – in later chapters of this Course Book. It also involves a moral or ethical dimension: the employment relationship has 'human and social implications', raising issues of human dignity, fairness and corporate social responsibility.

(b) It embraces not only 'soft' values to do with the well-being of people at work, but also 'hard' values to do with the **success of the enterprise**: the role of people and relationships in fostering efficiency, effectiveness and contribution. (These 'soft' and 'hard' perspectives, and HRM's role in seeking a 'fit' between them, are discussed in Part B of this Course Book.)

(c) It is a **'part of management'**. Organisation of the personnel function may require a specialist department or departments, but it has been suggested that a separate function need not exist: *all* managers in an organisation need to achieve results through the efforts of other people, and must therefore manage the employment relationship.

ACTIVITY 1   (30 MINS)

Check out the websites of two or three Professional HR associations, such as:

www.cipd.co.uk   Chartered Institute of Personnel & Development (UK)

www.shrm.org   Society for Human Resource Management (USA)

www.ahri.com.au   Australian Human Resources Institute

www.jshrm.org   Japan Society for Human Resource Management (you may have to use the translation tool in Google)

Browse through their home and mission statement pages, noting any useful definitions of 'personnel management' and 'Human Resource Management', and any statements of the philosophy underlying these concepts. How (and why) are people seen as important to the success of business? What cultural differences (if any) can you notice? What kinds of activity are seen as part of the personnel/HR professional's role?

2 THE HISTORICAL DEVELOPMENT OF PERSONNEL MANAGEMENT

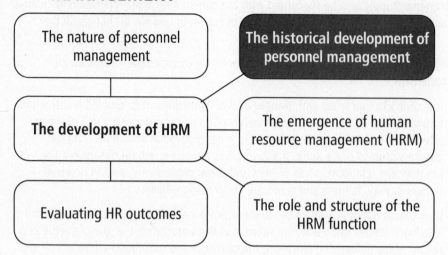

Tyson & Fell (1986) suggest that personnel management has its roots in four traditions, arising from developments in the employment environment over the last 150 years.

- The welfare tradition
- The industrial relations tradition
- The control of labour tradition
- The professional tradition

2.1 THE PERSONNEL PRACTITIONER AS WELFARE WORKER

It is generally agreed that the personnel function can be traced back to the benevolent attempts by some employers in the latter half of the 19th century to improve the working conditions and circumstances of workers, who had been hit hard by the first wave of industrialisation and urbanisation. Victorian entrepreneurs in the UK such as Rowntree, Cadbury and Lever initiated programmes providing such facilities as company housing, basic health care, canteens and education for workers' families, managed on behalf of the employer by 'industrial welfare workers'.

There was a dual motivation for these measures.

- They reflected a wider programme of **social reform and philanthropy**, led by political and religious movements of the day. Groups such as the Quakers, who in the USA were leaders in the abolition of slavery, strove to integrate successful business performance with the social, moral and spiritual betterment of their workers. (This may seem unduly paternalistic today, but at the time brought much-needed improvements in the quality of working life and the legal protection of workers.)

- Improved health and education, and the appreciation of their beneficiaries, secured an on-going pool of **suitable and willing labour** for the employer. Cadbury considered welfare and efficiency as 'two sides of the same coin' at his model factory at Bournville.

Nevertheless, the **welfare tradition** of personnel management arose from the time when much of the work and responsibility of the personnel officer was directed to the benefit of the employees, rather than to the strategic concerns of the enterprise and its management. Personnel management was in a sense the 'soft' or person-centred part or side of management. In specialised areas of personnel management today, such as occupational health, employee assistance schemes, workplace counselling services and so on, elements of this tradition persist with some force. However, as we see below, the personnel officer is not in any formal sense the representative of the workforce: (s)he is paid to be part of the organisation's management team, as both representative and adviser.

2.2 THE PERSONNEL PRACTITIONER AS INDUSTRIAL RELATIONS NEGOTIATOR

From the mid-19th century, the newly industrialised workers were also becoming increasingly organised. The legalisation of trade unions in 1871 raised the need for systematic frameworks for negotiation, conflict resolution and the management of relations between labour and employers.

The increasingly active role taken by labour organisations was reflected in political recognition. The Labour Party was formed in 1906, largely out of, and funded by, the trades union movement.

The industrial relations tradition of personnel management arose in response to the growing power of trade unions through to the 1960s and '70s, when much of the work and responsibility of the personnel officer involved mediating between the sides in industrial disputes, facilitating collective bargaining and negotiation, and ensuring compliance with industrial relations law and regulation.

Elements of this tradition may persist in the modern era in the perceptions of personnel officers and other parties to negotiations, conflict resolution, discipline and grievance procedures and so on. The 'diplomatic' role of personnel may also pose a dilemma of dual allegiance – particularly where there is lack of trust in the relationship between the personnel function and other members of the management team.

ACTIVITY 2 (20 MINS)

Whose 'side' is the personnel practitioner on? From your own experience or current knowledge of what a personnel officer does, suggest three examples of the conflict which might exist between his or her position as a member of the management team and his or her special relationship with the workforce, and discuss what you feel are the issues involved. Where would *you* stand on these issues?

2.3 THE PERSONNEL PRACTITIONER AS BUREAUCRAT

Meanwhile, in the boom following the industrial revolution, businesses had been growing larger and more complex. The '**control of labour**' tradition of personnel management arose in response to the increasing pace of organisational growth and change. The primary responsibility of the personnel officer came to be seen as supporting management by standardising, monitoring and controlling the range and complexity of workplace activity. This involved a range of activities such as: job allocation and performance monitoring; time-keeping and control of absenteeism; recording sick leave and holidays; administering pay and benefits, training and promotion; devising rules, regulations and compliance checklists; preparing workforce-related reports and returns and so on.

This is an essentially bureaucratic tradition, which is still evident in many personnel departments. It has been perpetuated, in part, by the ambiguity of personnel's perceived role and authority in the management team: where a department lacks direct positional or 'line' authority, the application of rules, regulations, procedures and forms is one of the key methods of exercising influence.

2.4 THE PERSONNEL PRACTITIONER AS PROFESSIONAL

The latter half of the 20th century saw a period of intense legislation in all areas of employment: health and safety, employment protection, equal opportunities and so on. (This has continued in the early 2000s, largely driven by the requirement to implement European social policy and EU Directives.)

The increasing complexity of legislation and regulation, together with the development of increasingly sophisticated behavioural and managerial theory, fostered **specialism** within the personnel function. The need for a specialised body of knowledge – drawing on law, economics, administrative management and the social sciences (sociology, psychology and so on) led to the establishment of a scheme of education and qualification, and the professionalisation of the work of the personnel practitioner.

Personnel management became recognised as a discipline in its own right, broadly applicable to all fields of employment. The Institute of Personnel Management (now the CIPD) made determined efforts to establish personnel management as a profession, through a programme of learning and examinations leading to qualification; opportunities for professional communication and networking; and requirements for continuing professional development.

EXAMPLE   TEAM PLAYERS WITH ENERGY AND VISION

Business Partner

My client is seeking an HR Business Partner to provide excellent front line generalist support across a complex and high profile business unit. The role will involve the individual working as a member of the management team with the experience and gravitas to challenge and support the business in an appropriate and effective manner.

The role responsibilities will include working in partnership with business leaders to align the people agenda and priorities to support the business strategy, building credibility with a key client base by becoming competent and fluent in the business service offerings. You will work with the wider HR community to meet business requirements and provide HR support on key business transformation programmes from inception through to implementation.

IT Systems Trainer

Reporting into the Training Manager, you will be responsible for designing, creating and delivering IT training solutions to system users within a designated client group, which will include staff within stores, retail support teams, support offices and the manufacturing and distribution sites. This role delivers training through a variety of Learning and Development interventions, to ensure high quality and relevant training to all systems users within the business, having minimal impact on store/business performance and to enable high performance.

HR Administrator

Reporting to the company HR Manager, the successful candidate will provide professional and proactive administration support. The ideal candidate will need to be results driven with a commitment to achieve against tight deadlines and have a positive and resilient attitude. On a daily basis you will be working closely with the HR manger in the production and development of appropriate HR policies and procedures, you will also carry our HR inductions for all new starters, deal with employee relations case management including note taking and the administration of grievance and disciplinary cases.

(Jobs advertised on the *People Management* website 2012)

ACTIVITY 3   (20 MINS)

Analyse the recruitment advertisements shown in the example above, in terms of the four 'traditions' of personnel management discussed above. What elements of each tradition can be seen, if any? Which key words stand out as foreign to these traditions, and what do they suggest about the organisation, its environment and the role of personnel management within it?

2.5 A SHIFT IN PERCEPTION OF THE PERSONNEL MANAGEMENT ROLE

By the 1950s, the personnel function appeared to have developed as 'a collection of incidental techniques without much internal cohesion': 'partly a file clerk's job, partly a housekeeping job, partly a social worker's job and partly "fire-fighting" to head off union trouble or to settle it.' (Drucker, 1955)

There was a widespread perception of personnel management as an essentially **reactive** – even defensive – role: avoiding or settling industrial disputes, preventing accidents and ill-health (and their associated costs) and so on.

Figure 1.1 illustrates this traditional perception of the role of the personnel function in the organisation.

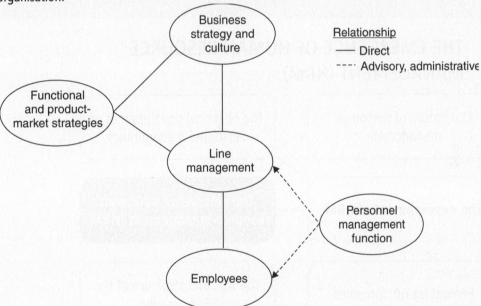

Figure 1.1: The personnel function in the organisation

The profession was becoming increasingly aware, however, that as long as personnel policy and practice were divorced from the strategy of the business, and failed to be proactive and constructive, personnel management would continue to be perceived by line management as having little to do with the 'real' world of business management and the 'bottom line' (profitability). Personnel specialists were commanding scant respect as business managers, and their influence continued to be limited to areas of little strategic impact.

A typical call, from the professional literature of the 1980s and '90s, was:

'The real requirement is **proactive** and **constructive**, rather than **defensive** and **reactive**. To discharge their true role, personnel managers must anticipate the needs of the organisation in the short and the long term. They must develop the policies to produce solutions to anticipated problems resulting from the external and internal environment, whilst influencing and creating the attitudes amongst employees needed for the enterprise's survival and success.' (Livy, 1988)

FOR DISCUSSION

'People may be regarded as a vital resource – at least plenty of lip service is paid to this concept by company chairmen in their annual statement – but many managers find it difficult to appreciate where the personnel department fits in, except in the simplest terms as a procurement (recruitment) and fire-fighting function.'

Role-play a discussion between the company CEO or line manager (in a field of your choice: say, Marketing or IT) and the personnel manager: what is the personnel function really *for,* from their respective points of view?

SIGNPOST

We have highlighted some of the key sources of discontent with the role of the traditional personnel function: its reactive/defensive (rather than proactive/constructive) nature, and its perceived irrelevance to the strategic and performance concerns of the business. We now look at some further factors which prompted a re-evaluation of the role of personnel management, and the emergence of the new term 'human resource management'.

3 THE EMERGENCE OF HUMAN RESOURCE MANAGEMENT (HRM)

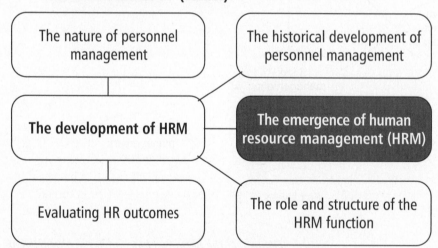

3.1 CONTEXT FOR A SHIFT IN PERSPECTIVE

Throughout the 20th century, new models and theories of **organisation and management** had been emerging to reflect the accelerating pace of change in the business environment, the diversity and expectations of workers and consumers, and the increasing sophistication of work psychology. The commitment, involvement and flexibility of the workforce was increasingly recognised as a key to organisational survival, challenging the personnel function to become involved in concerns of broader relevance to the business and its objectives.

(a) The management of change and changing business processes and structures (including the globalisation of business, and the advent of 'virtual organisations' enabled by Information and Communications Technology developments such as the internet)

(b)   Planning for long-term demographic challenges, such as the falling birthrate, increased immigration and skill shortages in the pool of available labour

(c)   Creating attractive 'employer brands' in the labour marketplace

(d)   Empowering workers; facilitating team-working and flexible working methods

(e)   Managing increasing diversity in the workforce: supporting equality of opportunity, developing family-friendly policies and so on

(f)   Creating and adapting organisational culture as a key to mobilising employee loyalty, commitment and creativity

Intensifying business competition was likewise demanding that personnel management justify itself in terms of **contribution** to the organisation's goals for growth, competitive gain and the improvement of bottom line performance. The payroll costs of many organisations today are of such magnitude (30-80% of total expenses) that senior managers must be concerned with human resources!

In the **social environment**, advances in education, technological skills and general affluence had raised employees' expectations of the quality of working life and awareness of their rights within the employment relationship. The need to compete in innovative, technology – and quality-sensitive markets put a premium on skilled **knowledge workers**, altering the balance of power in the employment relationship. Coercive and controlling psychological contracts of employment are no longer the norm (other than in very stable markets and/or areas of high unemployment): employees expect to have access to influence, responsibility and information related to their work. There has been a shift from **compliance** to **commitment** as the core of the psychological contract.

DEFINITION

A **psychological contract** is the set of values that determines what an organisation expects of its employees, and what they expect of it, in the employment relationship.

Politically, the UK government of the 1980s encouraged a shift away from trade union power and collective bargaining, instead emphasising entrepreneurialism, individualism and a 'unitary' which assumed that management and employees shared a common interest in the success of the enterprise. It seemed possible that industrial conflict and collective negotiation could be pre-empted – and ultimately replaced – by proactive people-focused personnel strategies such as participation and information-sharing.

Meanwhile, the popularity of the American anecdotal literature focusing on 'excellence' (for example, *In Search of Excellence* by Peters and Waterman) associated the success of high-performing companies with enlightened, people-focused management practices.

'All the **value** of this company is in its people. If you burnt down all of our plants and we just kept our people and information files, we would soon be as strong as ever. Take away our people and we might never recover.'

(Tom Watson, former president of IBM, quoted in Peters and Waterman, 1982)

This represented a conceptual shift away from regarding employees as a cost to be managed and controlled, and towards regarding them as an **asset** (or 'human **capital**') to be nurtured and developed. A former IBM President, Barry Curnow, further noted in the late 1990s that: 'We've moved through periods when money has been in short supply and when technology has been in short supply. Now it's the people who are in short supply. So personnel directors are better placed than ever before to make a real difference – a bottom-line difference. The **scarce resource**, which is the people resource, is the one that makes an impact at the margin, that makes one firm competitive over another.'

A variety of research studies has attempted to support the anecdotal evidence with hard data. Although the link to **business performance** is by no means clear cut, there is broad agreement that a greater use of 'human resource practices' (notably those focused on securing employee skills, motivation/commitment and flexible working) is associated with positive employee attitudes, higher levels of productivity and higher quality of service.

3.2 THE EMERGENCE OF HUMAN RESOURCE MANAGEMENT (HRM)

DEFINITION

Human Resource Management (HRM) may be defined as: 'a strategic approach to managing employment relations which emphasises that leveraging people's capabilities is critical to achieving sustainable competitive advantage, this being achieved through a distinctive set of integrated employment policies, programmes and practices.'   (Bratton & Gold, 2007)

As this definition suggests, the term HRM is often associated with both:

(a)   An orientation towards **personnel management**, viewing its role as proactive, system-wide interventions, linking HRM with strategic planning and cultural change

(b)   An orientation towards the **employment relationship**, embracing distinctive people-centred values such as trust, commitment, involvement and collaboration

The term Human Resource Management (HRM) gained recognition in the USA in the early 1980s as a label for the way certain blue-chip companies such as IBM, Xerox and Hewlett Packard were managing their people. The terms and its implications were subsequently explored by UK writers including David Guest, Karen Legge and John Storey, in the late 1980s and early 1990s. Despite heated debate about the nature, impact and morality of HRM (discussed briefly in Paragraph 3.5 below), the term has had widespread adoption in the last few years, and many of its underlying assumptions are now being incorporated into personnel management policy and practice.

3.3 CHARACTERISTICS OF HRM

The main features of HRM may be summed up as follows (Armstrong, 2009).

(a)   The attempt to achieve **strategic 'fit'** or integration between HR and business planning: HR policy should be formulated at the strategic level, and directly related to the organisation's competitive and value-adding objectives. (This may be called *'vertical'* integration.)

(b)   The development of coherent, mutually-supporting **HR policies and practices**: the strategic management of people will be reflected in all areas and systems of HRM. (This may be called *'horizontal'* integration.)

(c)   An orientation towards **commitment**: securing employee identification with the organisation's goals and values, not mere compliance with directives. This is often associated with management practices such as flexibility, teambuilding, empowerment, involvement and the creation of strong cultural values.

(d)   The **treatment of people as assets** rather than costs: regarding employees 'as a source of competitive advantage and as **human capital** to be invested in through the provision of learning and development opportunities'. This is often associated with a strong emphasis on the delivery of quality and customer satisfaction, and on rewarding performance, competence, contribution and added value.

(e)   A **unitarist approach to employee relations,** which assumes that there need be no inherent conflict of interest between employers and employees. This is often reflected in a shift from collective/representative to more individual employee relations.

(f)   The responsibility of **line management** for delivery of HRM objectives.

EXAMPLE	SELFRIDGES

'The **Selfridges** story is one of reinvention and growth, in which people management has played a vital role in creating a highly successful retail chain... One of the [new management] team's first critical choices was to decide what sort of retailer it should be – and how its people management should support that identity.

'Selfridges now markets itself as the "house of Brands", with its own strong image based on that presumption. In transforming its employment culture to complement the change, it adopted a series of new HR initiatives. It conducted culture surveys, organised focus groups and replaced its old Hay job evaluation scheme with a broadbanding pay arrangement. The Trafford Park store in Manchester... put great emphasis on communication, training and development.

'Behind all these innovations, Selfridges made an explicit effort to model the underlying stakeholder values required in its dealings with customers, employees, the local community, suppliers and other stakeholders. These values were expressed under four goals: to be "aspirational, friendly, accessible and bold"...

'Staff turnover, particularly in the first few years [of the Manchester store] was high... but the company did cut it from 78% in 2000 to 40% in 2001. There is a heavy reliance on part-time staff, making it more expensive to develop a sophisticated HR system, and another complication is that a large number of the sales associates are concession staff. The values matrix includes the statement "My concession staff are treated well and made to feel welcome". In practice, this means that they join the Selfridges sales teams, take the same training and are included in company communications...

'Staff at Selfridges displayed one of the highest levels of commitment out of the 12 organisations in our research. The factors they particularly linked to job satisfaction, motivation and commitment were challenging work; job security; teamwork; career opportunities; appraisal; and, most of all, communication, involvement and the way their managers managed.'

(Purcell *et al*, 2003)

In his influential work, Guest (1989) defined the four key policy goals of HRM as follows.

(a)   **Strategic integration** – 'the ability of organisations to integrate HRM issues into their strategic plans, to ensure that the various aspects of HRM cohere and for line managers to incorporate an HRM perspective into their decision-making.' This can be depicted as shown in Figure 1.2: compare this model with that shown in Figure 1.1.

(b)   **High commitment** – people must be managed in a way that ensures both their genuine 'behavioural' commitment to pursuing the goals of the organisation and their 'attitudinal' commitment, reflected in strong identification with the enterprise.

(c)   **Flexibility** – HRM policies must be structured to allow maximum flexibility for the organisation, so it can respond to ever-changing business needs: for example, by

encouraging functional versatility in employees and by creating 'an adaptable organisational structure with the capacity to manage innovation'. (This has since been further supported by technological developments such as laptops and the internet, allowing widely dispersed units and individuals to collaborate 'virtually' and on the move.)

(d)   **High quality** – the notion of quality must run through everything the organisation does, 'including the management of employees and investment in high-quality employees, which in turn will bear directly on the quality of the goods and services provided.'

The main conceptual difference between HRM and personnel management is, arguably, its focus on strategic integration.

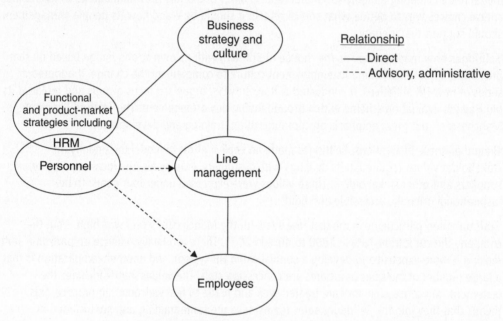

Figure 1.2: HRM: The strategic integration of personnel management

However, some commentators (Armstrong, 2009; Guest, 1989; Legge 1989) have suggested that that there are more similarities than differences between personnel management and HRM – and that HRM should perhaps been seen rather as a particular orientation to personnel management than as an alternative approach.

SIGNPOST

We discuss different perspectives on HRM itself in Chapter 8, where the ambiguities of the approach are explored in more detail.

ACTIVITY 4   (30 MINS)

Think of the business context(s) you are familiar with, or arrange to conduct a brief informal or telephone interview with any personal contacts you may have in the HR/Personnel field.

(a)   What label is given to the personnel management function in the organisation?

(b)   Is the term 'HRM' used – and if so, what is it understood to mean?

(c)   If the name 'HRM' was adopted in place of 'Personnel Management' (or something similar), how was this reflected in changes of philosophy, policy and practice?

(d)   Why do you think the name of the function might matter?

3.4 21ST CENTURY HRM?

Tyson (2006) suggests that the first decade of the 21st century has seen further – and more pronounced – changes to the way HR work is conducted, including:

(a)   The adoption of the **business partner** model (Figure 1.3), requiring HR specialists to operate effectively across a range of dimensions, as the desirable position for HR.

(b)   An increasing **consultancy orientation**, seeking to balance HR's roles in supporting – but also, where necessary challenging and changing – corporate strategy and practice. Among other effects, this has placed a premium on skills in organisational diagnosis, facilitation and coaching.

The business partner model (Figure 1.3) represents HR as operating across four key business dimensions: strategic and operational, processes and people.

Strategic

HR as: Strategic Partner	*HR as:* Change Agent

Processes ─────────────────────────── **People**

HR as: Administrative Experts	*HR as:* Employee Champions

Figure 1.3: The business partner model (adapted from Tyson, 2006)

'A business process focus with a strong strategic intent, coupled with the capacity to act as change agents may be one determinant, but HR specialists must show they can perform at the operational level as well, or they will never be given the chance to play the bigger strategic game.' (Tyson, *ibid.*)

FOR DISCUSSION

Tyson raises some interesting questions about this model.

•   Is it the role of HR to act as 'employee champions' – or is this only applicable in a North American context (where trade unions have less power than in Western Europe, say)?

•   Can an HR director be both a 'strategic partner' and a 'change agent'? What if it is the corporate strategy that needs changing?

Tyson summarises the **range of models** now embraced within HRM (which also reflect variation in the extent to which firms have adopted a full-blown HRM approach) as follows, showing progressive development from left to right.

	Administration	IR Systems	Business manager	Consultancy
Role	• Support to line management	• Policy	• Strategic	• Internal consultancy service
Focus	• Welfare • Personnel services • Records/ procedures • Unitary relations	• Industrial relations • Procedures/ systems • Rules • Pluralist relations	• Integration with corporate strategy • Business case/ relevance	• Service agreements • Projects • OD/change • External networks • Balanced interests
Objectives	• Service need of managers/ individuals	• Harmony • Legal compliance	• Results • Employee commitment	• Enable change • Organisational flexibility
Job title	• Welfare officer • Employment manager	• IR manager • Labour officer • Personnel manager	• HR manager (or director)	• Change manager • HR director

WEBLINK

CIPD 2011 Factsheet on HR Business Partnering.

▶▶ www.cipd.co.uk/hr-resources/factsheets/hr-business-partnering.aspx

3.5 ONGOING DEBATE ABOUT 'HRM'

The concept and terminology of HRM have fuelled ongoing debate among academics and practitioners.

(a) **Is HRM (in practice) really different from 'personnel management'?** The terms are often used interchangeably. One point of view is that 'HRM' is a term which practitioners have seized upon and applied to themselves, in the interests of their individual and professional status – whether or not they are in fact doing anything more than traditional personnel management: 'old wine in new bottles'. Another point of view, however, is that by continually focusing debate on the nature of the employment relationship and its role in business performance, HRM – whatever terminology is used – has helpfully altered both the orientation and practice of management and the expectation and experience of working life.

(b) **Is HRM a fair and ethical way to manage people?** One viewpoint is that HRM policies are merely a more subtle, psychologically-based form of manipulation than authoritarian or bureaucratic control. Another reservation is that acknowledging the importance of people in business success may simply be a more acceptable 'spin' on using or exploiting employees as a means to an end. 'Sadly, in a world of intensified competition and scarce resources, it seems inevitable that, as employees are used as a means to an end, there will be some who will miss out.' (Legge, 1998) On the other hand, 'it could be argued that if organisations exist to achieve ends, which they clearly do, and if those ends can only be achieved through people, which is clearly the case, the concern of managements for commitment and performance from those people is not unnatural. What matters is *how* managements treat people as ends and *what* managements provide in return.' (Armstrong, 2009)

(c) **Does it really make a difference to organisational performance?** Major research for the CIPD by Purcell, Kinnie and Hutchinson (2003) argue that 'organisations that support their employees by developing effective policies based on ability, motivation and opportunity will create higher levels of organisational commitment, motivation and job satisfaction', which in turn 'give (employees) the chance to help make their team, section and company better'.

However, there is a recognised argument that the piecemeal adoption of HR practices means that many organisations miss out on the perceived potential benefits if an integrated approach were to be taken, Marchington and Wilkinson (2008). So there is a disjunction between what senior management believe to be the role of the HR function, and the role it actually plays

FOR DISCUSSION

Set up a discussion or debate about any one of the three questions cited above, and justify the alternative points of view given (or your own viewpoints on the questions.

SIGNPOST

Having explored the nature of HRM, we now gather together some ideas on what HR practitioners typically do in practice, and how they operate within the organisation.

4 THE ROLE AND STRUCTURE OF THE HRM FUNCTION

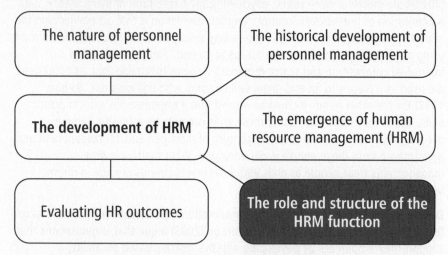

4.1 OPERATIONAL TASKS AND ACTIVITIES

The range of tasks and activities commonly carried out by human resource practitioners includes the following.

Organisation	• *Organisational design:* structuring the organisation, by grouping activities, assigning accountabilities and establishing communication and authority relationships
	• *Organisational development:* planning and implementing interventions in the organisation's social processes to improve effectiveness through techniques such as structural change, team-building, process consultancy, interpersonal skill development and role negotiation
	• *Job/role design and definition:* structuring the content and size of jobs (for efficient task performance, flexibility and worker satisfaction) and defining their component tasks, conditions and competency requirements (for recruitment, appraisal, reward and a number of other HR processes)
	• *Flexible working:* planning and implementing flexible structures and procedures to maximise the efficiency and adaptability of the organisation
Human resource planning and resourcing	• *Human resource planning:* forecasting the organisation's future requirements for labour, skills and competences, and planning to meet them through subsidiary plans for recruitment, deployment, development, retention and so on
	• *Talent management:* Ensuring that the organisation attracts, retains, motivates and develops the talented people it needs: the overall process of recruitment, integration, performance management, training and development and employee retention
	• *Recruitment:* Attracting employment applications from the number, type and calibre of people required by the HR plan

	• *Selection:* Assessing and selecting suitable employees from applicants
	• *Retention:* Planning rewards and incentives to control labour turnover and retain high quality staff
	• *Exit management:* managing the termination of contracts, retirements, resignations, dismissals and redundancies, in such a way as to comply with legal requirements and minimise human and financial costs
Performance management	• *Objective and competence requirement setting:* developing and agreeing frameworks of organisational, unit and individual goals to direct and motivate performance
	• *Performance monitoring and appraisal:* on-going monitoring and periodic assessment of performance within agreed requirements
	• *Discipline handling:* managing informal and formal processes to confront employee behaviour or performance which falls below organisational rules and standards
	• *Grievance handling:* managing informal and formal processes to address individual employee grievances or complaints
	• *Identifying learning and development needs:* as part of continuous improvement of performance
Reward management	• *Pay systems:* developing and managing salary structures, systems and scales that are equitable, fair and compliant with equal pay legislation
	• *Performance pay systems:* developing and managing ways of relating pay progression or bonuses to results, attainments (eg competence or skill), effort and other measures of performance
	• *Benefit schemes:* developing and managing employee entitlements (eg pensions, maternity and sick pay, annual leave) and 'fringe' benefits (eg allowances and services)
	• *Non-financial rewards:* building non-monetary rewards (such as recognition, challenge, personal development) into job design and management style, as part of a 'total reward' package
Human resource development	• *Learning organisation:* creating a culture and systems to support individual and organisational learning, information gathering and sharing and so on
	• *Education and training:* planning, implementing and evaluating on- and off-the-job learning opportunities and programmes to meet identified gaps in the skills required by the HR plan
	• *Personal development:* facilitating individual learning plans

	and opportunities, beyond the immediate job (eg for general employability) • *Career management:* identifying potential and planning career development opportunities; succession and promotion planning; guiding and mentoring individuals in career planning • *Managerial development:* providing education, training and opportunities to develop managerial competencies and support enhanced contribution
Health, safety and welfare	• *Occupational health and safety:* monitoring and managing work environments, practices and culture to ensure that employees are protected from health hazards and accidents; complying with relevant legislation; actively promoting health, fitness and 'work-life balance' to improve the wellbeing and performance of staff • *Welfare services:* providing services such as catering or recreational facilities, individual counselling and support (eg for illness, forthcoming redundancy or retirement, personal health problems)
Employee relations	• *Industrial relations:* managing informal and formal relationships with employee representatives (trade unions and staff associations); collective bargaining on terms and conditions; resolving collective disputes; implementing consultative committees and partnership agreements • *Employee communication:* informing employees about matters relevant to their work or of interest or concern to them • *Employee voice:* creating consultation opportunities for employees to contribute to decision-making in matters affecting them and their work
HR services	• *Managing the employment relationship:* contract management • *HR policies and procedures:* developing and administering guidelines and systems for all the above, to guide line managers and employees • *HR information systems:* developing and operating integrated systems for preparation of employee record-keeping, management reporting, statistical reports and returns and so on • *Compliance:* ensuring that all HR policies and practices are compliant with relevant law, regulation and codes of practice (and ideally, best practice) in areas such as employment protection (including dealing with employment tribunals), health and safety, equal opportunity and diversity, data protection and so on.

Graham and Bennett (1998) classify these activities into three dimensions of management.

(a)   The **utilisation of people at work**: recruitment, selection, transfer, promotion, separation, appraisal, training and development

(b)   The **motivation of people at work**: job design, remuneration, consultation, participation, negotiation and justice

(c)   The **protection of people at work**: working conditions, welfare services, safety, implementation of appropriate legislation

If this seems too employee-centred a classification, it must be added that the overall objective of these dimensions of management is maintained or enhanced **business performance**.

SIGNPOST

We cover many of these tasks and activities in detail, in the following chapters of this Course Book.

Another way of thinking about what HR practitioners do is to consider the various **processes** that are involved in performing the various activities and tasks listed above.

DEFINITION

A **process** is a sequence of activities (often crossing functional and organisational boundaries) involved in achieving goals, delivering services or adding value.

Armstrong (2009), for example, identifies a broad set of processes underpinning the HRM approach.

(a)   **Strategic HRM** – 'defining intentions and plans for the development of HRM practices, and ensuring that HR strategies are integrated with the business strategy and one another'

(b)   **Policy-making** – formulating and implementing HR policies which set guidelines on how personnel issues should be handled

(c)   **Competency, job and role analysis** – developing content and competency frameworks to support various activities such as organisation and job design, recruitment, appraisal, training and reward

(d)   **Change management** – advising on and facilitating the process of change in organisational structures and systems

(e)   **Knowledge management** – developing systems for obtaining and sharing knowledge, to foster organisational learning, innovation and performance.

ACTIVITY 5 (NO TIME LIMIT)

Use whatever online, work or personal contact sources you have at your disposal to obtain a copy of a job or role description of an HR manager. Such a document may be available – without breaching organisational confidentiality – as part of a job application package, on a careers/recruitment website, on a corporate internet or intranet site, or via your own business contacts.

Assess:

(a)   the objectives/outcomes of the role, as stated in the description
(b)   the tasks, activities and responsibilities set out in the description
(c)   any relationships with other roles in the organisation which are mentioned.

4.2   ROLES OF HR MANAGEMENT

HR practitioners may fulfil a range of roles, depending on the organisational context. Much of this work will be undertaken in partnership with line managers.

(a)   **Guidance role** – offering specialist recommendations and policy frameworks to guide line management decisions: for example, in regard to emerging HR issues, and the consistent and effective implementation of HR procedures.

(b)   **Advisory role** – offering specialist information and perspectives to line managers (and individual employees) on employment matters. Managers, for example, may be advised on training options, legislative provisions or how to handle specific people problems. Employees may be advised on their legal rights or development options, or counselled in relation to work or personal problems.

(c)   **Service role** – providing services to a range of internal customers. This includes administrative services (in areas such as payroll administration, employee records, reports and returns) and delivery of HRM programmes (recruitment and selection, training, health and welfare and so on).

(d)   **Control/auditing role** – analysing personnel indices (such as wage costs or labour turnover), monitoring performance, carrying out benchmarking or a local government review, say. This role has traditionally caused conflict with line managers, who felt they were being 'policed' – but line managers' discretion must be balanced with the need for consistency in applying HR policy, compliance with legal obligations, and ensuring that the strategic aims of HRM are being met.

(e)   **Planning/organising role** – for example, in human resource forecasting and planning, developing flexible working methods and so on.

At a more strategic and proactive level of HRM, HR practitioners may also take on roles as:

(a)   **Strategists**: helping to fulfil the business objectives of the organisation through strategic management of the human resource *and* influencing business planning by highlighting the human resource implications of objectives and strategies.

(b)   **Business partners**: sharing responsibility with senior and line management for the success of the enterprise, through the identification and exploitation of opportunities and the seeking of competitive advantage.

(c)   **Internal management consultants**: working alongside line managers in analysing business processes and systems, diagnosing and exploring problems, recommending solutions that the 'client' can own and implement, or implementing solutions and delivering services.

4.3 SHARED RESPONSIBILITY FOR HRM

DEFINITION

Centralisation and **decentralisation** refer to the degree to which the authority to make decisions is held centrally by a particular group of people *or* delegated and spread to a number of individuals and groups within the organisation.

Centralised control over human resource management generally implies the existence of an HR officer or department with authority over (or advisory input to) all personnel management tasks in the organisation.

Decentralised control over human resource management generally implies the delegation to line managers and team leaders of the authority for personnel management tasks affecting their own staff and activities.

In practice, there is a need for a mix of both, in order to gain the benefits of co-ordination and consistency as well as flair and flexibility.

FOR DISCUSSION

'Managers, if one listens to the psychologists, will have to have insights into all kinds of people. They will have to be in command of all kinds of psychological techniques. They will have to understand an infinity of individual personality structures, individual psychological needs, and individual psychological problems... But most managers find it hard enough to know all they need to know about their own immediate area of expertise, be it heat-treating or cost accounting or scheduling.'   (Drucker, 1955)

What does this say about the respective roles of line managers and HR specialists in managing people at work?

As the role of the HR function has become more strategic/proactive, rather than welfare/administrative/reactive, the following areas have commonly been retained as the responsibility of a centralised HR function.

(a)   **Strategic issues**, such as change management programmes and human resources planning, and all aspects of HR at the strategic level, including the formulating and communication of organisational policy. This ensures that the impact of human factors on strategic plans (and *vice versa*) is taken into account.

(b)   **Organisation-wide** communication and employee relations management. Centralisation has the advantage both of special expertise and a wider organisational viewpoint.

(c)   Provision of **specialist services** and **advice/consultancy**, where up-to-date specialist knowledge or input, or extra-departmental perspective, is required.

(d)   **Researching and auditing** of HR systems. This helps to co-ordinate and control HR functions across the organisation, to ensure that line departments are complying with policy and that policies are effective and relevant to the needs of line departments.

Such centralised functions create a coherent and integrated framework of policies, plans, systems and rules, developed by HR specialists, which help to maintain consistent practice and minimise redundant problem-solving and 're-inventing the wheel' by line managers. Within such a framework, a number of aspects of personnel management could be devolved to line departments.

ACTIVITY 6 (30 MINS)

You are a sales manager in Mpower Ltd, an organisation which develops and markets software and services for internet users: web page design, internet connection, browser programmes and so on. You are responsible for a team of 12 salespeople who work more or less 'independently' from home and 'on the road' and who service a remote rural area with a widely dispersed population.

What personnel management tasks would you wish to be *your* responsibility? What areas would you wish to have specialised or centralised help with? What other options might you consider?

(You might like to do this activity with a fellow student who can take the role of Mpower's head office HR manager. See what conflicts of interest come up, and how they might be resolved.)

4.4 THE ROLE AND RESPONSIBILITIES OF LINE MANAGERS IN HUMAN RESOURCE PRACTICES

Most commentators observe a trend toward greater **decentralisation** of personnel management roles, in line with 'slimmer' head office staffs, flatter management structures and the fostering of flexibility by giving greater autonomy to local business units.

The increase in the white-collar 'knowledge-based' workforce, with its mobility and higher expectations, has also supported a move toward individualism in career development, reward negotiation and other areas, which may be more flexibly managed by line managers and team leaders than by centralised personnel departments.

Meanwhile, integrated business processes and HR information systems have facilitated HR decision-making, on a day-to-day basis, by line managers.

The responsibility of line managers for delivering HR outcomes is a distinctive feature of the HRM approach, but even in a traditional personnel management model, line managers would often have responsibility for activities immediately concerned with the manager-team relationship: team selection, interviewing, and timekeeping management, performance appraisal, team motivation and so on.

EXAMPLE MANAGEMENT STYLES

'A key finding (of CIPD-funded research into 12 organisations to investigate how effective HRM creates competitive advantage) was the role of line managers in bringing HR policies to life... Their managerial behaviour – in implementing HR policies; in showing leadership by involving staff and responding to their suggestions; and in controlling quality, timekeeping and absence – makes a real difference to employees' attitudes...

'Looking at the information from our employee interviews, we found that there were frequent and statistically significant associations between people's approval of their managers' leadership style and a range of HR policies and practices. The way in which managers brought these HR policies to life and exercised leadership was strongly related to positive employee views on such areas as involvement, worker-management relations, communication, openness, coaching and guidance, performance appraisal, reward and recognition, training, job influence and quality control.

'Three of the case-study organisations made significant changes to the roles and competence profiles of their line managers after our first-year survey. One of these was Selfridges, where performance has continued to improve. We found similar remarkable results at the Royal United

Hospital at Bath. Despite difficulties at the top of the organisation, at ward level a new manager was appointed, a revised appraisal scheme was implemented and a stronger focus on work-life balance was achieved. Employee attitudes improved markedly and what once had been a retention blackspot ended the second year with no job vacancies.

'This was also true at Clerical Medical, now the life insurance arm of HBOS. We asked a manager in charge of a department that had achieved great progress which HR policies he had found most helpful. His answer was instructive: "It is the quality of team leaders that's important. If they take a close interest in people, it makes a big difference."'

(Purcell *et al*, 2003)

FOR DISCUSSION

Which 'side' do you naturally relate to: the line managers trying to get things done but hedged in by personnel rules and policies – or the HR manager having to beat his or her head against a brick wall to convince line managers of hard-won insights into people at work? Do you feel that as a line manager, you would be glad of expert help with complex people issues? Or as an HR manager, would you be glad that line managers are prepared to get on with their jobs, leaving you to more 'global' perceptions of the organisation's needs?

Set up a discussion between line and 'staff/advisory' functions: 'Why should we/you listen to the HR department?'

4.5 A SHARED SERVICES APPROACH

Shared services are support functions that are used by many different line departments or units in an organisation. A **shared service unit (SSU)** is a centralised, dedicated provider of such services to internal customers – on a quasi-'outsourced' basis. Functions such as HR (like procurement and IT) may be 'outsourced' by business units (such as regional divisions of a company) to the SSU, which:

(a)   Employs its own dedicated resources

(b)   Is responsible for managing the costs/quality of its services (like any external service provider)

(c)   Is often bound by contractual agreements with its internal customers, to provide guaranteed or target levels of service (via service level agreements or consultancy contracts)

Advantages claimed for the SSU approach include:

(a)   Consistency of practice and standards across the organisation

(b)   Strengthening of core competences

(c)   Significant cost savings (since there may be economies of scale and a reduction in the cost of back-office processes through centralisation eliminating duplication in individual units)

As with any form of centralisation, however, care must be taken to avoid the SSU's becoming isolated from end users and 'local' demands. Service level agreements must also be flexible enough to avoid the tendency to stifle innovation, initiative and above-specified performance.

EXAMPLE   IBM

Tyson (2006) outlines how: 'companies such as IBM have pioneered the division of HR activity
into three areas: the senior strategic role; the policy-making and consulting role; and the
transactional/administrative role. This latter role, and some of the consulting work, can then be
conducted through an HR call centre [or SSU] where there are HR staff who are fluent in
appropriate European languages, to deal with employee queries, or to refer them to the internal
consultant.'

4.6 OUTSOURCING HR TASKS

The need for organisational flexibility has supported the concept of the **core** organisation:
focusing in-house resources and expertise on the distinctive value-adding and competitive
advantage-gaining competences and functions of the organisation, and purchasing non-core
support services and functions from a range of 'peripheral' sources. We will discuss the 'core-
periphery' model in Chapter 9 of this Course Book, but for now, it is sufficient to note that a
number of HR activities may be regarded as 'peripheral' or complementary to the primary
functions of the business, and outsourced to external consultants or service providers.

The main areas identified as amenable to effective outsourcing include:

(a)   Training and development

(b)   Recruitment (and some aspects of selection, such as screening or testing)

(c)   Health and safety monitoring and advice (and related health and fitness promotion
        and services, if provided)

(d)   Employee welfare and counselling

(e)   Payroll management (and related benefit schemes, pensions administration and so
        on)

(f)   Legal advice on compliance

ACTIVITY 7   (20 MINS)

Why might it be beneficial to outsource the particular activities listed above? What sort of
external service providers would be suitable to take on each activity?

In addition, the HR function may have *de facto* responsibility for a range of ancillary activities –
such as on-site catering, security, office/facility management, child care, company care fleet
management and so on – which could be more effectively outsourced to external specialists.

The advantages and disadvantages of outsourcing may be summarised as follows.

Advantages	Disadvantages
HR costs are reduced by downsizing the HR function and potentially cheaper provision of services by specialists	External advisers/providers must be carefully chosen, contracted and managed, in order to maintain standards and organisational values
HR specialists are freed up to focus on core value-adding and business-specific tasks and knowledge	External advisers/providers may lack understanding or flexibility to be able to tailor their offering to reflect the organisation's objectives, culture or brand
Specialist knowledge and expertise may be easier to buy in than to develop within the organisation	Outsourcing may be carried out for short-term cost saving without defining which activities are (or may become) 'core' to the business or role of HRM in the organisation
External specialists may have access to infrastructure development (eg website or application software, purpose-built facilities) that the business lacks	The horizontal integration and consistency of application across the range of HR policy and practice may be lost
The objectivity of external service/advice providers may improve the quality of solutions and their acceptability to members of the organisation	

4.7 SUMMARY

As we have suggested, HRM is perhaps most helpfully seen as a broadly distributed organisational competence or orientation, rather than a 'function' in the sense of a department of specialists. The HR function may be thought of as the integration of people management systems throughout the organisation, rather than a particular set of roles and activities.

The diagram below (Figure 1.4), loosely based on the work of Schuler *et al* (1995), may be read from the bottom-up (following the classical planning hierarchy) or from the top-down (from a functional perspective).

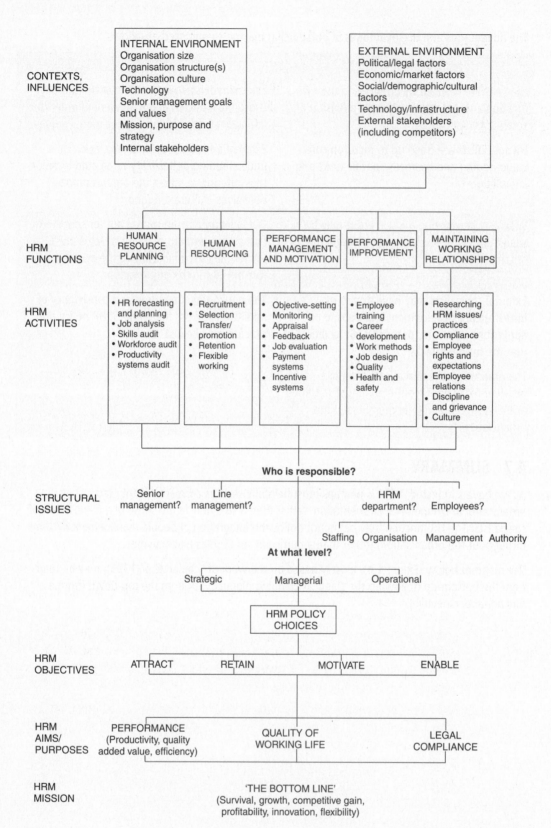

Figure 1.4: HRM in context

5 EVALUATING HR OUTCOMES

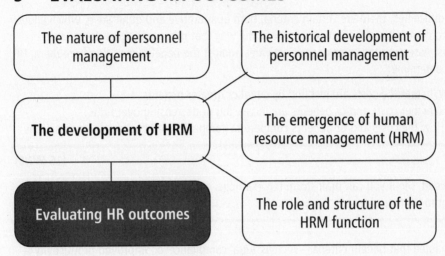

5.1 THE PROBLEM OF EVALUATION

If HRM is to be taken seriously at a strategic level as a contributor to bottom line business performance, it must be subject to evaluation. However, there are considerable difficulties attached to the evaluation of the HR function.

(a) While some performance-based criteria (profitability, productivity, error reduction, compliance and so on) are relatively easy to measure and compare, having to do with units and monetary values, others are not (for example, innovation or flexibility).

(b) Effective HRM should, over the long term, measurably impact on improved business performance. However:

   (i) Its short-term activities may not show such effects

   (ii) It is difficult to attribute these effects to HR activity alone: organisational performance involves many other variables, including technology, management effectiveness, market conditions, competitor initiatives and so on

(c) Subjective criteria such as the quality of working life, employee motivation, team spirit, openness to change, job satisfaction, the quality of employee relations and so on are notoriously difficult to measure, let alone to attach monetary values to, as a means of comparison.

(d) Benchmarking (standard-setting on the basis of best practice in other organisations) is difficult because of the wide differences in the environmental and internal variables affecting different organisations.

(e) HRM itself is a wide-ranging activity, and therefore requires a wide range of criteria for evaluation.

5.2 COST-BENEFIT ANALYSIS

Despite these difficulties, there are certain criteria, both quantitative and qualitative, which allow HR managers to demonstrate their effectiveness in the way that other managers do: by cost-benefit analysis. Assessing the costs of their activities against the benefits resulting from them, HR managers can determine:

(a)   Whether the costs are justified by equal or greater benefits

(b)   Whether costs and/or benefits are increasing or decreasing over time

(c)   How the costs and/or benefits compare to competitor or benchmark organisations

ACTIVITY 8   (15 MINS)

Before we proceed, see if you can brainstorm ten examples each of benefit criteria and cost criteria relevant to HR management.

You may have noted that benefit criteria – such as 'legal compliance' or 'improved productivity' – may apply to all HRM activities, while costs tend to be more specific to each activity: the cost of training, for example, which might include training resources, teacher payroll, coaches' and trainees' time in lost production and so on. Costs are more easily measurable, because they have a monetary value attached, but benefit criteria can usually be given a monetary value, if required: 'reduced accidents and illness', for example, can be expressed as a saving of the potential costs of lost production, benefits and compensation payments, training of replacement workers and so on.

5.3 QUANTITATIVE MEASURES

Quantitative or statistical indices of the HR function's activities may be available in relation to areas such as the following.

(a)   Staff turnover/labour wastage (or labour stability) ratios

(b)   Absenteeism rates

(c)   Unit labour costs (useful in comparison to previous periods and/or competing businesses)

(d)   Incidences of grievance procedures, disciplinary procedures, appeals to employment tribunals, compensation claims, proceedings for non-compliance and so on

(e)   Number of days production (and associated costs) lost through accidents, sickness, industrial disputes etc

(f)   Number of applications attracted by recruitment methods and/or lead time to recruit an employee

(g)   Number of selected recruits remaining in the job, achieving performance targets, achieving promotion and so on

(h)   Number of staff (including HR staff) achieving professional or other qualifications, or undertaking training programmes

(i)   Success of training (and other) programmes in achieving their objectives

(j)   Number of requests for information handled by the HR department, lead time in responding to requests, ability to answer technical personnel questions on demand and so on

(k)   The costs of any and all of the above

SIGNPOST

We look at means of evaluating specific HR activities, such as recruitment and training, in relevant chapters.

5.4 QUALITATIVE MEASURES

Qualitative, or subjective, criteria may be harder to measure, but may be equally important in the field of HRM. Examples include the following.

(a)   Employee motivation, team spirit, job satisfaction, acceptance of change and so on – as gauged by attitude surveys, interviews, psychological testing and other tools of behavioural science, as well as presumed observed effects on productivity, communication, absenteeism and so on

(b)   The extent to which HR proposals, policies, documentation and so on are accepted by line managers – as suggested by implementation rates, questions and objections

(c)   The perception of the HR function's value, service, expertise, quality of advice, professionalism and so on by its internal customers: senior management, line managers and employees

5.5 THE FOUR Cs

The Four Cs model was developed by researchers at the Harvard Business School as a means of investigating HRM issues (Beer *et al,* 1984). It suggests that the effectiveness of the outcomes of HRM should be evaluated under four headings.

(a)   **Commitment** – that is, employees' identification with the organisation, loyalty and personal motivation in their work. This, like the qualitative criteria mentioned above, may be assessed through methods such as attitude surveys, exit interviews and analysis of presumed effects (such as absenteeism and labour turnover).

(b)   **Competence** – that is, employees' skills and abilities, training needs and potential for performance improvement and career development. This may be measured through skill audits, competency testing and performance appraisal systems.

(c)   **Congruence** – that is, the harmonisation of the goals, values and efforts of management and employees (or at least the *perception* by employees that they have a mutual vision and purpose, to mutual benefit). This may be estimated by the quality of employee relations, the incidence of grievance and disciplinary action, conflict and communication and so on.

(d)   **Cost-effectiveness** – that is, efficiency, whereby HRM objectives are met and benefits obtained at the lowest input cost.

The Harvard model does not solve the problems of the accurate measurement of qualitative criteria; nor of the incompatibility of varying criteria (cost-effectiveness achieved by downsizing, for example, might not encourage commitment or congruence); nor of the sheer variety of HR activity and contexts (since there are organisations and areas of organisational activity in which low-skilled monotonous jobs and authoritarian management styles are still possible and indeed appropriate). However, it does offer a simple framework for thinking about HR effectiveness.

ACTIVITY 9 (30 MINS)

Think about your own work organisation, or an organisation you know well.

(a) How would you go about assessing the effectiveness of its HRM, according to the Four Cs model?

(b) Without doing a detailed assessment, how do you estimate it would rate on each of the Four Cs?

5.6 INTERNAL SERVICE AND CONSULTANCY AGREEMENTS

The effectiveness of HR projects and services may also be measured more explicitly against defined **performance indicators** and service standards set out in contractual agreements with internal customers.

Service agreements may be used by HR departments (or external providers) which provide day-to-day HR administration and operations to business units. They establish clear agreement on the nature and level of service to be provided – acting as an incentive to HR performance *and* as a way of managing user expectations! Service-level issues may include: how often the service is to be provided; during what hours it is to be available; what number and grade of staff will be available; how far the service does (and does not extend); and what speed of response can be guaranteed.

Consultancy agreements may be appropriate where an HR practitioner or project team acts in an internal consultancy capacity to a line department or business unit. An **internal consultant** works inside one part of an organisation to help another part. Although this is a complex role – since the consultant is working within the same system and culture as the client – they both have the same *external* customers and shared goals; the increased effectiveness of the organisation.

Internal (and external) consultants may be called in to propose or design something, or solve a problem, outside the expertise of the client unit, or to introduce and manage change in the client unit. (Examples of potential consultancy projects in HR include reorganisation, training, introduction of flexible working or performance management, or employee relations problem-solving.)

A consultancy agreement may therefore include matters such as:

(a) The client's expectation, needs and wants

(b) An agreed definition of the problem

(c) Specific objectives, outcomes or deliverables

(d) A working approach that will suit both parties (what will be reported back, how, how often and to whom? What co-operation and access to information will be supplied by the client? and so on)

(e) A preliminary time (and where appropriate, cost) schedule for the process

CHAPTER ROUNDUP

- The personnel function may take different forms in different organisations. Traditionally, it has been regarded as a primarily administrative, reactive, problem-handling function, concerned with hiring and firing, employee welfare and industrial relations.

- Four traditions colour perceptions of personnel management: the welfare tradition, the industrial relations tradition, the control of labour tradition and the professional tradition.

- Human Resource Management (HRM) is a concept which seeks to recognise employees as an asset to be nurtured, rather than a cost to be controlled, and which views the sourcing, deploying and developing of these human resources as a key integrated element of business strategy.

- HRM developed out of influences such as: the increased complexity of business processes and their dependence on employee flexibility and commitment; the need for competitive advantage; the increased power and expectations of highly-skilled knowledge workers; and the identification of human relations policy as the key to management effectiveness and business 'excellence'.

- Key areas of operational HR activity include: organisation; human resource planning and resourcing; performance management; reward management; human resource development; health, safety and welfare; employee relations; and HR services.

- One of the distinctive characteristics of an HRM orientation is the devolution of responsibility for delivering HRM outcomes to line management. In practice, strategic, specialised and organisation-wide activities are often centralised under the control of an HR function, while day-to-day aspects of people management are often devolved to line managers, who are able to manage the employment relationship in a more individualised and flexible way. Other options are the outsourcing of peripheral HR functions or the adoption of a shared services approach.

- The HR function can only establish credibility by systematic evaluation of its activities in the light of business objectives, and any internal service or consultancy agreements drawn up with internal customers/clients.

QUICK QUIZ

1   List the four 'traditions' of personnel management.

2   To what groups of people does the HR practitioner have responsibilities?

3   List a number of factors which contributed to the shift towards an HRM orientation.

4   What are the main features of HRM?

5   What, according to Guest, are the four key policy goals of HRM?

6   List eight broad areas into which the operational activities of HRM may be grouped.

7   List the possible roles of HR practitioners.

9   Summarise the arguments for and against outsourcing HR activities.

10   What are the Four Cs of the Harvard model?

ANSWERS TO QUICK QUIZ

1   Welfare, industrial relations, control of labour, professional.   (see Section 2)

2   To the employer, to the workforce (in part), to the profession.   (Para 2.4)

3   Dissatisfaction with the reactive role of personnel management; developments in organisation/management theory; competition putting pressure on contribution; social changes raising employee expectations of the psychological contract; political support for proactive employee relations; focus on the value of people as a scarce resource and source of value.   (Para 2.5)

4   Strategic fit; integrated HR policies and practices; commitment orientation; people as assets; unitarist employee relations; involvement of line managers.   (Para 3.3)

5   Strategic integration, high commitment, flexibility, high quality.   (Para 3.3)

6   Organisation; HR planning and resourcing; performance management; reward management; human resource development; health, safety and welfare; employee relations; HR services.   (Para 4.1)

7   Guidance, advice, service, control/auditing, planning/auditing, strategy, business partnership, internal consultancy.   (Para 4.2)

8   Delivering HR policies to employees (explicit in HRM orientation); interpersonal processes of team management and motivation; specific devolved personnel management tasks at the interface between the employer and the team (eg team selection, individual discipline, absence management, motivation).

9   See Paragraph 4.6 for a complete answer.

10   Commitment, congruence, competence, cost-effectiveness.   (Para 5.5)

ANSWERS TO ACTIVITIES

1   There is no suggested answer to this activity: it is intended to stimulate your awareness of:

(a)   Some of the research sources available to you in exploring this topic further

(b)   The variety of ways in which HRM concepts are expressed

(c)   Cultural, legal and other variations in HRM principles and practices in different parts of the world

2   Examples of conflicts of interest might include the following.

(a)   The need for downsizing or delayering for organisational efficiency. The workforce may well see this as a betrayal, yet it is part of resource management to know when to liquidate assets: organisational survival may even depend on increased efficiency/flexibility or cost reduction.

(b)   The negotiation of reward packages. As a member of management, you may wish to minimise increases in the cost of labour, or rationalise them in some other way. The workforce perceives pay rises as a 'right' or as an indication of the value the organisation puts on its services, and may be disappointed.

(c)   Disciplinary procedures. The interests of management may best be served by 'clamping down' on absenteeism, poor time-keeping and so on in order to keep general discipline and efficiency – but the workforce, or particular individuals, will often feel that rules are unfair or unfairly applied.

Broadly, these are issues of the way power is used in organisations. The personnel function can go a long way to minimising the potential hurt and conflict caused by applying and communicating the decisions of management fairly and sensitively.

3   *Welfare tradition:* very little sign of such an orientation in the job descriptions – except perhaps in the HR officer's responsibility for 'assisting with the induction process': even this seems more likely to be performance-oriented rather than for the psychological comfort of the recruits.

Industrial relations tradition: very little of this either, in the traditional sense. The word 'negotiations' crops up (Resource Manager), but more in the sense of collaborative responsibility for project resourcing. The phrase 'enthusiastic and passionate employees' (Training Advisor) suggests a unitarist perspective on the employment relationship: no inherent conflict anticipated.

Control of labour tradition: targets, competence frameworks, plans, co-ordination, the 'tracking' (monitoring) of employees against appraisal objectives, the requirement for computer literacy: this suggests the presence of administrative control systems in the organisation. However, these elements are tempered with more 'dynamic' elements.

Professional tradition: the Training Adviser and HR officer are required to have CIPD qualifications and the Training Adviser additionally requires specific specialist experience. However, more general managerial skills and experience are also mentioned: time management, languages, communication and so on.

Non-traditional concepts: the key word seems to be integration. 'In negotiation with departmental heads and project managers... links with other offices... overall management...' (Resource Manager). 'Driving the development strategy together with the company' (Training Adviser). 'Integral part' (HR Officer).

4   Terminology clearly matters to some of the people who perform the function, for their own sense of self-esteem and the status of their profession. An important consideration is whether the employees view the idea of themselves as 'resources' positively or negatively, and whether practice justifies the more 'enlightened' sounding title, or is indeed viewed cynically as the same 'old wine' in 'fancy new bottles'. Adoption of the title may be a sign of conflict and power struggles within the organisation (with HR trying to boost its status, credibility and influence) or it may enhance the organisation's reputation or 'brand' as an employer in the labour market.

5   This is a research activity. (Keep written evidence of your information search for your portfolio or assignment bibliographies!)

6   The answer to this activity is personal to you. However, the case scenario suggests some areas for consideration.

    (a)   As sales manager, you are responsible for staff who have particular needs: notably for motivation, encouragement and supervision while 'on the road'. You need to think about whether team-building would be best served by *your* maintaining contact with them on HR matters (such as appraisal, reward, training) or through a (possibly anonymous) personnel department. On the other hand, you might like some expert briefing on how to manage 'virtual teams', on problems suffered by team members (eg suffering isolation or stress) and so on.

    (b)   You have quite specific requirements for your staff. They need to be technically aware (in order to advise customers), highly knowledgeable about the company's products, proactive sales people (since the customers are dispersed, and likely to be somewhat traditional – although ideal candidates for the products). You might feel, given the difficulties of team building, that you would like to retain responsibility for selection and training – or you may prefer a more organisation-wide perspective: perhaps it would be good to have centrally selected/trained people who are close to the product and its technical possibilities – and then train them in sales?

These are just some suggestions to show you how widely and deeply an organisation needs to think through these issues.

7   *Training:* specialist facilities/equipment/resources, specialist knowledge of learning techniques, suitable for 'off-the-job' training. Providers: eg colleges, training companies, online campuses, publishers of books and software

Recruitment: specialist techniques (eg in psychometric testing), networks of contacts, savings in advertising media buying, online facilities (e-recruitment), removes routine pre-screening etc. Providers: eg recruitment consultants, e-recruitment sites, Job Centres, careers officers.

Health/safety: specialist knowledge of law/regulation, removes perception of 'policing' from team leaders, special facilities (medical testing, fitness etc). Service providers: consultants, fitness/medical facilities.

Welfare/counselling: specialist training, access to networks/referrals, removes 'personal' issues from workplace. Providers: counsellors, welfare agencies, Employee Assistance providers.

Payroll/benefits/pensions: specialist software/knowledge, removes routine peripheral tasks, avoids legal responsibility for financial advice. Providers: specialist agencies, financial service providers.

Legal advice: specialist knowledge, removes 'policing' on compliance from the HR department. Providers: law firms.

8   Some examples are as follows.

(a)   **Benefit criteria**: increased productivity, increased quality/reduced error/wastage, reduced absenteeism, reduced labour turnover, increased job satisfaction, legal compliance, reduced accidents/ illness, reduced employee stress, increased job involvement, increased innovation, reduced costs of fines, reduced grievance/ disciplinary actions, reduced industrial disputes, enhanced response to recruitment, enhanced community goodwill.

(b)   **Cost criteria**: costs of health and safety activity, training, recruitment, consultancy, remuneration, HR department training, welfare provision, computerisation, HR salaries, ergonomic improvements, compliance.

9   Suggested methodologies include attitude surveys, questionnaires, observation, interviews (eg exit interviews, counselling interviews, appraisal interviews), and analysis of the presumed effects of more or less 'C' factors (positive or negative labour stability, absenteeism rates, incidence of conflict and so on).

In terms of the evaluation of your chosen organisation's HRM function, you are on your own! Do attempt this exercise, however, even if it is just a brief mental survey of your college, your favourite fast food outlet or whatever. This will get you thinking not just about how to evaluate the success of HRM policy and practice, but about how HRM goes about fostering, maintaining and increasing the 'C' factors in the organisation.

Chapter 02

Human resource planning

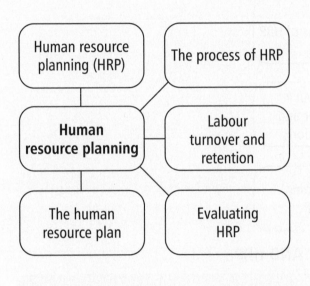

- Human resource planning (HRP)
- The process of HRP
- **Human resource planning**
- Labour turnover and retention
- The human resource plan
- Evaluating HRP

Introduction

As we saw in Chapter 1, human beings are one of the resources that a business must obtain and manage in pursuit of its objectives. Human resource (previously 'manpower') planning is the task of assessing and anticipating the skill, knowledge and labour time requirements of the organisation, and initiating action to fulfil or 'source' those requirements. If the organisation (or a particular area of its activity) is declining, it may need to plan a reduction or redeployment of the labour force. If it is growing, or moving into new areas of activity, it will need to find and tap into a source of suitably skilled labour.

It may already have occurred to you that this cannot be as easy as it sounds! External factors – particularly over the long term – create fluctuations in the demand for and supply of labour. So do internal factors, such as individual and team productivity, training, and labour turnover through retirements, resignations, parental leave and so on.

If anything, as we shall see, the uncertainties of human resource planning make it even more important – and certainly, it becomes more important to approach it systematically: in this chapter, we consider how this can be done.

Your objectives

In this chapter you will learn about the following.

- The purpose of human resource planning

- The processes and stages involved in human resource planning

- The need for human resource planning and the difficulties involved in accurately predicting HR requirements

- Limiting factors in the external environment, and changes in the external environment, which influence the human resource planning process

1 HUMAN RESOURCE PLANNING (HRP)

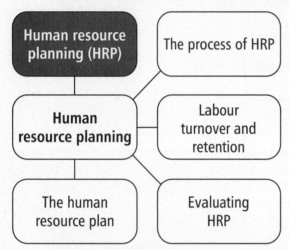

1.1 'MANPOWER PLANNING' AND HRP

DEFINITION

Human resource planning may be defined as 'a strategy for the acquisition, utilisation, improvement and retention of the human resources required by the enterprise in pursuit of its objectives.'

The traditional 'manpower planning' model may be broadly outlined as follows.

(a) Forecast **demand** for specific skills, competences or grades of employee.

(b) Forecast **supply** of these skills, competences or grades, both within and outside the organisation.

(c) Plan to remove any **discrepancy** between demand and supply. If there is a shortage of labour, for example, you would need to reduce demand (say, through improved productivity), or improve supply (through training and retention of current staff, or recruitment from outside, for example).

Apart from the sexist connotations of the term 'manpower', this traditional model has, in the light of HRM, come to seem too narrow in three key respects.

(a) It is heavily reliant on calculations of employee numbers, with insufficient attention to skills, competences and other factors in productivity contribution or value.

(b) It is insufficiently integrated with other key factors in the management of the human resource: motivation and productivity; organisational culture and systems; job and organisation design; and so on.

(c) It is based on matching people with 'jobs', in an era when traditional job designs are being eroded by the emphasis on functional, temporal and numerical flexibility in the workforce.

Liff (2000) notes that 'there has been a shift from reconciling numbers of employees available with predictable, stable jobs, towards a greater concern with skills, their development and deployment'.

(a) **Recruiting** the required number and type/quality of staff.

(b) **Retaining** the required number and type/quality of staff – and therefore letting go those who are not required (by natural labour turnover and/or by planned downsizing).

(c) **Utilising** staff in the most efficient and effective manner: increasing productivity, introducing multiskilling and other forms of flexibility and so on.

(d) **Improving** the skills, capabilities and motivation of staff, so that they become a more flexible resource, capable of fulfilling emerging requirements.

It is arguable that forecasting staff and skill requirements has become more *difficult* in recent times because of the increasing uncertainty and rate of change in the business environment. However, it has also arguably become more *necessary*, because the risks of 'getting it wrong' (particularly in an era of global economic recession) are correspondingly greater.

Human resource planning (HRP) is a form of **risk management**. It involves realistically appraising the present and anticipating the future (as far as possible) in order to get the **right people** into the **right jobs** at the **right time** *and* managing employee behaviour, organisational culture and systems in order to **maximise the human resource** in response to anticipated opportunities and threats.

ACTIVITY 1 (15 MINS)

We have noted that the supply (and demand) of skilled human resources is subject to a number of factors outside and within the organisation. Suggest three possible reasons why a business might find itself experiencing a *shortage* of a particular skill or type of employee.

1.2 HRP AND CORPORATE PLANNING

As suggested in Chapter 1, human resources are an important input into the overall corporate strategy, and the two are mutually interdependent. If the corporate plan envisages a cut in output, for example, or the closure of a particular plant, then the human resource plan will need to consider redeployment of staff, redundancies and so on. If the corporate plan specifies a move into a new product market, the human resource plan will have to source the required labour from outside or within the organisation, through recruitment, training or sub-contracting.

In turn, the availability of labour resources can act as a constraint on, or spur to, the achievement of corporate goals. If there are skill shortages and employees cannot be recruited or developed cost-effectively, plans for expansion or diversification may have to be curtailed. The availability of multiskilled or expert teams, on the other hand, may inspire innovative strategies for growth and change.

1   **Creates a link between business and HR plans**. People planning ensures that the strategic plan has to be understood in order that the people plan can fit; and demonstrates to the organisation that the people planning needs to considered and incorporated.

2   **Better control over staffing costs and numbers employed**. Whatever the future prospects may be for an organisation, whether they be growth or reduction in headcount, an organisation needs a plan. If the future is unknown, it may be prudent to recruit temporary or agency workers and so design flexibility into the organisation and so, in turn, partition off the permanent workforce from the turbulent period.

3   **More informed judgements about the skills and attitude mix in the organisation**. While headcount numbers will always be a concern, attention also needs to be given to the skills mix within the workforce. Does the current workforce have the skills and attitudes that will ensure organisational success in the future?

4   **Maintain a profile of current staff**. If HR does not know what resources it has currently, how can it plan for the future? To enhance planning, the organisation would benefit from not only knowing the numbers, position, grade etc but this would be greatly enhanced by knowledge of skills, experience etc.

(Marchington and Wilkinson, 2008)

The strategic impact of HRM in general and HRP in particular is such that we should expect to see a senior HR manager at the organisation's strategic apex, alongside the heads of other major functions such as finance and marketing.

SIGNPOST

Some people might still argue that proactive forward planning to meet human resource requirements is a waste of time, especially for small to medium-sized businesses. Why does it have to be so complicated? Surely, if you are short of staff, you hire some – or train or promote some of your existing staff? And if business declines and you find yourself with superfluous staff, you make some redundancies? In fact, it is not quite so simple. We suggest why.

1.3 WHY IS HRP NECESSARY?

An attempt to look beyond the present and short-term future, and to prepare for contingencies, is increasingly important. Some manifestations of this are outlined below.

'the need for strategic workforce planning and execution of workforce planning has never been greater as organisations…operate in more turbulent environments and confront the key challenges of competing for key skills and talents and of containing payroll costs..'

(Lavelle 2007, cited in Torrington *et al*, 2011)

(a)   Jobs in innovative and fast-changing contexts may require experience and skills which cannot easily be bought in the market place, and the more complex the organisation, the more difficult it will be to supply or replace highly specialised staff quickly. The need will have to be anticipated in time to initiate the required development programmes. The decline of the 'job for life' and the common desire to gain wide and rounded experience have contributed to rates of staff turnover. Leavers must be replaced with suitable staff. At senior levels, succession planning should identify potential replacements, internal or external, for those expected to retire or simply move on.

(b)   Employment protection legislation and increasing public demand for corporate social responsibility make downsizing, redeploying and relocating staff (eg in response to economic recession) a slow and costly process.

(c)   Rapid technological change is leading to a requirement for human resources that are both more highly skilled and more adaptable. Labour flexibility is a major issue, and means that the career and retraining **potential** of staff is at least as important as their actual qualifications and skills. Thus, 'trainability' is now a major criterion for selection.

(d)   The scope and variety of markets, competition and labour resources are continually increased by environmental factors such as the expansion of the European Union, the globalisation of business and the explosive growth of e-commerce.

(e)   Information and Communication Technology (ICT) has made available techniques which facilitate the monitoring and planning of human resources over fairly long time spans: accessing of demographic and employment statistics, trend analysis, 'modelling' of different scenarios and variables, and so on.

(f)   Labour costs are a major proportion of total costs in many industries and must be carefully controlled. Cost control action will involve carefully planned remuneration schemes, strict control of headcount and avoidance of waste in such forms as over-manning and unnecessary activity. Business process reengineering and the deskilling of jobs may lead to redundancies, especially among over-qualified staff.

Armstrong (2009) sums up the aims of HRP as follows.

(a)   To attract and retain the number of people required, with the skills, expertise and competences required.

(b)   To anticipate potential surpluses or shortfalls which will need to be adjusted.

(c)   To develop a well-trained and flexible workforce which will support organisational adaptation to external changes and demands.

(d)   To reduce dependence on external recruitment to meet key skill shortages (by formulating retention and development strategies).

(e)   To improve the utilisation of people (most notably by developing flexible working systems).

ACTIVITY 2   (15 MINS)

To what extent would HRP be possible and desirable for:

(a)   A company designing, manufacturing and selling personal computers?
(b)   A large local government authority?
(c)   An international airline?

1.4   A CONTINGENCY APPROACH TO HRP

We have suggested that **long-range, detailed human resource planning** is a necessary form of risk management, preparing businesses for foreseeable contingencies. However, there has been some disillusionment about the feasibility and value of such planning, given the rapidly evolving and uncertain business environment and the kinds of highly flexible organisational structures and cultures that have been designed to respond to it.

(a)   The trend in **organisation and job design** is towards functional feasibility (multi-skilling), team working, decentralisation (or empowerment) and flexibly-structured workforces (discussed later in this Course Book), to facilitate flexible deployment of labour. Peters (1994) cites successful US businesses like management consultancy – McKinsey, news broadcaster – CNN and manufacturer – Titeflex as examples of 'unglued' structures made up of small, functionally versatile units that come together and disband constantly, according to task requirements; that find their own customers, set up their own networks and generate their own projects; that continuously re-educate themselves to meet new demands. Such structures are entirely flat, output/customer-focused, business-generating, information-seeking, continuously learning and shifting. They sweep aside traditional barriers to innovation, customer service and creative problem-solving – but also effectively abolish 'jobs' and predictability of labour utilisation.

(b)   Within flexible structures and markets, where manipulating information – not making things – is the primary business activity, the traditional concepts of 'job' and 'career' are being eroded. Bridges (1995), for example, foresaw a workforce made up of **'vendor workers'** who sell their services to a variety of clients and work for them on a project basis. This fundamentally changes the nature of 'job vacancies' and of the labour pool.

(c)   With new emphasis on continuous improvement, customer service and product innovation, organisations are striving to be more adaptive, visionary, fluid in their structures and holistic in their thinking. The **'learning organisation'** embraces learning at all levels and in all areas, focusing on the process of learning and adapting to what is learned: HRP is thus seen as an opportunity to explore different scenarios, without preconceived requirements or solutions.

In such environments, a different, less prescriptive approach to HRP may be required. Kane and Stanton (1994) suggest three broad approaches that respond to these uncertainties.

(a)   **The staff replacement approach**. Staff are recruited or promoted to fill a vacancy as and when it occurs – if it is still required – with little formal planning. While this is essentially reactive, and does not provide for much change in the knowledge and skill base of the organisation, it allows a degree of flexibility on an *ad hoc* basis. Organisations or units with relatively stable environments may have little difficulty filling vacancies as they arise, while in volatile environments and organisations with high staff mobility and turnover, it may be recognised that longer-range projections of labour requirements are in any case meaningless.

(b)   **Short-term Human Resource Strategy**. In environments where long-term forecasting of future requirements is quickly rendered obsolete by change and uncertainty, yet the ability to adapt the skills and knowledge of the workforce is required, a short-term strategic model may be more suitable. This approach has a 'key issues' orientation: HR and line managers collaborate to determine what the organisation's **key HR issues** are in the short term, emphasising flexibility and speed of response to emerging threats and opportunities. HR plans are thus more likely to be:

- Focused on short-term action planning and implementation
- Based on simpler data analysis
- Owned by line managers.

(c)   **Vision-driven Human Resource Development**. This approach is long term in its orientation and is appropriate when the nature of the future environment is uncertain. It is driven by organisational vision, mission and core values, rather than detailed staffing forecasts and targets. Such an approach is often employed where a major cultural shift is required, calling for corresponding shifts in employee attitudes, skills and behaviours.

When the future environment can be described with some certainty, traditional long-range HRP remains a useable approach.

The process of choosing the appropriate approach may be shown as follows (adapted from Kane and Stanton (1994):

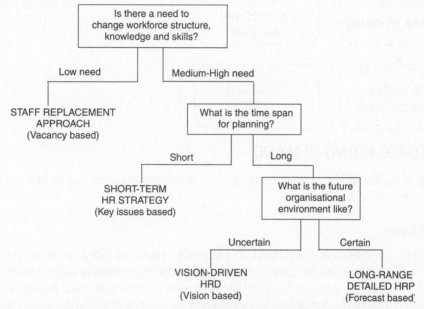

Figure 2.1: Approaches to human resource planning

Note that an alternative (and possibly confusing) terminology emphasising time scale would be to use 'short-term', 'medium-term' and 'long-term' as equivalent to the three possibilities outlined above. Confusion might arise from the contrasting uses of the phrase 'short-term'. The terminology equivalents are tabulated below.

Kane and Stanton terminology	Alternative terminology
Staff replacement approach	Short-term HRM
Short-term HR strategy	Medium-term HRM
Vision-driven HRD (and long-range HRP)	Long-term HRM

SIGNPOST

Let us now look at the HR planning process in more detail. We have already suggested that it is a form of 'supply and demand management', aiming to minimise the risk of either surplus (and therefore inefficiency) or shortage (and therefore ineffectiveness) of the labour resource. We shall now see how that works in practice.

2 THE PROCESS OF HRP

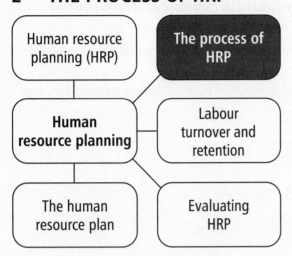

2.1 FORECASTING DEMAND

Forecasts of the **demand** for labour, competences and productivity levels will be affected by both internal and external factors.

Internal factors

(a) **Organisational objectives**. Organisational objectives will drive requirements for resources and the long- and short-term plans in operation to achieve them. Where plans are changed, the effect of the changes must be estimated: proposed expansion, contraction, innovation or diversification of the organisation's activities will affect the demand for labour in general or for particular skills. Typical changes include:

- Changed levels of demand
- Introduction of new products and services
- Entry into new markets
- Technological change of all kinds
- Changes to geographical locations

The probable extent of change may be estimated by market research, competitive analysis, trends in technological advances and so on (although sudden changes in market conditions complicate the process: the effect of global terrorism on defence spending, for example or the 2008 collapse of global financial markets).

(b) **Staff characteristics and utilisation**. Labour requirements will depend in part on the expected productivity or work rate of different types of employee and the expected volume of business activity. Productivity, in turn, will depend on a range of factors, such as capital expenditure, technology, work organisation, employee motivation, management style and negotiated productivity deals. Employee characteristics to be considered include:

- Age
- Sex
- Ethnicity
- Abilities
- Skills

Ethical and legal considerations relating to discrimination must be respected.

(c) **The cost of labour** – including overtime, training, benefits and so on – and therefore what financial constraints there are on the organisation's labour or skill levels.

External factors

(a) **Demand in the relevant labour markets**. In recent years, economic recession and developments in ICT, for example, have encouraged downsizing and delayering, thus reducing demand for labour generally in advanced economies. At the same time, ICT developments have created new markets, products and business processes creating demand for new skills (such as network management or website design).

(b) **Government policy**. Government economic policy can have a significant influence on the demand for labour, both by influencing the availability of credit and by the expansion or reduction of staff numbers in government departments and related bodies.

(c) **The changing nature of work**. Advanced nations are seeing a continuing decline in manufacturing industry and significant growth in service industries of all kinds. These changes have obvious effects on the demand for a range of categories of labour. Demand is falling for manufacturing production labour of all grades, but particularly for unskilled and semi-skilled workers. At the same time, there is expanding demand for labour in such areas as care of the elderly, the ICT-based work already mentioned and knowledge workers of all kinds.

(d) **Technological developments**. Quite apart from the impact of ICT, technological developments are likely to continue to have significant effect in a number of areas.

- Improvements in productivity
- Emergence of new industries
- Requirements for training
- Reduced requirements for maintenance

EXAMPLE   **TESCO**

Tesco is a company that has seen continuous growth for a number of years and needs to recruit on a regular basis for both the food and non-food parts of the business. For example, in 2008/09 4,000 new managers were required to support business growth. Tesco regards workforce planning as vital for the company.

Tesco identifies three main causes for vacancy creation:

- Opening new stores in the UK and internationally

- Retirement, resignation and internal promotion

- The creation of new types of jobs due to changes in its processes and developments in technology

Tesco uses a workforce planning table to establish the likely demand for new staff. This considers both managerial and non-managerial positions.

This planning process runs each year from the last week in February. There are quarterly reviews in May, August and November, so Tesco can adjust staffing levels and recruit where necessary. This allows Tesco sufficient time and flexibility to meet its demands for staff and allows the company to meet its strategic objectives, for example, to open new stores and maintain customer service standards.

Tesco seeks to fill many vacancies from within the company. It recognises the importance of motivating its staff to progress their careers with the company. Tesco practises what it calls "talent planning". This encourages people to work their way through and up the organisation. Through an annual appraisal scheme, individuals can apply for "bigger" jobs. Employees identify roles in which they would like to develop their careers with Tesco. Their manager sets out the technical skills, competencies and behaviours necessary for these roles, what training this will require and how long it will take the person to be ready to do the job. This helps Tesco to achieve its business objectives and employees to achieve their personal and career objectives.

(*Times* 100 Business Case Studies)

ACTIVITY 3 (30 MINS)

Bratton and Gold (2007) note that many HR departments practise 'e-HR': using the internet and related ICT systems (including internal networks or intranets) to support their activities.

(a)   How might e-HR be used in HR planning?

(b)   What other sources of information can you brainstorm, that might be used in supply and demand forecasting for HRP?

2.2 FORECASTING SUPPLY

The available **supply** of labour, competences and productivity levels may be forecast by considering internal and external factors.

Internal factors

(a)   The competences, skills, trainability, flexibility and current productivity level of the existing workforce.

(b)   The structure of the existing workforce in terms of age distribution, skills, hours of work, rates of pay and so on.

(c)   The likelihood of changes to the productivity, size and structure of the workforce. Such changes may come through:

(i)   Wastage (turnover through resignations and retirements), promotions and transfers, absenteeism and other staff movements. This will require information on:

- The age structure of staff (forthcoming retirement or family start-up)
- Labour turnover for a comparable period
- The promotion potential and ambitions of staff

(ii)   Employee trainability, morale and motivation, which may influence productivity and flexibility

(iii)   Organisational, technological, cultural, managerial and other changes which may positively or negatively affect employee productivity, loyalty etc

External factors

The present and potential future supply of relevant skilled labour in the **external labour market** will be influenced by a range of factors, including some already discussed under the heading of demand. These certainly include economic conditions generally, government policy and actions and the changing nature of work. In addition, the HR planner will have to assess and monitor factors such as those given below.

(a) **Skill availability**: locally, nationally and also internationally: labour mobility within the EU has had a major influence on the UK workforce, for example.

(b) **Changes in skill availability**, due to education and training trends, resources and initiatives (or lack of these), and rising unemployment (worker availability) due to economic recession.

(c) **Competitor activity**, which may absorb more (or less) of the available skill pool.

(d) **Demographic changes**: areas of population growth and decline, the proportion of younger or older people in the workforce in a particular region, the number of women in the workforce and so on.

(e) **Wage and salary rates** in the market for particular jobs. ('Supply' implies *availability:* labour resources may become more or less affordable by the organisation).

FOR DISCUSSION

Select an organisation you are familiar with. Is its need for labour growing, shrinking, or perhaps moving into new skill areas? What, if anything, is the organisation doing about this? What other key strategic issues is the organisation facing – and what challenges do they present for human resource management? What specific challenges are posed by the current economic recession for HR planning?

2.3 CLOSING THE GAP BETWEEN DEMAND AND SUPPLY

Shortfalls or surpluses of labour/skills/productivity which emerge may be dealt with in various ways, in accordance with the organisation's specific HR and business objectives and policies (for example, equal opportunities), cultural values (for example encouraging commitment, quality focus or developing people within the organisation) and available structures and technologies. Detailed action programmes may be drawn up for the following strategies.

Shortfalls may be met by:	*Surplus* may be met by:
Internal transfers and promotions, training and development (including individual career management and succession/promotion planning)	Running down manning levels by natural wastage or 'accelerated wastage' (encouraging labour turnover by with-holding incentives to loyalty: eg pay freezes or barriers to promotion)
External recruitment or improvement of recruitment methods (eg diversity programmes to encourage more applicants)	Restricting or 'freezing' recruitment
The extension of temporary contracts, or the contracts of those about to retire	Redundancies (voluntary and/or compulsory)
Reducing labour turnover, by reviewing possible causes (including pay and conditions), improving induction/ socialisation measures	Early retirement incentives
The use of freelance/temporary/agency staff to cover fluctuating demand	Short-contract and flexible-hours (eg annual hours contracts) to cover fluctuating demand

Shortfalls may be met by:	*Surplus* may be met by:
Reducing labour turnover, by reviewing possible causes (including pay and conditions), improving induction/ socialisation measures	Eliminating overtime and 'peripheral' workforce groups (freelance and temporary workers)
The extension of temporary contracts, or the contracts of those about to retire	Retraining and/or redeployment of staff to other areas of skill/productivity shortage. This may involve diversification by the organisation, to utilise existing skills/knowledge; retraining of employees in newly-needed skill areas; and/or multi-skilling, so that the workforce can be flexibly deployed in areas of labour shortage as and when they emerge
Outsourcing appropriate activities to external contractors	
The development of flexible (or otherwise more productive) working methods and structures: multi-skilling, project structures, delayering	
Productivity bargaining encouraging overtime working or offering bonuses and incentives to increase productivity	
Review and adjustment of corporate culture, management style and organisation to increase productivity	
New technology (increasing productivity, and/or reducing the need for human labour)	
Adjustment of corporate objectives: contracting in recognition of the constraints	

Bear in mind that there are also **external constraints** on HR planners in considering any or all of the above: UK legislation and EU directives, regulations and court rulings, the organisation's employer brand (reputation in the labour market) and other factors must be taken into account when planning to hire, 'fire', or alter working terms and conditions.

SIGNPOST

Note that the sources of labour are both internal (the current workforce and its future potential) and external (people in the 'labour pool'). We discuss the external labour market and the internal labour market (and related issues of promotion and succession) in Chapter 3. Another key issue of HRP – flexibility – is discussed in detail in Part B of this Course Book. Here we look at a major factor in forecasting the internal supply of labour: turnover and retention.

3 LABOUR TURNOVER AND RETENTION

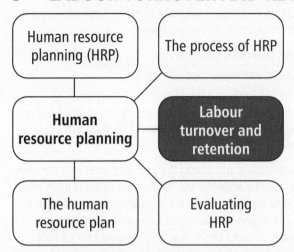

3.1 MEASURING LABOUR TURNOVER

DEFINITION

Labour turnover is the number of employees leaving an organisation and being replaced. The rate of turnover is often expressed as the number of people leaving, as a *percentage* of the average number of people employed, in a given period. The term '*natural wastage*' is used to describe a 'normal' flow of people out of an organisation through retirement, career or job change, relocation, illness and so on.

There are different ways of measuring labour turnover. Most simply, actual gross numbers of people leaving may provide a basis for recruitment/replacement – but this statistic does not say anything about whether or not these people need replacing! To measure labour turnover in a more systematic and useful way, an index such as the following may be used.

(a) **Crude labour turnover rate** (*the BIM Index, British Institute of Management*, 1949)

Here we express turnover as a percentage of the number of people employed.

$$\frac{\text{Number of leavers in a period}}{\text{Average number of people employed in the period}} \times 100 = \% \text{ turnover}$$

This is normally quoted as an annual rate and may be used to measure turnover per organisation, department or group of employees. The *advantage* of this index is that it can alert HR planners to unusually high percentages of the workforce leaving – compared with the HR plan, or with the industry average, say – which would suggest that something is wrong, or that more effort is needed to retain employees. The *disadvantage* of this index is that it does not indicate *who* is leaving the department or organisation: even a high turnover rate may not reflect any real instability if the core of experienced staff consistently remains. (In fact, most wastage occurs among young people and those in the early stages of their employment in an organisation: stability tends to increase with length of service.)

(b) **Labour stability**

Here we try to eliminate short-term employees from our analysis, thus obtaining a better picture of the significant movements in the workforce.

$$\frac{\text{Number of employees with one or more years' service}}{\text{Number of employees employed at the beginning of the year}} \times 100\%$$

$= \%$ *stability*

Particularly in times of rapid expansion, organisations should keep an eye on stability, as a meaningful measure.

(c) The labour stability index ignores new starts during the year and does not consider actual length of service, which may be added to the measurement via **length of service analysis**, or **survival rate analysis**. Here, the organisation calculates the proportion of employees who are engaged within a certain period who are still with the firm after various periods of time. There may be a survival rate of 70% after two years, for example, but only 50% in year three: the distribution of losses can be plotted on a survival curve to indicate trends.

ACTIVITY 4 (20 MINS)

Suppose a company has 20 employees at the beginning of 2012, and 100 at the end of the year. Disliking the culture created by the expansion, 18 of the original experienced labour force resign.

Calculate:

(a) The crude labour turnover rate

(b) The stability rate

Comment on the significance of your results.

3.2 CAUSES OF LABOUR TURNOVER

Some reasons for leaving will be largely unavoidable, or unforeseeable. **'Natural wastage'** occurs through:

(a) Illness or accident (although transfer to lighter duties, excusing the employee from shiftwork or other accommodations might be possible)

(b) A move from the locality for domestic, social or logistical reasons

(c) Changes to the family situation: for example, when an individual changes job or gives up work to accommodate parental responsibilities

(d) Retirement

(e) Career change

Other causes of labour turnover, however, may be to do with the organisation, management, terms and conditions and so on: in other words, **job dissatisfaction**.

ACTIVITY 5 (15 MINS)

Suggest a number of factors that might contribute to labour turnover, which might broadly be grouped under the heading of 'job dissatisfaction'.

Which of these factors would be sufficient to make you leave an organisation: a) in a market where you were reasonably sure of finding other employment b) in a market where other employment was scarce?

Labour turnover is also influenced by:

(a) **The economic climate and the state of the job market**. When unemployment is high and jobs are hard to find, labour turnover will be much lower.

(b) **The age structure and length of service of the workforce**. An ageing workforce will have many people approaching retirement. However, it has been found in most companies that labour turnover is highest among:

(i) Young people, especially unmarried people with no family responsibilities

(ii) People who have been in the employment of the company for only a short time

The employment life cycle usually shows a decision point shortly after joining, when things are still new and perhaps difficult. This is called the **'first induction crisis'**. There is then a period of mutual accommodation and adjustment between employer and employee (called the **'differential transit'** period): in the settling of areas of conflict, there may be further turnover. A second (less significant) induction crisis occurs as both parties come to terms with the new *status quo*. Finally, the period of **'settled connection'** begins, and the likelihood of leaving is much less.

SIGNPOST

So far, you may have got the impression that 'labour turnover' equals 'instability', and that, since it is caused by job dissatisfaction, it must be a bad thing for the organisation. But remember: earlier in this chapter we noted that an organisation may from time-to-time have a surplus of labour or particular skills, which it would like to be able to 'lose' through natural wastage instead of costly redundancies. And some organisations may be constantly creating and disbanding projects: forming loose, temporary or 'virtual' networks of people – without tying themselves to expectations of 'jobs' or 'careers'. So should organisations fight to retain employees – or not?

3.3 IS TURNOVER A 'BAD THING'?

The following table puts labour turnover in perspective.

Potential *advantages* of labour turnover	Potential *disadvantages* of labour turnover
Opportunities to inject 'new blood' into the organisation: new people bringing new ideas and outlooks, new skills and experience in different situations	Broken continuity of knowledge, relationships, culture and succession, where continuity could offer stability and predictability

Potential *advantages* of labour turnover	Potential *disadvantages* of labour turnover
Balance in the age structure of the workforce. Absence of labour turnover would create an increasingly aged workforce, often accompanied by an increasing wage/salary cost	Lead time and lost performance while a replacement is found and brought 'on line' to the level of expertise of the previous job-holder
The creation of opportunities for promotion and succession which offers an important incentive to more junior employees	Morale problems. Turnover may be perceived by other employees as a symptom of job dissatisfaction, causing the problem to escalate The costs of turnover, including: • **Replacement costs**: recruiting, selecting and training; loss of output or efficiency • **Preventive costs**: the cost of retaining staff, through pay, benefits and welfare provisions, maintaining working conditions
The ability to cope with labour surpluses, in some grades of job, without having to make redundancies	

It is common to hear that turnover is bad when it is high – but this cannot be assessed in isolation. What is an acceptable rate of turnover and what is excessive? There is no fixed percentage rate of turnover which is the borderline between acceptable and unacceptable. Labour turnover rates *may* be a signal that something is wrong when:

(a) They are higher than the turnover rates in another similar department of the organisation; for example, if the labour turnover rate is higher at branch A than at branches B, C and D in the same area, something might be wrong at branch A.

(b) They are higher than they were in previous years or months; in other words, the situation might be deteriorating.

(c) The costs of labour turnover are considered too high – although they will be relative to the costs of preventing high turnover by offering employees incentives to stay.

Otherwise, the organisation may live with high rates because they are the norm for a particular industry or job (think about call centres, for example); because the organisation culture accepts constant turnover (as in a project-based or 'virtual' network organisation); or because the cost of keeping employees is greater than the cost of replacing them!

SIGNPOST

So, if an organisation does decide that it needs to control or reduce its labour turnover rate, what can it do?

3.4 RETENTION PLANNING

A systematic **investigation** into the causes of unusually or undesirably high turnover will have to be made, using various methods, as outlined below.

(a) Information given in **exit interviews** with leaving staff, which should be the first step after an employee announces his/her intention to leave. (It must be recognised, however, that the reasons given for leaving may not be complete, true, or those that would be most useful to the organisation. People may say they are 'going to a better job', for example, while the real reason for the move is dissatisfaction with the level of interest in the current job.)

(b) **Attitude surveys**, to gauge the general climate of the organisation, and the response of the workforce as a whole to working conditions, management style and so on.

(c) Information gathered on the number of (interrelated) **variables** which can be assumed to **correlate** with labour turnover – such as an ageing workforce, higher rates of pay outside the organisation etc.

The causes of turnover should be addressed by HR planning, where it is practical and cost-effective to do so.

(a) If particular managers' practices or styles are creating significant dissatisfaction, performance improvement measures may be implemented.

(b) Coherent policies may be introduced (or more consistently applied) with regard to training and development and promotion from within the organisation.

(c) Induction or orientation programmes for new recruits should address the issues that cause problems at the 'first induction crisis' stage.

(d) Selection programmes should be reviewed to ensure that future recruits are made aware of (and ideally are compatible with) the demands of the job and culture of the organisation.

(e) Problems with working conditions should be solved – especially if they also concern health and safety.

(f) Pay levels and structures may be reviewed in the light of perceived fairness and/or market rates.

FOR DISCUSSION

'Accelerated wastage' is the practice of allowing (or using) job dissatisfaction to encourage people to leave in higher numbers than they would by 'natural wastage', in order to reduce a labour surplus.

How do you respond to this concept? Do you think it has a place in an ethical HRM policy? How would you justify it?

SIGNPOST

The apparently simple 'supply and demand' equation, discussed in Section 2 above, makes HRP look scientific – but there are so many 'messy' human factors involved that its feasibility and reliability have been questioned. This raises the further question of how the success and value of HRP can be measured by the organisation. We examine some of these issues below.

4 EVALUATING HRP

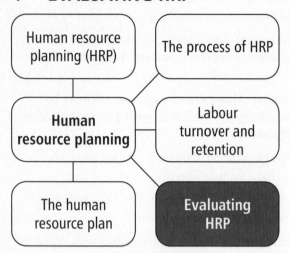

4.1 HOW RELIABLE IS HRP?

Human resource planning is regarded as a scientific, statistical exercise, but it is important to remember that statistics in themselves are limited in value.

Forecasting is not an exact science. Few exponents of even the most sophisticated techniques would claim that they are wholly accurate, although:

(a) The element of guesswork has been substantially reduced by the use of computer models to test various assumptions and to indicate trends

(b) The general principles can still be applied to indicate problems and stimulate control action

ACTIVITY 6   (15 MINS)

HR planners are human beings, and so are the human resources or people-assets themselves: what might be the major limitations on the reliability or objectivity of statistical methods in HR planning?

Statistical methods can be used to create a more accurate model of the future than simple subjective estimates. Computerisation has greatly enhanced the speed, ease and accuracy with which they can be applied, and many PC-based HR software packages are now available. Even so, there are a number of assumptions involved, and the results are purely **quantitative** – for example, numbers of staff required – where **qualitative** information may be required for meaningful decision-making: the effects of change, re-staffing or management style on the culture of the organisation and individual/group behaviour and so on.

WEBLINK

If you are curious about PC-based HR software, you might like to check out Software Source, a site established by the CIPD to provide information on HR software suppliers and products.

▶▶ http://softwaresource.co.uk

Where end products are measurable, **work-study techniques** can offer a reasonably accurate forecast of staffing requirements. In service sectors and 'knowledge work', however, end products and output may not be easily subject to standard-setting. For example, the number of telephone calls, interviews, customers served, or ideas generated is likely to fluctuate widely with the flow of business and the nature of particular transactions.

DEFINITION

Work study methods break down and measure the elements of a given task in order to define the standard number of staff hours per unit of output.

Managerial estimates form the simplest and cheapest method of assessment. As such, they may be the most appropriate – and are the most common – method for small organisations. At the best of times, however, this method has the disadvantage of a high degree of subjectivity, and although this can be controlled to an extent (by requiring managers to support their estimates with reasons and to reconcile their estimates with those of senior management), it is a source of potential risk.

A measure of flexibility will need to be built into any HR plan, so that it can be adapted to suit likely or even unforeseen contingencies. Above all, it should not be seen or communicated as an inflexible plan, as if it were based on certainty.

> 'Clearly, the more precise the information available, the greater the probability that HR plans will be accurate. But, in practice, they are subject to many imponderable factors, some completely outside an organisation's control... international trade, general technological advances, population movements, the human acceptance of or resistance to change, and the quality of leadership and its impact on morale. The environment, then, is uncertain, and so are the people whose activities are being planned. HR plans must therefore be accepted as being continuous, under constant review, and ever-changing. Since they concern people, they must also be negotiable.'

(*Cuming*, 1993)

4.2 IS HRP WORKING?

DEFINITION

A **human resource audit** is an investigation designed to:

(a) Give a picture of the current structure, size and productivity of the organisation's labour force.

(b) Check that HR plans, systems, policies and procedures have been and are being carried out.

The best test of the accuracy and effectiveness of HRP is to check whether the reality has in fact conformed to the forecasts and plans: a basic system of control.

    (a) **Actual staffing levels and trends** should be checked against budgets.

        (i) If HR planners have allowed for reductions in staffing levels through natural wastage, it is important to ensure that such wastage is allowed to happen. (It is a natural tendency for managers to seek replacements for any staff losses, even those which have been budgeted for.)

        (ii) The budgets themselves may be (or may have become) inappropriate. The HR plan must constantly be reviewed and revised in the light of changes and actual (unanticipated) events.

(b) **HR records** should be checked to identify that any change (promotion, transfer, redundancy, recruitment, etc) has been properly approved, in line with the HR plan.

This process may uncover:

(i) Inadequate authorisation of particular types of change; for example, it may be common to transfer employees within the same department without proper approval or reference to the overall staffing plan.

(ii) Unauthorised or unnecessary use of agency or temporary personnel.

(c) **Staff utilisation** should be reviewed: how efficiently is the human resource employed? This process may uncover a need for fundamental change (such as a complete restructure or automation of work). Under-utilisation of a skill category is an inefficient use of the organisation's resources, as well as a common source of personal dissatisfaction among staff.

4.3 IS HRP COST-EFFECTIVE?

Although labour costs in many manufacturing companies are falling as a proportion of total costs, as processes are increasingly automated, HR costs are still significant and may form a large proportion of total costs in labour-intensive sectors such as services.

An organisation should therefore assess the **cost** effect of any HR plan – recruitment drive, training initiative or downsizing exercise – in proportion to the **expected benefits** to be derived from it.

DEFINITION

A **cost-benefit analysis** is a comparison of the cost of an actual or proposed measure with an evaluation or estimate of the benefits gained from it. This will indicate whether the measure has been, or is likely to be, cost-effective – or 'worthwhile'.

There are a number of reasons why a cost-benefit analysis of the HR plan might be useful.

(a) It emphasises the **total cost** of the plan, including wages and related costs, in relation to gains in efficiency or effectiveness.

(b) It allows costs of the plan to be **compared** with other options. For example, once the cost of recruitment has been evaluated, the organisation can assess the merits of alternative plans such as:

(i) Outsourcing the activity

(ii) Developing and multi-skilling existing staff

(iii) Buying capital equipment or altering work processes in other ways to enhance productivity

(c) It emphasises that **cost-effectiveness** – not cost-minimisation – is the aim. For example, temporary or part-time workers may be 'cheaper' for the organisation – but if long-term gains in stability, expertise, management succession, business relationships, knowledge preservation and motivated output are lost (compared with employing full-time, permanent staff), this would be a false economy.

FOR DISCUSSION

Do a cost-benefit analysis of your present studies. Is education and training a good investment – and if so, for whom?

SIGNPOST

It should be clear that HRP, at the stage of closing the gap between supply and demand, actually involves planning in a number of areas of HRM. We end this chapter with a summary of the Human Resource Plan.

5 THE HUMAN RESOURCE PLAN

Once the analysis of human resource requirements has been carried out, and the various options for fulfilling them considered, the **human resource plan** will be drawn up. This may be done at a strategic level (and indeed, as we saw in Section 1.2 above, it will have strategic impact). It will also involve tactical plans and action plans for various measures, according to the strategy that has been chosen. Typical elements might include:

(a) **The resourcing plan**: approaches to obtaining skills/people within the organisation, and by external recruitment

(b) **Internal resource plan**: availability of skills within the organisation; plans to promote/redeploy/develop

(c) **The recruitment plan**: numbers and types of people, and when required; sources of candidates; the recruitment programme; desired 'employer brand' and/or recruitment incentives

(d) **The training plan**: numbers of trainees required and/or existing staff who need training; training programme

(e) **The redevelopment plan**: programmes for transferring or retraining employees

(f) **The flexibility plan**: plans to use part-time workers, jobsharing, homeworking, outsourcing, flexible hour arrangements etc

(g) **The productivity plan**: programmes for improving productivity, or reducing manpower costs; setting productivity targets

(h)   **The downsizing plan**: natural wastage forecasts; where and when redundancies are to occur; policies for selection and declaration of redundancies; redevelopment, retraining or relocation of employees; policy on redundancy payments, union consultation and so on

(i)   **The retention plan**: actions to reduce avoidable labour wastage

The plan should include budgets, targets and standards. It should allocate responsibilities for implementation and control (reporting, monitoring achievement against plan).

CHAPTER ROUNDUP

- HRP is a strategy for the acquisition or reduction, utilisation, improvement and retention of an enterprise's human resources in response to the requirement of the organisation's strategic plan.

- A systematic approach to HRP would be as shown in the diagram below.

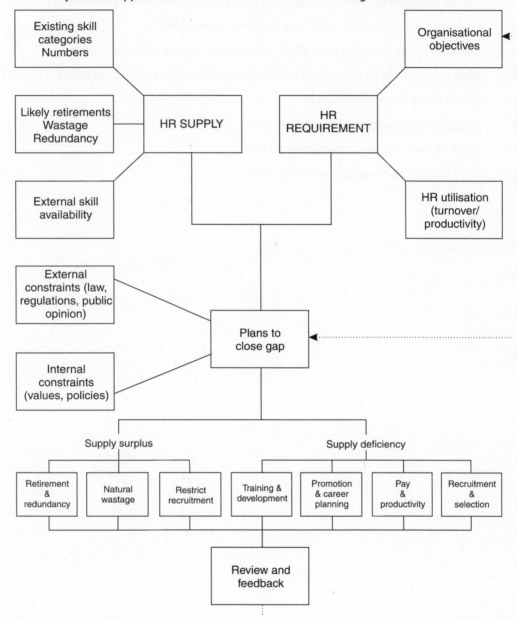

QUICK QUIZ

1   List the elements of human resource planning.

2   Outline the items commonly contained in an organisation's corporate or strategic plan as they affect HRP.

3   List the reasons why human resource planning has increased in importance in recent years.

4   List three basic approaches to HRP in a changing environment

5   Outline the three major stages involved in the human resource planning process.

6   What are the major areas of information required by the human resource planner?

7   How is labour turnover measured?

8   What are the *advantages* of labour turnover?

9   List three methods used in forecasting for HRP.

10 What is meant by the human resource audit?

ANSWERS TO QUICK QUIZ

1   Recruitment, retention, utilisation, improvement and downsizing of staff.   (see Para 1.1)

2   Predicted financial situation; intended product markets and market share; desired output and productivity; changes in location; employee numbers.   (Para 1.2)

3   Difficulty in replacing specialised staff; employment protection legislation; rapid technological change; need for effective utilisation of staff; national skills shortages in certain areas; international competition; computer technology.   (Para 1.3)

4   The staff replacement approach; short-term; HR strategy; vision-driven HRD approach.   (Para 1.4)

5   Forecasting demand; forecasting supply; closing the gap between demand and supply.   (Section 2)

6   Organisational objectives; staff utilisation; labour costs; environmental factors; staff turnover; production levels.

7   Crude labour turnover rate; labour stability index; survival rate analysis.   (Para 3.1)

8   Opportunities for 'new blood'; balanced age structure; promotion/ succession opportunities; reduction of labour surplus.   (Para 3.3)

9   Statistical methods; work study; managerial estimates.   (Para 4.1)

10 The process whereby an organisation ensures that its human resource planning systems work, and that the plans they incorporate are properly implemented.   (Para 4.2)

ANSWERS TO ACTIVITIES

1   A skill shortage might be caused by:

    (a)   Long-term declines in education and training, or in population (nationally or in the local area).

    (b)   The immediate effects of a competitor entering the market or area and employing some of the pool of skilled labour.

    (c)   Increases in demand for the product or service for which the skill is required; or the relocation, resignation or demotivation of key skilled people – for all sorts of personal and circumstantial reasons.

2   (a)   The computer company is operating in an extremely volatile and changing market, which will present HRP difficulties. The technology, and associated skills, are constantly changing, together with competitive pressures: an innovative competitor could 'steal' the market. This is also a highly-skilled business, however, with skill shortages in the labour market, and long training times: despite the difficulties, long-term planning will be important.

    (b)   Some years ago, the local authority would have represented a fairly stable (not to say 'ponderous') bureaucratic structure, with fairly rigid, predictable HR plans. Reductions in funding, and the contracting out of services, have made HRP more difficult and desirable: workforce reduction and flexibility, and the use of HRP to change organisational culture, will be key issues.

(c)   The airline is a business which is potentially volatile, and sensitive to barely controllable factors such as price wars, political/terrorist action, industrial action, airspace restrictions, crashes affecting image, global recession affecting travel, and so on. At the same time it is dependent on several categories of employees (airline pilots, aerospace engineers) who are scarce and have long training cycles: planning ahead for selection and retention will be crucial.

3   (a)   The internet is a rich source of statistical, environmental, benchmarking and other relevant information for HRP. Internal corporate databases (possibly integrated into Human Resource Information Systems) should provide data on current skills, workforce structure, productivity and so on. Expert and decision-support software is also available for manpower and 'Enterprise Resource Planning' (ERP). (You may like to do a web search on 'ERP' or 'Human Resource Planning' and check out some of the resources for yourself.)

       (b)   This may be useful as the beginnings of a research/information database. There are many potential sources of labour and environmental information. Just a few suggestions:

    - CIPD and other HR journals (and their websites)

    - News media

    - Employment and industry journals (*Employment Gazette, Employment Digest,* specific industry journals, *Industrial Relations Review, Labour Market Quarterly*)

    - Government statistical publications (census information, *Social Trends*)

    - Publications, websites and contacts of relevant bodies: trade unions, trade associations, employers' associations, training bodies

    - Competitors and other employers (websites, annual reports and accounts, personal contacts)

4   At the end of 2012, the company works out that it has:

BIM Index: $\dfrac{18 \text{ leavers}}{60 \text{ (average) employees}} \times 100 = 30\%$ **turnover**

This is not uncommon, and would cause no undue worries. However:

Stability index: $\dfrac{2 \text{ year servers}}{20} \times 100 = 10\%$ **stability**

Only 10% of the labour force is stable (and therefore offering the benefits of experience and acclimatisation to the work and culture of the organisation). A crude turnover rate has disguised the significance of what has happened.

5   Common factors include the following.

       (a)   **Incompatibilities with the organisation climate or culture, or its style of leadership**. An organisation might be formal and bureaucratic, where employees are expected to work according to prescribed rules and procedures. Other organisations are more flexible, and allow more scope for individual expression and creativity. Individuals will prefer – and stay with – one system or the other.

       (b)   **Unsatisfactory pay and conditions of employment**. If these are not good enough according to people's needs (or in comparison with others), people will leave to find better terms elsewhere, or will use this as a catalyst to express their discontent in other areas.

(c)   **Poor physical working conditions**. If working conditions are uncomfortable, unclean, unsafe, or noisy, say, people will be more inclined to leave.

(d)   **Lack of career prospects and access to training**. If the chances of advancement before a certain age are low, an ambitious employee is likely to consider leaving to find a job where promotion is likely to come more quickly. The same may be true where an employee wants training for a qualification or skill development, and opportunities are limited in his/her current job.

The second part to this activity is personal to you.

6   (a)   Statistics are not the only element of the planning process, and are subject to interpretation and managerial judgements that are largely qualitative and even highly speculative (involving future growth, say, or potential for innovation).

(b)   Trends in statistics are the product of social processes, which are not readily quantifiable or predictable. Staff leave for various social reasons in (unpredictable) individual cases, to get married, relocate or whatever. The growth of the temporary and freelance workforce is a social trend, as are the buying patterns which dictate demand for goods and services.

Chapter 03 Recruitment

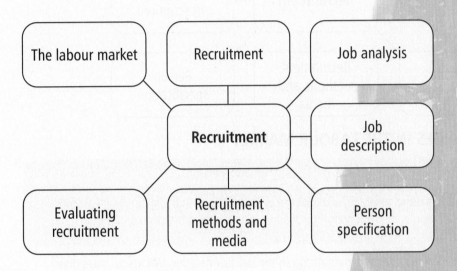

The labour market — Recruitment — Job analysis

Recruitment

Job description

Evaluating recruitment — Recruitment methods and media — Person specification

Introduction

In Chapter 2 we noted that there were sources of labour supply both **inside** the organisation and in its **environment**. In this chapter, we look briefly at the labour market (external and internal) and at some of the issues affecting the **resourcing and recruitment plan**.

Recruitment is the process whereby an organisation communicates opportunities and information to the labour market in order to attract the quantity and quality of potential employees it requires to fulfil its human resource plan. This chapter outlines a systematic approach to this task.

The process of deciding which of the candidates short-listed by the recruitment process are suitable is called **selection**: this will be discussed in Chapter 4.

Your objectives

In this chapter you will learn about the following.

- The structured approach to recruitment (highlighting 'best practice')
- Recruitment policies and procedures, including job analysis, job description and person specification

- Recruitment methods and media, including job advertisements, application forms and e-recruitment

- The legislative framework and benchmark evidence guiding recruitment policy and practice

1 THE LABOUR MARKET

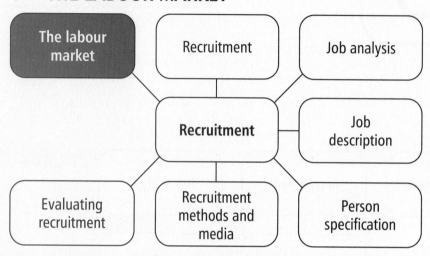

1.1 CHANGES IN THE LABOUR MARKET

DEFINITION

The **labour market** is the sphere in which labour is 'bought' and 'sold', and in which market concepts such as supply, demand and price operate with regard to human resources.

The **labour market** has changed dramatically in the last few decades. Writers on manpower planning (as it was then called) in the 1970s suggested that a 'seller's market' had been established, as technology increased the skills and, therefore, scarcity value of employees in certain jobs, and as the scale of state benefits blunted the fear of unemployment; the initiative seemed to be with the employee, or with organised groups of employees.

The decline of manufacturing, the increase of women in employment, the globalisation of business (allowing offshoring of production and service provision to low-cost labour countries) and the more general application of technology, among other factors, have changed that situation. A 'buyer's market' for labour now gives employers considerable power, with a large pool of available labour created by unemployment and non-career (temporary, freelance) labour.

On the other hand, even in conditions of high overall employment, particular skill shortages still exist and may indeed be *more* acute because of economic pressures on education and training. Engineers and software designers, among other specialist and highly trained groups, are the target of fierce competition among employers, forcing a re-evaluation of recruitment and retention policies.

SIGNPOST

We discuss labour market in other contexts in this Course Book: as a spur to flexibility (in Chapter 9) and as a globalised phenomenon (in Chapter 12).

Here we note some of the key labour market trends that may affect the recruitment plan.

BPP
LEARNING MEDIA

The following have been identified (Torrington *et al*, 2011) as the three major trends in the UK labour market as a whole:

- Demographic trends
- Diversity
- Skills and qualifications

1.2 DEMOGRAPHIC TRENDS

DEFINITION

Demography is an analysis of statistics on birth and death rates, the age structure of populations, ethnic groups within communities, population movements and so on.

(a) The **number of people who are economically active** in the UK has steadily increased over recent decades , principally due to immigration and the expanding number of women returning to, and remaining in, paid work (supported by diversity and family-friendly HR policies). Over the long term, however, the proportion of the population that is available for work is expected to shrink: birth-rates continue to fall, and life-expectancy to increase, creating a retired population which is larger in proportion to the population of those of working age.

(b) As a result, the **age profile of the workforce** is also changing: the population as a whole is getting older, with fewer young people entering the workforce (especially as a greater proportion of them remain longer in full-time education). This was reinforced by the introduction of age diversity legislation in the UK encouraging the selection and retention of mature workers. (See Chapter 10 for a greater description of the legislation relating to discrimination)

UK national statistics

The population of the UK is growing in size and becoming increasingly older. Ageing refers both to the ageing of the population and the increasing number of people reaching older age.

Over the period 1984 – 2009 the number of people aged 65 and over in the UK increased by 20% to 10.1 million; in 2009, 16% of the population were aged 65 and over. The number of people aged 85 and over more than doubled over the same period to 1.4 million and the percentage aged under 16 fell from 21% to 19%.

In 2009 the median age for women (40 years) was higher than for men (38 years). This is because, on average, women live longer than men. However, the gender gap has narrowed; in 1984 the median ages for women and men were 36 and 33 years respectively, a difference of 3 years.

Population ageing will continue for the next few decades. By 2034 the number of people aged 85 and over is projected to be 2.5 times larger than in 2009, reaching 3.5 million and accounting for 5% of the total population. The population aged 65 and over will account for 23% of the total population in 2034, while the proportion of the population aged between 16 and 64 is due to fall from 65% to 59%.

ACTIVITY 1 (10 MINS)

What can you see as the main implications for employers of the demographic changes identified above, in terms of challenges in attracting and retaining quality workers?

1.3 DIVERSITY

The workforce is becoming increasingly diverse in its make-up, in several respects.

(a) **Sex**. Increased female participation in the workforce has been a significant social trend since the Second World War. The employment rate for women of working age is currently just under 70%. Although a majority of managerial posts are still occupied by men, and there is a continued gap in overall pay levels, there has been an increase in the representation of women at all levels. There is still significant segregation in terms of the types of work performed, with particular areas of work dominated by either men or women. Women currently account for over 80% of part-time workers in the UK. One of the effects of the financial crisis has been the growth of part-time jobs, and the number of people in part-time jobs who want to work more hours but are unable to – referred to as 'underemployed'.

(b) **Ethnic diversity**. Multi-racial representation has greatly increased in the UK workforce. The Workplace Employee Relations Survey (2004) suggested that over 50% of workplaces are multi-racial compared to only 30% in 1980.

> In February 2012 *The Guardian* newspaper reported:
>
> The big number in today's story is the net migration of 250,000 people – the difference between the 593,000 people who came into the country in the year to June 2011 and the 343,000 who left the country to live abroad for more than 12 months.
>
> Although the numbers of people coming into the country are up by about 2% on the previous year, the reason the balance has grown may be more due to the 1.2% drop in people emigrating.
>
> Estimates shows India as the top country for people coming to the UK with 11.9% of all immigrants. It's followed by Pakistan, (5.8%), Poland (5.4%), Australia (5.2%) and China (5.2%). That has changed a lot since the early-1990s, when Germany was the top country. It also shows that most people emigrating from the UK go to Australia, followed by the USA.
>
> In the year to June 2011 the estimated number of long-term migrants whose main reason for entering the UK was work-related was 185,000 – 22% lower than the peak of 239,000 in the year to June 2008. The estimated number of long-term migrants whose main reason for entering the UK was formal study was 237,000 in the year to June 2011 – lower than the peak of 248,000 arriving to study in the year to September 2010.

Major implications for employee resourcing include the need to take account of:

(a) **Anti-discrimination legislation** and **best practice** in recruitment (discussed further in Paragraph 2.4 below). As well as legal protection for groups which have traditionally been under-represented in the workplace, heightened sensitivity to such matters means that positive equal opportunity and diversity policies play an important part in building an employer brand which will enable organisations to attract quality labour.

(b) The needs of increasingly diverse family shapes and circumstances, in order to attract and retain people. Legislation has begun to address the needs of dual income families (eg parental leave and time off for emergencies) but proactive HR initiatives – such as career breaks and childcare support – contribute importantly to a 'family-friendly' employer brand.

FOR DISCUSSION

(Grant Thornton International Business Report, 2012)

- Businesses in Russia, followed by Botswana, the Philippines and Thailand have the most women in senior management; those in Germany, India and Japan the least

- Less than 1 in 10 businesses has a female CEO, with women largely employed in finance and human resources (HR) roles

What do you think accounts for these practices?

What actions could organisations take to change these current practices?

SIGNPOST

Other issues in the management of diversity are covered in detail in Chapter 10 of this Course Book.

1.4 SKILLS AND QUALIFICATIONS

There has been a steady decline in the demand for skills in the manufacturing and agricultural sectors, and a corresponding growth in managerial and professional occupations and service industries. A new premium has been placed on interpersonal skills (such as team-working, customer service and communication) and on personal skills (such as flexibility, time-management and self-motivation).

Since the early 1990s, there has been an increase in the number of **graduates** entering the labour market. However:

(a) Taylor (2010) points out that although more and more people are going to university in the UK, insufficient numbers are going to meet the potential future demand; the shortfall is around 15%.

(b) '...the future is likely to involve a substantial tightening of skilled labour market, lifting still further the advantages that will accrue to those who are best placed to recruit and then retain the limited number of people who have the most sought-after skills.'   (Torrington *et al*, 2011)

The implications for recruiters may be the need to:

(a) Compete more aggressively for skilled candidates

(b) Re-define jobs to maximise the use of scarcer (or more expensive) skills

(c) Recruit (or relocate work) overseas

(d) 'Lower' recruitment requirements for specific skills and qualifications and invest in employee training and development in the required skills

EXAMPLE   CHINA TURNS TO SOCIAL MEDIA TO RECRUIT STAFF

Companies in the Middle Kingdom are increasingly using social media to find the top talent – especially among foreign workers.

Chinese employers are increasingly turning to social media to recruit staff as they struggle to find the right talent.

Such a move may give the upper hand to expatriates (expats), many of whom are already familiar with social media tools such as LinkedIn as a recruitment tool among Western companies.

Interestingly, the driving force isn't coming from the head offices of multinationals but their Chinese operations, who complain about not being able to find the right candidates, especially among foreign workers.

Traditional recruitment methods are proving less effective when it comes to expats, who increasingly use social networks to search for employment opportunities.

The China division of accountancy firm Deloitte Touche Tohmatsu recently offered a virtual office tour on Weibo, China's equivalent of Twitter. Candidates could choose to tour either its Shanghai, Beijing or Hong Kong offices, and go to meeting rooms and offices where they could talk to existing employees.

About 17,000 people signed up to play the office tour game, helping to build up a useful database of candidates, including a large percentage of foreigners who are already familiar with such exercises.

Later this year hotel chain Marriott is launching a social game on Renren – China's equivalent of Facebook – which will allow users to manage a hotel or restaurant so they can become familiar with the hospitality industry.

Marriott needs to hire 20,000 people in the Middle Kingdom within the next three years as it expands its hotel empire from 60 to 100.

Jidi Guo, of Shanghai-based Maximum Employment Marketing Group, said: 'Job boards and corporate career sites will remain important recruitment channels, but they are very different from social media. In the West, this space is dominated by LinkedIn, but China does not yet have a widely used business social network.

Nor is there a Chinese equivalent to BranchOut, the Facebook-based app that recently nabbed US$25 million in funding for social recruitment. Social networks are a promising recruitment channel but the tools available in China today are still in their infancy.'

Weibo recently launched a service for job searchers to post mini CVs on its website with a limit of 140 Chinese characters.

The mini CVs were used by computer giant Lenovo in a recruitment drive which led to a number of people being hired.

(*The Independent*, 2012)

FOR DISCUSSION

Select an organisation or business sector that you know well, and identify the key issues facing human resourcing in that organisation or sector.

(Alternatively, you may wish to interview a contact in business, and write a report on the recruitment issues in his or her firm.)

BPP
LEARNING MEDIA

ACTIVITY 2 (45 MINS)

Outline a simple HRP procedure (refer to Section 2 of Chapter 2 if you need to) which will take into account demographic and educational trends in the country of your choice.

SIGNPOST

When forecasting the supply of labour and skills available to the organisation to meet the demands of its activities and objectives, the HR planner must take into account:

- The current skill base, size and structure of its existing workforce
- The potential for change in that skill base, size and structure

This constitutes an internal labour market.

1.5 INTERNAL SOURCES OF LABOUR

If the organisation faces a demand for a particular skill, that demand may be satisfied from within the existing labour force by:

(a) **Retaining** skilled individuals, against the flow of labour turnover

(b) **Transferring** or deploying individuals with the relevant skills from their current job to the job where those skills can be utilised more effectively

(c) **Training and developing** individuals in the required skills and abilities

(d) **Exploiting contacts** with present employees, friends and family of employees, and former external applicants, who might be referred (and to an extent, pre-appraised) for vacancies.

If the organisation experiences **fluctuating** demand for a particular skill or for numbers of workers, it may need to approach the above strategies somewhat differently, in order to be able to deploy labour flexibly. If a retail business requires extra sales people in the pre-Christmas period, for example, or a factory requires trained specialists in a particular field only at certain stages of a project – or in the event of problems – what do they do? Train, retain and transfer sufficient people for the busiest scenario? You should be able to see that this would be costly and inefficient – and unlikely to enhance the credibility of the HR planner! This is, in essence, what **labour flexibility** – in terms of numbers and skills deployed – is about.

SIGNPOST

Retention was discussed in Chapter 2. Flexibility is discussed in Chapter 9. Here we briefly discuss *promotion* as a form of internal 'recruitment'.

1.6 PROMOTION AND SUCCESSION

DEFINITION

Succession is the act, process or right by which one person 'succeeds to' or takes over the office or post of another person. In a business organisation, there may be a policy whereby a 'successor' is developed to replace a more senior manager who retires or leaves.

Promotion and succession policies are a vital part of the human resource plan, as a form of risk management associated with the internal supply of labour. The planned development of staff (not just skills training, but experience and growth in responsibility) is essential to ensure the **continuity of performance** in the organisation. This is particularly so for **management succession planning**: the departure of a senior manager with no planned or 'groomed' successor could leave a gap in the organisation structure and the lead time for developing a suitable replacement may be very long.

A comprehensive **promotion programme**, as part of the overall HR plan will include:

(a)   Establishing the relative significance of jobs by analysis, description and classification, so that the line and consequences of promotion are made clear.

(b)   Establishing methods of assessing staff and their potential for fulfilling the requirements of more senior positions.

(c)   Planning in advance for training where necessary to enhance potential and develop specific skills.

(d)   Policy with regard to internal promotion or external recruitment and training.

A coherent **promotion policy** may vary to include provisions such as the following.

(a)   All promotions, as far as possible, and all things being equal, are to be made from within the firm. (For the argument for this, see our answer to Activity 4.)

(b)   Merit and ability (systematically appraised) should be the principal basis of promotion, rather than seniority (age or years of service) – although this may vary in cultures where seniority is a key value.

(c)   Vacancies should be advertised and open to all employees.

(d)   There should be full opportunities for all employees to be promoted to the highest grades.

(e)   Training should be offered to encourage and develop employees of ability and ambition in advance of promotion.

(f)   Scales of pay, areas of responsibility, duties and privileges of each post etc should be clearly communicated so that employees know what promotion means – in other words, what they are being promoted *to*.

ACTIVITY 3   (15 MINS)

What problems with line/departmental managers can you foresee for an HR manager who attempts to implement a policy such as the one outlined above?

1.7   INTERNAL OR EXTERNAL RECRUITMENT?

Promotion is useful from the firm's point of view in establishing a management succession, filling more senior positions with proven, experienced and loyal employees. It is also one of the main forms of reward the organisation can offer its employees.

The decision of whether to promote from within or fill a position from outside will hinge on many factors. If there is simply no-one available on the current staff with the expertise or ability required (say, if the organisation is venturing into new areas of activity, or changing its business processes), the recruitment manager may have to seek qualified people externally. If there is time, a person of particular potential in the organisation could be trained in the necessary skills, but that requires an analysis of the costs as compared with the possible (and often less quantifiable) benefits.

ACTIVITY 4 (15 MINS)

Outline what you think would be the advantages of promoting from within the organisation, instead of recruiting someone from outside. What would be the main disadvantages?

2 RECRUITMENT

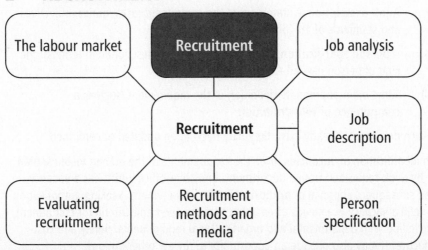

DEFINITION

Recruitment is the part of the human resourcing process concerned with finding the applicants: it is a positive action by management, going into the labour market, communicating opportunities and information, and encouraging applications from suitable candidates.

Aims of the recruitment process

We can analyse the aims of the recruitment process into three main areas.

- **The creation of a pool of suitable candidates**. Recruitment is about attracting applications from sufficient candidates with the appropriate qualifications, skills, experience and personal qualities. The aim is to create a pool of candidates for each vacancy that arises so that the most suitable can be appointed.

- **The management of the recruitment process itself**. Those responsible for recruitment will also be charged with the development and refinement of the procedures and practices in use. These must be clear, effective and applied consistently. All applicants must be treated fairly and equitably and, in particular, a satisfactory equal opportunities policy must be applied.

- **The basis of selection**. The recruitment process feeds into selection and must support the requirement that selection is made on merit and in accordance with the stated requirements of each job vacancy.

2.1 A SYSTEMATIC APPROACH

The overall aim of the recruitment process in an organisation is to obtain the quantity and quality of candidates required to fulfil the objectives of the organisation.

A systematic approach to recruitment will involve the following stages.

(a) Detailed **human resource planning** defining what resources the organisation needs to meet its objectives.

(b) **Job analysis** (or variants), so that for any given job or role there is a definition of the skills, knowledge and attributes required to perform the job.

   (i) A **job description**: a statement of the component tasks, duties, objectives and standards of the job

   (ii) A **person specification**: a reworking of the job description in terms of the kind of person needed to perform the job

   (iii) Some other appropriate definition of the requirement, such as a **competence or role definition**

   If such documents already exist, they may need to be updated or confirmed.

(c) An identification of **vacancies**, from the requirements of the human resource plan or by a job requisition from a department, branch or office which has a vacancy, and subsequent approval or **authorisation** for engagement. Seeking authorisation to refill a vacancy is a means of ensuring that the need and criteria for recruitment, are in line with departmental and organisational requirements, timely and cost-effective. It may also provide an opportunity to review other options.

(d) Evaluation of the **sources of skills**, which again should be identified in the human resource plan. Internal and external sources, and media for reaching them (eg through **job advertisement** or e-recruitment, say) will be considered.

(e) Preparation and publication of recruitment **information**, which will:

   (i) Attract the attention and interest of potentially suitable candidates

   (ii) Give a favourable (but accurate) impression of the job and the organisation

   (iii) Equip interested candidates to make an application (how and to whom to apply, desired skills, qualifications etc).

(f) **Processing applications** prior to the selection process. This may include:

   (i) Screening replies at the end of the specified period for application
   (ii) Short-listing candidates for initial consideration
   (iii) Advising applicants of the progress of their application
   (iv) Drawing up a programme for the selection process which follows

ACTIVITY 5 (30 MINS)

Which features of the recruitment process suggest that it might be most efficient and effective if *centralised* within the HR function, rather than delegated to line managers in their own departments? (Refer back to Chapter 1 if you need some hints.) Suggest five advantages of centralised recruitment.

Trends towards flexibility and multi-skilling have encouraged a slightly different approach, which is oriented more towards '**fitting the job to the person**' than 'fitting the person to the job' in a highly innovative market, technological environment or organisational culture. For example, rigid

BPP
LEARNING MEDIA

job descriptions would not be suitable. In order to creatively exploit the opportunities of such environments, organisations should be able to look at the skills and attributes of the people they employ, and those of gifted outsiders, and ask: 'What needs doing, that this person would do best?'

In a relatively informal environment, where all-round knowledge/skills and experience are highly valued and suitable external labour resources are scarce (say, in management consultancy), this approach would give much-needed flexibility. The organisation would try to recruit excellent, flexible, motivated and multi-skilled personnel, without reference to any specific job, as defined by a job description. They would form an available resource for any task or requirement that arose on a project or 'virtual project team' basis.

However, the **'selection' approach** ('fitting the person to the job') is still by far the most common, and is suitable for most organisations with fairly defined goals and structures.

2.2 RECRUITMENT POLICY AND BEST PRACTICE

Detailed procedures for recruitment should only be devised and implemented within the context of a coherent **policy**, or code of conduct.

A typical recruitment policy might deal with:

(a) Internal advertisement of vacancies

(b) Efficient and courteous processing of applications

(c) Fair and accurate provision of information to potential recruits

(d) Selection of candidates on the basis of qualification, without discrimination on any grounds

(e) Recruitment of labour reflecting the composition of society as a whole, and perhaps local labour where possible (supporting diversity and social sustainability targets, eg in the public sector)

Detailed **procedures** should be devised in order to make recruitment activity systematic and consistent throughout the organisation (especially where it is devolved to line managers). Apart from the resourcing requirements, which need to be effectively and efficiently met, there is a **marketing** aspect to recruitment, as one 'interface' between the organisation and the outside world: applicants who feel they have been unfairly treated, or recruits who leave because they feel they have been misled, do not enhance the organisation's reputation in the labour market.

ACTIVITY 6 (1 HOUR)

Find out what the recruitment and selection procedures are in an organisation of your choice. These may be stated on the corporate website, or you may be able to ask a recruitment or HR officer. (Alternatively, do a web search on the phrase 'Recruitment Code of Practice' – and browse some of the varied examples of good practice…)

If you are employed, get hold of and examine some of the documentation your own organisation uses. Illustrations are given in this chapter, but practice and terminology vary.

2.3 INFLUENCES ON RECRUITMENT POLICY

Recruitment policy will be influenced by the following considerations.

(a) The organisation's **image** in the community, marketplace and labour market: its **'employer brand'** and identity as an employer. Recruitment advertising, in particular, is a public relations exercise: it must reflect the organisation's values and professionalism – and, where appropriate, its marketing message (quality, products/services etc)

(b)   The **human resource plan** and subsidiary plans

(c)   **Fairness**, **courtesy and professionalism** in dealing with applicants, as defined by 'best practice' benchmark evidence

(d)   **Legislation and regulations** affecting:

    (i)   **Terms and conditions** able to be offered to (or imposed on) potential employees (for example, minimal wage, working hours, holiday entitlements)

    (ii)   **Equal opportunities** and **diversity** – the prevention of direct and indirect discrimination by:

- The wording and placing of recruitment advertisements which imply or tend towards a preference for a particular group

- Indicating or implying intention to discriminate in internal planning, advertising or instructions to recruitment agencies

This is discussed further below.

    (iii)   **Labour mobility** – for example, discrimination on the basis of nationality or national origin against candidates from the European Economic Area

(e)   The **cultural values** of the organisation, as well as the national culture in which it operates. These are often reflected in the attributes considered essential or desirable in candidates; the importance attached to educational, vocational or professional qualifications; and/or identification with the organisation's self-image (responsible, fun, fast-paced, flexible or whatever)

WEBLINK

If you are interested in the concept of 'employer brand', see:

CIPD 2012 Factsheet on Employer Brand

▶▶ www.cipd.co.uk/hr-resources/factsheets/employer-brand.aspx

2.4 THE LEGISLATIVE FRAMEWORK ON RECRUITMENT

We discuss **equal opportunity** and the **management of diversity** in detail in Chapter 10, as one of the critical HRM issues. However, the key points in relation to recruitment, are as follows.

The Equality Act 2010 consolidated all the previous discrimination legislation, and introduced the concept of 'protected characteristics':

- Age
- Disability
- Gender reassignment
- Marriage and civil partnership
- Pregnancy and maternity
- Race
- Religion or belief

- Sex
- Sexual orientation

These 'characteristics' are protected by the provisions of the Act, consequently employers need to ensure they do not discriminate against someone who possess one or more of these protected characteristics.

The Equality and Human Rights Commission (EHRC)

The EHRC replaced the former Commission for Racial Equality, the Equal Opportunities Commission and the Disability Rights Commission. The EHRC provides the following advice about recruitment. It is unlawful for an employer to discriminate against a candidate for a job because of their age, disability, race, religion or belief, sexual orientation, background or gender in any part of the recruitment process – in job descriptions, person specifications, application forms, during interviews, in tests, or in shortlisting.

For example, application forms should not ask for details that are not relevant to the job, such as country of birth or sexual orientation (except where such questions are contained in monitoring forms that are separated from application forms before assessment). During interviews, questions about a woman's plans for starting a family, or asking an applicant whether they think that they will 'fit in' with the organisation, may also be evidence of discrimination.

However, an employer can ask if the person has a disability so any special arrangements can be made, as necessary, for them to attend an interview.

Evidence of discrimination

There is no obligation on an employer to show that they have selected the best candidate for the job. However, all employers are recommended to keep records that allow them, if challenged, to justify their decisions to select particular candidates and reject others.

Employers need to be able to show that each selection is based on objective evidence of a person's ability to do the job satisfactorily, and not on assumptions or prejudices about race, gender, disability, sexual orientation, religion or belief, or age. An employer is unlikely to say that they rejected the person for any of these reasons. But if the person believes there is evidence of discrimination, they may be able to make a case.

A key point that is worth highlighting is that the Act contains a general principle that health-related inquiries are not permitted until a job offer has been made. However, the recruiter is allowed to ask questions to establish whether the candidate is able to perform the tasks and functions 'intrinsic' to the work. This would allow questions relating to a person's ability, for example, to lift and carry where that would be necessary for the job, but would not permit questions about general impairments, for example past mental illness. It should not be overlooked that the employer still has a duty regarding reasonable adjustments.

FOR DISCUSSION

'For those employers who ignore or fail to comply with [diversity and equal opportunity] legislation, the consequences will be severe,' says [employment lawyer] Richard Lister.

'Damage can also be inflicted on a company's reputation', according to [diversity manager for financial services group, HBOS] Jones. 'Forget about legal claims: it is about treating people with respect.

'It's also about the war for talent. Employers will also miss out on a talented and diverse workforce and lose their competitive edge if they ignore this legislation', believes Dinah Warman, CAP adviser, diversity. 'These new legal obligations will help employers stamp out the kinds of prejudices that stop organisations from accessing the talent they need and that keep talented people out of the job,' she said.'   (Higginbottom, 2003)

What are the HRM values behind each of these three statements? You might like to take each of the three positions and argue them against opposing or resistant viewpoints.

SIGNPOST

We now discuss some of the recruitment procedures listed in Paragraph 2.1 in more detail.

3 JOB ANALYSIS

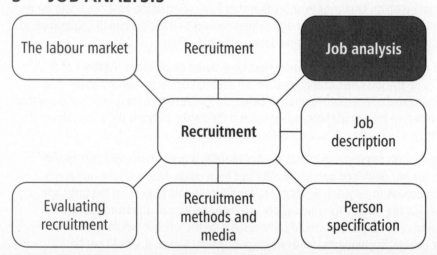

The labour market — Recruitment — **Job analysis**

Recruitment — Job description — Person specification — Recruitment methods and media — Evaluating recruitment

DEFINITION

Job analysis is 'the determination of the essential characteristics of a job', the process of examining a job to identify its component parts and the circumstances in which it is performed.
(British Standards Institute).

The product of the analysis is usually a **job specification** – a detailed statement of the activities (mental and physical) involved in the job, and other relevant factors in the social and physical environment.

3.1 USES OF JOB ANALYSIS

Job analysis, and the job specification resulting from it, may be used by managers:

(a) In **recruitment and selection** – for a detailed description of the vacancy to provide a source of information for the preparation of job descriptions and personnel specifications

(b) For **appraisal** – to assess how well an employee has fulfilled the requirements of the job

(c) In devising **training programmes** – to assess the knowledge and skills necessary in a job

(d) In establishing **rates of pay** – this will be discussed later in connection with job evaluation

(e) In eliminating **risks** – identifying any hazards in the job

(f) In reorganisation of the **organisational structure** – by reappraising the purpose and necessity of jobs and their relationship to each other

3.2 CONTENT OF JOB ANALYSIS

Information which should be elicited from a job appraisal is both task and worker-oriented, including:

(a) **Initial requirements of the employee**: aptitudes, qualifications, experience, training required; personality and attitudinal considerations

(b) **Duties and responsibilities of the job**: physical aspects; mental effort; routine or requiring initiative; difficult and/or disagreeable features; degree of independence of discretion; responsibilities for staff, materials, equipment or cash etc; component tasks (where, when, how frequently, how carried out); standards of output and/or accuracy required; relative value of tasks and how they fit together

(c) **Environment and conditions of the job**: physical surroundings, with notable features such as temperature or noise; hazards; remuneration; other conditions such as hours, shifts, benefits, holidays; career prospects; provision of employee services – canteens, protective clothing etc

(d) **Social factors of the job**: size of the department; teamwork or isolation; type of people dealt with – senior management, the public; amount of supervision; job status

3.3 METHODS OF JOB ANALYSIS

Opportunities for analyses occur when jobs fall vacant, when salaries are reviewed, or when targets are being set, and the HR department should take advantage of such opportunities to review and revise existing job specifications.

Job analysis can be carried out by:

(a) **Observation of working practice**, where jobs are relatively routine and repetitive. The analyst watches and records the job holder's activity, task times and performance standards, working conditions etc. A proforma question sheet listing the factors to be recorded is normally used, incorporating range statements (circumstances in which each task is carried out and standards of competence required) and rating scales.

(b) **Questionnaires and interviews**, for jobs with longer task cycles and invisible work (planning, problem-solving and so on). The job holder is asked to explain, describe and quantify (as far as possible) the job. His or her manager, and other third parties, may be asked to complete the same exercise.

(c) **Diaries, time sheets and other self-recording techniques**. The job holder may be asked periodically to record activity, or may include **critical incidents** highlighting key aspects of the job.

ACTIVITY 7 (15 MINS)

The fact that a job analysis is being carried out may cause some concern among employees: they may fear that standards will be raised, rates cut, or that the job may be found to be redundant or require rationalisation.

How might the analyst need to carry out his or her work in order to gain their confidence?

4 JOB DESCRIPTION

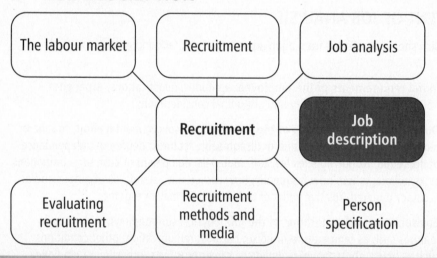

DEFINITION

A **job description** is a broad outline of a job or position at a given time (since jobs are dynamic, subject to change and variation). 'It is a written statement of those facts which are important regarding the duties, responsibilities, and their organisational and operational interrelationships.'

(Livy, 1988)

4.1 PURPOSES AND USES OF JOB DESCRIPTIONS

In **recruitment**, a job description can be used to:

(a) Decide which skills (for example, technical, human, conceptual, design) and qualifications are required of the job holder. When formulating recruitment advertisements, and interviewing an applicant for the vacancy, the interviewer can use the resulting specification to match the candidate against the job.

(b) Assess whether the job will efficiently utilise the abilities and provide scope for the aspirations of the prospective job holder.

(c)   Determine a rate of pay which is fair for the job, if this has not already been decided by some other means.

4.2 THE CONTENTS OF A JOB DESCRIPTION

A job description should be clear and concise, and so ought not to be lengthy. A standard format for a job description should provide the information listed below.

(a)   **Job title**, department and job code number; the person to whom the job holder is responsible; possibly, the grading of the job.

(b)   **Job summary** – detailing in a few paragraphs the major functions and any tools, machinery and special equipment used; possibly also a small organisation chart.

(c)   **Job scope and content** – for manual work, a list of the sequence of operations that constitute the job, noting main levels of difficulty. In the case of management tasks there should be a list of the main duties and responsibilities of the job, indicating frequency of performance – typically between 5 and 15 main duties listed. This includes the degree of initiative involved, and the nature of responsibility (for other people, machinery and/or other resources).

(d)   The extent (and limits) of the job holder's authority and responsibility.

(e)   Statement showing relation of job to other closely associated jobs, including superior and subordinate positions and liaison required with other departments.

(f)   Working hours, basis of pay and benefits, and conditions of employment, including location, special pressures, social isolation, physical conditions, or health hazards.

(g)   Opportunities for training, transfer and promotion.

(h)   Possibly, also, objectives and expected results, which will be compared with actual performance during employee appraisal – although this may be done as a separate exercise, as part of the appraisal process.

(i)   Any formal qualifications required.

e.g.   **EXAMPLE**   **JOB DESCRIPTION**

MIDWEST BANK PLC

1.   *Job title.*   Clerk (Grade 2)

2.   *Branch.*   All branches and administrative offices

3.   *Job summary.*   To provide clerical support to activities within the bank

4.   *Job content.*   Typical duties will include:

          (a)   Cashier's duties
          (b)   Processing of branch clearing
          (c)   Processing of standing orders
          (d)   Support to branch management

5.   *Reporting structure.*

              Administrative officer/assistant manager

              Supervisor (Grade 3)

              Clerk (Grade 2)

---

6.   *Experience/Education:* Experience not required; minimum 3 GCSEs or equivalent

7.   *Training to be provided:* Initial on-the-job training plus regular formal courses and training

8.   *Hours:* 38 hours per week

9.   *Objectives and appraisal:* Annual appraisal in line with objectives above

10.   *Salary:* Refer to separate standard salary structure

Job description prepared by: Head office HR department (October 2012)

4.3 LIMITATIONS OF JOB DESCRIPTIONS

Townsend (1985) suggested that job descriptions are of limited use.

(a)   They are only suited for jobs where the work is largely repetitive and therefore performed by low-grade employees.

(b)   Jobs are likely to be constantly changing as turbulent business environments impact upon them, so a job description is constantly out-of-date or limiting.

(c)   Job descriptions stifle flexibility and encourage demarcation disputes, where people adhere strictly to the contents of the job description, rather than responding flexibly to task or organisational requirements.

Where job descriptions are used, it should be remembered that:

(a)   A job description is like a photograph, an image 'frozen' at one point in time

(b)   A job description needs constant and negotiated revision

(c)   A job description should be secondary in importance to a customer requirement, quality improvement or problems solved

4.4 ALTERNATIVES TO JOB DESCRIPTION

It has been suggested that work requirements should be defined in terms of the contribution or outcomes expected of the job holder.

Some organisations are therefore moving towards:

(a)   **Goal, competence or accountability profiles**, setting out the outputs and performance levels expected of the individual (or team). We examine competence profiles a little later.

(b)   **Role definitions**, defining the part played by the job holder in meeting organisational and departmental objectives. A role definition is therefore wider than a job description, focusing less on 'content' than on how the job holder contributes to business processes and results through competent and flexible performances.

A role profile or definition will therefore specify the overall purpose of the role, what role holders are expected to achieve (key results) and what they will be accountable for, and the behavioural/technical competences required to achieve the defined level of contribution.

BPP
LEARNING MEDIA

5   PERSON SPECIFICATION

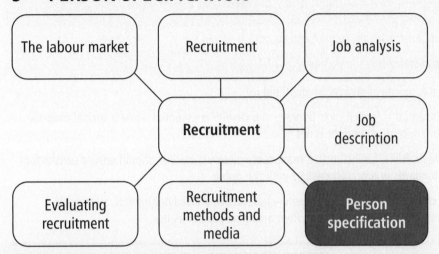

 DEFINITION

A **person specification** profiles the type of person the organisation should be trying to recruit for a given position: that is, the 'ideal' candidate.

Professor Alec Rodger (1970) was a pioneer of the systematic approach to recruitment and selection in the UK. He suggested that:

> If matching *[ie of demands of the job and the person who is to perform it]* is to be done satisfactorily, the requirements of an occupation (or job) must be described in the same terms as the aptitudes of the people who are being considered for it.

This was the basis for the formulation of person specification as a way of matching people to jobs on the basis of comparative sets of data: defining job requirements and personal suitability along the same lines.

5.1   MODELS FOR PERSON SPECIFICATION

Two influential models were adopted as the basis of person specification.

The Seven Point Plan (Rodger, 1970)	Five Point Pattern of Personality (Munro Fraser, 1971)
Physical attributes (such as neat appearance, ability to speak clearly and without impediment)	Impact on others, including physical attributes, speech and manner
Attainment (including educational qualifications)	Acquired knowledge or qualifications, including education, training and work experience
General intelligence	Innate ability, including mental agility, aptitude for learning
Special aptitudes (such as neat work, speed and accuracy)	Motivation: individual goals, demonstrated effort and success at achieving them
Interests (practical and social)	Adjustment: emotional stability, tolerance of stress, human relations skills

The Seven Point Plan (Rodger, 1970)	Five Point Pattern of Personality (Munro Fraser, 1971)
Disposition (or manner: friendly, helpful and so on)	
Background circumstances	

Each feature in the specification may be classified as:

(a) **Essential** – for instance, honesty in a cashier is essential while a special aptitude for conceptual thought is not

(b) **Desirable** – for instance, a reasonably pleasant manner should ensure satisfactory standards in a person dealing with the public

(c) **Contra-indicated** – some features are actively disadvantageous, such as an inability to work in a team when acting as project leader.

EXAMPLE   **PERSON SPECIFICATION: CUSTOMER ACCOUNTS MANAGER**

	ESSENTIAL	DESIRABLE	CONTRA-INDICATED
Physical attributes	• Clear speech • Well-groomed • Good health		Chronic ill-health and absence
Attainments	• 2 'A' levels • GCSE Maths and English • Thorough knowledge of retail environment	• Degree (any discipline) • Marketing training 2 years' experience in supervisory post	No experience of supervision or retail environment
Intelligence	High verbal intelligence		
Aptitudes	• Facility with numbers • Attention to detail and accuracy • Social skills for customer relations	• Analytical abilities (problem solving) • Understanding of systems and IT	• No mathematical ability • Low tolerance of technology
Interests	Social: team activity		• Time-consuming hobbies • 'Solo' interests only
Disposition	• Team player • Persuasive • Tolerance of pressure and change	Initiative	• Anti-social • Low tolerance of responsibility
Circumstances	Able to work late, take work home	Located in area of office	

5.2 LIMITATIONS OF PERSON SPECIFICATIONS

As our example suggests, a wide number of variables may be included in a person specification. If it is not used flexibly, however, and the specification fails to evolve as business and employment conditions change, it may swiftly lose its relevance. For example:

(a) Attainments are often focused on educational achievements, since there has traditionally been a strong correlation between management potential and higher education. However, this does not necessarily reflect the range of learning and experience available, nor the increasing diversity of educational backgrounds and qualification standards in a global labour market.

(b) 'Physical attributes' and 'background circumstances' may suggest criteria which can now be interpreted as discriminatory, to the disabled (in the case of a speech impairment, say) or to women (for example, the ability of women with family responsibilities to undertake full-time employment).

(c) The category of 'general intelligence' has traditionally been based on 'IQ', a narrow definition of intelligence as mental dexterity. It is now accepted that there are at least seven different intelligences, not least of which are emotional, intuitive, practical and interpersonal intelligence, which are key factors in the new fluid, horizontal business world.

FOR DISCUSSION

'Forget loyalty and conformity. We can't afford narrow-skill people' (Rosabeth Moss Kanter). What does this say about the concept of the desirable **disposition** for an employee? What kind of characteristics may now take the place of loyalty and conformity as desirable attributes for success and contribution in today's business environment (or in an industry or occupation of your choice)?

5.3 COMPETENCE PROFILES

DEFINITION

Competences are transferable personal qualities, which draw from a range of skills, abilities, traits, job knowledge, experience and other qualities needed to perform a job effectively. (Redman and Wilkinson, 2009)

Competence frameworks, definitions or profiles are based on **key success factors** in a given business or sector (through benchmarking exercises or definitions formulated by standard-setting lead bodies). They may also be developed within organisations, linked to their specific strategic objectives, cultural values and task requirements.

The advantage of competence-based profiles include the following.

(a) They can be linked directly to the strategic objectives of an organisation.

(b) They reflect best practice in the relevant occupation or profession (if defined by standard-setting bodies).

(c) They are flexible in the face of changing conditions and requirements, as they are menu-driven and non-prescriptive about job/organisational specifics.

(d)   They can be applied at all levels of the organisation (although the behaviours expected will obviously vary), which helps to foster core values and consistent practice in the organisation.

(e)   They directly relate candidates' attainments and attributes to the demands of the job, and should, therefore, be both accurate (in predicting job performance) and non-discriminatory.

ACTIVITY 8   **(5 MINS)**

Think of an example of competences that are (a) likely to have been demonstrated in candidates' academic or working life; (b) likely to predict successful job performance; and (c) readily assessable in an interview or other selection test.

6   RECRUITMENT METHODS AND MEDIA

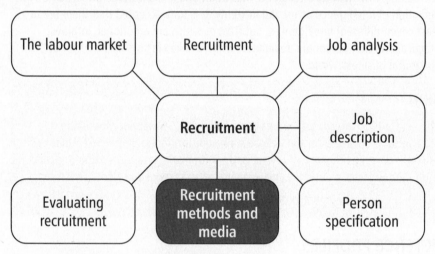

6.1   EXTERNAL RECRUITMENT

A number of methods are available to organisations to contact (and attract) potential candidates. These can be summarised as follows.

Method	Evaluation
The internet: Wide range of recruitment databases, plus web advertising/ application	*Advantages:* <ul><li>IT-literate users</li><li>Preselection by database, low cost</li><li>Worldwide catchment</li></ul> *Disadvantages:* <ul><li>Difficulty of verification</li><li>Competition</li></ul>
Unsolicited requests: Write-ins or walk-ins (Media: word-of mouth, recommendation, previous recruitment advertising, general employer branding)	*Advantages:* <ul><li>Inexpensive</li><li>Preselected for enthusiasm, initiative</li><li>Open **walk-in** policy may encourage application where job difficult to fill</li></ul>

Method	Evaluation
	Disadvantage: • Needs control and systematic application handling
Existing contacts: Previous (re-employable) employees; retirees; career break; previous applicants of suitable general quality held on file	*Advantage:* • Work behaviour/attributes known; may be amenable to part-time, temporary or flexible working *Disadvantage:* • Needs systematic database management
Referrals: Registers of members seeking employment, kept eg by trade unions and professional bodies	*Advantage:* • Preselection at low cost *Disadvantage:* • Indirectly discriminative
Job centres: Network of agencies provided by central government: particularly for manual and junior positions in admin/clerical/retail	*Advantages:* • Free • Local and national • Socially responsible (not-for-profit) *Disadvantages:* • Register limited to unemployed • Require relationship/selection management
Resettlement services: Finding civilian positions for armed forces personnel at end of service	*Advantage:* • Can be highly trained/experienced *Disadvantage:* • Inexperience in civilian culture?
Careers services: Placing graduates of schools and training institutions	*Advantages:* • Potential for young unsocialised recruits • Potential for preview through work placements • Financial incentives (government schemes such as YT, Apex) • Potential for strong relationship – selection preference, curriculum influence *Disadvantages:* • Recruits may lack experience • Administration of work-experience • Possible indirect discrimination

Method	Evaluation
Employment agencies: Wide range of specialising agencies; temporary agencies for one-off requirements and short-term cover	*Advantages:* • May undertake prescreening • Temp agencies facilitate flexible working *Disadvantages:* • Quality can vary • Cost
Selection consultants: Recruit and select for positions; may cover clerical/admin staff, specialist staff (media, financial etc), or managerial	*Advantages:* • Reduces administration for employer • Specialist selection skills • Wide-ranging contacts *Disadvantages:* • Cost • May lack awareness of organisation's culture, values, detailed criteria • Excludes internal applicants • Lack of accountability
Outplacement consultants: Registers, retraining etc to help redundant and early-retired employees	*Advantages:* • Perceived socially responsible • Provide some training *Disadvantage:* • Quality varies
Search consultants: 'Head hunters'. Networking to track highly employable individuals: candidates proactively approached	*Advantage:* • Selects for high employability net-working, exploration opportunity *Disadvantages:* • Cost • Limited range • Organisation may be victim as well as beneficiary!
Direct to source: Schools, colleges, universities (Media: advertisement, 'milk-round' presentation)	*Advantages:* • Networking relationships • Opportunities to preview via work placement, 'gap' year etc • Access to graduates in desirable (scarce) disciplines *Disadvantages:* • Local catchment area • Tends to be annual 'season' • Recruits lack experience • Potential for indirect discrimination

EXAMPLE

A survey reported in *People Management* (31 May 2007) showed that only 18% of employers use recommendations from employees as a recruiting tool – and thereby 'throw away millions of pounds on recruitment advertising'.

A company hiring 250 people a year could save £80,000 if 10% of hires came from referrals by employees of people they know – even if a £250 reward was offered for a successful referral!

ACTIVITY 9 (1 HOUR)

We have already mentioned some of the 'media' by which an organisation can advertise or make known its staffing needs by the methods listed above. Brainstorm as full a list as you can of advertising/information media relevant to recruitment. For each of the media you mention, add any advantages or disadvantages you can think of.

WEBLINK

Virgin Group

Check out the 'Jobs' section of this (and other corporate sites) for examples of e-recruitment. The Virgin site has helpful information on the recruitment process, equality and diversity policies and so on.

http://careers.virgin.com/

6.2 E-RECRUITMENT

E- (or internet or online) recruiting has exploded in recent years, having been used mainly for IT jobs in the early stages of internet adoption. E-recruitment can be subdivided into organisations' own corporate websites and commercial job boards.

The internet is a useful tool in a number of ways.

(a) To post or advertise vacancies, either on the employer's own website (or intranet, for internal advertising) or on specialist online recruitment sites.

(b) To provide information about the employer, recruitment policies and jobs (often available on the employer's own website, as well as recruiter databases).

(c) To allow database searches, matching employers' requirements and job seekers' CVs.

(d) To facilitate communication (via e-mail) between enquirers/applicants and employers.

(e) To complete recruitment applications electronically (online application forms, computerised screening of essential matching criteria, online psychometric tests etc).

Organisations using their own website to recruit is now predominant; however the use of commercial job boards by organisations has seen a lower take up. The main users of job boards appear to be recruitment agencies who wish to communicate to the largest possible audience.

Research also indicates that recruiting organisations will often supplement their online campaign with other techniques such as recruitment agencies or printed advertising.

Advantages of e-recruitment

(a)   Its cost-effectiveness, compared to traditional forms of advertising

(b)   Its ability to reach a wide and geographically dispersed (even global) audience of potential candidates

(c)   The advert may be seen by suitable candidates who may not have considered or even been aware of the recruiting organisation

(d)   Its ability to offer more information (for self-selection) about the organisation and the job, potentially in a more attractive (interactive, multi-media) format

(e)   Its demonstration of basic computer literacy (where desired) by applicants

(f)   Electronic support for application, CV matching, short-listing and so on – more swiftly and cost-effectively than by human agency

(g)   The provision of application information for use in Human Resource Information Systems, eg to analyse applications received, monitor equal opportunities etc

(h)   The ability to monitor traffic (hits on the site, pages viewed etc) to derive information on the effectiveness of the site, levels of interest etc

While the use of e-recruitment has many advantages, research indicates that these factors are not the only ones driving the adoption, other causes are:

- Industry culture, if both the organisation and workers tend to be online then there will be a greater likelihood of using e-recruitment

- If it is perceived that the industry and type of employees sought are orientated to online working

- Where employers are inundated with unsuitable applicants, the use of online filters will reduce the burden

- HR managers believe that to be seen as current and progressive practitioners they are expected to use e-recruitment, even though they may be sceptical as to the measurable benefits

Disadvantages of e-recruitment

(a)   Many applications are unsuitable (especially if the organisation only wants to recruit locally or nationally)

(b)   Technical problems with the site risks losing suitable candidates

(c)   Insufficient information about the job or the company encourages speculative applications or fails to fully inform and engage potentially suitable applicants

(d)   Screening and short-listing software relies heavily on matching keywords, and can disqualify suitable candidates on this basis

(e)   The impersonal nature of the process does not start the development of the psychological contract on a positive note

(f)   May still screen out otherwise suitable applicants for whom it is not the preferred job-seeking tool

(g) Poor quality sites are interpreted by some applicants as representing poor quality organisations and so are deterred from applying

EXAMPLE · BENEFITS OF INTERNET RECRUITMENT

In 2006 the Welsh Local Government Association published the results of a project to promote the use of the internet for its recruitment rather than traditional newspapers. It found the following benefits:

- The quality of applicants was as good or better than obtained from previous conventional advertisements for the same post. This indicated a degree of self-selection via the information on the web.

- The approach attracted a broader 'web savvy' class of applicant.

- Due to ease of accessing websites there was evidence that job seekers were returning time and again to check current vacancies.

- Less administrative support was needed for the recruitment process as applicants were downloading documents from the web rather than telephoning for a pack.

- Many more applicants were applying via the web.

- The spread of grades and types of post where people applied via the web was very broad, and included ex-manual posts and junior clerical posts.

- Savings of between 50% and 70% were achieved on the cost of conventional newspaper advertisements.

- Outcomes in terms of appointments made were comparable.

ACTIVITY 10 (1 HOUR)

Use the internet to appraise the e-recruitment strategies of two or more firms, using the checklist suggested by the benchmarking study cited above.

(a) Start with your own organisation or place of study.

(b) Browse the sites of Google, or any other top companies you are interested in.

(c) Browse the 'jobs' or 'careers' channels of your preferred search engine, or the specialist careers/jobs agencies/sites advertised.

6.3 THE RECRUITMENT ADVERTISEMENT

The object of recruitment advertising is to home in on the target market of labour, and to attract interest in the organisation and the job.

In a way, it is already part of the selection process. The advertisement will be placed where suitable people are likely to see it (say, internally only – immediately preselecting members of the organisation – or in a specialist journal, preselecting those specialists). It will be worded in a way that further weeds out people who would not be suitable for the job (or for whom the job would not be suitable). Be aware, however, that some such forms of preselection may be construed as discriminatory if they disadvantage some groups more than others. (Advertising internally only, where the current workforce is overwhelmingly male, may be construed as indirectly discriminatory to women, for example.)

The way in which a job is advertised will depend on the type of organisation and the type of job.

A factory is likely to advertise a vacancy for an unskilled worker in a different way from a company advertising for a CIPD-qualified person for a senior HR position. Managerial jobs may merit national advertisement, whereas semi- or un-skilled jobs may only warrant local coverage, depending on the supply of suitable candidates in the local area. Specific skills may be most appropriately reached through trade, technical or professional journals.

The advertisement, based on information set out in the job description, (or variants) and recruitment policy, should contain the following information.

    (a)   The organisation: its main business and location (at least)

    (b)   The job: title, main duties and responsibilities and special features

    (c)   Conditions: special factors affecting the job

    (d)   Qualifications and experience (required, and preferred); other attributes, aptitudes and/or knowledge required

    (e)   Rewards: salary and benefits (negotiable, if appropriate), opportunities for training and career development

    (f)   Application: how to apply, to whom, and by what date.

The advertisement should encourage a degree of **self-selection**, so that the target population begins to narrow itself down. (The information contained in the advertisement should deter unsuitable applicants as well as encourage potentially suitable ones.) It should also reflect the desired image of the organisation in the outside world: its employer brand.

AT MILTON KEYNES
'NO' ISN'T A WORD WE LIKE TO USE

We'd much rather give the thumbs up to new ideas and new innovations. And in our forward-thinking HR department, that's exactly what we're doing.

It's all part of the Council's wider aims to change the way local government operates. Embracing new legislation and bringing our services closer to internal and external clients alike, we're adopting a real business focus - and shaping some bold plans for the future. If you're MCIPD qualified, have a record of continued professional development and you're aware of the wider issues confronting a Council like ours, they're plans you could share in.

HUMAN RESOURCES OFFICER - OPERATIONS
£22,194 - £26,091 REF: R01331

You'll be part of our central HR operation, ensuring that all our services run smoothly and effectively - as well as contributing to the overall development of the department. We'll also look to you to provide Council-wide advice on everything from employment legislation to HR procedure, calling on at least 3 years' generalist human resources experience, a background in trade union liaison and proven communication skills. Requests for full/part-time or term-time only are welcome.

HUMAN RESOURCES OFFICER - EMPLOYEE RELATIONS
£22,194 - £26,091 REF: R01332

You'll be reviewing, developing and undertaking briefings on HR policies; advising managers and HR colleagues on policies and employment legislation; trade union consultation; reviewing and monitoring the Occupational Health contract. You will have at least 3 years' human resources experience.

CLOSING DATE: 16 OCTOBER 2000.

Further information and application forms are available by telephoning (01908) 253344 or 253462 (answerphone service available 24 hours per day) or by writing to HR Recruitment Team, Milton Keynes Council, Saxon Court, 502 Avebury Boulevard, Milton Keynes MK9 3HS. Minicom (01908) 252727 (office hours only) or e-mail: Helen.Davey@milton-keynes.gov.uk

PLEASE QUOTE THE APPROPRIATE REFERENCE.

The Council is an Equal Opportunities Employer. Applications are invited from candidates with the necessary attributes regardless of gender, colour, ethnic origin, nationality, creed, disability or sexual orientation. Many Council jobs are suitable for job sharing.

The aim of the recruitment process is *applications* by suitably qualified candidates. What form might an application take, in order for it to be fed into the selection process?

6.4 APPLICATIONS

Applications for a particular advertised (or unadvertised) vacancy, or for employment in the organisation as and when vacancies arise, may be received in various forms.

(a) **Unsolicited letter**, **e-mail**, **'walk-in' or other enquiry**. This would normally be responded to with a request for the following.

(b) **Application form**

    (i) For lower-level, relatively standardised jobs, for which a high volume of applicants is expected, this may be a brief, directly targeted form (focusing on qualifications and experience considered essential to the job) in order to facilitate ruthless weeding out of unsuitable applicants, and requiring minimal discretion, self-expression and time in both completion and interpretation.

    (ii) For managerial, specialist or culturally-driven jobs, a more complex application form or package may be used, in order to elicit more complex responses: biographical/psychological ('biodata') questionnaires, guided self-expression, samples for hand-writing analysis, preliminary testing (description of previous work-related problem-solving, or response to case-study scenarios, say) and so on. Such in-depth tools for preselection save time and effort at the interview stage, but are time-consuming to prepare and analyse, and should be subjected to cost-benefit considerations.

(c) **Curriculum vitae (CV)** or **résumé**, usually accompanied by a **covering letter** drawing the recruiter's attention to specific aspects of the applicant's' CV which are relevant to the vacancy or organisation. The CV is essentially a brief, systematic summary of the applicant's qualifications, previous work experience and relevant skills/interests/requirements, plus details of individuals willing to vouch for his or her performance, character and employability (**referees**).

The application form or CV will be used to find out relevant information about the applicant, in order to decide, at the initial sifting stage:

(a) Whether the applicant is obviously unsuitable for the job; or

(b) Whether the applicant might be of the right calibre, and worth inviting to interview.

The application form will be designed by the organisation (or recruitment agency) to fulfil the following criteria.

(a) It should elicit information about the applicant which can be directly compared with the requirements of the job.

(b) For managerial, interpersonal and culturally-driven jobs – requiring particular values, orientations and attributes – it should give applicants the opportunity to describe (briefly) their career ambitions, why they want the job, perceived strengths and weaknesses etc.

(c) It should convey a professional, accurate and favourable impression of the organisation, a public relations and employer branding tool.

(d) It should extract any data required to enable the organisation subsequently to monitor and evaluate the success of its recruitment procedures (in regard to numbers of female, minority and disabled applicants, number of applications per source and other issues).

BPP LEARNING MEDIA

An example of a basic application form is given here.

AOK PLC

APPLICATION FORM

Post applied for ….

PERSONAL DETAILS

Last name Mr/ Mrs/ Miss/Ms

First name

Address

Post code

Telephone   (Daytime)   (Mobile)

Date of birth

Nationality

Marital status

Dependants

Education (latest first)

Date		Institution	Exams passed/qualifications
From	To		

TRAINING AND OTHER SKILLS

Please give details of any specialised training courses you have attended.

Please note down other skills such as languages (and degree of fluency), driving licence (with endorsements if any), keyboard skills (familiarity with software package).

EMPLOYMENT

Dates		Employer	Title
From	To	name and address	and duties

Current salary and benefits …

INTERESTS
Please describe your leisure/hobby/sporting interests.

YOUR COMMENTS
Why do you think you are suitable for the job advertised?

ADDITIONAL INFORMATION
Do you have any permanent health problems? If so, please give details.

When would you be able to start work?

REFERENCES
Please give two references. One should be a former employer.

Name	Name
Address	Address
Position	Position

Signed	Date

ACTIVITY 11 (20 MINS)

Suggest four ways in which an application form could be *badly* designed (both in appearance and content). You may be able to do this from personal experience.

6.5 INTERNAL RECRUITMENT

Internal advertising of vacancies may be a requirement for some organisations, under agreements negotiated with trade unions. Advertising media include noticeboards (paper and electronic – for example via corporate intranet), in-house journals, memoranda to supervisors/managers soliciting recommendations and observation and word-of-mouth (the **grapevine**).

Methods of **internal recruitment** include:

(a) Advertising for self-applicants
(b) Soliciting recommendations from supervisors/managers and training officers
(c) Soliciting referrals by existing employees to family, friends and contacts
(d) Formal succession, promotion and transfer planning.

Most of these methods incur little extra cost, being based on existing or easily accessible information about the candidate's abilities, attitudes and so on.

7 EVALUATING RECRUITMENT

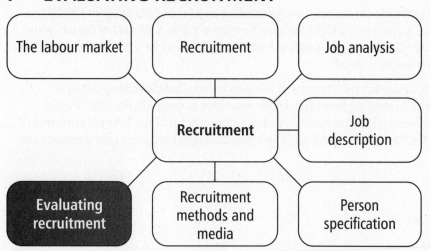

An evaluation of recruitment (and selection) procedures will aim to determine whether the procedures succeeded in getting a *suitable* person into a job, at the *time* when the person was required and at an acceptable *cost*. At a more strategic level, it determines whether recruitment is succeeding in achieving the organisation's overall HR plan.

Connock (1991) suggests that the recruitment process can be audited at four levels.

(a) **Performance indicators** should be established and measured at each stage of the process including:

- Total numbers of applications received
- Time taken to locate applicants
- Cost per applicant
- Time taken to process applications/per application
- Number of female/minority/disabled/mature-age applicants
- Number of qualified applicants (matching advertised criteria)
- Number of qualified female/minority/disabled/mature-age applicants

These metrics basically assess the effectiveness and cost-efficiency of recruitment advertising, equal opportunities policy and recruitment administration. Post-entry criteria – such as number of offers extended per source/method or in relation to applications received, cost and time of training recruits, subsequent job performance and length of service of recruits and so on – may only be applied after the selection process, but still reflect on recruitment.

(b) **Cost-effectiveness** of the various methods used should be measured. For example, it may be that a certain advertising medium is too costly for the number of worthwhile responses it generates.

ACTIVITY 12 (20 MINS)

What kind of information would you need to record in order to appraise the cost-effectiveness of a recruitment method/medium? Aim to end up with a meaningful figure for the cost per person appointed (and actually entering employment).

(c) **Monitoring the make up of the workforce** and the impact of new recruits is essential as part of an equal opportunities policy to identify areas where certain groups are under-represented.

(d) An **attitude survey** may be conducted amongst recruits to measure satisfaction and gather feedback: did the job advertisement give a fair idea of the job, were they frustrated by the length of time they had to wait for a decision or the calibre of any feedback given?

Other methods of evaluating recruitment and selection include **'benchmarking'** which is comparing the organisation's systems with known examples of good practice used in other organisations. Where the HR department has adopted the concept of the **'internal customer'**, it can also gather feedback from internal customers (line managers) and users (job applicants and recruits).

CHAPTER ROUNDUP

- The labour market consists of potential employees, both internal and external to the organisation.

- Demographic trends have important implications for HR planning, especially the falling number of young people in the workforce, the rising number of female and older workers, increasing ethnic diversity and national/regional education trends.

- Recruitment is concerned with defining job requirements and attracting suitable applicants. Selection is concerned with fitting the person to the job.

- A systematic recruitment procedure can be summarised in diagrammatic form as shown in the following page.

The recruitment process

```
┌─────────────────────────┐
│     Job requisition     │
│     (replacement or     │
│       new position)     │
└─────────────────────────┘
             │
             ▼
┌─────────────────────────┐
│     Check need for      │                    ┌──────────────────────┐
│      replacement -      │        No          │  Obtain authority or │
│    is the engagement    │───────────────────▶│  adopt alternative   │
│       authorised?       │                    │  (such as overtime,  │
└─────────────────────────┘                    │    reorganisation)   │
       │                                        └──────────────────────┘
     Yes                                                   │
       ▼                                                   │
┌─────────────────────────┐                                │
│   Does a job description│◀───────────────────────────────┘
│     and personnel       │
│   specification exist?  │
└─────────────────────────┘
                                                 ┌──────────────────────┐
┌──────────────┐      Yes           No           │      Analyse job:    │
│  Review and  │◀─────────────────────────────▶ │       prepare        │
│    update    │                                 │     description/     │
└──────────────┘                                 │    specification     │
      │                                          └──────────────────────┘
      │        ┌─────────────────────────┐                 │
      └───────▶│   Are the terms/conditions │◀─────────────┘
               │   of employment agreed?    │
               └─────────────────────────┘
                                                 ┌──────────────────────┐
                        No                       │     Agree terms      │
                ─────────────────────────────▶  │    and conditions    │
                    Yes                          └──────────────────────┘
                     ▼                                      │
               ┌─────────────────────────┐                 │
               │       Is there a        │◀────────────────┘
               │   suitable supply of    │
               │   internal candidates?  │
               └─────────────────────────┘
                                                 ┌──────────────────────┐
┌──────────────┐     Yes            No           │      Evaluate        │
│    Place     │◀─────────────────────────────▶ │     alternative      │
│   internal   │                                 │        media         │
│ advertisement│                                 └──────────────────────┘
└──────────────┘                                            │
      │                                          ┌──────────────────────┐
      │                                          │  Preparation and     │
      │                                          │   publication of     │
      │                                          │    information       │
      │                                          └──────────────────────┘
      │        ┌─────────────────────────┐                 │
      └───────▶│       Determine         │◀────────────────┘
               │       selection         │
               │        methods          │
               └─────────────────────────┘
                            │
                            ▼
               ┌─────────────────────────┐
               │        Select           │
               │       candidate         │
               └─────────────────────────┘
```

? QUICK QUIZ

1. Why is the shift towards an ageing population important for HRP?

2. Suggest two ways in which recruiters can avoid discrimination on the basis of (a) race and (b) gender.

3. List three methods by which job analysis may be carried out.

4. What is a job description?

5. What three criteria make 'competences' effective in guiding recruitment and selection?

6. List five methods of recruitment of candidates from the external job market.

7. What are the *drawbacks* of e-recruitment?

8. List four methods of receiving applications.

9. List four methods by which vacancies could be filled from the internal labour pool.

10. List three methods by which recruitment procedures may be evaluated.

ANSWERS TO QUICK QUIZ

1   Because the workforce will reflect the proportion of older workers, and because of the corresponding decline in the number of young people available to work.

(see Para 1.2)

2   (a)   Avoid asking country of birth
      (b)   Avoid asking women questions about wanting to start a family   (Para 2.4)

3   Observation, questionnaire/interview, diaries/self-recording   (Para 3.3)

4   A broad description of the purpose, scope, duties and responsibilities of a particular job.

(Para 4)

5   Focusing on demonstrable areas; likely to predict job performance; readily assessable.

(Para 5.3)

6   Agencies, consultancies, internet, direct to source, existing contacts

(Para 6.1)

7   Too many unsuitable applicants; technical problems; insufficient job or company information; poor software; impersonal nature of the process; candidates don't like applying online; poor quality site reflects poor quality organisation in mind of candidates

(Para 6.2)

8   CV; application form; unsolicited enquiry; web application   (Para 6.4)

9   Retention, transfer or redeployment, training and development, promotion, exploiting employee contracts and/or flexible working methods   (Para 6.5)

10   By determining key performance indicators and monitoring performance against them; by measuring cost-effectiveness; by monitoring the make-up of the workforce; by conducting attitude surveys; by benchmarking   (Section 7)

ANSWERS TO ACTIVITIES

1   (a)   The falling number of younger workers will make it increasingly difficult to recruit and retain skilled younger people, with intense competition – particularly among organisations that have traditionally recruited school leavers and new graduates. Organisations will either have to revise strategies to compete for younger workers – or change their resourcing policies and culture to accept older workers (a process supported by age diversity legislation).

      (b)   In the UK, the ratio of people 65+ to those of working age is 21 : 100. By 2030, this is anticipated to be 25+ : 100, adding to the difficulties of the state to provide pensions for the retired population. Employers are likely to find the provision of occupational pension benefits an increasingly important tool in attracting and retaining employees.

2   Connock (1991) suggests six steps by which organisations can cope with these demographic and educational trends.

      •   Establish what labour market the organisation is in.

      •   Discover the organisation's catchment areas (ie location of potential recruits).

- Discern the supply-side trends in the catchment area labour force. (For example, how many school leavers are expected? What is the rate of growth/decline of local population?)

- Examine education trends in the location.

- Assess the demand from other employers for the skills you need. (If there is a large concentration of, say, electronics companies in the region, they will be interested in hiring people with similar skills.)

- Try to assess whether some of your demand can be satisfied by a supply from other sources.

3   It is often difficult to persuade departmental managers to agree to the promotion of a subordinate out of the department, especially if (s)he has been selected as having particular ability: the department will be losing an able member, and will have to find, induct and train a replacement. Moreover, if the manager's resistance were revealed, there might be a motivational issue to contend with. The HR manager will have to be able to justify a recommendation with sound policies for providing and training a replacement with as little impact on the department's efficiency as possible.

4   Where the organisation has the choice, it should consider the following points.

(a)   Management will be familiar with an internal promotee: there will be detailed appraisal information available from employee records. The external recruit will to a certain extent be an unknown quantity – and the organisation will be taking a greater risk of unacceptable personality or performance emerging later.

(b)   A promotee has already worked within the organisation and will be familiar with its:

(i)   Culture, or philosophy; informal rules and norms as well as stated policy
(ii)   Politics; power-structures and relationships
(iii)   Systems and procedures
(iv)   Objectives
(v)   Other personnel (who likewise will be familiar with him/her)

(c)   Promotion internally is visible proof of the organisation's willingness to develop people's careers. This may well have an encouraging, motivating and loyalty-inducing effect.

(d)   Internal advertisement of vacancies contributes to the implementation of equal opportunities policies. Many women are employed in secretarial and clerical jobs from which promotion is unlikely – and relatively few are in higher-graded roles. Internal advertising could become a route for opening up opportunities for women at junior levels.

(e)   On the other hand, an organisation must retain its ability to adapt, grow and change, and this may well require new blood, wider views, fresh ideas. Insiders may be too socialised into the prevailing culture to see faults or be willing to 'upset the apple cart' where necessary for the organisation's health.

5   Some ideas:

(a)   The overall priorities and requirements of the organisation will be more clearly recognised and met, rather than the objectives of sub-systems such as individual departments.

(b)   There will be a central reference point for communication, queries and applications from outside the organisation.

(c)   Communication with the environment will also be more standardised, and more likely to reinforce the organisation's overall corporate image.

(d)   Potential can be spotted in individuals and utilised in the optimum conditions – not necessarily in the post for which the individual has applied, if (s)he might be better suited to another vacant post.

(e)   The volume of administration and the need for specialist knowledge (notably of changing legal and industrial relations requirements) may suggest a specialist function.

(f)   Standardisation and central control should arguably be applied to, for example, equal opportunities, pay provisions and performance standards, where fairness and consistency must be seen to operate.

6   This task is intended to develop your research skills and your awareness of HR practice in a specific organisation. Make it an ongoing assignment to gather case study information about the recruitment policies and practices of organisations that interest you…

7   The job analyst will need to gain their confidence by:

(a)   Communicating: explaining the process, methods and purpose of the appraisal

(b)   Being thorough and competent in carrying out the analysis

(c)   Respecting the work flow of the department, which should not be disrupted

(d)   Giving feedback on the results of the appraisal, and the achievement of its objectives. If staff are asked to co-operate in developing a framework for office training, and then never hear anything more about it, they are unlikely to be responsive on a later occasion

8   Competences:

- Likely to be demonstrated: eg leadership, initiative, ability to work with others, ability to work under (or without) supervision

- Likely to predict job performance: eg motivation to achieve, specific technical skills related to the job (numeracy, computer use)

- Assessable: eg team building (asking candidates to describe when they have successfully built a team), problem analysis (asking candidates to analyse and suggest solutions to a case study scenario), conflict resolution (asking a candidate to role play a mediator in an industrial conflict scenario)

9   Some of the media you may have come up with should include the following.

Newspapers and journals (trade, professional) – ie 'Press' media	• Journals better targeted, papers offer wider local or national coverage • Wider and more targeted coverage – higher cost: cost-effectiveness must be monitored, controlled • May offer opportunity to produce own artwork – may not (control required)
Cinema, radio, TV – ie 'broadcast' media	• Can offer general marketing opportunity • Powerful all-senses effect • Expensive (especially TV) • Mass coverage (option of local) • Appeal to young audience

Posters, leaflets, notices on notice boards (+ multi-media equivalents: cassettes, videos)	• Targeting through positioning only • Can be expensive, hit-and-miss, long timescale • Content/style controlled by organisation
Exhibitions, conferences, roadshows, open-days, presentations	• If well targeted location, can reach large number of relevant people • Opportunities for non-committal networking, exploration • Immediacy of face-to-face communication – but also a risk • Can be expensive to organise/delegate
Websites	• Untargeted (except to IT-literate) • Controllable • Relatively low-cost • Opportunity for general marketing

10   This is a research exercise. You may like to print out some of your findings for your portfolio or assignment bibliography.

11   (a)   Answer spaces too small to contain the information asked for

(b)   Forms which are (or look) so lengthy or complicated that prospective applicants either complete them perfunctorily or give up (and apply to another employer instead)

(c)   Illegal (eg discriminatory) or offensive questions

(d)   Lack of clarity as to what (and how much) information is required

12   Connock suggests that a framework such as that shown below be used to determine the cost per person appointed for each method.

Source of application	Number of applications	Number of shortlisted candidates	Number offered job	Number commenced employment	Total cost	Cost per head appointed
Local press advert						
National press advert						
Specialist press advert						
Leaflet drop etc						
Total						

Chapter

04

Selection

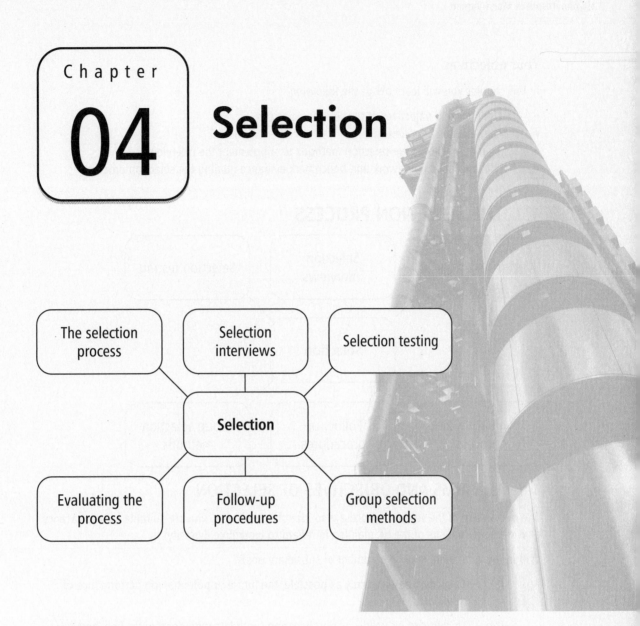

Introduction

The introduction to Chapter 3 outlined the idea of selection: the part of the employee resourcing process which leads naturally on from recruitment. Selection involves identifying the most suitable of the candidates attracted by recruitment efforts. (In practice, this may be a negative process of weeding out people who are *unsuitable* for the job or organisation – or people for whom the job or organisation may be unsuitable.)

The selection of the right candidate(s) is of vital importance. No organisation would like to find a 'star' employee for a competing organisation on its rejection list, any more than it wants an employee who can't do the job and doesn't 'fit in' – however perfect they may have seemed in the interview! Various selection methods are used to try to reduce the risks of either event by gathering as much relevant information about the candidate as possible. In this chapter we look at how this can be done.

Your objectives

In this chapter you will learn about the following.

- The aims and objectives of the selection process
- The selection interview
- A range of alternative selection methods to supplement the interview
- The legislative framework and benchmark evidence guiding the selection process

1 THE SELECTION PROCESS

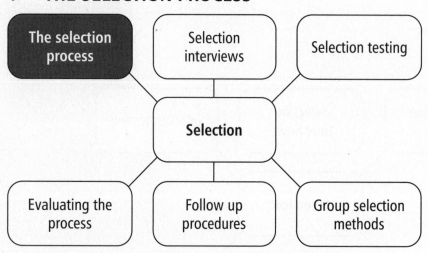

1.1 THE AIMS AND OBJECTIVES OF SELECTION

The overall aim of the selection process is to identify candidates who are suitable for the vacancy or wider requirements of the HR plan (eg in regard to workforce diversity).

Within this aim, there may be a number of subsidiary goals.

(a)   To predict, as accurately as possible, the future or potential job performance of candidates.

(b)   To compare, as validly as possible, one candidate with another, to find 'best fit' between applicants and the organisation's needs.

(c)   To inform candidates, as accurately and attractively as possible, about the organisation, the job, the psychological contract of employment and likely future prospects, in order to facilitate:

(i)   Self-selection by the candidates

(ii)   Subsequent adjustment to the role by the successful candidate, minimising disappointment and induction crisis and supporting retention

(d)   To give the best possible impression of the organisation as a potential employer: creating a brand as 'employer of choice' in an industry or sector, or in competition with other potential employers.

(e)   To comply with legislation, policy and organisational values in regard to equal opportunity, fair treatment and professionalism in dealing with candidates.

(f)   To provide information for other HRM processes, such as employee induction and development, or the evaluation of the selection process itself.

1.2 A SYSTEMATIC APPROACH TO SELECTION

A typical selection system will include the following basic procedures.

(a) Take any **initial steps** required. If the decision to interview or reject cannot be made immediately, a standard letter of acknowledgement should be sent, as a courtesy, to each applicant. It may be that the job advertisement requires applicants to write to the personnel manager giving personal details and requesting an application form: this would then be sent to applicants for completion and return.

(b) Set each application against **key criteria** in the job advertisement and specification. Critical factors may include qualifications, experience or competences.

(c) **Sort applications** into 'possible', 'unsuitable' and 'marginal'.

(d) 'Possibles' will then be more closely scrutinised, and a **shortlist for interview** drawn up. Ideally, this should be done by both the HR specialist and the prospective manager of the successful candidate, who will have more immediate knowledge of the type of person that will fit into the culture and activities of the department.

(e) Invite candidates for **interviews** (requiring them to complete an application form, if this has not been done at an earlier stage).

(f) Interview potentially qualified candidates.

(g) Reinforce interviews with **selection testing** and other mechanisms where required.

(h) Check the **references** of short-listed candidates.

(i) Institute **follow-up procedures** for successful applicants.

   (i) Make an **offer of employment**, negotiating terms and conditions if appropriate.

   (ii) Draw up a **contract** or **written particulars of employment**.

   (iii) Arrange **work permits** and related issues of residency, if required by cross-border recruitment.

   (iv) Plan initial **induction** into the organisation and provide preparatory information.

(j) Review un-interviewed 'possibles', and 'marginals', and put potential future candidates on **hold** or in reserve.

(k) Send standard letters to **unsuccessful applicants**, informing them that they have not been successful. Best practice now also includes the offering of feedback to unsuccessful applicants, on request, as to why their application was unsuccessful.

(l) Keep **records** of criteria and processes used in decision-making, both for evaluation – and to provide evidence of fair dealing if required to counter a claim of discrimination.

1.3 THE LEGAL FRAMEWORK ON SELECTION

Discrimination

Detailed provisions in regard to equal opportunities are discussed in Part B of this Course Book, since it is an area of relevance throughout HR policy and practice. However, in regard to selection, you should be aware of the following.

(a) **Application forms** as general guidance should not ask for details that are not relevant to the job, such as country of birth or sexual orientation (except where such questions are contained in monitoring forms that are separated from application forms before assessment).

Where employers are monitoring such information then this should be included on a tear-off slip which is removed before those involved in the selection process review the application form. The existence of monitoring or its absence may be taken into account in tribunal proceedings.

(b) **Interview procedures** and documentation should be carefully controlled to avoid discrimination. For example:

(i) A non work-related question must be asked of all candidates, if any, and even then, should not imply discriminatory intent (by asking only women about care of dependants, or about hormonal influences on moods, say)

(ii) At least one representative of both sexes and all races of applicants should be invited for interview

(iii) Detailed notes of proceedings, criteria and decisions should be made in order to furnish justification in the event of a claim of discrimination.

(c) Selection tests should demonstrably avoid favouring particular groups (although this is a contentious area, as outlined see in Paragraph 3.2 below).

Remember, as mentioned in Chapter 3, current UK legislation outlaws discrimination on the grounds of sex, or change of sex, sexual orientation, marital and civil partnership status; pregnancy, race, nationality, ethnic or national origin; disability; religious belief and age. In the selection context, there is also legislation protecting offenders whose convictions have been 'spent' after a period of time (which varies according to the severity of the offence).

ACTIVITY 1   (15 MINS)

The following is a classic IQ test question.

'Which is the odd man out?

MEASLES, STEAMER, LEAVE, OMELETTE, COURAGE.'

(a) What is the answer?
(b) How might this question discriminate against certain tested groups?

Privacy and data protection

The gathering of data in the application and selection process is also a sensitive area. In the UK, the *Data Protection Act 1998* was implemented in stages up to 2007 – but retrospectively affects all record systems set up on or after 24 October 1998. Major provisions include the following.

(a) The right of employees to access their personnel files, to be informed of the purpose for which data is being collected about them, and to approve the use of that data for any other purposes.

(b) Requirements for the adequacy of information, keeping it up-to-date and the security of information (particularly if it is to be exported outside the European Economic Area).

(c) Additional safeguards on the collection of data about race, ethnic origin, religious or political beliefs, union membership, health, sexual orientation or criminal activities (except for the purposes of monitoring racial equality).

FOR DISCUSSION

'A US retailer testing some 2,500 applicants for security jobs, required applicants to answer intimate personal questions in a pre-employment psychological examination, but was later forced to pay more than $2 million to settle a lawsuit over the test, which included 'true or false?' questions such as:

- I have never indulged in any unusual sexual practices
- I am very strongly attracted by members of my own sex
- I believe my sins are unpardonable
- I feel sure there is only one true religion

The employer argued in court that the test was necessary to screen out applicants who were emotionally unstable, unreliable, and resistant to established rules, as well as applicants with addictive or violent tendencies who might put customers or other employees at risk.'...

Aside from the actual outcome of this case, how far do you think a test of this kind is:

(a) Useful or effective (and with what intention)?
(b) Ethically reprehensible (and on what grounds)?

To the extent that the employer's concerns are genuine, what other means of screening might or should they employ?

SIGNPOST

We now go on to outline some of the methods by which selections can be made.

1.4 SELECTION METHODS

Various techniques are available, depending on the policy and criteria of selection in each case.

(a) **Interviews**. These may be variously structured (one-to-one, panel, sequential), and using various criteria of job relevance (application details, skills and competences, critical incident/situational questions) and scoring methods (general impressions, criteria ratings). As the most popular of methods, interviews are considered in detail below.

(b) **Evaluation of education and experience**, comparing application data to job requirements.

(c) **Selection testing**. Written tests of ability and aptitude (cognitive and/or mechanical), personality and so on are increasingly used, alongside work sample tests which simulate job-related activities (such as typing or copy writing tests) and examination of portfolios of work (eg for architects or photographers). Tests are also discussed in more detail below.

(d) **Background and reference checks**, in order to verify application claims as to qualifications, previous employment record and reasons for leaving etc. References are discussed in Section 5 of this chapter.

(e) **Biodata analysis**. Biodata (biographical data) is gathered via multiple choice questions on family background, life experiences, attitudes and preferences. The results are compared with an 'ideal' profile based on correlations with effective job performance.

(f) **Handwriting analysis**, or graphology. Handwriting is said to indicate up to 300 character traits of the individual. There is no scientific evidence of its predictive accuracy, but it is popular in Europe and to a lesser extent in the USA and Australia. (In general, handwritten covering letters are requested as a useful general indicator of orderly thinking, presentation and so on.)

(g) **Group selection methods**, or **assessment centres**, allowing the assessment of team-working, leadership, problem-solving and communication skills through the use of group discussions, role plays, business games and 'in-tray' simulations. These are discussed below.

ACTIVITY 2 (20 MINS)

How accurate do you think the above-listed methods are at predicting job performance and suitability?

A number of research studies have attempted to measure how popular and how effective various techniques are.

- **Effectiveness** is measured according to the '**predictive validity**' scale, which ranges from 1 (the technique unfailingly predicts candidates' subsequent job performance) to 0 (the technique is no better than random chance at predicting candidates' subsequent job performance).

- **Popularity** is measured by the percentage of surveyed companies that use the technique.

(a) Rank the following techniques in order from most popular to least popular, from what you might anticipate.

(b) For each, add a number between 0.00 and 1.00 to indicate what you think their predictive validity might be.

Techniques: Personality tests, references, work sampling, interviews, assessment centres, cognitive tests, graphology, biodata.

SIGNPOST

We now look at each of the three major techniques in turn.

2 SELECTION INTERVIEWS

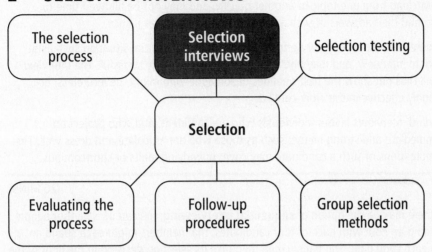

2.1 TYPES OF INTERVIEW

Individual or **one-to-one interviews** are the most common selection method. They offer the advantages of direct face-to-face communication, and the opportunity to establish **rapport** between the candidate and interviewer: each has to give their attention solely to the other, and there is potentially a relaxed atmosphere, if the interviewer is willing to establish an informal style.

The disadvantage of a one-to-one interview is the scope it allows for a biased or superficial decision.

(a)   The candidate may be able to disguise lack of knowledge in a specialist area of which the interviewer themself knows little.

(b)   The interviewer's perception may be selective or distorted (see Paragraph 2.4 below), and this lack of objectivity may go unnoticed and unchecked.

(c)   The greater opportunity for personal rapport with the candidate may cause a weakening of the interviewer's objective judgement.

Panel interviews are designed to overcome the above disadvantages. A panel may consist of two or three people who together interview a single candidate: most commonly, an HR specialist and the candidate's future boss. This may be more daunting for the candidate (depending on the tone and conduct of the interview) but it has several advantages.

(a)   The HR and line specialists can gather the information they each need about the candidate and give him or her the various information (s)he requires from each of them at one sitting.

(b)   The interviewers make a joint assessment of the candidate's abilities, and behaviour at the interview. Personal bias is more likely to be guarded against, and checked if it does emerge.

Large formal panels, or **selection boards**, may also be convened where there are a number of individuals or groups with an interest in the selection. This has the advantage of allowing a number of people to see the candidates, and to share information about them at a single meeting; similarly, they can compare their assessments on the spot, without a subsequent effort at liaison and communication.

Offsetting these administrative advantages, however, are some drawbacks:

(a)   Questions tend to be more varied, and more random. Candidates may have trouble switching from one topic to another quickly, and may not be allowed time to expand their answers in such as way as to do themselves justice.

(b)   Some candidates may not perform well in a formal, artificial situation such as a board interview, and may find such a situation extremely stressful. The interview will thus not show the best qualities of someone who might, nevertheless, be highly effective in the work context.

(c)   Board interviews favour individuals who are confident, and who project an immediate and strong image, such as those who are articulate and dress well. First impressions of such a candidate may cover underlying faults or shortcomings.

ACTIVITY 3 (20 MINS)

In some cases, there may be the option of **sequential interviewing**: instead of, say, four people on a panel spending an hour with each of four candidates, the members might each spend an hour alone with each candidate. The panel could then take its selection decision in the light of the information obtained at the separate interviews.

What do you think would be the pros and cons of this approach?

2.2   PREPARING INTERVIEWS

In brief, the factors to be considered with regard to conducting selection interviews are:

(a)   The impression of the organisation given by the interview arrangements

(b)   The psychological effects of the location of the interview, seating arrangements and manner of the interviewer(s)

(c)   The extent to which the candidate can be encouraged to talk freely (by asking open questions) and honestly (by asking probing questions), in accordance with the organisation's need for information

(d)   The opportunity for the candidate to learn about the job and organisation

(e)   The control of bias or hasty judgement by the interviewer

The interview is a two-way process, but the **interviewer** must have a clear idea of what it is intended to achieve, and must be in sufficient control of the process to cover the required ground.

The **interview** agenda and questions will be based on:

(a)   The job description, competence profile and/or person specification setting out the job/role requirements

(b)   The information supplied by the candidate in the application form, CV and covering letter

The interview process should be efficiently run to make a favourable impression on the candidates and to avoid unnecessary stress (unless ability to handle pressure is a selection criterion!). The interview room should be free from distraction and interruption.

2.3 INTERVIEWER SKILLS AND QUESTIONING TECHNIQUES

ACTIVITY 4 (30 MINS)

Think back to a selection interview you have had, for a job, school or place at your university/college.

(a) What sort of interview did you have: one-to-one, panel, formal or informal?

(b) What impression of the organisation did you get from the whole process?

(c) How well-conducted was the interview, looking back on it?

(d) What efforts (if any) were made to put you at your ease?

'Interviews are so common that they are often taken for granted. People view interviews as simply conversations during which information is gathered. While interviews are similar to conversations, there are important differences. An interview is a specialised form of conversation conducted for a specific task-related purpose.' (Whetton and Cameron, 2002)

In 2009 a survey by the CIPD showed that interviews are still the most common method of selection:

69%	Competency-based interview
68%	Interviews following the contents of a CV/Application form
59%	Structured interview

Whetton and Cameron identify the following key skills for interviewers.

(a) Creating **effective questions**, arising out of a clear purpose and agenda, with the aim of eliciting the information required.

(b) Creating an **appropriate climate** for information sharing, using supportive communication techniques, such as:

    (i) Rapport building, establishing trust and relationship

    (ii) Active listening, using attentive body language and responsive verbal behaviours (eg summarising, clarifying)

    (iii) Introducing the interview in a way that establishes a positive tone and familiarises the candidate as to how the interview will be conducted

(c) Using **question types** intentionally, in order to control the pace and direction of the interview, remaining responsive to the replies given by the candidate. (This is discussed further below.)

(d) Using and interpreting **non-verbal cues**, or 'body language' (dress, posture, eye contact, gestures, facial expressions).

(e) Being willing, and able, to identify shallow or unconvincing responses, and to **probe and challenge** when necessary: in other words, critically evaluating the candidate's responses.

(f) Being alert to the influence of first impressions, stereotypes and other forms of potential **bias**.

EXAMPLE   **THE PEOPLE PROCESS**

Whetton & Cameron (2002) cite a six-step process used by an unidentified major firm outlining an effective interview process.

'PEOPLE-oriented Selection Interview Process'

P   Prepare

    1   Review application, CV and other background information
    2   Prepare both general and individual-specific questions
    3   Prepare suitable physical arrangements

E   Establish Rapport

    1   Try to make applicant comfortable
    2   Convey genuine interest
    3   Communicate supportive attitude with voice and names

O   Obtain Information

    1   Ask questions
    2   Probe
    3   Listen carefully
    4   Observe the person (dress, mannerisms, body language)

P   Provide Information

    1   Describe current and future job opportunities
    2   Sell positive features of firm
    3   Respond to applicant's questions

L   Lead to Close

    1   Clarify responses
    2   Provide an opportunity for final applicant input
    3   Explain what happens next

E   Evaluate

    1   Assess match between technical qualifications and job requirements
    2   Judge personal qualities (leadership, maturity, team orientation)
    3   Make a recommendation

A variety of question styles may be used, to different effects.

(a)   **Open questions** or open-ended questions ('Who...? What...? Where...? When...? Why...?') force interviewees to put together their own responses in complete sentences. This encourages the interviewee to talk, keeps the interview flowing, and is most revealing ('Why do you want to work in HR?')

(b)   **Probing questions** are similar to open questions in their phrasing but aim to discover the deeper significance of the candidate's experience or achievements. (If a candidate claimed to have had 'years of relevant experience', in a covering letter, the interviewer might need to ask 'How many years?', or 'Which particular jobs or positions do you consider relevant and how?')

(c)   **Closed questions** are the opposite, inviting only 'yes' or 'no' answers: ('Did you...?', 'Have you...?'). A closed question has the following effects.

(i)   It elicits answers only to the question asked by the interviewer. This may be useful where there are small points to be established ('Did you pass your exam?') but there may be other questions and issues that (s)he has not anticipated but will emerge if the interviewee is given the chance to expand ('How did you think your studies went?').

(ii)   It does not allow interviewees to express their personality, so that interaction can take place on a deeper level.

(iii)   It makes it easier for interviewees to conceal things ('You never *asked* me....').

(iv)   It makes the interviewer work very hard!

(d)   **Multiple questions** are just that: two or more questions are asked at once. ('Tell me about your last job? How did your knowledge of HRM help you there, and do you think you are up-to-date or will you need to spend time studying?') This type of question can be used to encourage the candidate to talk at some length, but not to stray too far from the point. It might also test the candidate's ability to listen and handle large amounts of information, but should be used judiciously in this case.

(e)   **Problem-solving or situational questions** present candidates with a situation and asks them to explain how they would deal with it or how they have dealt with it in the past. ('How would you motivate your staff to do a task that they did not want to do?' or 'Can you tell us about a time when you were successful about setting a goal and achieving it?') Such questions are used to establish whether the candidate will be able to deal with the sort of problems that are likely to arise in the job, or whether (s)he has sufficient technical knowledge. Whetten and Cameron (2002) suggest asking negative questions as well as positive ('Now tell us about a time you *failed* to meet a goal you set. How could you have done better?') in order to expose hidden bias.

(f)   **Leading questions** direct the interviewee to give a certain reply. ('We are looking for somebody who likes detailed figure work. How much do you enjoy dealing with numbers?', or 'Don't you agree that...?', 'Surely...?')

The danger with this type of question is that interviewees will give the answer they think the interviewer wants to hear, but it might legitimately be used to deal with highly reticent or nervous candidates, simply to encourage them to talk.

ACTIVITY 5   (20 MINS)

Identify the type of question used in the following examples, and discuss the opportunities and constraints they offer the interviewee who must answer them.

(a)   'So you're interested in a business studies degree, are you, Jo?

(b)   'Surely you're not interested in business studies, Jo?'

(c)   'How about a really useful qualification like a business studies degree, Jo? Would you consider that?'

(d)   'Why are you interested in a business studies degree, Jo?'

(e)   'Why *particularly* business studies, Jo?'

Candidates should also be given the opportunity to **ask questions**. Indeed, well-prepared candidates will go into an interview knowing what questions they want to ask. Their choice of questions might well have some influence on how the interviewers finally assess them. Moreover, there is information that the candidate will need to know about the organisation and the job, and about:

(a) Terms and conditions of employment (although negotiations about detailed terms may not take place until a provisional offer has been made)

(b) The next step in the selection process – whether there are further interviews, when a decision might be made, or which references might be taken up

SIGNPOST

Having said all this, why did interviews score so badly on the predictive validity scale? (See the answer to Activity 2, if you have not already done so.) Despite their popularity, they have a number of limitations…

2.4 LIMITATIONS OF INTERVIEWS

Interviews are criticised because they fail to provide accurate predictions of how a person will perform in the job. The main reasons why this might be so are:

(a) **Limited scope**. An interview is necessarily too brief to 'get to know' candidates in the kind of depth required to make an accurate prediction of their behaviour in any given situation.

(b) **Limited relevance**. Interviews that lack structure and focus may fail to elicit information that is relevant to the candidate's likely future performance in the job and compatibility with the organisation.

(c) **Artificiality**. An interview is an artificial situation: candidates may be 'on their best behaviour' or, conversely, so nervous that they do not do themselves justice. Neither situation reflects what the person is 'really like'.

(d) **Errors of judgement** by interviewers. These include:

   (i) The **halo effect** – a tendency for people to make an initial general judgement about a person based on a single obvious attribute, such as being neatly dressed, or well-spoken, which may colour later perceptions.

   (ii) **Contagious bias** – a process whereby an interviewer changes the behaviour or responses of the applicant by suggestion, through the wording of questions or non-verbal cues.

   (iii) **Logical error**. For example, an interviewer might place too much emphasis on isolated strengths or weaknesses, or draw unwarranted conclusions from facts (confusing career mobility with disloyalty, say).

(e) Lack of skill and experience by interviewers. For example:

   • Inability to take control of the direction and length of the interview
   • A reluctance to probe into facts and challenge statements where necessary

3 SELECTION TESTING

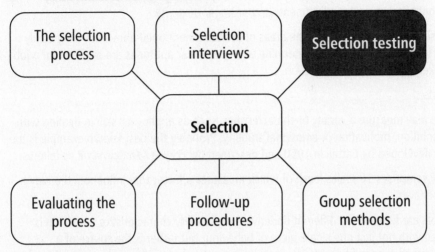

3.1 TYPES OF TESTS

In many job selection procedures, an interview may be supplemented by some form of selection test.

Cushway (1994) lists six criteria which such tests should satisfy.

1   A sensitive measuring instrument that discriminates between subjects
2   Standardised, so that an individual's score can be related to others
3   Reliable, in that it always measures the same thing
4   Valid, in that the test measures what it is designed to measure
5   Acceptable to the candidate
6   Non-discriminatory

The science of measuring mental capacities and processes is called 'psychometrics'; hence the term **'psychometric testing'**. There are five types of test commonly used in practice.

Intelligence or cognitive ability tests

These are tests of general cognitive ability which typically test memory, ability to think quickly (perceptual speed, verbal fluency) and logically (inductive reasoning), and problem-solving skills. Reliance on such criteria has shown steady increase, perhaps because of uncertainty in UK employers' minds about the validity of A-level and GCSE results, the wide variation in degree classes between higher educational institutions and the difficulties of comparing international qualifications.

Most people have experience of IQ tests, and few would dispute their validity as good measures of general intellectual performance.

Aptitude tests

Aptitude tests are designed to predict an individual's **potential** for performing a job or learning new skills. There are various accepted areas of aptitude:

(a)   **Reasoning** – verbal, numerical and abstract/visual (eg accuracy and speed in arithmetical calculations, naming or making words, identifying shapes)

(b)   **Spatio-visual ability** – practical intelligence, non-verbal ability and creative flair (eg skill to solve mechanical puzzles)

(c)   **Perceptual speed and accuracy** – eg clerical ability (identifying non-identical pairs of numbers)

(d)   **'Psycho-motor' ability** – mechanical, manual, musical and athletic: ability to respond accurately and rapidly to stimuli (eg pressing lighted buttons), using controlled muscular adjustments and/or finger dexterity.

With a few possible exceptions, most of the areas of aptitude mentioned above are fairly easily measurable. So long as it is possible to determine what particular aptitudes are required for a job, such tests are likely to be useful for selection.

Personality tests

Personality tests may measure a variety of characteristics, such as applicants' skill in dealing with other people, ambition, motivation or emotional stability. Probably the best known example is the 16PF, originally developed by Cattell in 1950 and described (in *People Management*) as follows.

The 16PF comprises 16 scales, each of which measures a factor that influences the way a person behaves.

The factors are functionally different underlying personality characteristics, and each is associated with not just one single piece of behaviour but rather is the source of a relatively broad range of behaviours. For this reason the factors themselves are referred to as source traits and the behaviours associated with them are called surface traits.

The advantage of measuring source traits, as the 16PF does, is that you end up with a much richer understanding of the person because you are not just describing what can be seen but also the characteristics underlying what can be seen.

The 16PF analyses how a person is likely to behave generally, including, for example, contributions likely to be made to particular work contexts, aspects of the work environment to which the person is likely to be more or less suited, and how best to manage the person.

Other examples include the Myers-Briggs Type Indicator® (mostly intended for self-development purposes), the Minnesota Multiphasic Personality Inventory (MMPI) and the FIRO-B personality profile. The validity of such tests has been much debated, but it seems that some have been shown by research to be valid predictors of job performance, so long as they are used and interpreted properly. A test may indicate that a candidate is introverted, has creative ability and is pragmatic – but this is only of use if this combination of characteristics can be linked to success or failure in the type of work for which the candidate is being considered.

Another area of current interest (which falls somewhere between personality, aptitude and intelligence testing) is the concept of **emotional intelligence**.

DEFINITION

The capacity for **emotional intelligence (EQ)** is recognising our own feelings and those of others, for motivating ourselves, and for managing emotions well in ourselves and in our relationships.   (Goleman, 1998)

Goleman argues that: 'the more complex the job, the more emotional intelligence matters – if only because a deficiency in these abilities can hinder the use of whatever technical expertise or intellect a person may have'. Emotional competence accounts for some 70% of the competences listed by an organisation as essential for effective performance. They also correlate strongly with managerial success, labour stability completion of training and promotability (Whetten & Cameron, 2002; Goleman, 1998).

Goleman (and others) have published **Emotional Competence Assessment** questionnaires for each of the five key domains of EQ: self-awareness, self-regulation, motivation, empathy and social skills.

BPP
LEARNING MEDIA

Proficiency and attainment tests

Proficiency tests are perhaps the most closely related to an assessor's objectives, because they measure ability to do the work involved. An applicant for an audio typist's job, for example, might be given a dictation tape and asked to type it. This is a type of attainment test, in that it is designed to measure abilities or skills already acquired by the candidate.

ACTIVITY 6 (30 MINS)

What kind of work sample or proficiency tests would you devise for the following categories of employee? For each, state whether your test is a physical, verbal or mental test.

- (a) Administrative assistants
- (b) Construction supervisors
- (c) Airline pilots
- (d) Magazine editors
- (e) Telephone operators

EXAMPLE PSYCHOMETRIC TESTS

'A government agency has adopted innovative recruitment techniques by using psychometric tests to measure how well candidates fit in with the public-sector culture.

'And other public-sector organisations could soon follow suit, after the *Environment Agency* revealed the move had dramatically reduced staff turnover rates.

'The agency overhauled its recruitment for environmental officers, following retention problems. Candidates are now sent to assessment centres specifically to evaluate whether they have the "personality and qualities to work in the public sector" …

' "Understanding the public-sector ethos is being increasingly recognised as important and as necessary to getting the right skills … It is certainly harder to train people in those behavioural attributes than it is to train them in the technical side." '

Watkins (2003)(b)

3.2 LIMITATIONS OF PSYCHOMETRIC TESTING

Psychometric testing has grown in popularity in recent years, but you should be aware of certain drawbacks.

- (a) There is not always a direct (let alone predictive) relationship between ability in the test and ability in the job: the job situation is very different from artificial test conditions.

- (b) The interpretation of test results is a skilled task, for which training and experience is essential. It is also highly subjective (particularly in the case of personality tests), which belies the apparent scientific nature of the approach.

- (c) Additional difficulties are experienced with particular kinds of test. For example:

  - (i) An aptitude test measuring arithmetical ability would need to be constantly revised or its content might become known to later applicants.

  - (ii) Personality tests can often give misleading results because applicants seem able to guess which answers will be looked at most favourably.

(iii)   It is difficult to design intelligence tests which give a fair chance to people from different cultures and social groups and which test the *kind* of intelligence that the organisation wants from its employees. The ability to score highly in IQ tests does not necessarily correlate with desirable traits such as mature judgement or creativity, merely mental agility. In addition, 'practice makes perfect': most tests are subject to coaching and practice effects.

(d)   It is difficult to exclude discrimination and bias from tests. Many tests (including personality tests) are tackled less successfully by women than by men, or by immigrants than by locally-born applicants because of the particular aspects chosen for testing. This may make their use indirectly discriminatory.

The most recent edition of the 16PF test, for example, has been scrutinised by expert psychologists 'to exclude certain types of content, such as dated material, content that might lead to bias, material that might be unacceptable in an organisational setting and anything considered to be strongly socially desirable or undesirable'.

FOR DISCUSSION

'Among the qualities which neither the interview nor intelligence tests are able to assess accurately are the candidate's ability to get on with and influence his [or her] colleagues, to display qualities of spontaneous leadership and to produce ideas in a real-life situation.'

(Plumbley, 1991)

Why might this be a drawback? What can be done about it?

4   GROUP SELECTION METHODS

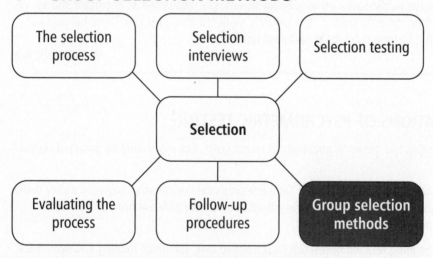

4.1   TECHNIQUES IN GROUP SELECTION

Group selection methods or **assessment centres** might be used by an organisation as the final stage of a selection process for high-value jobs (since they are comparatively expensive to run). They consist of a series of tests, interviews and group situations normally held over a period of two days, involving a small number of candidates (typically six to eight).

Group selection methods are appropriate for assessing the following.

(a) **Social skills** such as sensitivity to the views and opinions of others, reaction to disagreement and criticism, and the ability to influence and persuade others.

(b) **Intellectual skills** such as the consideration of the merits and demerits of other arguments put forward and the ability to think clearly (particularly at short notice), situational problem-solving and so on.

(c) **Attitudes** such as political, racial or religious views, attitude to authority, or willingness to take risks (initiative).

Typical techniques used in group selection include:

(a) Group **role-play** exercises, in which candidates can explore (and hopefully display) interpersonal skills and/or work through simulated managerial tasks.

(b) **Case studies**, where candidates' analytical and problem-solving abilities are tested in working through described situations/problems, as well as their interpersonal skills, in taking part in (or leading) group discussions of the case study.

(c) **'In-tray' exercises**, simulating a typical work-load to be managed.

(d) **Leaderless discussion groups** (LDGs), allowing leadership skills and issues to emerge freely.

Often what are termed '**leaderless group activities**' will be conducted. Such activities can be used to assess the leadership potential of job applicants in uncertain situations with no formal power structure. The group is presented with a topic for discussion and given a defined period of time to reach a conclusion. The topic may be related to the job in question, and may either be of a problem-solving nature ('Should product X be developed given the following marketing and financial information?') or more general ('Is capital punishment an effective deterrent?'). The contribution made by individual candidates will be scored according to factors such as assertiveness, quality of thought and expression, analytical skill, and the ability to lead the group towards a decision.

Another method of assessment involves giving candidates a typical job problem to solve individually in a set time, at the end of which each candidate has to present and justify his or her solution to the other members of the group.

EXAMPLE   VIRGIN ATLANTIC

The **Virgin Atlantic** careers website outlines its selection methods for prospective candidates as follows.

Assessment Centres

An Assessment Centre is a method of assessing the strengths and development needs of candidates. They generally last for all or part of a day and they're made up of a number of exercises.

For positions in Cabin Crew, In-Flight Beauty Therapist, Airports and Contact Centre there will be some kind of assessment centre, which will contain some of the following elements:

- Group decision
- Role plays
- Analysis presentation
- Ability tests, such as numerical reasoning
- Behavioural/biographical interview

Group discussions

These are useful in assessing candidates who are applying for roles with a strong element of teamwork.

Ability tests

These measure certain abilities or aptitudes and usually involve some kind of scoring that will indicate the level of your ability in the area being tested or your potential to learn more.

Behavioural/biographical interviews

In a behavioural interview you will be asked to give specific examples of situations that you have dealt with and what the outcomes were.

At a biographical interview you will be asked to discuss your CV and employment history, outlining what you have done, what your achievements are and how/why you have made your career choices.

4.2 PURPOSES OF GROUP SELECTION

Group sessions might be useful because:

(a)   They give selectors a longer opportunity to study the candidates.

(b)   They reveal more than application forms, interviews and tests alone about the ability of candidates to persuade, negotiate and explain ideas to others and also to investigate problems efficiently. These are typically management skills.

(c)   They reveal more about how candidates' personalities and attributes will affect the work team and their own performance.

(d)   They achieve some measure of comparability between candidates.

(e)   The pooled judgement of the panel of assessors is likely to be more accurate than the judgement of a single interviewer.

SIGNPOST

We now look at some of the later considerations in the selection process, bringing the candidate through to a contract of employment.

ACTIVITY 7   (60 MINS)

For an organisation of your choice, find out:

(a)   What selection methods are used, and for what kinds of jobs
(b)   The policies or guidelines given for the use of these methods

5 FOLLOW-UP PROCEDURES

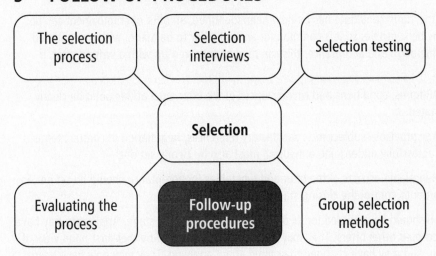

5.1 REFERENCE CHECKING

References provide further confidential information about the prospective employee, although they may be of varying value; the reliability of all but the most factual information must be questioned. A reference should contain:

(a)   Straightforward factual information confirming the nature of the applicant's previous job(s), period of employment, pay, and circumstances of leaving.

(b)   Opinions about the applicant's personality and other attributes. These should obviously be treated with some caution. Allowances should be made for prejudice (favourable or unfavourable), charity (withholding detrimental remarks), and possibly fear of being actionable for libel (although references are privileged, as long as they are factually correct and devoid of malice).

At least two **employer** references are desirable, providing necessary factual information, and comparison of personal views. (**Personal** references tell the prospective employer little more than that the applicant has a friend or two.)

If a judgement of character and suitability is desired, it might be most tellingly formulated as the question: 'Would you re-employ this individual? (If not, why not?)'

Telephone references may be time-saving, if standard reference letters or forms are not available. They may also elicit a more honest opinion than a carefully prepared written statement. For this reason, a telephone call may also be made to check a very glowing or very reluctant reference.

(Note that when **giving** references, caution is also required. A landmark legal judgement in *Spring v Guardian Assurance plc 1995*, decided that an employer owes a duty of care to employees in relation to giving a reference, and in obtaining the information upon which the reference is based. On the other hand, an employer could face civil liability from a company which suffered economic loss as a result of hiring an employee on the basis of a false complimentary reference!)

ACTIVITY 8   (10 MINS)

At the end of a recent selection process one candidate was, in the view of everyone involved, outstanding. However, you have just received a very bad reference from her current employer. What do you do?

5.2 THE OFFER OF EMPLOYMENT

Assuming that the 'right' candidate has by now been identified, an offer of employment can be made. Time may be sensitive, so it is common for an **oral offer** to be made, with a negotiated period for consideration and acceptance: this can then be followed-up with a written offer, if appropriate.

(a) All terms, conditions and circumstances of the offer must at this point be clearly stated.

(b) Any provisos ('subject to… satisfactory references, negotiation of contract terms', successfully undergoing a medical) must also be clearly set out.

(c) Negotiable aspects of the offer and timetables for acceptance should be set out, in order to control the closing stages of the process.

The organisation should be prepared for its offer to be rejected at this stage. Applicants may have received and accepted other offers. They may not have been attracted by their first-hand view of the organisation, and may have changed their mind about applying. They may only have been testing the water in applying in the first place, gauging the market for their skills and experience for future reference, or seeking a position of strength from which to bargain with their present employers. A small number of eligible applicants should, therefore, be kept in reserve.

5.3 CONTRACTS OF EMPLOYMENT

Once the job offer has been confirmed and accepted, the contract of employment can be prepared and offered.

A contract of employment may be written, oral or a mixture of the two. Senior personnel may sign a contract specially drafted to include complex terms on matters such as performance-related pay, professional indemnity, confidentiality and restraint of trade. Others may sign a standard form contract, exchange letters with the new employer or supply agreed terms orally at interview. Each of these situations, subject to the requirements (outlined below) as to written particulars, will form a valid contract of employment, as long as there is mutual agreement on essential terms.

5.4 WRITTEN PARTICULARS OF EMPLOYMENT

Although the contract need not be made in writing, the employer must give an employee (who works at least eight hours a week) a written statement of certain particulars of his or her employment, within two months of the beginning of employment (*Employment Rights Act 1996*).

The statement should identify the following.

(a) The names of employer and employee

(b) The date on which the employee's continuous employment began

(c) The scale or rate of remuneration provided to the employee, the method of calculating the remuneration and the intervals at which payment is made

(d) Hours of work and normal working hours

(e) Entitlement to holiday and holiday pay

(f) Any terms and conditions relating to incapacity for work owing to sickness or injury, including any provision for sick pay

(g) Terms and conditions relating to pensions and pension schemes

(h) Notification as to whether a contracting-out certificate is in force

(i) The length of notice to which the employee is entitled (such notice must be at least equal to the statutory requirement)

(j) The employee's job title or a brief description of the employee's duties

(k) Where the employment is temporary, the period for which it is expected to continue or, if it is for a fixed term, the date when it is to end

(l) The place of work and whether the employee may be expected to work at various locations

(m) Any collective agreements which may affect the terms of the contract

(n) Details of disciplinary and grievance procedures, works rules, union of staff association membership

(o) Information relating to the terms of employment where the employee is required to work outside the UK for longer than one month

It is sufficient to refer to separate booklets or notices (on matters such as pension schemes and disciplinary/grievance procedures) where the relevant details can be found; not all the information needs to go in the written statement! The point is to give new employees clear, precise information about their employment.

5.5 DEALING WITH UNSUCCESSFUL APPLICANTS

In order to maintain a positive reputation and employer brand, and to support overall labour development, a best practice approach to selection will also ensure the equitable and supportive treatment of unsuccessful applicants.

(a) All applicants should be informed as promptly as possible of the status of their application. Candidates who have been interviewed should be personally informed that their application has not been successful.

(b) The 'rejection' should be as positive as possible, bearing in mind the possibility that an unsuccessful applicant may be eligible for future vacancies (with or without further personal or skill development): known previous candidates 'kept on file' are a cost-effective recruitment pool.

(c) Candidates may be offered the opportunity to receive feedback, on request, as to why their application was unsuccessful. This demonstrates the employer's transparency (and compliance with equal opportunity requirements). It also compels selectors to justify their decisions on objective grounds. It supports job-seekers in developing their CVs, portfolios of skills, interview technique etc, enabling them to become more readily employable. It also encourages more discerning self-selection by seekers in response to job advertisements, making the whole process (in the long run) more efficient and effective.

6 EVALUATING THE PROCESS

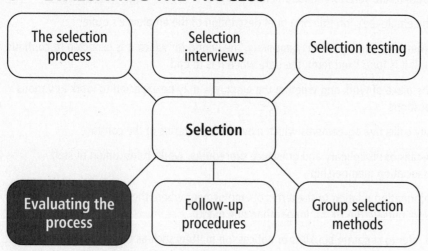

6.1 EVALUATING SELECTION

Much the same method can be used to evaluate selection as recruitment: see Section 7 of Chapter 3.

Selection procedures can further be evaluated by determining whether selection decisions seem to have been 'correct' in the light of subsequent job performance, cultural impact and service longevity of the successful candidate.

(a) If tests were used to assess likely potential to perform certain tasks, the retained test results can be compared with actual performance in the job. Regular discrepancies may suggest that the tests are flawed.

(b) Similar comparisons may be made using interview ratings and notes. Interviewers who consistently fall short in the accuracy of their judgements should be trained accordingly.

Other performance criteria for evaluating selection procedures include:

(a) Number of candidates (and/or minority/female/disabled candidates) interviewed in relation to applications

(b) Number of offers made in relation to number of interviews (especially to minority/female/disabled candidates)

(c) Number of acceptances in relation to offers made

(d) Number of successful applicants subsequently appraised as competent in the job

(e) Lead time for successful applicants to be trained to competence

(f) Number of starters still employed after one year (two years or an appropriate period of measurement)

(g) Cost of selection methods per starter employed one year later

CHAPTER ROUNDUP

- The contents of this chapter may be summarised in diagrammatic form.

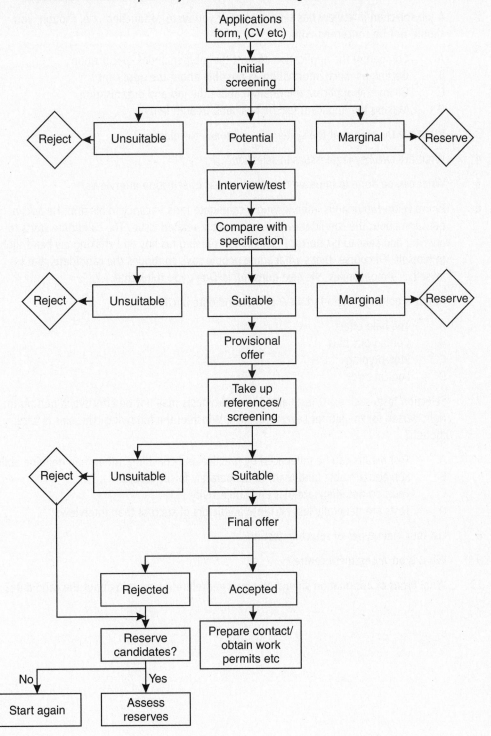

QUICK QUIZ

1   What are the aims of selection?

2   A job selection interview has several aims. If you were conducting one, though, you
     should **not** be concerned with:

     A   Comparing the application against the job/personnel specification
     B   Getting as much information as possible about the applicant
     C   Giving the applicant information about the job and organisation
     D   Making the applicant feel he has been treated fairly

3   What are the stages of the systematic approach to selection?

4   What are two key legal issues in selection?

5   What can be done to improve the effectiveness of selection interviews?

6   Amon Leigh-Hewman is interviewing a candidate for a vacancy in his firm. He asks a
     question about the candidate's views on a work-related issue. The candidate starts to
     answer, and sees to his horror that Amon in pursing his lips and shaking his head slightly
     to himself. 'Of course, that's what some people say', continues the candidate, 'but I
     myself…' Amon smiles. His next question is 'Don't you think that…?

     Amon is getting a distorted view of the candidate because of:

     A   The halo effect
     B   Contagious bias
     C   Stereotyping
     D   Logical error

7   Selection tests such as IQ tests and personality tests may not be effective in getting the
     right person for the job for several reasons. Which of the following criticisms is false,
     though?

     A   Test results can be influenced by practice and coaching rather than genuine ability
     B   Subjects are able (and tend) to deliberately falsify results
     C   Tests do not eliminate bias and subjectivity
     D   Tests are generally less accurate predictors of success than interviews

8   List four main types of selection testing.

9   What is an 'assessment centre'?

10   What types of information should an employer reference contain about the candidate?

ANSWERS TO QUICK QUIZ

1   Filling vacancies with best person; informing applicants (to facilitate self-selection and adjustment); creating employer brand; upholding values of fairness and professionalism
(see Para 1.1)

2   B. Information needs to be relevant   (Para 2.1)

3   Set key criteria; compare applications (forms, CV) against criteria; sort and shortlist; acknowledge all responses; invite candidates to interview/selection testing or other methods; check references; issue offer of employment; draw up contract; obtain work permits (if necessary); plan induction; send standard letters to 'rejects' and 'reserves'
(Para 1.2)

4   Discrimination/equal opportunity and privacy/data protection   (Para 1.3)

5   Planning; relevant criteria; interviewer training and appraisal; structured style of questioning; awareness of potential for bias   (Paras 2.2 – 2.3)

6   B   (Para 2.4)

7   D. Interviews are generally less accurate   (Para 3.1)

8   Cognitive, aptitude, personality, proficiency   (Para 3.1)

9   A group selection process, using a series of tests, interviews and group situations and exercises over a period of two days, typically involving 6 – 8 candidates for a job (Para 4.1)

10   Factual information confirming the nature of the applicant's previous job, period of employment, pay and circumstances of leaving. Opinions (cautious) about the applicant's attributes and employability   (Para 5.1)

ANSWERS TO ACTIVITIES

1   (a)   'Steamer'. (The others share national connotations: German measles, French leave, Spanish omelette, Dutch courage.)

    (b)   The answer presupposes a knowledge of expressions which are rooted in a European context and, in some cases, are old-fashioned and dependent on a middle-class upbringing and education.

2   Marchington and Wilkinson (2008) include an analysis of the accuracy of selection methods. As can be seen combining methods produces the most reliable outcome.

1.00	Perfect selection	0.40	Personality tests
0.65	Intelligence tests and integrity tests	0.37	Assessment centres
0.63	Intelligence tests and structured interviews	0.35	Biodata
0.60	Intelligence tests and work sampling	0.26	References
0.54	Work sample tests	0.18	Years of job experience
0.51	Intelligence tests	0.10	Years of education
0.51	Structured interviews	0.02	Graphology
0.41	Integrity tests	0.00	Selection with a pin

Employers appear to rely *most* heavily on the least *valid* selection methods! Interviews, in particular, seem not much better than tossing a coin…

3   Rees (1996) suggested the following points. You may not agree with all of them.

    (a)   The method need take no more time for the organisation: in fact single interviews may turn out to take less than an hour.

    (b)   Candidates would have to spend more time being interviewed but 'might not mind this if they felt it was a more effective method of selection'.

    (c)   It is normally easier to create rapport and coax information out of a person when you are seeing him or her alone.

    (d)   However, inexperienced interviewers will be far more 'exposed' than they would be in a panel interview. They may prefer merely to observe.

    (e)   The method is liable to create more argument about the final decision: the interviewee may be flagging by the end of the session and give a totally different impression to later interviewers.

4   This is personal to your experience: it will help you develop the evidence to show your competence in investigating selection procedures in organisations.

5   (a)   Closed. (The only answer is 'yes' or 'no', unless Jo is prepared to expand on it, at his or her own initiative.)

    (b)   Leading. (Even if Jo was interested, (s)he would get the message that 'yes' would not be what the interviewer wanted, or expected, to hear.)

    (c)   Leading closed multiple! ('Really useful' leads Jo to think that the 'correct' answer will be 'yes': there is not much opportunity for any other response, without expanding on it unasked.)

    (d)   Open. (Jo has to explain, in his or her own words.)

    (e)   Probing. (Jo has to defend his or her decision.)

6   Here are some suggestions.

Test

(a)   Admin assistants   Use of specific software or equipment (physical)
                                   Dictation (physical)
                                   Filing (physical)
                                   Letter proofreading/correction (mental)
                                   Telephone answering (verbal)

(b)   Construction supervisors   Plan error recognition (mental)
                                   Role play dealing with worker problems (verbal)

(c)   Airline pilots   Rudder control, direction control (physical)
                                   Navigational reading (mental)
                                   Radio procedures (verbal)

(d)   Magazine editors   Writing headlines (mental)
                                   Proofreading/correction (mental)
                                   Page layout (mental/physical)

(e)   Telephone operators   Switchboard handling (physical/mental)
                                   Role play incoming calls (verbal)

7   This is another investigation opportunity: keep a record for your portfolio.

8   It is quite possible that her current employer is desperate to retain her. Disregard the reference, or question the referee by telephone, and seek another reference from a previous employer if possible.

Chapter

05

Reward management

Introduction

'Reward management is about deciding how people should be rewarded and ensuring that reward policies and practices are implemented. Strategic reward aligns reward strategies, systems and processes with the fundamental need of the business for high performance. It involves developing total reward strategies, which provide for both financial and non-financial rewards, determining levels of pay, base pay management, the management of contingency pay schemes and the provision of employee benefits.'   Armstrong (2012)

Reward management strategies are designed to support the achievement of business objectives, by helping to ensure that the organisation can attract, retain and motivate competent and committed employees.

In this chapter, we look briefly at the role of reward in the context of **motivation theories**. We then go on to explore some key aspects of *reward management:* how the value of work is determined (by job evaluation) and other factors affecting pay. We also examine at a variety of financial and non-financial reward systems, as part of the 'total reward' concept.

This chapter discusses several ways in which people can be rewarded differentially according to their *performance*. This theme is explored further in Chapter 6, where we cover the monitoring of performance – partly for the purposes of allocating rewards.

Your objectives

In this chapter you will learn about the following.

- The relationship between motivation theory and reward
- The process of job evaluation
- The main factors determining pay levels
- Different types of reward systems, including performance-related pay
- Flexible benefits

1 MOTIVATION AND REWARD

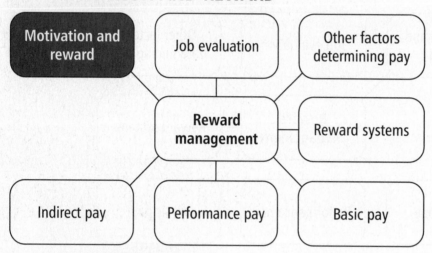

1.1 WHAT IS MOTIVATION?

The word 'motivation' is commonly used in different contexts to mean:

(a) The **mental process** of choosing desired outcomes, deciding how to go about them, assessing whether the likelihood of success warrants the amount of effort that will be necessary, and setting in motion the required behaviours. This is sometimes called '**intrinsic motivation**', as it arises from factors and processes within the individual.

(b) The **social process** by which the behaviour of an individual is influenced by others. 'Motivation' in this sense usually applies to the attempts of organisations to maintain or increase workers' effort and commitment by using rewards and punishments. This is sometimes called '**extrinsic motivation**', as it arises from actions done to or for the individual by others.

Theories of motivation are often categorised as 'content theories' and 'process theories'

Content theories assume that human beings have an innate package of motives (needs or desired outcomes) which they take action to pursue. They ask: '*What* motivates people?' Maslow's Hierarchy of Needs and Herzberg's two-factor theory are two of the most important approaches of this type. McClelland's work on high achievers offers an interesting sidelight on pay and motivation.

Process theories explore the psychological process through which outcomes become desirable and are pursued by individuals. They ask: '*How* are people motivated?' This approach assumes that people are able to select their goals and choose the paths towards them, by a conscious or unconscious process of calculation. Expectancy theory is a key example.

> **SIGNPOST**
>
> We look briefly at these key motivational theories in turn, highlighting the nature of 'rewards' in each.

1.2   NEED THEORY

Need theories suggest that individuals have certain innate needs. When a need is unsatisfied, the individual experiences tension – and acts in pursuit of goals that will satisfy the need.

Abraham Maslow (1954) developed the original and most famous need theory. He argued that human beings have five innate needs, which he suggested could be arranged in a 'hierarchy of relative pre-potency' as shown in Figure 5.1.

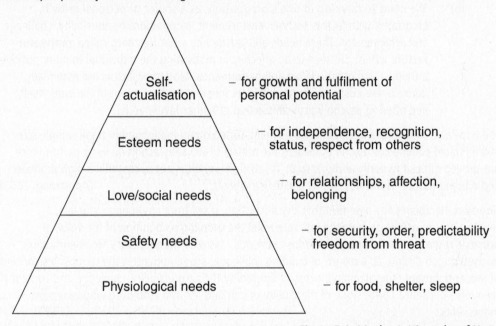

Figure 5.1: Maslow's Hierarchy of Needs

Each level of need is dominant until satisfied: only then does the next level of need become a motivating factor. Maslow regarded self-actualisation as the ultimate human goal: 'the desire to become more and more what one is, to become everything that one is capable of becoming'. It can never be satisfied in full.

Maslow's hierarchy is simple and intuitively attractive: you are unlikely to worry about respect if you are starving! However, it is only a theory, and not derived specifically from work psychology. Empirical verification of the hierarchy is hard to come by. Individuals may select any number of specific goals to satisfy their needs: for example, esteem needs may be satisfied by promotion, or a pay increase – or neither, depending on the individual's values and vocation. Research has also suggested that the hierarchy reflects UK and US cultural values, which may not transfer to other contexts.

Nevertheless, the hierarchy underpins a recognition that people can be motivated at work by **rewards which offer satisfaction of their 'higher order needs'**: social belonging (relationships, teamwork, collaboration), esteem (competence, achievement, independence, confidence and their reflection in the perception of others: recognition, appreciation, status, respect) and self-actualisation (challenge, personal development, fulfilment).

1.3 TWO-FACTOR THEORY

Frederick Herzberg (1966) interviewed Pittsburgh engineers and accountants about 'critical incidents' which made them feel good or bad about their work. He identified two basic need categories of individuals at work.

(a) The **need to avoid unpleasantness**, associated with fair treatment in compensation, supervision, working conditions and administrative practices. These needs are satisfied by what Herzberg called '**hygiene**' **factors**: they may minimise dissatisfaction and poor job performance, but have little ability to motivate the individual to higher levels of job satisfaction or extra performance. Hygiene factors are essentially extrinsic rewards, deriving from factors in the environment or context of work, and offering satisfaction of lower-level needs.

(b) The **need to develop in one's occupation**, as a source of personal growth, associated with factors such as advancement, recognition, responsibility, challenge and achievement. These needs are satisfied by what Herzberg called '**motivator**' **factors**, which are seen to be effective in motivating the individual to more positive attitudes, and greater effort and performance. Motivator factors are essentially intrinsic rewards, deriving from factors inherent in the content of the work itself, and offering psychological satisfaction of higher-level needs.

The two-factor model has been criticised as being based on an inadequately small sample size and a limited cultural context. In particular, the impact of job satisfaction on work performance has proved difficult to verify and measure: 'A satisfied worker is not necessarily a high producer, and a high producer is not necessarily a satisfied worker.' (Armstrong, 2003)

However, Herzberg's key assertion that 'dissatisfaction arises from environment factors: satisfaction can only arise from the job' confirmed the growing recognition of the value of **intrinsic rewards** – as opposed to extrinsic rewards – as motivating factors. Herzberg's work focused on job design, as a means of building challenge, scope and interest into jobs: his concept of **job enrichment** ('the planned process of upgrading the responsibility, challenge and content of the work') became a cornerstone of the quality of working life and employee empowerment movements.

1.4 McCLELLAND – ACHIEVEMENT MOTIVATION THEORY

David McClelland (Human Motivation, 1987) identified four main needs-based motives.

- Achievement
- Power
- Affiliation
- Avoidance

The first three correspond, roughly, to Maslow's self-actualisation, esteem and love needs. People who have a high need for achievement are motivated far more by challenging opportunities than they are by money. However, these high achievers also have a strong need for feedback on their performance and monetary rewards are valued as a means of keeping score. Such people are unlikely to remain in jobs that do not pay them well for their high achievement, which reinforces the view that pay is a hygiene factor.

1.5 TOTAL REWARD

Today's '**total reward**' concept recognises that a reward system offering a mix of both extrinsic and intrinsic rewards is likely to be the most effective way of motivating employees.

Torrington *et al* (2011), add additional perspective as to why total reward is attractive 'As a result (of the recession) employers are having to think more creatively and more broadly about the rewards that they offer, looking for ways of motivating and retaining valued staff, without increasing their pay bills. For these reasons the concept of 'total reward' has become attractive and significant in recent years. This involves thinking about the reward package in a very broad sense, not only the aspects that involve payment, but a range if other elements too. Organisations may be increasingly constrained in terms of how much more they can pay someone, but there is much less constraint when it comes to providing them with career development opportunities, flexible work patterns or even a stimulating and pleasant working environment'

DEFINITION

Reward refers to 'all of the monetary, non-monetary and psychological payments that an organisation provides for its employees in exchange for the work they perform.'

(Bratton & Gold, 2007)

ACTIVITY 1   (30 MINS)

What 'intrinsic' or internal satisfactions and rewards do you value in your own job (as opposed to the 'extrinsic' or external things the organisation can give you, like pay, comfortable working environment or likeable management)? Why do you work? What do you get out of your work that you most value? What would you miss most if you didn't work? (If you've never been employed, ask these questions of someone who has.)

Try putting each of these satisfactions into (a) Maslow's categories of needs and (b) Herzberg's categories of hygiene and motivator factors.

Did you have any hesitation about where to put 'pay' in these categories? If so, why?

1.6 PROCESS THEORIES

While content theories of motivation, such as those of Maslow and Herzberg, focus on the satisfaction of needs, process theories are concerned with the mental processes, conscious or unconscious, that determine the extent and nature of an individual's motivation.

1.7 VROOM – EXPECTANCY THEORY

The expectancy theory of motivation basically states that the strength of an individual's motivation to do something will be influenced by:

(a)   The perceived link between individual effort, performance and particular outcomes (will reward follow effort?)

(b)   The importance of those outcomes to the individual (will the reward make the effort worthwhile?)

Vroom (1964) suggested a formula by which motivation could be assessed and measured, based on an expectancy theory model. In its simplest form it may be expressed as:

Force or strength of motivation to do x	=	Valence (Strength of the individual's preference for outcome y)	×	Expectancy (Individual's perception of the likelihood that doing x will result in outcome y)

Figure 5.2: Vroom's Expectancy Theory Formula

Valence is represented as a positive or negative number, or zero – since outcomes (or rewards) may be desired, avoided or considered with indifference. *Expectancy* is expressed as a probability (in the perception of the individual): any number between 0 (no chance) and 1 (certainty).

So, for example, an employee may have a high expectation that behaviour x (say, increased productivity) will result in outcome y (say, promotion) – because of a performance contract, perhaps – so E = 1. However, if (s)he is indifferent to that outcome (say, because (s)he doesn't want the responsibility), V = 0 (or less) and (s)he will not be motivated to increase productivity. Similarly, if the employee has a great desire for promotion – but doesn't believe that more productive behaviour will secure it (say, because (s)he has been passed over previously), E = 0 and (s)he will still not be highly motivated.

This model helps to explain why performance incentives and rewards work most effectively when:

(a) **The link between effort and reward is clear**. (This is a key criterion in designing performance-based pay schemes – but would also apply to the giving of non-financial rewards such as praise and recognition, for example.)

(b) **Intended results and goals are made clear**, and especially when individuals share in setting goals (so they can complete the calculation).

(c) **The reward is perceived to be worth the effort**. (This is part of the rationale for flexible benefit schemes, allowing employees to choose from a menu of incentives and rewards.)

1.8 GOAL THEORY

Locke (1968) (cited in Mullins, 2007) suggests that people's personal goals play an important role in determining their behaviour, in that they guide people's responses and actions, since they recognise that goal-oriented success is likely to lead to the satisfaction of their emotions and desires.

Locke (1975) (cited in Mullins, 2007) 'Goal setting is more appropriately viewed as a motivational technique rather than as a formal theory of motivation'.

Goal theory suggests that people's performance in their jobs is related to the difficulty of their goals, the extent of their commitment to them and the degree of feedback they receive on their relative performance. This has implications for management that is described in the next chapter.

FOR DISCUSSION

There has been ongoing debate about the role of job satisfaction in motivated performance. Some authorities have argued that 'happy bees make more honey': others counter that this cannot be proved.

Huczynski & Buchanan (2001) further note that:

'There is less talk about "the quality of working life" when there is little work to be had…'

What is your own view on how far employees need – and employers should offer – 'higher order' satisfactions at work, especially in times of economic recession?

What motivates *you*?

1.9 PARTICIPATION AND INVOLVEMENT

Need theories, such as those of Maslow and Taylor, emphasise the intrinsic rewards of work. The concepts of self-actualisation and the need to develop in one's work lead naturally to the idea that an increased level of autonomy in the work situation will enhance motivation. In particular, it is suggested that workforce motivation will be enhanced by involvement in decisions affecting worker and work. This concept runs alongside and complements political ideas about industrial democracy and the role of trade unions. We do not explore these topics further here since they are fully covered in the companion BPP Business Essentials Course Book *Human resource development and employee relations*.

1.10 PAY AS A MOTIVATOR

Monetary reward has a central, but ambiguous, role in motivation theory.

Scientific management and instrumentality

It is almost intuitive to suppose that people enter into employment with the specific aim of securing an income. Simple economic theory is based on the maximisation of utility, which may be understood in terms of maximum economic reward for minimum economic activity. This simple approach is one of the bases upon which Taylor and his contemporaries developed the approach known as **Scientific Management**. One of Taylor's fundamental assumptions was that his methods would increase the cash returns to both worker and employer and would therefore be eagerly taken up by both. He said:

What the workmen want from their employers beyond anything else is high wages, and what employers want from their workmen most of all is a low labour cost of manufacture.

Taylor (1911)

The 'Affluent Worker' research of Goldthorpe, Lockwood *et al* (1968) explained the role of pay as a motivator in terms of **instrumentality**. Instrumentality is the attitude adopted by people when they do one thing in order to achieve or bring about another. An instrumental orientation to work sees it purely as a source of income that may then be expended in obtaining the things that the worker really wants. Goldthorpe *et al* found that highly-paid Luton car assembly workers accepted that their work was tedious and unfulfilling, but had made a rational decision to enter employment offering high monetary reward rather than intrinsic interest. However, the research also suggested that people will seek a suitable balance of:

(a)   The rewards that are important to them

(b)   The deprivations they feel able to put up with in order to earn them

Even those with an instrumental orientation to work have limits to their purely financial aspirations, and will cease to be motivated by money if the disadvantages of their employment – in terms of long working hours, poor conditions and so on – become too great.

EXAMPLE   JOHN LEWIS TO SHARE NEARLY £200M IN BONUSES AFTER SUCCESSFUL YEAR

Shopworkers at the John Lewis Partnership on Monday scooped a bonus worth more than nine weeks' pay after business boomed last year at its department stores and sister chain Waitrose – despite the high-street downturn.

The strong performance means its 76,500 staff who **co-own** the retail group, receive a bonus equal to 18% of their annual salary in this month's wages. All permanent employees or "partners", from its chairman Charlie Mayfield to shop assistants and shelf-stackers, receive the same percentage payout from this year's bonus pot of £194.5m.

Mayfield said comparing the partnership bonus with recent bankers' bonuses was "talking apples and something that wasn't in the fruit category". However, he said the *espirit de corps* generated by employee ownership was a competitive advantage, which had helped to produce the 20% jump in pre-tax profits to £367.9m in the year to 29 January.

At John Lewis' flagship store on Oxford Street, the staff cheered when the bonus figure was announced. Last year they received a £151m bonus, equivalent to nearly eight weeks' pay. The payout was then equal to 15% of salary, compared with 13% in 2009 and 20% in 2008, before the high street was hit by the recession. The group's operating profits have now more than recovered from the slump.

John Lewis' managing director Andy Street, who is considering buying a car or a painting with his bonus, said the "crucial thing" about the bonus was that it was the same percentage for every single partner. "Also, it is totally driven by the results of the organisation, he added. "Everyone has put the bonus pot of £195m together and collectively they are sharing in it."

Christine Hewitt, who works as an administration assistant at the London store and plans to spend the money on singing lessons and a music summer school, was thrilled by the payout: "I thought it would be 15% – even 16% – I didn't even dare to allow myself to expect 17% in case I was disappointed. So, when it was 18% I shrieked; and I am not the kind of person who shrieks."

(*The Guardian*, March 2011)

Pay and group processes

Taylor's approach to management was, in part, based on his early experience of workers' practice of taking as long as possible to do a piece of work. He called this 'soldiering' because of its resemblance to marking time as opposed to making progress. Soldiering took advantage of management's incomplete knowledge of how long a given piece of work should, in fact, take. Workers soldiered, Taylor felt, partly from a natural human tendency to avoid exertion, but more importantly, to **defend their income**, since they were generally paid at piecework rates and faster work would inevitably lead to **rate cuts**. There was great solidarity among the workforce in this respect and, when he first became a supervisor at Midvale Steel, Taylor struggled to increase output. The essence of Scientific Management is **efficiency**: the greatest output per unit of input. This principle led Taylor and his peers to a system in which management optimised all the variables in the work situation and the workforce did exactly as they were told, receiving good rates of pay for doing so. When it worked, this system abolished soldiering, but it could not do away with the inherent processes of human behaviour.

This was demonstrated by the long series of experiments at the Western Electric Company's works at Hawthorne in Chicago, carried out by Roethlisberger and Dickson under the general

BPP LEARNING MEDIA

supervision of Elton Mayo. The experiments started in a typically Scientific Management way when the company carried out an experiment to assess the effect of lighting on productivity. They were astonished to find that productivity shot up, whatever they did with the lighting. This led to further experiments that clearly demonstrated that output was determined by a range of factors other than pay. These factors included, as assumed by Taylor, shared anxiety about piecework rates and the prospects of layoff or dismissal in the then prevailing poor economic conditions. **Social pressure** was exerted to discourage over-enthusiasm in individual workers. (Roethlisberger and Dickson, 1939)

Assessing the importance of pay

Pay is not mentioned explicitly in any need list, but clearly it can allow or support the satisfaction of various needs. According to Herzberg, it is the most important of the hygiene factors: valuable not only in its power to be converted into a wide range of other satisfactions, but also as a consistent measure of worth or value, allowing employees to compare themselves with other individuals or occupational groups. However, it is still only a hygiene factor: it gets taken for granted, and often becomes a source of dissatisfaction (particularly by comparison with others) rather than satisfaction.

Individuals may have needs unrelated to money, to which the pay system of the organisation is irrelevant or even conflicting (eg overtime bonuses conflicting with the need for work-life balance). Although the size of their income will affect their standard of living, most people tend not to be concerned to *maximise* their earnings. They may like to earn more but are probably more concerned to:

(a) Earn *enough* to meet their needs and aspirations

(b) Know that their pay is *fair* in comparison with the pay of others in comparable groups both inside and outside the organisation. This is sometimes known as the principle of *distributive equity* (Adams, 1963): it has been highlighted in recent decades by expectation and legislation in regard to equal pay for men and women (discussed later in the chapter).

Pay should be seen as only one of several intrinsic and extrinsic rewards offered by work. If it is used to motivate, it can only do so in a wider context of the job and other considerations. The significance in motivation theory of high-order needs, intrinsic rewards and subjective factors (such as expectancy and valance) suggests that HR managers need to:

(a) Develop reward systems which offer both financial and non-financial bonuses, rather than relying on simplistic assumptions of instrumentality

(b) Support job redesign, employee involvement and ongoing development planning which offer intrinsic satisfactions (particularly in the area of potential self-actualisation)

(c) Support an organisational and managerial culture which consistently values and expresses appreciation for employee contribution.

SIGNPOST

We return to the influence of rewards on performance in Section 4 of this chapter. First, we look in more detail at 'pay' and how pay levels are determined.

2 JOB EVALUATION

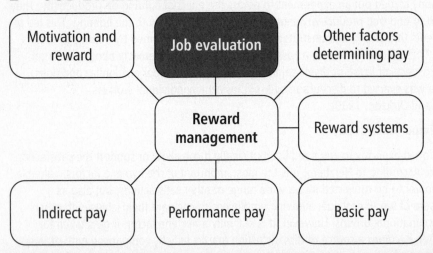

> **DEFINITION**
>
> **Job evaluation** is the process of analysing and assessing the content, worth or size of jobs within an organisation, in order to rank and group them as a basis for an equitable remuneration system.

2.1 THE PURPOSE AND AIMS OF JOB EVALUATION

Job evaluation is intended to create a rational and fair framework for job gradings and the pay decisions arising from them. It aims to:

(a) Assess the value of jobs to the organisation in relation to one another

(b) Support the development of job gradings and pay structures that are objective, balanced and equitable

(c) Ensure that the organisation is able to give (and demonstrate that it gives) equal pay for work of equal value, as required by law

2.2 ARGUMENTS FOR AND AGAINST FORMAL JOB EVALUATION

Formal job evaluation fell out of favour in the 1980s, being seen as too bureaucratic and inflexible for business environments which increasingly emphasised flexibility and reward for individual performance. However, in recent years, a renewed focus on equity – and specifically, on equal pay – has encouraged widespread adoption of formal job evaluation schemes.

The arguments for and against job evaluation may be summarised as follows.

Advantages	Disadvantages/limitations
• Job evaluation can offer a systematic approach to determining relative job values, without which it is difficult to justify the fairness of pay differentials. • Job evaluation offers a framework for consistent ongoing decision-making about job grades and rates of pay. • A properly designed and applied job evaluation process is more likely to be *felt* to be fair by employees. • An analytical job evaluation scheme is the only acceptable defence in equal pay cases, as a means of achieving equal pay for work of equal value.	• Job evaluation can be bureaucratic, inflexible and time-consuming. • Job evaluation can inhibit the development of a flexible, 'high-involvement' workplace (Bratton & Gold, 2007), because it adds 'rigidity' to the job and the pay structure, and imparts a 'top-down' ethos. • Job evaluation ratings can be gender biased, eg if job factors to be valued are based on jobs dominated by men. • Job evaluation is at best 'systematic' rather than 'scientific': there is an element of subjective judgement. • Job evaluated salary structures get out-of-date, unless attention is given to periodic review and maintenance.

In general, the criticisms focus on badly designed or applied job evaluation, rather than the concept of job evaluation itself.

ACTIVITY 2 (60 MINS)

Do you feel your salary is fair for the job you do, and in relation to others? (Remember, job evaluation concerns the content, size and value of the *job* to your organisation – not on how much you put into it or how well you perform it.) Do you know how your job is evaluated? Do you know how your salary is worked out? What could the organisation do to make the system (a) clearer and (b) fairer?

Either answer these questions yourself, or ask them of an employed person who is willing to be interviewed by you on this topic.

2.3 THE PROCESS OF JOB EVALUATION

The process of job evaluation covers four basic steps.

Step 1 **Select compensable factors**

Compensable factors represent the aspects of jobs for which the organisation is willing to pay. Armstrong (2009) suggests that effective factors should:

- Apply equally well to different types of work (including specialists and generalists, lower level and higher level jobs, and jobs performed by men and women)

- Refer to relevant and important differences between jobs, in order to allow comparison for ranking purposes

- Be understandable by, and acceptable to, all those who will be covered by the scheme

Examples of compensable factors include: knowledge and skills, judgement and decision-making, freedom to act and responsibility for financial resources.

Step 2   **Gather data on jobs**

Some information for evaluation may already be available in the form **of job descriptions**, or may have to be gathered by **job analysis** (see Chapter 3).

Step 3   **Evaluate jobs**

There are two basic types of job evaluation scheme.

- **Non-analytical schemes** make largely subjective judgements about the whole job, its difficulty, and its importance to the organisation relative to other jobs.

- **Analytical schemes** systematically analyse how far compensable factors are present in each job, in order to arrive at appropriate weightings and rankings.

These methods are discussed further below.

Step 4   **Assign specific pay values to the job**

The output of a job evaluation scheme is a **pay structure**: a ranking or hierarchy of jobs in terms of their relative value to the organisation. The organisation must then make policy decisions to assign pay values to jobs or job grades within the structure. This is generally done with reference to market rates of pay, how the organisation's pay levels compare with those of its competitors, and how aggressively it must compete to attract and retain quality labour. (This is discussed in Section 3 below.)

2.4 JOB EVALUATION SCHEMES

Non-analytical schemes

Job classification is the most common non-analytical approach. The organisation decides what grades of pay there should be and defines the requirements of each grade. Jobs are allocated to an appropriate grade by matching job descriptions to grade definitions.

Job ranking compares jobs with one another and ranks them in accordance with their relative importance or contribution to the organisation. Having established a hierarchy of jobs, they can be divided into groups for grading purposes.

Analytical schemes

Analytical schemes break jobs down into their component elements, for more detailed analysis. It is now the accepted procedure that if claims are made arising to Equal Pay that job evaluations must use analytical methods in order to demonstrate that the organisation is offering equal pay for 'work of equal value'. They must examine 'the demands on a worker under various headings (for instance, effort, skill, decision)'.

Points rating is currently the most popular method of formal job evaluation.

(a)   It begins with the definition of about 8 – 12 compensable factors: these will vary according to the type of organisation and can be adapted to its changing needs and key values.

(b)   A number of *points* is allocated to each compensable factor, as a maximum score, across a range of '*degrees*' which reflect the level and importance (or weighting) of the factors within a job.

(c)   A comprehensive *points rating chart* is therefore established, covering a range of factors and degrees which can be applied to a variety of specific jobs. An example of such a chart is shown in Figure 5.3.

(d)   Each *job* is then examined, analysed factor by factor according to the points rating chart, and a points score is awarded for each factor, up to the maximum allowed. The total points score for each job provides the basis for ranking the jobs in order of importance, for establishing a pay structure and for pricing the pay structure. An example of a **job evaluation form** for points rating is shown in Figure 5.4.

Factor comparison involves the selection of key *benchmark jobs*, for which the rate of pay is considered to be fair (perhaps in comparison with similar jobs in other organisations).

(a)   Each of these jobs is analysed, using compensable factors, to decide how much of the total salary is being paid for each factor. So if technical skill is 50% of a benchmark job paying £32,000, the *factor pay rate* for technical skill (within that job) is £16,000.

(b)   When this has been done for every benchmark job, the various factor pay rates are correlated, to formulate a *ranking and pay scale* for each *factor*.

(c)   Other (non-benchmark) jobs are then evaluated factor by factor, to build up a *job value*. For example, an analysis for a skilled administrative job might be:

Factor	*Proportion of job*		*Pay rate for factor (as established by analysis of benchmark jobs)*	*Job value* £
Technical skills	50%	×	£32,000 pa	16,000
Mental ability	25%	×	£24,000 pa	6,000
Responsibility for others	15%	×	£20,000 pa	3,000
Other responsibilities	10%	×	£16,000 pa	1,000
				26,000

FOR DISCUSSION

The 'transparency' or openness of a job evaluation exercise is critical to its effectiveness. Why might employees and their representatives be suspicious, or feel threatened, by a job evaluation programme (particularly if it is being introduced for the first time)? What kinds of information and messages will the HR manager want to give them in order to support effective job evaluation and preserve employee relations? (You may like to role play this as a discussion between staff, union representatives and an HR manager.)

Compensable factor	DEGREE (Weighting)				
	1	2	3	4	5
GENERAL					
Job knowledge	10	25	50	70	-
Practical experience	15	30	50	70	-
Physical effort	5	10	15	-	-
Complexity	15	20	25	30	-
Judgement/initiative	15	20	30	40	50
Job conditions	5	10	15	-	-
Contact with peers	5	10	20	40	-
Contact with clients	10	20	30	40	50
Attention to detail	5	10	15	20	-
Potential for error	5	10	20	40	-
Confidential data	5	10	15	20	30
.....	...	...	...	...	...
SUPEVISORY					
Nature of supervision	5	10	20	-	-
Scope of supervision	10	15	25	-	-
Resource allocation	10	15	25	30	-
Trust	15	20	30	40	50
Management reporting	10	15	25	30	-
Quality	15	30	90	50	60
.....	...	...	...	...	...

Degree definitions

- **Job knowledge**

1. Maintain basic procedures; operate and maintain basic machinery; undertake range of tasks under supervision; comply with rules and policies.

2. Administer a routine area of work, under supervision; operate and maintain basic machinery to proficient standard; understand purpose of rules and policies and be able to identify compliance issues.

3. Supervise a small number of staff in routine and non-routine tasks; be responsible for checking of work; manage own routine and non-routine workload; control maintenance of range of machinery and compliance with rules and policies, including coaching/briefing of staff; certificate-level qualification in job-related area.

4. Supervise staff in routine and non-routine tasks; manage quality and customer service issues; plan and co-ordinate own and section workload; systematic view of rules and procedures, with ability to propose improvements; diploma-level qualification in job-related area.

5. –

Figure 5.3: Points rating chart (excerpt)

Job evaluation form

Key job code _____   Department _____

Job type _____   Job holder studied _____

Date _____   Employee number _____

Task number

Description

Factor	Rating			Comments
	Points	Weighting	Total	

Skills and knowledge
  Education/qualifications
  Experience
  Dexterity				

Skills sub-total				
Initiative				

Responsibility
  People
  Equipment
  Resources				

Responsibility sub-total				

Effort
  Mental
  Physical				

Effort sub-total				

Communication
  Oral
  Written				

Communication sub-total				
Interpersonal skills				

Conditions of work
  Hazards
  Isolation
  Monotony				

Conditions sub-total				
TOTAL				
RANKING				
COMMENTS				

Figure 5.4: Points rating form

SIGNPOST

Job evaluation only determines a job's relative worth to the organisation, by ranking or grading. It does not reflect its monetary worth to the organisation. We now consider a number of other factors influencing the setting of actual pay levels.

3 OTHER FACTORS DETERMINING PAY

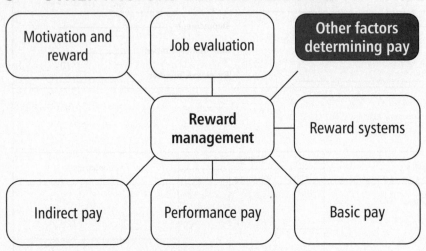

3.1 MARKET RATES OF PAY

In order to arrive at pay rates which support recruitment, retention and motivation, a pay structure should be a combination of:

(a) The results of job evaluation, based on relative worth of jobs to the organisation and internal equity; and

(b) The results of market pay analysis, based on the 'absolute' worth of jobs to the organisation and competitiveness in the labour market.

The concept of the market rate is not exact: different employers will pay a range of rates for similar job titles – particularly in the case of managerial jobs, whose scope and nature will vary according to context and culture. However, most organisations use **pay surveys** of key or 'benchmark' jobs to get a broad indication of the 'going rate' of pay for a job. Sources of information on market rates include:

(a) Published surveys

(b) Surveys carried out by HR specialists or commissioned from management consultants

(c) Business network or 'club' surveys, where organisations exchange pay information on a regular basis

(d) General market monitoring and intelligence: recruitment advertising, government statistics, recruitment consultancies etc.

Market rate information on benchmark jobs can be used to add monetary values to 'similar' jobs within the organisation's job-evaluated rankings. Other jobs can then be placed on the pay scale according to their relative positions in the ranking, and priced accordingly.

ACTIVITY 3 (30 MINS)

You may like to check out some of the sources of published pay surveys available online, such as the *Annual Survey of Hours and Earnings* (ASHE).

(a) How reliable do you think each of the sources of market rate data listed in Paragraph 3.1 would be?

(b) How would you go about 'job matching': comparing the jobs cited in market rate data with jobs in your own organisation, as 'like with like' in terms of the type and size of the job and the type of organisation?

The market rate of pay will vary with supply/demand factors such as:

(a) The **relative scarcity of special skills** in the particular market from which the organisation draws its labour

(b) The **sensitivity of employees** to pay levels or differentials. Pay may, or may not, act as an incentive to change employers, depending on the availability of work elsewhere, the employee's loyalty and the non-financial rewards offered by the organisation or the job.

Market rates of pay will have most influence on pay structures where there is a standard pattern of supply and demand in the open labour market. If an organisation's rates fall below the benchmark rates in the local or national labour market from which it recruits, it may have trouble attracting and holding employees. Management has three basic policy choices:

(a) To **lead** the competition: often used for key or scarce skills, or to establish a leading employer brand as part of the organisation's competitive strategy

(b) To **match** what other employers are paying: the least-risk approach

(c) To **lag** behind the market: may be cost-effective where vacancies can be easily filled in the local labour market (minimising direct competition with other employers)

ACTIVITY 4 (45 MINS)

What do you think are the arguments *for* and *against* an organisation's offering above-market rates of pay?

Other factors which may distort or dilute the effect of the forces of supply and demand on labour pricing (in addition to job-evaluated equity criteria) include:

(a) **Affordability**: the organisation's ability to pay the market rate.

(b) The **culture and value system** of the organisation, which will influence the attitude of management towards the market rate, and whether age, length of service, motivation, employee aspirations and/or other factors are taken into account in the determination of pay, rather than fluctuations in supply and demand. (You may note from some of the International Comparisons in this chapter that national cultural differences also influences salary strategy.)

(c) The bargaining strength of trade unions (where applicable) in **collective bargaining** negotiations. Pay scales, differentials and minimum rates may be negotiated at plant, local or national level.

(d)   **Government intervention**, including incomes policies and anti-inflationary measures (limiting the size of pay increases by pay controls). UK governments have often used control of public sector pay to influence general pay trends. The UK also has a national minimum wage (*National Minimum Wage Regulations 1998,* the enforcement of which was strengthened by the *Employment Act 2008)* and equal pay legislation (discussed further below).

EXAMPLE   **INTERNATIONAL COMPARISON**

Reward policy in **Germany** is highly collectivised. Each trade union (organised on broad industry lines) negotiates with the employers' federation on a state by state basis – allowing for the relative prosperity of the region. Companies (such as Volkswagen) which are not part of a trade association may negotiate separately with the relevant trade union. Many HR managers will therefore not be involved in wage negotiation at all, but will simply implement the agreement locally.

The system of industrial democracy known as 'co-determination' gives a plant-level Works Council the right to co-determine company policy on matters including how wages and salaries are to be paid (method, time), the use of incentives (bonus schemes, piece work, performance-related pay). Traditionally, popular elements of reward systems include holiday and long-service bonuses, suggestion schemes, incentive/merit pay (for manual grades) and profit sharing (for managerial grades), with employee share ownership schemes attracting tax incentives.

3.2 INDIVIDUAL PERFORMANCE

Job-evaluated pay structures are generally designed to allow increasing rewards for seniority (eg by using incremented rates for age or length of service), competence (eg by applying competence-based bands) and/or performance (eg by applying merit or contribution bands). The **incentive** role of pay in motivating employees to higher levels of performance may also be built into the reward system through separate bonus schemes, performance-related pay, employee share ownership schemes and so on. We discuss these aspects in detail later in the chapter.

3.3 EQUAL PAY

The *Equal Pay Act 1970* was the first major attempt 'to prevent discrimination as regards terms and conditions of employment between men and women.' Women were entitled to claim equal pay and conditions of service for:

- Jobs rated as equivalent under a job evaluation scheme

- Work that was 'the same as or broadly similar' to the work of a man in the same establishment, where job evaluation was not used

The *Equal Pay (Amendment) Regulations 1984* established the right to equal pay and conditions for work of equal value (that is, not necessarily 'similar' work, but work of equivalent evaluation). If job evaluation is not used in an organisation, the employee can apply to an Employment Tribunal for a (legally enforceable) order to have an evaluation carried out by an independent expert. The *Equality Act 2010* included an important addition, that if an individual is to make a claim when choosing a comparator, a claimant is able to name a predecessor.

3.4 NATIONAL MINIMUM WAGE

The *National Minimum Wage Act 1998* provided for a minimum hourly wage for nearly all workers. The rates are amended from time to time.

FOR DISCUSSION

Why do you think there has been continuing sensitivity in recent years to the issue of equal pay?

Why is it important for 21st century business organisations to take this into account?

SIGNPOST

We now look briefly at reward systems and how they can be structured.

4 REWARD SYSTEMS

DEFINITION

A **reward system** is 'the mix of extrinsic and intrinsic rewards provided by the employer... [It] also consists of the integrated policies, processes, practices and administrative procedures for implementing the system within the framework of the human resources (HR) strategy and the total organisational system.' (Bratton & Gold, 2007)

4.1 OBJECTIVES OF THE REWARD SYSTEM

The key objectives of any reward system can be summed up as follows.

(a) **Recruiting and retaining quality labour** in line with the human resource plan. External competitiveness with market rates may be the strongest influence on recruitment, while internal equity may be the strongest influence on retention.

(b) **Motivating individual and team performance**, to maximise return on investment from the human resource. There are various forms of reward system which link reward to performance (discussed below).

(c) **Supporting organisational culture**, by conveying messages about the values, behaviours and outcomes that the organisation prizes and is willing to pay for.

(d) **Supporting flexibility**, by responding to changing organisational skill and performance requirements.

4.2 COMPONENTS OF THE REWARD SYSTEM

Three broad components can be identified within the reward system.

(a) **Direct or base pay**: a fixed salary or wage that constitutes a standard rate for the job, as defined by market pricing and job evaluation. This amount is paid at intervals of a week or month and reflects 'hours of work': the amount of *time* spent at the workplace or on the job. It is appropriate as a basic pay component in jobs where outputs are less meaningful or measurable. It also provides a relatively consistent and predictable basic income. Pay *progression* (increases in basic pay over time) may be related to age or length of service, or to performance-related criteria such as competence or skill attainment.

The key advantages of direct pay are that it is easy to implement and administer; it is generally felt to be fair (especially if established by job evaluation); and it helps to establish mutual commitment in the employment relationship.

(b) **Performance or variable pay**: a method or component of pay directly linked to work-related behaviour, such as performance or attainments. There are various types of variable pay, including:

(i) **Payment by results (PBR)**, which links pay directly to the quantity of output produced by the individual (or team): piecework, commission (usually a percentage of sales value generated) or output or target-based bonuses

(ii) **Performance-related pay (PRP)**, offering additional payments for individual or team performance according to a range of possible performance criteria (quality, customer service, teamworking, innovation)

(iii) **Organisation performance pay**, based on the profitability of the firm: eg value added schemes, profit-sharing schemes and employee shareholding

The key advantage of such rewards (in theory) is that they motivate employees to higher levels of performance and foster a culture in which performance, competence and contribution (and specific criteria such as teamworking or innovation) are valued and rewarded. However, as we noted in Section 1 of this chapter, the assumption that people are motivated and managed solely by pay is simplistic.

(c) **Indirect pay or 'benefits'**: non-cash items or services. These may include 'deferred pay' in the form of pension contributions, legal entitlements (for example, to sick pay, maternity pay, maternity/paternity leave, and annual leave), and so-called 'fringe' benefits such as company cars, housing assistance, medical insurance and allowances.

4.3 THE 'TOTAL REWARD' CONCEPT

The sum of the components discussed above is known as **'total remuneration'**. The concept of **'total reward'** is based on the premise that monetary payments are not the only, or necessarily the most effective, form of reward and that financial and non-financial rewards should be linked together as an integrated reward package: Figure 5.5.

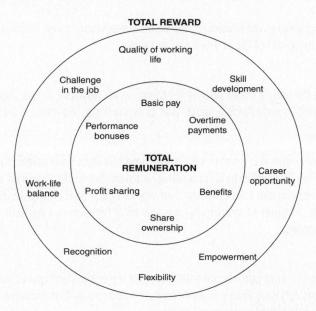

Figure 5.5: Total reward package

A total reward orientation seeks to integrate reward strategy both vertically (with business strategy) and horizontally (with a range of other HRM strategies).

Armstrong (2003) cites a study by WorldatWork which suggests the following benefits of a total reward approach:

(a) **Increased flexibility**: tailoring rewards to changing circumstances

(b) **Recruitment and retention**: offering employees the 'total value' of the employment package (and monitoring its true cost to the organisation)

(c) **Potential for low-cost reward solutions**

(d) **Heightened visibility in tight labour markets**: offering valued rewards

EXAMPLE   ACCENTURE WEBSITE 2012

We understand that what you earn and the benefits you receive have an enormous impact on your quality of life. Because we're always competing to attract and retain the very best people, we continuously review our rewards strategy to make sure it's the best it can be.

On this page, we want to give you a brief taste of what could be coming your way as a member of the Accenture team.

Generous holiday allowance
Interest-free season ticket loan
Generous pension scheme
Employee share purchase plan
Charity work option (three days per year)
Subsidised gym membership
Private healthcare
Life assurance
Critical illness cover
Hotel and travel discounts
Generous maternity leave
Paternity leave
Generous car cash allowance (manager level and above)

Besides making sure you're well rewarded, we also have a whole range of initiatives designed to help you get even more out of life at work and at home.

Flexible working

Our people told us this was a major priority for them, so it's now one for us. Just some of the options we're offering include flexible hours, part-time working, job-sharing and home-working.

Leaves of absence

There may be a time when you want to take some time out from your career – perhaps you want to write a novel, work in another field for a while or travel the world. If you've worked here for more than two years, you can take between four weeks and a year of unpaid leave and return to your job afterwards. At times of oversupply, we also offer flex-leave: a partially-paid sabbatical for six to twelve months.

Working parents

Our commitment to working parents goes way beyond decent maternity and paternity leave. Our Working Parents Advisory Forum is an Accenture-wide group that provides support, shares practical information and shapes company policy.

Fitness & health

We have a range of health and welfare initiatives on the go. Everything from occupational health and safety programmes through to regular health screens and discounted gym membership.

Counselling

Whether it's work or home worries, our independent counselling service offers confidential telephone or face-to-face advice for you and your family.

WEBLINK

For more details, see:

▶ ▶ http://careers.accenture.com/gb-en/working/overview/benefits/Pages/index.aspx

SIGNPOST

We now look at each of the three components of the total remuneration package in turn.

BPP
LEARNING MEDIA

5 BASIC PAY

5.1 SALARY AND WAGE SYSTEMS

The terms 'wages' and 'salaries' are sometimes used interchangeably to refer to monetary rewards, but there are traditional distinctions between them.

Wages	Salaries
• Manual/'blue collar' workers – historically on short contract terms	• White-collar workers – historically with greater security of tenure
• Paid weekly	• Paid monthly, as a proportion of an annual fixed sum
• Based on a weekly or hourly rate for time/output	• Related to seniority, qualifications, performance, with progression over time
• Premium rates paid for overtime	• Overtime not usually paid

In the UK and US, wage payment systems have increasingly been replaced by salaries as part of **single status** schemes. These represent an attempt to harmonise the payment systems operating in an organisation, and in the process to remove barriers between workers and management and to encourage commitment and co-operation.

ACTIVITY 5   (10 MINS)

What advantages and disadvantages for the organisation and its workers can you see from single status schemes?

EXAMPLE

Severn Trent Water introduced performance-related pay for all front-line staff in 2005, so they are assessed in the same way as managers and directors.

The new pay structure, introduced in 2006, linked total award to overall company performance based on profit, safety and attendance records.

Previously, the company had mixed pay practices, with staff on different rates. (And some rather outdated policies such as a 'Sheepdog allowance' for staff patrolling reservoirs!)

(*People Management*, 13 October 2005)

5.2 SALARY SYSTEMS

A salary system generally consists of a:

(a) **Grade structure**, consisting of a hierarchy of bands or levels ('grades') to which are allocated groups of jobs that are broadly comparable in value: Figure 5.6.

(b) **Pay structure**, defining pay ranges or scales for each grade, allowing scope for *pay progression* or increases according to length of service and performance.

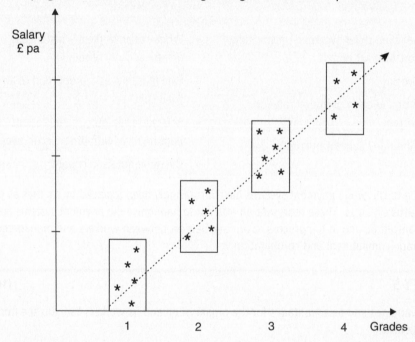

Figure 5.6: Grade structure

The grade structure requires careful design, because of the consequences for promotions and transfers between grades.

(a) **Differentials** between pay ranges should recognise increases in job value between one grade and another.

(b) The **range** of each grade should be wide enough to allow for progression, offering rewards for lateral career development (where promotion opportunities are few) and competence development. 'Broad banding' (having few grades of 'bands', each spanning a wide range) also allows rates of pay to be more flexibly adapted to market rate fluctuations, individual performance and flexible roles.

(c)   There should be some **overlap**, in recognition that an experienced person performing well in a given job may be of more value than a new or poor performer in the next grade up.

Progression or pay increases within a grade may be achieved by fixed increments linked to age or length of service (common in the public sector) or by various forms of performance-related increases.

Flexibility will be required: changes in job content or market rates should prompt regrading. Individual growth in competence should also be allowed for. In the case of an individual whose performance is outstanding, but for whom there are no immediate openings for promotion, discretionary payment above the grade maximum may be made.

ACTIVITY 6   (NO TIME LIMIT)

(a)   Is there a salary policy and structure in your organisation (or an organisation of your choice?) Find out and record the salient details.

(b)   If you had trouble finding out, what does this say about the political aspects of salary administration?

5.3 WAGE SYSTEMS

A typical wage structure will include:

(a)   A basic (time or piecework) rate; *plus*

(b)   Overtime premium rates for work undertaken outside normal hours

(c)   Shift pay at premium rates for employees who work unusual or socially disruptive hours or shift patterns (a form of *compensatory* pay)

(d)   Compensatory payments for abnormal working conditions (eg 'danger money', 'dirt money', 'wet money'), although these may be built into basic rates during job evaluation

(e)   Allowances (eg to employees living in high cost-of-living areas like London)

(f)   Merit or length-of-service bonuses

(g)   Payment by results bonuses and incentives (discussed below).

6 PERFORMANCE PAY

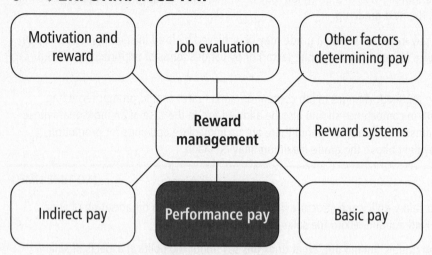

6.1 EFFECTIVE PERFORMANCE PAY SYSTEMS

Effective performance (or 'contingent') pay systems should fulfil the following criteria.

(a) Targets and standards of performance required to earn the rewards must be made clear to the people involved.

(b) The formulae used to calculate rewards, and any conditions that apply, should be easily understood.

(c) The rewards should be – and perceived to be – significant enough to make the effort worthwhile (perhaps 10% of basic salary).

(d) Rewards should be related to performance indicators over which people have control or influence, through their own behaviour or decision-making.

(e) There should not be a lengthy time lag between performance and reward.

6.2 PERFORMANCE-RELATED PAY (PRP)

Individual performance-related pay (IPRP) relates monetary bonuses and/or the rate and extent of pay progression (increases in basic pay over time) to the performance of individuals, assessed according to defined criteria.

For managerial and other salaried jobs, a form of **performance management** is usually applied so that:

(a) Key results can be identified and agreed, for which merit awards will be paid

(b) The exact conditions and amounts of awards can be made clear to employees

(c) Performance indicators can be regularly monitored and evaluated, in order to establish when targets have been reached and awards earned

For service and other departments, a PRP scheme may involve **bonuses** for achievement of key results, or **points schemes**, where points are awarded for performance on various criteria (efficiency, cost savings, quality of service) and a certain points total (or the highest points total in the unit, if a competitive system is used) wins cash or other awards.

PRP is not appropriate for all organisations. It requires conditions where individual performance can be objectively and meaningfully measured, where individuals are in a position to control the outcomes of their work, where close teamworking or co-operation with others is not central to successful job performance and where there is an individualistic organisational culture.

(Torrington *et al*, 2011)

A table detailing the advantages and limitations of IPRP is given below.

Advantages of IPRP	Disadvantages/limitations of IPRP
• Encourages the setting, clarification and communication of key task behaviours and performance criteria	• Based on over-simplistic belief in instrumentality: not all employees motivated by financial incentives
• Encourages the monitoring, gathering and sharing of feedback on current performance	• Fosters instrumentality: creates a culture where employees expect to be rewarded for everything
• Integrates organisational and individual priorities and objectives	• Fosters a manipulative management culture based on 'carrot and stick' rather than intrinsic rewards
• Promotes a results-focused culture and behaviours: flexibility, customer service, quality and 'entrepreneurial' thinking	• Undermines teamworking by focusing on individual effort
• Reduces the need for other types of managerial control (direct supervision, technology), fostering self-motivation	• May focus on quantitative outputs, at the expense of quality
• Attracts and retains people who expect to be rewarded for delivering results	• May focus on established ways of doing things, inhibiting creativity and innovation
• Provides a concrete means of rewarding performance	• May focus on short-term productivity gains rather than long-term strategic goals
	• May frustrate employees, where they are not able to control all factors in their performance
	• Relies heavily on effective performance management for objective performance definition and assessment

FOR DISCUSSION

'Managers who insist that the job won't get done right without rewards have failed to offer a convincing argument for behavioural manipulation. Promising a reward to someone who appears unmotivated is a bit like offering salt water to someone who is thirsty. Bribes in the workplace simply can't work.'   (Kohn, 1993 cited by Torrington *et al*, 2011)

Do incentives only secure temporary compliance – or can they change underlying attitudes?

EXAMPLE   INTERNATIONAL COMPARISON

A key feature of employment in **Japan** has traditonally been the seniority system, which links reward with length of service rather than with job or performance factors. This is a subtler distinction than it may appear, since length of service is equated with commitment, skill development and status. 'It is a scale of 'person-related' payments – as opposed to 'job-related' payments... an intricate set of rules, based on the exponential principle that the higher you go, the faster you rise, designed to give recognition to both seniority and merit. The seniority principle requires that everybody goes up a notch every year' (Dore, cited by Beardwell and Holden, 1997). This concept of 'performance-related pay' is very different from the Western concept of performance as individual achievement: it reflects the complexity of the relationship between the individual, the organisation, the job and socio-cultural values of status, commitment and belonging.

6.3 SUGGESTION SCHEMES

Another variant on performance-based pay is the **suggestion scheme**, where payments or non-cash rewards are offered to staff to formulate workable ideas on improving efficiency or quality, new marketing initiatives or solutions to production problems. The theory is that there is, in any case, motivational value in getting staff involved in problem-solving and planning, and that staff are often in the best position to provide practical and creative solutions to their work problems or the customer's needs – but that an added incentive will help to overcome any reluctance to put forward ideas (because it is seen as risky, or doing management's job for them, or whatever).

Wherever possible, the size of the payment should be related to the savings or value added as a result of the suggestion – either as a lump sum or percentage. Payments are often also made for a 'good try' – an idea which is rejected but considered to show initiative, effort and judgement on the part of the employee.

Suggestion schemes usually apply only to lower grades of staff, on the grounds that devising improvements is part of the manager's job, but with the increase of worker empowerment and 'bottom-up' quality initiatives, they are becoming more widespread in various forms.

6.4 TEAM-BASED PAY

Group incentive schemes typically offer a bonus for a group (distributed equally, or proportionately to the earnings or status of each individual) which achieves or exceeds specified targets. Offering bonuses to a whole team may be appropriate for tasks where individual contributions cannot be isolated, workers have little control over their individual output because tasks depend on each other, or where team-building is required.

One key objective of team reward is to enhance team spirit and co-operation as well as to provide performance incentives – but it may also create pressures or conflict within the group, if some individuals are 'not pulling their weight'.

Long-term, large-group bonus schemes may be applied plant- or organisation-wide. **Gain sharing** schemes allocate additional awards when there has been an increase in profits or a decrease in costs.

(a) **Value-added** schemes, for example, work on the basis that improvements in productivity (indicated by a fall in the ratio of employment costs to sales revenue) increases value added, and the benefit can be shared between employers and employees on an agreed formula.

(b) **Scanlon plans** pay frequent, plant-wide bonuses, based on improvements in productivity and reduction in labour costs which are brought about through collective bargaining and the participation of employee representatives.

Profit-sharing schemes offer employees current or deferred bonuses (paid in cash or shares) based on company profits. The formula for determining the amounts may vary, but in recent years, a straightforward distribution of a percentage of profits above a given target has given way to a value-added concept.

The link between individual effort and profitability is recognised to be remote, so profit sharing does not constitute a direct incentive. However, it is based on the belief that all employees can contribute to profitability, and that their contribution should be recognised. It may foster profit-consciousness and commitment to the future prosperity of the organisation. The greatest effect on productivity resulting from the scheme may, in fact, arise from its use as a focal point for discussion with employees about the relationship between their performance and results, and areas and targets for improvement.

An **employee stock plan** or **employee share ownership scheme** (such as an *All Employee Share Ownership Plan* or *Savings-Related Share Option Scheme)* allows employees to acquire shares in their employing company. The key advantage of such systems may be to encourage employees to take 'ownership' of the long-term success of the business – although the collapse of corporations such as Enron, and the global economy's sudden plunge into recession in 2008, has highlighted the extent to which this may be a double-edged sword…

ACTIVITY 7 (15 MINS)

Are you motivated by monetary incentives? At what point would the offer of more money cease to motivate you to longer hours, greater efforts (or whatever)? Try and identify three likely problems with, or limitations of, cash/monetary incentives.

EXAMPLE SPORTS DIRECT STAFF REWARDS ARE IN A DIFFERENT LEAGUE

Here's an idea for Philip Clarke, the Tesco boss seeking to invigorate his UK stores and his UK staff: super-charge your shop-floor share incentive arrangements.

The strategy seems to have paid off in spades for Mike Ashley's Sports Direct, a business that became a stock market joke after various post-flotation calamities in 2007 and 2008: the share price descended from 300p to 36p.

The price was back to 100p by the time Ashley introduced a three-year employee bonus scheme in 2009 – but the timing was still excellent for qualifying staff. All the profit targets have been met and today's trading update spelled out what it means for members of the scheme.

More than 2,000 staff will receive an average of 5,000 shares this summer and a further 12,000 next summer if they are still employed at Sports Direct. At the current share price of 291p, 17,000 shares are worth almost £50,000. That's a chunky sum in a business where average salaries are around the £20,000 mark.

Many retailers, including Tesco, like to boast every year about the rewards their staff earn via various bonus and profit-share arrangements. Sports Direct's numbers, however, are in a different league. The 2009 scheme "proved an excellent tool to encourage and motivate the entire organisation while helping to retain staff," notes the company.

(*The Guardian*, 2012)

6.5 NON-CASH INCENTIVES

Incentive and recognition schemes are increasingly focused not on cash, but on non-cash rewards. Traditionally aimed at sales people, non-cash gifts and incentives are now widely used to add interest to quality and suggestion schemes, enabling managers to recognise staff contribution flexibly, informally and at relatively low cost. Incentive awards include vouchers, air miles, the choice of gift from a catalogue, travel experiences and so on.

Tulip (2003) suggests that incentive schemes need to be up-to-the-minute, fresh and flexible, if they are to be effective.

'An incentive scheme has to be achievable, but people also have to be rewarded with the sort of things they want. Call centre workers, for example, tend to be a young market, often making a first home, and so tend to select electrical merchandise or kitchen goods. These are less likely to incentivise high-flyers, older workers and managers, who typically go for an "experience", whether that be a holiday or something more extreme.'

A range of ideas for incentives is highlighted, including:

- Experience-based incentives (particularly effective as rewards for successful teams or team-based projects) such as snowboarding or dolphin watching events.

- Gift vouchers traditionally backed by major retailers such as Marks & Spencer and John Lewis Partnership: some of these offer a wider range of opportunities such as those offered by the Virgin brand (from CDs to hot air ballooning).

Such schemes can be regarded by some staff as manipulative, irrelevant or just plain gimmicky. However, they can be effective as team-building exercises and as part of a total reward programme.

FOR DISCUSSION

Which of the non-cash incentive examples mentioned above do you think would be a good investment for the organisation, and why? Which would you, as an employee, find most attractive? (Explore any personal and cultural differences in the answers from your discussion group.)

7 INDIRECT PAY

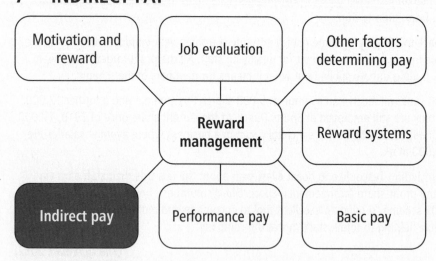

7.1 BENEFITS

Employee benefits consist of items or awards which are supplementary to normal pay. Some – such as sick pay, maternity/paternity leave and statutory maternity/paternity/adoption pay – are legal entitlements, so the common term 'fringe' benefits is perhaps misleading. Other benefits are more in the nature of optional extras and, as such, may be part of the total remuneration package.

QUICK QUIZ

1   Explain the formula F = E × V in terms of motivational theory.

2   What is 'instrumentality' and what is its relevance to reward management?

3   Outline the advantages and disadvantages of job evaluation.

4   List the four basic steps in job evaluation.

5   List four sources of information on market rates of pay.

6   What are the implications of the Equal Pay and the subsequent Equality Act for setting pay levels?

7   Define a 'grade structure' and a 'pay structure' in a salary system.

8   What are the advantages and disadvantages of performance-related pay?

9   List three options for organisation-wide performance rewards.

10 What are the advantages of flexible benefits?

ANSWERS TO QUICK QUIZ

1   Force of motivation to do X = valence (important of outcome Y) x expectancy (perceived probability that doing X will lead to Y).   (see Para 1.4)

2   The concept that people will do something as a means to an end: eg work for money. Lies behind monetary/extrinsic reward systems, but is simplistic: instrumentality is not universal or straightforward as a motivating factor.   (Para 1.5)

3   For a full answer, see the table in Paragraph 2.2.

4   Select compensable factors, gather data on jobs, evaluate jobs (using non-analytical or analytical methods), assign pay values to jobs.   (Para 2.3)

5   Published surveys; special surveys; business network/club surveys; general marketing monitoring and intelligence.   (Para 3.1)

6   Women are entitled to claim equal pay for work of equal value. This should be justified by analytical job evaluation, which uses both non-gender-biased compensable factors and non-gender-biased evaluation.   (Para 3.3)

7   Grade structure: a hierarchy of bands or levels ('grades') to which are allocated groups of jobs that are in the same value range.

     Pay structure: pay ranges or scales for each grade, allowing scope for pay progression within the grade.   (Para 5.2)

8   For a full answer, see Paragraph 6.2.

9   Gain sharing schemes, profit-sharing, employee share ownership.   (Para 6.4)

10   For a full answer, see Paragraph 7.3.

ANSWERS TO ACTIVITIES

1   The answers to this activity will be personal to you, and should clarify your thinking about need theories and rewards. The issue of pay is discussed in Paragraph 1.5.

2   Again, the answer to this activity will be personal to you, but remember to draw out the relevant learning. Your subjective experience of job evaluation (your own sense of the fairness of your salary *and* the transparency and perceived fairness of your organisation's job evaluation scheme) should highlight some of the issues for HR managers. You will also be building up your 'case study' file of examples of HR practices in the real world.

3   (a)   Published surveys are quick and relatively inexpensive – but may not be relevant to the organisation's jobs, and may be out of date.

Special surveys may be time-consuming and costly, but they directly compare jobs in the market place with jobs in the firm.

Network/club surveys are a cost-effective way of accessing surveys, and are regularly updated.

Recruitment ads and consultancies may be misleading: the job descriptions are unlikely to be sufficient to match jobs accurately, and salaries offered/cited may not be reflected in practice.

(b)   Job matching may be done by using job titles, but this is likely to be very misleading. Job descriptions are likely to offer greater accuracy in identifying directly comparable jobs: the fuller the description, the greater the comparability. Comparing full job evaluations of different jobs would be most valuable – if such data were available (eg through commissioned or published surveys).

4   One may list the general arguments for paying over market rate as follows.

(a)   The offer of a notably higher remuneration package than market rate may be assumed to generate greater interest in the labour market. The organisation will therefore have a wider field of selection for the given labour category, and will be more likely to have access to the most skilled/experienced individuals. If the organisation establishes a reputation as a 'wage leader' it may generate a consistent supply of high-calibre labour.

(b)   There may be benefits of high pay offers for employee loyalty, and better performance resulting from the (theoretically) higher calibre and motivation of the workforce.

(c)   Even if a cheap supply of labour were available, and the employer could get away with paying a low rate, its ideology or ethical code may make it reluctant to do so. A socially responsible employer may wish to avoid the exploitation of labour groups, such as immigrants, who may not be aware of general market rates.

(d)   An employer might adopt a socially responsible position not purely for ethical reasons but to maintain a respected image and good relations with government, interest groups, employee representatives and the general public (potential customers/ consumers).

(e)   Survival and immediate profit-maximisation are not necessarily the highest objective of any organisation. Employers in growth markets, or hoping to diversify into new markets, cannot afford a low-calibre, high-turnover workforce. Notably innovative organisations can be seen to be offering higher than market rate on salaries (eg Mars) or remuneration packages including profit-related bonuses (eg Sainsbury's): moreover, their financial performance bears out their view that pay is an investment. To an extent, this pay strategy stems from the culture or value system of the organisation, the importance it attaches to loyalty, innovation and initiative, and its willingness to pay more to attract and retain such higher-level attributes: quantity may not be the prime employment criterion.

On the other hand, there are substantial cost savings in paying lower rates. It cannot be assumed that high remuneration inevitably leads to higher motivation and better performance. Not everybody has an instrumental orientation to work: money may not be the prime incentive – and pay is often a source of dissatisfaction rather than satisfaction, whatever its level.

If the organisation's ability to maintain high rewards in the future is in doubt (eg in times of recession), management ought also to be aware that the disappointment and culture shock of reversing a high-remuneration policy is very great.

5   Single status schemes can save an organisation administrative and overtime costs, and may improve employee flexibility and industrial relations. For manual workers, there are clear advantages in receiving a wider range of benefits and an annual salary (which at least improves their borrowing position).

However, there may be an increase in labour costs overall. For the workers, too, there is a drawback, in monthly – instead of weekly – payments. There is also a perceived loss of status for salaried workers, in the achievement of parity by previous wage-earners: this may affect their morale, although the organisation culture will have a lot to do with whether harmonisation is perceived as threatening or equitable and exciting.

6   If you are not employed in a work organisation, ask a salaried acquaintance. Do not neglect to think about part (b) of this activity: research has shown that in the absence of information about salaries, people become dissatisfied by what they *think* they are earning in relation to others. Some people seem genuinely not to want to know how their salary is determined, as long as it progresses year on year: what might the consequences of such an attitude be for loyalty, motivation and the salary bill of the organisation?

7   There are a number of difficulties associated with incentive schemes based on monetary reward.

(a)   Increased earnings simply may not be an incentive to some individuals. An individual who already enjoys a good income may be more concerned with increasing their leisure time, for example.

(b)   Workers are unlikely to be in complete control of results. External factors, such as the general economic climate, interest rates and exchange rates may play a part in *profitability* in particular. In these cases, the relationship between an individual's efforts and their reward may be indistinct.

(c)   Greater specialisation in production processes means that particular employees cannot be specifically credited with the success of their particular products. This may lead to frustration amongst employees who think their own profitable work is being adversely affected by inefficiencies elsewhere in the organisation.

(d)   Even if employees *are* motivated by money, the effects may not be altogether desirable. An instrumental orientation may encourage self-interested performance at the expense of teamwork. It may encourage attention to output at the expense of quality, and the lowering of standards and targets (in order to make bonuses more accessible).

Workers remain suspicious that if they achieve high levels of output and earnings, management will alter the basis of the incentive rates to reduce future earnings. Work groups, therefore, tend to restrict output to a level that they feel is 'fair' and 'safe'.

8 In a survey of 2,000 people in full-time employment in France, Britain, Germany and Italy, it was discovered that:

(a) Most workers think a staff restaurant is a more important benefit than a company car (84% of workers, in 'cuisine-conscious' France!)

(b) Company cars were also rated less important than pensions or private health insurance

Monitoring and managing performance

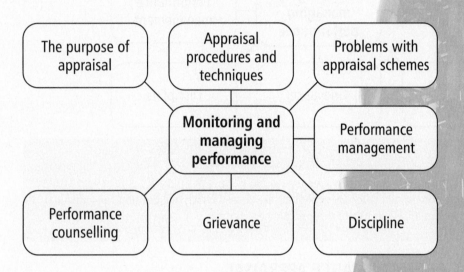

Introduction

The process of monitoring individual and group performance, and giving helpful feedback for improvement, is generally called **performance appraisal**. The purpose of appraisal was traditionally regarded as constructive criticism of an employee's performance by the line manager, but nowadays it has a more forward-looking approach.

- Helping the employee to overcome any problems or obstacles to performance

- Identifying where an employee's potential for improved performance and greater challenge could be better fulfilled

- Setting goals and priorities for further monitoring and development

Your objectives

In this chapter you will learn about the following.

- Organisational approaches to monitoring performance, including appraisal and performance management

- The role, purpose and types of appraisal

- 360-degree feedback
- Skills in appraisal and giving feedback
- Performance management interventions including discipline, grievance and counselling

1 THE PURPOSE OF APPRAISAL

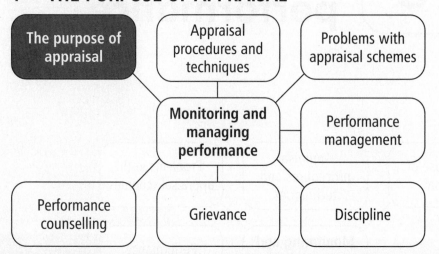

DEFINITION

Performance appraisal is the process whereby an individual's performance is reviewed against previously agreed goals, and whereby new goals are agreed which will develop the individual and improve performance over the forthcoming review period.

1.1 ROLE OF PERFORMANCE APPRAISAL

Monitoring and evaluating the performance of individuals and groups is an essential part of human resource management. It has several key aims.

(a) To identify individuals' learning/development and performance improvement needs

(b) To identify problems or barriers to performance which require intervention

(c) To identify people with potential for future promotion, supporting succession planning

(d) To provide a basis for reward decisions: eligibility for results-related bonuses, competence-related increments, merit awards and so on

(e) To improve communication about work issues, performance and development opportunities between managers and team members

SIGNPOST

It may be argued that a particular, deliberate stock-taking exercise is unnecessary, since managers are constantly monitoring progress and giving subordinates feedback from day-to-day. Why have a formal appraisal system?

1.2 WHY HAVE A FORMAL APPRAISAL SYSTEM?

It must be recognised that, if no system of formal appraisal is in place:

(a)   Managers may obtain random impressions of subordinates' performance (perhaps from their more noticeable successes and failures), but not a coherent, complete and objective picture.

(b)   Managers may have a fair idea of their subordinates' shortcomings – but may not have devoted time and attention to the matter of improvement and development.

(c)   Different managers may be applying a different set of criteria, and varying standards of objectivity and judgement, undermining the value and credibility of appraisal.

(d)   Managers rarely give their subordinates systematic or constructive feedback on their performance.

Common practice is to provide for formal appraisal at least annually, however, appraisal at six monthly intervals is not unusual. It will be normal for supervision to be closer and appraisal more frequent during the initial phase of employment, especially where satisfactory completion of a period of probation is required.

ACTIVITY 1   (15 MINS)

List four disadvantages to the *employee* of not having an appraisal system.

1.3 THE SYSTEMATIC APPROACH TO APPRAISAL

A typical appraisal system should involve:

(a)   Identification of **criteria** for assessment

(b)   The preparation of an **appraisal report**

(c)   An **appraisal interview**, for an exchange of views about the results of the assessment, targets for improvement, solutions to problems etc

(d)   The preparation and implementation of **action plans** to achieve improvements and changes agreed

(e)   **Follow-up**: monitoring the progress of the action plan

SIGNPOST

We now look at each stage in turn.

2 APPRAISAL PROCEDURES AND TECHNIQUES

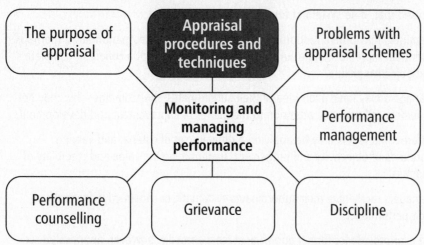

2.1 WHAT SHOULD BE MONITORED AND ASSESSED?

Assessments must be related to a common set of standards, so that comparisons can be made between individuals. On the other hand, they should be related to meaningful and specific performance criteria, which take account of the critical variables in each job.

ACTIVITY 2	**(20 MINS)**

Think of some criteria which you would want to use in assessment of some jobs – but which would not be applicable in others.

Personal qualities like reliability or outgoingness have often been used as criteria for assessing people. However, they are not necessarily relevant to job performance: you can be naturally outgoing, but still not good at communicating with customers, if your product knowledge or attitude is poor. Also, personality judgements are notoriously vague and unreliable: words such as 'loyalty' and 'ambition' are full of ambiguity and moral connotations.

In practical terms, this has encouraged the use of **competence or results-based appraisals**, where performance is measured against specific, job-related performance criteria.

Most large organisations have preprinted assessment forms setting out all the relevant criteria and the range of possible judgements. (Figure 6.2 illustrates such a form later in this chapter.) Even so, a manager should critically evaluate such schemes to ensure that the criteria for assessment are relevant to his or her team and task – and that they remain so over time, as the team and task change.

Relevant criteria for assessment might be based on the following.

(a) **Job, role or competence descriptions** as a guide to what competences, responsibilities and results might be monitored and assessed.

(b) **Departmental or team plans, performance standards and targets**. If the plan specifies completion of a certain number of tasks, or production of a certain number of units, to a particular quality standard, assessment can be focused on whether (or how far) those targets have been achieved.

(c) **Individually negotiated goals and standards** for performance and/or improvement. This is a feature of 'performance management', discussed in Section 4 of this chapter.

2.2 BENCHMARKING

DEFINITION

Benchmarking is the 'establishment, through data gathering, of targets and comparators, that permit relative levels of performance (and particularly areas of underperformance) to be identified. Adoption of identified best practices should improve performance.

(Chartered Institute of Management Accountants (CIMA) *Official Terminology*)

Benchmarking is generally undertaken in order to improve corporate rather than individual performance. However, it may be seen as related to performance management since it involves much similar activity.

The benchmarking process

Benchmarking can be divided into stages.

Stage 1

The first stage is to **ensure senior management commitment** to the benchmarking process. This will only be genuinely available when the senior managers have a full appreciation of what is involved: senior staff are quite capable of changing their minds when it becomes apparent that they did not anticipate the actual levels of cost or inconvenience, for example.

Stage 2

The areas to be benchmarked should be determined and objectives set. Note that here, the objectives will not be in the form of aspirations for improvement to specific processes and practices, but more in the nature of stating the extent and depth of the enquiry.

Stage 3

Key performance measures must be established. This will require an understanding of the systems involved, which, in turn, will require discussion with key stakeholders and observation of the way work is carried out.

Stage 4

Select organisations to benchmark against. Internal benchmarking may be possible but, where internal departments have little in common, comparisons must be made with equivalent parts of other organisations.

Stage 5

Measure own and others' performance. Negotiation should take place to establish just who undertakes the measurement: ideally, a joint team should do it, but there may be issues of confidentiality or convenience that mean each organisation does its own measuring.

Stage 6

Compare performance. Raw data must be carefully analysed if appropriate conclusions are to be drawn. It will be appropriate to discuss initial findings with the stakeholders concerned: they are likely both to have useful comment to offer and to be anxious about the possibility of adverse reflection upon them.

Stage 7

Design and implement improvement programmes. It may be possible to import complete systems; alternatively, it may be appropriate to move towards a synthesis that combines various elements of best practice. Sometimes, improvements require extensive reorganisation and restructuring. In any event, there is likely to be a requirement for training. Improvements in administrative systems often call for investment in new equipment, particularly in IT systems.

Stage 8

Monitor improvements. The continuing effectiveness of improvements must be monitored. At the same time, it must be understood that improvements are not once and for all and that further adjustments may be beneficial.

Reasons for undertaking benchmarking

Benchmarking has the following advantages.

(a) Benchmarking can assess a firm's existing position, and provide a basis for establishing standards of performance.

(b) The comparisons are carried out by the managers who have to live with any changes implemented as a result of the exercise.

(c) Benchmarking focuses on improvement in key areas and sets targets which can be challenging but evidently achievable.

(d) The sharing of information can be a spur to innovation.

(e) The result should be improved performance, particularly in cost control and delivering value.

Drawbacks of benchmarking

Many companies have gained significant benefits from benchmarking but it is worth pointing out a number of possible dangers.

(a) It can cloud perception of strategic purpose by attracting too much attention to the detail of what is measured, since it concentres on doing things right rather than doing the right thing: the difference between efficiency and effectiveness. A process can be efficient but its output may not be useful.

(b) Benchmarking does not identify the reasons why performance is at a particular level, whether good or bad.

(c) It is a catching-up exercise rather than the development of anything distinctive. After the benchmarking exercise, the competitor might improve performance in a different way.

(d) It depends on accurate information about comparator companies.

(e) It is not cost-free and can divert management attention.

(f) It can become a hindrance and even a threat: sharing information with other companies can be a burden and a security risk.

SIGNPOST

We now examine at some of the performance monitoring and reporting methods used in organisations.

2.3 REPORTING METHODS

Overall assessment

The manager writes in narrative form their judgements about the appraisee. There will be no guaranteed consistency of the criteria and areas of assessment, and managers may not be able to convey clear, effective judgements in writing.

Guided assessment

Assessors are required to comment on a number of specified characteristics and performance elements, with guidelines as to how terms such as 'application', 'integrity' and 'adaptability' are to be interpreted in the work context. This is a more precise, but still rather vague method.

Grading

Grading adds a comparative frame of reference to the general guidelines, whereby managers are asked to select one of a number of defined levels or degrees to which an individual displays a given characteristic. These are also known as rating scales, and have been much used in standard appraisal forms. (See Figure 6.2.)

Numerical values may be added to gradings to give rating scores. Alternatively, a less precise graphic scale may be used to indicate general position on a plus/minus scale, as in Figure 6.1.

Factor: job knowledge

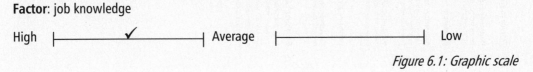

Figure 6.1: Graphic scale

Performance Classification

Outstanding performance is characterised by high ability which leaves little or nothing to be desired. Personnel rated as such are those who regularly make significant contributions to the organisation which are above the requirements of their position. Unusual and challenging assignments are consistently well handled.

Excellent performance is marked by above-average ability, with little supervision required.

Satisfactory Plus performance indicates fully adequate ability, without the need for excessive supervision. Personnel with this rating are able to give proper consideration to normal assignments, which are generally well-handled. They will meet the requirements of the position. **Satisfactory plus'** performers may include those who lack the experience at their current level to demonstrate above-average ability.

Marginal performance is in instances where the ability demonstrated does not fully meet the requirements of the position, with excessive supervision and direction normally required. Employees rated as such will show specific deficiencies in their performance which prevent them from performing at an acceptable level.

Unsatisfactory performance indicates an ability which falls clearly below the minimum requirements of the position.

'Unsatisfactory' performers will demonstrate marked deficiencies in most of the major aspects of their responsibilities, and considerable improvement is required to permit retention of the employee in the current position.

Personal Characteristic Ratings

1.- Needs considerable improvement - substantial improvement required to meet acceptable standards

2.- Needs improvement - some improvement required to meet acceptable standards

3.- Normal - meets acceptable standards

4.- Above normal - exceeds normally acceptable standards in most instances

5.- Exceptional - displays rare and unusual personal characteristics

4168B/1

Figure 6.2: Standard appraisal form

Personnel Appraisal: Employees in Salary Grades 5-8

Date of review	Time in position Yrs Mths	Age Yrs	S.G.	Name
Period of Review	Position Title			Area

Important : Read guidance notes carefully before proceeding with the following sections

Section One

	Performance Factors						Section Two	Personal Characteristics
	N/A	U	M	SP	E	O		1 2 3 4 5 6
Administrative Skills							Initiative	
Communications - Written							Persistence	
Communications - Oral							Ability to work with others	
Problem Analysis							Adaptability	
Decision making							Persuasiveness	
Delegation							Self-confidence	
Quantity of Work							Judgement	
Development of Personnel							Leadership	
Development of Quality Improvements							Creativity	

Section Three Highlight Performance Factors and particular strengths/weaknesses of employee which significantly affect Job Performance

| | Overall Performance Rating (Taking into account ratings given) | |

Prepared by: Signature _____ Date _____ Position Title _____

Section Four Comments by reviewing authority

| | | HR Review Initial |

Signature _____ Date _____ Position Title _____

Section Five Supervisor's Notes on Counselling Interview

| | | Date |

Signature _____ Date _____ Position Title _____

Section Six Employee's Reactions and Comment

Signature _____ Date _____

Behavioural incident methods

These concentrate on employee behaviour, which is measured against typical behaviour in each job, as defined by common **'critical incidents'** of successful and unsuccessful job behaviour reported by managers. The analysis is carried out for **key tasks**, which are identified as critical to success in the job and for which specific standards of performance *must* be reached. This makes scales highly relevant to job performance, and facilitates objective assessment because ratings are described in behavioural terms.

The behavioural equivalent of the graphic scale for a manager's key task of 'marketing initiative' might appear as follows.

Produces no new ideas for marketing. Appears apathetic to competitive challenge	Produces ideas when urged by head office. Ideas not clearly thought out nor enthusiastically applied	Produces ideas when urged by head office and gives full commitment to new programmes	Spontaneously generates new ideas for marketing and champions them through head office approval. Ideas related to identified needs and effective in practice

Figure 6.3: Critical incident scale

Results-oriented schemes

All the above techniques may be used with more or less results-oriented criteria. A wholly results-oriented approach sets out to review performance against specific targets and standards of performance, which are agreed in advance by a manager and subordinate together.

Key advantages of such an approach include the following.

(a) The subordinate is more involved in appraisal, and performance, because (s)he is able to evaluate progress in achieving clear, jointly-agreed measures.

(b) The manager is relived of the 'critic' role and becomes more of a 'counsellor', jointly defining solutions to performance issues.

(c) Clear and known targets are beneficial in motivation, especially in maximising the effectiveness of financial incentives.

(d) The emphasis of appraisal becomes forward-looking (focusing on improvements and incentives), rather than purely retrospective.

FOR DISCUSSION

Which of the above reporting methods would you consider:

(a) Fairest
(b) Most easily justified to the person being appraised
(c) Most suitable for determining performance pay awards?

SIGNPOST

We have just raised the possibility that an employee might be involved in monitoring and evaluating his or her own performance. Let's look at some of the sources of assessment feedback *other* than the appraisee's immediate boss.

2.4 SOURCES OF PERFORMANCE FEEDBACK

Organisations have begun to recognise that the employee's immediate boss is not the only (or necessarily the best) person to assess his or her performance. Other options include:

(a)   The employee him or herself (self-appraisal)

(b)   Peers and co-workers (peer appraisal)

(c)   Subordinates (upwards appraisal)

(d)   A combination of sources (360-degree feedback).

Self-appraisal

Self-appraisal allows individuals to carry out a self-evaluation as a major input to the appraisal process.

The advantages of such an approach include the following.

(a)   It **saves the manager time**, as employees identify the areas which are most relevant to the job and their relative strengths.

(b)   It offers **increased responsibility** to the individual, which may improve motivation.

(c)   It helps to integrate the goals of the individual with those of the organisation.

On the other hand, of course, people are often not the best judges of their own performance! They may deliberately over- (or under-) estimate their performance, in order to gain approval or reward – or to conform to group norms, say.

Upward appraisal

This is a notable modern trend, adopted in the UK by companies such as BP and British Airways, whereby the subordinates/team appraise their manager/leader.

The advantages of such an approach might be as follows.

(a)   Subordinates tend to know their superior (particularly in the area of leadership skills) better than anyone.

(b)   Multiple ratings (from a group of subordinates) have greater statistical validity than a single view.

(c)   Upward appraisal encourages subordinates to give feedback and raise problems they may have with their boss, which otherwise would be too difficult or risky for them to voice.

(d)   It supports upward communication in general, which may have knock-on benefits for creativity, problem-solving and employee relations.

ACTIVITY 3   (15 MINS)

Imagine you had to do an upward appraisal on your boss, parent or lecturer. Suggest the two major problems that might be experienced with upward appraisal.

Customer appraisal

In some companies, part of the appraisal process may take the form of feedback from 'customers' (internal or external). This may be taken further into an influence on remuneration: at Rank-Xerox, for example, 30% of a manager's annual bonus is conditional upon satisfactory levels of customer feedback.

Feedback from customers (external and internal) is particularly valuable in:

(a)   Encouraging and monitoring the customer care orientation of the organisation as a whole – in line with modern thinking about business processes, quality management etc.

(b)   Showing a commitment to respond meaningfully to customer feedback.

(c)   Focusing areas of an employee's performance that are recognised to have real impact on the business.

(d)   Encouraging the 'internal customer' concept within the organisation, as an aid to co-ordination.

360-degree feedback

360-degree feedback (also known as 'multi-rater instruments' and 'multi-source assessment') is the most radical recognition of multiple **stakeholders** in an individual's performance. As described by Peter Ward (who introduced the system at Tesco):

> *Traditional performance measurement systems have rarely operated on more than one or two dimensions. However, 360-degree feedback is designed to enable all the stakeholders in a person's performance to comment and give feedback. This includes the current (and perhaps previous) boss (including temporary supervisors), peers and co-workers, subordinates and even external customers. Finally, the employee's own self-assessment is added and compared.*

Information is usually collected (anonymously) through questionnaires, either on paper or online.

The advantages of 360-degree feedback are as follows.

(a)   It offers the opportunity to build up a rounded picture of an employee's performance: the more relevant parties contribute, the more complete the picture.

(b)   Multiple appraisal may reduce or at least balance the element of subjectivity which inevitably enters appraisal of one individual by another.

(c)   360-degree feedback increases the amount and openness of multi-directional task and performance-related communication in the organisation. This is particularly beneficial in the case of cross-functional communication, creating opportunities for improved integration, co-ordination and knowledge/ideas sharing.

(d)   The extensive information-gathering process, and feedback from key performance areas and contacts (including customers and suppliers, where relevant), signals the seriousness with which appraisal is regarded by the organisation, reinforcing commitment to performance management and improvement.

However, the approach has a number of disadvantages.

(a)   Subjectivity is not eliminated by the process: a number of subjective viewpoints is arguably no fairer than just one!

(b)   There are still difficulties in gathering feedback from peers (fear of being 'disloyal' and subordinates (fear of reprisals).

(c)   It is not easy to define performance criteria that will be meaningful and measurable for each appraiser, nor to weight the evaluations of the different appraisers, nor to reconcile or prioritise contradictory evaluations by different appraisers.

(d)   There is extra organisation, paperwork and evaluation to be done, although this is now minimised by a range of software packages for the process, allowing computer or online 'form' filling, integration and reporting. (Do a web search on '360-degree appraisal' for a huge sampling of providers...)

EXAMPLE

W H Smith is often used as a case study for 360-degree appraisal. The company had operated upwards appraisal (covering some 1,200 managers) since 1990, but in 1996 it trialled a 360-degree system in its HR function.

Between eight and fifteen people filled in forms covering each manager's competences and personal objectives. The appraisers were asked to rate them on a scale of one to five and give anecdotal examples to support the marks (ie 'critical incidents'). The forms were sent to an independent third party for collating.

The company found that the system sharpened the developmental aspects of its appraisal meetings, but that it also caused a significant administration load. Many appraisers found it hard to comment on the individual manager's performance objectives, and to come up with anecdotal evidence for ratings.

When the system was rolled out to the IT function, the processing was done in-house (to save costs). When it was extended to the rest of the organisation, a computerised system was developed to reduce bureaucracy.

ACTIVITY 4   (20 MINS)

In a 360-degree feedback questionnaire a skill area like 'communicating' might be defined as the 'ability to express oneself clearly and to listen effectively to others'. Guiding descriptions might then include 'Presents ideas or information in a well-organised manner' or 'Allows you to finish what you have to say'; followed by rating scales.

Rate yourself on the two descriptions mentioned here, on a scale of 1–10. Get a group of friends, fellow-students, even a tutor or parent, to write down (anonymously) *their* rating for you on the same two comments. Keep these notes in an envelope, unseen, until you have gathered a few.

Compare them with your self-rating, if you dare... What drawbacks did you (and your respondents) find to such an approach?

SIGNPOST

Having reported on an individual's performance – whether in a written narrative comment, or on a prepared appraisal form – a manager must discuss the content of the report with the individual concerned.

2.5 THE APPRAISAL INTERVIEW

There are basically three ways of approaching appraisal interviews (Maier, 1958).

(a)   The **tell and sell** method. The manager tells the subordinate how (s)he has been assessed, and then tries to 'sell' (gain acceptance of) the evaluation and any improvement plans. This requires unusual human relations skills, in order to convey feedback in a constructive manner, and to motivate behavioural change.

(b)   The **tell and listen** method. The manager tells the subordinate how (s)he has been assessed, and then invites comments. The manager therefore no longer dominates the interview throughout, and there is greater opportunity for counselling as opposed to pure direction. The employee is encouraged to participate in the assessment and the working out of improvement targets and methods. Change in the employee may not be the sole key to improvement, and the manager may receive helpful feedback about job design, methods, environment or supervision.

(c)   The **problem-solving** approach. The manager abandons the role of critic altogether, and becomes a counsellor and helper. The discussion is centred not on assessment of past performance, but on future solutions to the employee's work problems. The employee is encouraged to recognise the problems, think solutions through, and commit to improvement. This approach is more involving and satisfying to the employee and may also stimulate creative problem-solving.

Many organisations waste the opportunity represented by appraisal for **upward communication**. If an organisation is development-focused, it should harness the aspirations and abilities of its employees by asking positive and thought-provoking questions such as: Could any changes be made in your job which might result in improved performance? Have you any skills, knowledge, or aptitudes which could be made better use of in the organisation?

2.6 FOLLOW-UP

After the appraisal interview, the manager may complete his or her report with an overall assessment and/or the jointly-reached conclusion of the interview, with recommendations for follow-up action. This may take the following forms.

(a)   Informing appraisees of the results of the appraisal, if this has not been central to the review interview.

(b)   Carrying out agreed actions on reward, training, problem-solving and so on.

(c)   Monitoring the appraisee's progress and checking that (s)he has carried out agreed actions or improvements.

(d)   Taking necessary steps to help the appraisee to attain improvement objectives, by guidance, providing feedback, upgrading equipment, altering work methods or whatever.

ACTIVITY 5   (5 MINS)

What would happen if there was no follow-up action? (Think past the obvious.)

EXAMPLE   INTERNATIONAL COMPARISON

Some key cultural issues are involved in appraisal and its uses. Budwhar & Mellahi (2006), for example, highlight the inequitable application of promotion criteria in some Middle Eastern countries.

Nepotism, known usually as *wasta*, is perceived to be widespread in **Saudi Arabia**. Anecdotal evidence suggests that the promotion of people with tribal or family connections is very common… This is especially true in large and public sector organisations. It is a result of the tribal-based collectivist culture, where an individual's loyalty to the tribe, family and friends is valued over and above that to the organisation.

2.7 SKILLS IN GIVING FEEDBACK

Giving feedback on performance is a key leadership skill. Many people find receiving positive feedback (compliments, praise) just as hard to receive as negative feedback. However, the purpose of feedback is to help people learn by increasing their awareness of what they do, how they do it and its impact on other people. There are two main types of feedback, both of which are valuable in enhancing performance and development.

(a) **Motivational feedback** is used to reward and reinforce positive behaviours, progress and performance by praising and encouraging the individual. Its purpose is to increase *confidence*.

(b) **Developmental feedback** is given when a particular area of performance needs to be changed and to suggest how this might be done. Its purpose is to increase *competence*.

'Constructive' feedback (of either type) is designed to widen options and increase development. It does *not* mean giving only positive or 'encouraging' feedback about what a person did well: feedback about undesirable behaviours and their effects, given skilfully, is in many ways more useful.

The following are some brief guidelines on giving constructive developmental feedback.

(a) **Be intentional**. Emotions may be running high: feedback is ideally communicated calmly. There may be other people present: feedback is best given confidentially.

(b) **Start with positives**. People will more readily accept that criticism is objective and constructive if it is balanced with praise for positive aspects of their behaviour or performance.

(c) **Focus on the behaviour**. Feedback needs to refer clearly and objectively to behaviours, actions and results – *not* the person or their personality. ('Tough on the problem, soft on the person' is a good general rule.)

(d) **Be precise**. Feedback needs to be specific, avoiding vague and global statements: *not* 'you are always late' but 'on two occasions this week you have been more than five minutes late for meetings'.

(e) **Gain co-operation**. First, try asking people how *they* think they acted or handled a particular situation: you may find that, in giving feedback, you are able to confirm what they are already aware of. This encourages collaborative problem-solving.

(f) **Don't tackle everything at once**! Give the person one or two priority areas to deal with at a time.

(g) **Close with encouragement**. Balance negative feedback with positive encouragement that change is possible and will be supported.

FOR DISCUSSION

Consider a situation in the past when you had to give feedback to someone about their performance or behaviour.

(a) How did you feel about it?

(b) What do you think makes giving (i) positive feedback on good performance and (ii) negative feedback on poor performance difficult for you (and others)?

SIGNPOST

In theory, systematic appraisal schemes may seem fair to the individual and worthwhile for the organisation, but in practice the system often goes wrong. Let's see how, and what can be done.

3 PROBLEMS WITH APPRAISAL SCHEMES

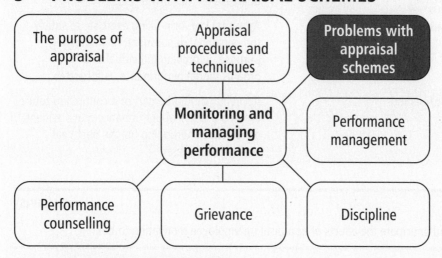

3.1 PROBLEMS IN PRACTICE

Lockett (1992) lists a number of reasons why appraisal may not always be effective in practice.

Appraisal barriers	Comment
Appraisal as confrontation	Many people use appraisals 'as a sort of show-down, a good sorting out or a clearing of the air.' In this kind of climate: • There is little collaboration in problem-solving. • The feedback is subjective (often hostile). • The feedback is badly delivered. • Appraisals are 'based on yesterday's performance not on the whole year'. • There is lack of attention to positive development potential.
Appraisal as judgement	The appraisal 'is seen as a one-sided process in which the manager acts as judge, jury and counsel for the prosecution'. This puts the subordinate on the defensive. Instead, the process of performance management 'needs to be jointly operated in order to retain the commitment and develop the self-awareness of the individual.'

Appraisal barriers	Comment
Appraisal as chat	The appraisal is conducted as if it were a friendly chat 'without … purpose or outcome … Many managers, embarrassed by the need to give feedback and set stretching targets, reduce the appraisal to a few mumbled "well dones!" and leave the interview with a briefcase of unresolved issues.'
Appraisal as bureaucracy	Appraisal is a form-filling exercise, to satisfy the personnel department. Its underlying purpose, improving individual and organisational performance, is forgotten.
Appraisal as unfinished business	Appraisal should be part of a continuing future-focused process of performance management, not a way of 'wrapping up' the past year's performance issues.

ACTIVITY 6 (15 MINS)

What would you anticipate the effects of appraisal on employee motivation to be?

Redman and Wilkinson (2009) identify other reasons as to why appraisals are not as accurate as hoped for:

Halo effect	This is where one positive criterion distorts the assessment of others. Similarly, the horns effect is where a single negative aspect dominates the appraisal rating.
Doppelganger effect	This is where the rating reflects the similarity between appraiser and appraised.
Crony effect	Is the result of appraisal being distorted by the closeness of the relationship between the appraiser and appraised.
Veblen effect	Is named after the economist Veblen; where all appraisees are given the same rating regardless of the quality of their efforts.
Impression effect	Is the problem of distinguishing between actual performance from calculated 'impression management'. Employees often attempt to manage their reputations by substituting measures of performance eg effort, for measures of outcome eg results, particularly when the results are less than favourable.
Recency effect	Where only events that have happened recently are remembered and commented upon.

3.2 EVALUATING APPRAISAL

The appraisal scheme should itself be assessed (and regularly reassessed), according to the following general criteria.

(a) **Relevance**

- Does the system have a useful purpose, relevant to the needs of the organisation and the individual?

- Is the purpose clearly expressed and widely understood by all concerned, both appraisers and appraisees?

- Are the appraisal criteria relevant to the purposes of the system?

(b) **Fairness**

- Is there reasonable standardisation of criteria and objectivity throughout the organisation?

- Has attention been given to the potential for direct or indirect discrimination in the criteria and methods of appraisal?

(c) **Serious intent**

- Are managers committed to the system – or is it just something the personnel department thrusts upon them?

- Who does the interviewing, and are they properly trained in interviewing and assessment techniques?

- Is reasonable time and attention given to the interviews – or is it a question of 'getting them over with'?

- Is there a genuine demonstrable link between performance and reward or opportunity for development?

(d) **Co-operation**

- Is the appraisal a participative, problem-solving activity – or a tool of management control?

- Is the appraisee given time and encouragement to prepare for the appraisal, so that he can make a constructive contribution?

- Does a jointly-agreed, concrete conclusion emerge from the process?

(e) **Efficiency**

- Are all the above achieved with a justifiable investment of time and cost?

ACTIVITY 7 (15 MINS)

Look up the procedures manual of your organisation, and read through the appraisal procedures – or ask someone about their organisation.

How effective are these appraisal procedures? Measure them against the criteria given above.

If you can get hold of an appraisal report form, have a go at filling one out for yourself – a good exercise in self-awareness!

---

4   PERFORMANCE MANAGEMENT

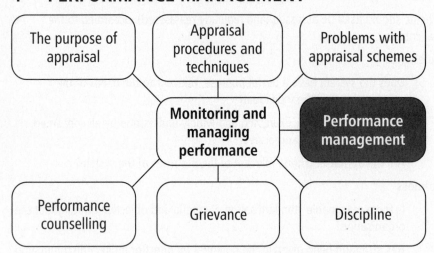

4.1   WHAT IS PERFORMANCE MANAGEMENT?

Performance management as an approach to management may be seen as an application of Locke's goal setting theory as described in the previous chapter. There we said that goal theory suggests that people's performance in their jobs is related to the difficulty of their goals, the extent of their commitment to them and the degree of feedback they receive on their performance relative to them.

Mullins (2007) discerns four practical applications of goal theory that are relevant to the practice of performance management.

(a)   Managers should systematically identify and set specific performance goals.

(b)   Goals should be challenging but not so difficult to achieve as to be seen as irrelevant to real world performance.

(c)   Detailed and timely feedback on progress towards goal achievement must be provided.

(d)   Employee participation in setting goals may enhance commitment to them and so lead to higher performance.

> **DEFINITION**
>
> **Performance management** is an approach in which there is a dual emphasis: on setting key accountabilities, objectives, measures, priorities and time scales for the following review period *and* monitoring, appraising and adjusting performance on an ongoing basis.

Torrington *et al* (2011) summarise a typical performance management system in Figure 6.4.

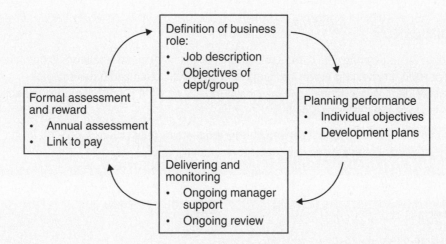

Figure 6.4: Typical performance management system

4.2 WHY PERFORMANCE MANAGEMENT?

In the late 1980s, the emphasis moved from (largely retrospective) performance appraisal to (on-going) performance management, as increasing global competition created strong pressure for organisations to continually improve their performance and capabilities. The new focus on quality, customer service and added value meant that quality standards had to be set or refined – and this fed through to the performance management processes.

There are a number of advantages to a performance management orientation.

(a) Objective-setting gives employees the security and satisfaction of both understanding their jobs and knowing exactly what is expected of them. (A report by the Audit Commission, entitled *'Calling the Tune'*, showed that local authorities who operated a comprehensive performance management system scored highly in staff attitude surveys on 'know how' and 'feel good' factors. In other words, objective-setting and appraisal help staff to feel that they understand more about their work, and 'feel good' about it.)

(b) Joint-objective setting and a developmental approach are positive and participatory, encouraging regular and frequent dialogue, a shared results focus; helping employees' to own and commit to change and improvement.

(c) Performance management focuses on future performance planning and improvement rather than retrospective performance appraisal, so it contributes to an output, customer flexibility and continuous improvement focus.

However, it should also be noted that such a system depends on the integration of goal-setting, development planning, appraisal and reward planning activities. Performance management is also not immune to the problems of appraisal: inconsistent use of ratings, appraiser bias, lack of training by line managers implementing the scheme and so on.

FOR DISCUSSION

Armstrong (2012) describes the purpose of performance management as follows. Performance management is a systematic process for improving individual, team and organisational performance. Strategic performance management focuses on what needs to be done to help the organisation achieve its business goals.

How is this different from performance appraisal? What are its implications for the HR function: recruitment, reward, training and development and its own role?

SIGNPOST

How does this work in practice?

4.3 PERFORMANCE MANAGEMENT ACTIVITIES

There are four key performance management activities.

- Preparation of performance agreements
- Preparation of performance and development plans
- Management of performance throughout the year
- Performance reviews

Preparation of performance agreements or contracts

These set out individual or team objectives; how performance will be measured; the knowledge, skills and behaviour needed to achieve the objectives; and the organisation's core values.

Objectives may be either:

(a) Work/operational (results to be achieved or contribution to be made to the accomplishment of team, departmental and/or organisational objectives); or

(b) Developmental (personal or learning objectives).

Objectives and their wider role in the organisation are discussed further below.

Performance measures should be objective and capable of being assessed: relevant data should be readily available. They should relate to results (not to effort) and those results should be within the individual's control.

Some typical areas for the setting of performance targets are listed below.

(a) Sales (for sales representatives)
(b) Growth in turnover, profitability or shareholder value (for the most senior executives)
(c) Waiting times (for hospital executives)
(d) Pass rates (for teachers and lecturers)
(e) Punctuality and attendance (for junior workers)

Discussions should ensure that individuals fully understand what is expected of them and that if they fulfil those expectations they will be regarded as having performed well.

Preparation of performance and development plans

These set out detailed performance and personal development needs, and action plans to address them, in order to meet individual objectives.

Management of performance throughout the year

This involves the continuous process of providing feedback on performance, conducting informal progress reviews and dealing with performance problems as necessary. This may include the planning and implementation of:

(a) Learning, coaching or training interventions, to address competence gaps or other shortfalls (or opportunities).

(b) Disciplinary action, to improve individual behaviours and attitudes.

(c) Counselling interventions, to guide individuals in defining and solving problems.

(d) Managerial intervention to improve resources, systems, work organisation or other barriers to performance.

It is worth noting that 'performance management' has become associated with the management of 'problem' performers and situations: disciplinary and performance counselling interventions and so on. We discuss these in the following sections of this chapter – but there is also a strong overlap with the topic of 'employee welfare', since performance problems may be caused by the illness, stress or difficulties of an employee. These issues are discussed in Chapter 11.

Performance reviews

Performance reviews involve both taking a view of an individual's progress to date *and* reaching an agreement about what should be done in the future. The performance review provides the means by which:

(a) Results can be **measured** against targets

(b) The employee can be given **feedback**

(c) An **agreement can be reached** on ongoing development needs and future performance targets

(d) The **link** between results and performance-related pay can be made

4.4 THE WIDER USE OF GOALS AND OBJECTIVES

An understanding of the organisation's mission is invaluable for setting and controlling the overall functioning and progress of the organisation. However, it is possible for an organisation to operate reasonably effectively even if most of the people within it have only an **intuitive or vague understanding of its purpose**. Most people's work is defined in terms of far more specific and immediate things to be achieved: if these things are related in some way to the wider purpose, the organisation will function. Loosely speaking, these 'things to be achieved' are the goals, objectives and targets of the various departments, offices, and individuals that make up the organisation. In more effective organisations **goal congruence** will be achieved: all these disparate goals, objectives and targets will be consistent with one another and will operate together to support progress with the mission.

Goals can be related in several ways: **hierarchically**, as in the pyramid structure outlined below; **functionally**, as when colleagues collaborate on a project; **logistically**, as when resources must be shared or used in sequence; and in **wider organisational senses**, as when senior executives make decisions about their operational priorities. A good example of the last category is the tension between long- and short-term priorities in such matters as the need to contain costs while at the same time increasing productivity by investing in improved plant.

A hierarchy of objectives

A simple model of the relationship between the various goals, objectives and targets is a **pyramid** analogous to the traditional organisational hierarchy. At the top is the **overall mission**;

this is supported by a small number of **wide ranging goals**, which may correspond to overall departmental or functional responsibilities. For a business, a primary, corporate objective will be the return offered to shareholders, however this is measured. There may be other primary objectives and there will certainly be supporting objectives for costs, innovation, markets, products and so on.

Each of the high level goals is supported in turn by more detailed, **subordinate goals**. These may correspond, perhaps, to the responsibilities of the senior managers in the function concerned. The pattern is continued downwards until we reach the **work targets** of individual members of the organisation.

We owe the concept of a hierarchy or cascade of objectives to the great management thinker and writer *Peter Drucker*, who outlined the system now known as **management by objectives** (MbO) in the middle of the twentieth century. MbO is still in use as a management tool, though no longer promoted as a universal solution. Its importance for this discussion of goals and objectives is that Drucker was the first to suggest that objectives should be SMART. This acronym originally stood for the qualities listed below.

Specific   **M**easurable   **A**chievable   **R**ealistic   **T**ime-related

Today, *realistic* is often replaced with *results-focused*, for two reasons.

(a)   The pursuit of innovation as a route to competitive advantage makes it very important that managerial attention is directed towards **achieving results** rather than just **administering established processes**.

(b)   Realistic means much the same thing as achievable, anyway.

There are other variants: *achievable* may be replaced with *attainable*, which has an almost identical meaning, and *relevant* (meaning appropriate to the group or individual concerned) has been proposed as a third option for *R*.

The role of culture

The concept of organisational culture is a very useful element in the understanding of behaviour in organisations. It is, however, a very large topic and not one that we need to discuss in depth here. However, some aspects of corporate culture are particularly relevant to the management of both individual and collective performance.

Earlier in this section we mentioned that people's performance depends, in part, on the strength of their **commitment** to their goals. If management wishes to improve performance, it is not enough simply to announce goals; if stated goals are to have an effect on performance, staff must adopt them as their own. This process of adoption is sometimes referred to as **internalisation**. Clearly, it will be to the benefit of performance if managers are able to encourage this process.

One of the ways in which this can be achieved is the promotion of a corporate culture whose ethos and values respect and support corporate goals. This is not a simple matter. Culture develops within organisations in an almost organic way: it is not generally amenable to bureaucratic processes, being far more a matter of leadership and example on the part of influential members of staff. However, the existence of a clear **mission statement** may assist the process and the performance management system itself, if perceived as reasonable and not oppressive, may have benign cultural effects.

4.5   EXTERNAL ACCREDITATION

Performance management, like other aspects of organisational management, can benefit from a rational and systematic approach. Several schemes of external accreditation exist that can help organisations to improve their systems and methods.

(a)   **Investors in People** is a scheme for business improvement sponsored by the UK government. It has ten dimensions, each with a range of performance indicators.

- Business strategy
- Learning and development strategy
- People management strategy
- Leadership and management strategy
- Management effectiveness
- Recognition and reward
- Involvement and empowerment
- Learning and development
- Performance measurement
- Continuous improvement

Assessment is based on interviews with staff and depends on evidence of satisfactory policy and practice outcomes

(b)   **Customer Service Excellence** '…tests in great depth those areas that research has indicated are a priority for customers, with particular focus on delivery, timeliness, information, professionalism and staff attitude. There is also emphasis placed on developing customer insight, understanding the user's experience and robust measurement of service satisfaction. ' www.customerserviceexcellence.uk.com/

(c)   **ISO 9001:2008 series** is the latest version of a general scheme of organisational accreditation in quality management that began with the UK's BS 5750 standard in 1979.

All of these schemes are, to a greater or lesser extent, rather bureaucratic in application. Nevertheless, they do offer guidance on improvement in their specific areas of concern and accreditation can have a benign influence on the organisation's standing with its peers. In the case of ISO 9001:2008, it is impossible to do business in some areas without accreditation.

SIGNPOST

The area of individual performance management is vast, and covered by a vast literature practitioners: disciplinary and grievance handling, and performance counselling.

5   DISCIPLINE

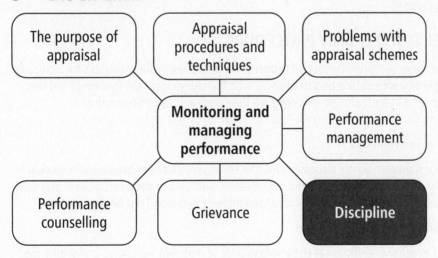

DEFINITION

Discipline can be considered as: 'a condition in an enterprise in which there is orderliness, in which the members of the enterprise behave sensibly and conduct themselves according to the standards of acceptable behaviour as related to the goals of the organisation'.

Discipline is often imposed in organisations through the definition of rules and standards of conduct, and through the threat of sanctions for non-conformance (this is sometimes called 'negative' discipline, although it need not be applied in a negative way.) Disciplinary action may be **punitive** (punishing an offence), **deterrent** (warning people not to behave in that way) or **reformative** (ensuring that the behaviour will not happen again). Its goal is nevertheless always to improve the future behaviour of the employee concerned, and other members of the organisation.

5.1 TYPES OF DISCIPLINARY SITUATIONS

There are many types of disciplinary situations which may require intervention. The most frequently occurring are:

(a)   Excessive absenteeism

(b)   Repeated poor timekeeping

(c)   Defective and/or inadequate work performance

(d)   Poor attitudes which influence the work of others or which reflect on the public image of the firm

ACTIVITY 8   **(15 MINS)**

Suggest five more reasons for management taking disciplinary action. (You might be able to draw on your own experience at work, school or college.)

In addition, managers might be confronted with disciplinary problems stemming from employee behaviour *off* the job: abuse of alcohol or drugs, or involvement in some form of law-breaking activity. If off-the-job conduct has an impact upon performance *on* the job, the manager must be prepared to deal with it.

5.2 MODEL DISCIPLINARY PROCEDURE

Many enterprises have accepted the idea of **progressive discipline**, which provides for increasing severity of the penalty with each repeated offence: a bit like the yellow card (warning), red card (sent off) system used in football. The following are the suggested steps of progressive disciplinary action.

(a)   **The informal talk**

The manager simply discusses with the employee his or her behaviour in relation to the standards expected by the organisation, and tries to get a recognition that such behaviour is unacceptable, with a commitment that it will not be repeated.

(b)   **Oral warning or reprimand**

The manager emphasises the undesirability of repeated violations, and warns the offender that it could lead to more serious penalties.

BPP
LEARNING MEDIA

(c) **Written or official warning**

A written warning is a formal matter, and becomes a permanent part of the employee's record. (It may also serve as evidence in case of protest against the later dismissal of a repeat offender.)

(d) **Suspension without pay**

Disciplinary lay-offs may extend over several days or weeks, and may only be used if provided for in the contract of employment.

(e) **Dismissal**

This should be reserved for the most serious offences. For the organisation it involves waste of a labour resource, and potential loss of morale in the work team.

Employers are required by Employment Tribunals to observe the non-statutory *ACAS* (Advisory, Conciliation and Arbitration Service) Code of Practice *Disciplinary & Grievance Procedures* 2009, an excerpt of which is reproduced in the boxed text below.

- Fairness and transparency are promoted by developing and using rules and procedures for handling disciplinary and grievance situations. These should be set down in writing, be specific and clear.

- Employment tribunals will take the size and resources of an employer into account, in deciding what measures are practicable. However, it is important to deal with issues fairly.

  - Employers and employees should raise and deal with issues promptly, without unreasonable delay.

  - Employers and employees should act consistently.

  - Employers should carry out any necessary investigations to establish the facts of the case.

  - Employers should inform employees of the basis of the problem and give them an opportunity to put their case in response before any decisions are made.

  - Employers should also permit employees to be accompanied at any formal disciplinary or grievance meeting.

  - Employers should allow an employee to appeal against any formal decision made.

(ACAS, 2009)

FOR DISCUSSION

How (a) accessible and (b) clear are the rules and policies of your college: do people really know what they are and are not supposed to do? Have a look at the student regulations. How easy is it to see them – or were you referred elsewhere? Are they well-indexed and cross-referenced, and in language that all students will understand?

How (a) accessible and (b) clear are the disciplinary procedures? Who is responsible for discipline?

SIGNPOST

The crucial interpersonal event in disciplinary action will be the interview. The following advice takes into account both procedural guidelines and interpersonal issues.

5.3 DISCIPLINARY INTERVIEWS

Preparation for the disciplinary interview will include the following.

(a) Gathering facts about the alleged infringement.

(b) Determination of the organisation's position: how valuable is the employee, potentially? How serious are the offences/lack of progress? How far is the organisation prepared to go to support or impose improvement?

(c) Identification of the aims of the interview: punishment? deterrent to others? problem-solving? Specific standards for future behaviour/ performance need to be determined.

(d) Notification of the employee concerned, with time to prepare for the disciplinary interview and seek representation if desired.

The disciplinary interview will then proceed as follows.

Step 1 The manager will explain the purpose of the interview.

Step 2 The manager will explain the organisation's position with regard to the issues involved and the organisation's expectations with regard to future behaviour/ performance.

Step 3 The employee should be given the opportunity to comment, explain, justify or deny.

Step 4 Improvement targets should be jointly agreed (if possible).

   (i) They should be specific and quantifiable, performance-related and realistic.

   (ii) They should be related to a practical but reasonably short time period. A date should be set to review progress.

   (iii) Measures should be proposed to help the employee where necessary (eg mentoring, extra supervision or coaching, counselling and so on).

Step 5 The manager should explain any penalties imposed on the employee, the reasons behind them and, if the sanctions are ongoing, how they can be withdrawn (eg at what point and at what terms the employee could expect the removal of the formal warning from their record). There should be a clear warning of the consequences of failure to meet improvement targets or breaching expected codes of behaviour.

Step 6 The manager should explain the appeals procedure.

Step 7 The manager should ensure the employee understands fully steps 1 – 6 above and then should briefly summarise the proceedings.

Records of the interview will be kept on the employee's personnel file for the formal follow-up review and any further action necessary, until such time as it is agreed they should be removed.

6 GRIEVANCE

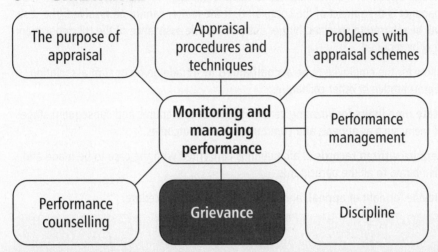

> **DEFINITION**
>
> A **grievance** occurs when an individual feels that (s)he is being wrongly or unfairly treated by a colleague or supervisor: picked on, unfairly appraised, discriminated against and so on.

6.1 PURPOSE OF A GRIEVANCE PROCEDURE

Ideally, grievances should be solved informally by the individual's manager. However, if this is not possible, a formal grievance procedure should be followed, to:

(a) Allow objective grievance handling – including 'cooling off' periods and independent case investigation and arbitration

(b) Protect employees from victimisation – particularly where a grievance involves their immediate superiors

(c) Provide legal protection for both parties, in the event of a dispute resulting in claims before an Employment Tribunal

(d) Encourage grievance airing – which is an important source of feedback to management on employee problems and dissatisfactions

(e) Require full and fair investigation of grievances, enabling the employer–employee relationship to be respected and preserved, despite problems

6.2 GRIEVANCE PROCEDURES

Formal grievance procedures, like disciplinary procedures, should be set out in **writing** and made available to all staff. These procedures should:

(a) State what **grades of employee** are entitled to pursue a particular type of grievance.

(b) **Distinguish between individual grievances and collective grievances** (which might be pursued through industrial relations processes).

(c) State the **rights of the employee** for each type of grievance: what actions and remedies may be claimed.

(d)   State what the **procedures for pursuing a grievance** should be. They will typically involve appeal in the first instance to the line manager (or next level up, if the line manager is the subject of the complaint). If the matter cannot be resolved, the case will be referred to specified higher authorities. The assistance of the HR department may be required.

(e)   Allow for the employee to be **accompanied** by a trade union or staff association representative or other colleague.

(f)   **State time limits** for initiating certain grievance procedures and subsequent stages of them, such as appeals and communication of outcomes.

(g)   **Require written records** of all meetings concerned with the case to be made and distributed to all the participants.

(h)   Provide for right of **appeal**, and specify the appeals procedure.

SIGNPOST

As with disciplinary action, the focus of conflict resolution will be in an interview between the manager and the subordinate.

6.3 GRIEVANCE INTERVIEWS

The dynamics of a grievance interview are broadly similar to a disciplinary interview, except that it is the subordinate who primarily wants a positive result or improvement in someone else's behaviour. (Remember *discipline* is where an employee does wrong: *grievance* is where an employee feels wronged.)

Prior to the interview, the manager should gain some idea of the complaint and its possible source. The meeting itself can then proceed through the following stages.

Step 1   **Exploration**. What is the problem: the background, the facts, the causes (obvious and hidden)? At this stage the manager should simply try to gather as much information as possible, without attempting to suggest solutions or interpretations: the situation must be seen to be open.

Step 2   **Consideration**. The manager should:

- Check the facts

- Analyse the causes – the problem of which the complaint may only be a symptom

- Evaluate options for responding to the complaint, and the implication of any response made

It may be that information can be given to clear up a misunderstanding, or the employee will withdraw the complaint – having 'got it off his chest'. However, the meeting may have to be adjourned (say, for 48 hours) while the manager acquires extra information and considers extra options.

Step 3   **Reply**. The manager, having reached and reviewed various conclusions, reconvenes the meeting to convey (and justify, if required) his or her decision, and hear counter-arguments and appeals. The outcome (agreed or disagreed) should be recorded in writing.

ACTIVITY 9   **(20 MINS)**

Think of a complaint or grievance you have (or have had) at school or college. Have you done anything about it? If so, was it on your own, or through some kind of grievance procedure? If so, what happened: were you satisfied with the process and outcome? If not, why not? How could the procedure have been improved?

WEBLINK

CIPD (2012 Factsheet: Discipline & Grievances at Work)

▶ ▶ www.cipd.co.uk/hr-resources/factsheets/discipline-grievances-at-work.aspx

ACAS (2009 Code of Practice)

▶ ▶ www.acas.org.uk/index.aspx?articleid=2174

7   PERFORMANCE COUNSELLING

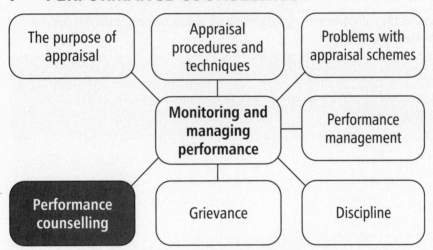

Where problems are identified in an individual's performance – whether through annual appraisal or ongoing monitoring – a line manager may need to intervene.

7.1 REASONS FOR POOR PERFORMANCE

Not all performance problems will be disciplinary in nature, or due to training/ competence gaps. Other factors the manager may need to consider include:

(a)   Job changes which have left the job-holder less suited for the work

(b)   Personality factors or clashes with team members

(c)   Factors outside the work situation (eg marital or financial problems)

(d)   Problems with job design, work layout, management style and other factors outside the individual's own control

7.2 PERFORMANCE COUNSELLING PROCESS

In order to deal with the issue, the following four-step process could be implemented.

(a) Counsel the individual through a basic problem-solving process.

    (i) **The facts**. The manager should help the individual to accept and define the problem, through constructive feedback and supportive questioning.

    (ii) **The causes**. The individual and the manager should explore and agree on the causes of the problem. A collaborative, problem-solving orientation is needed.

    (iii) **The remedies**. The individual and the manager should explore and agree on the remedies to the problem.

(b) Ensure the individual understands the consequences of persistent poor performance, where relevant; this might involve invoking the firm's disciplinary procedures.

(c) Set and agree clear improvement targets and action plans and agree a period of time over which performance is expected to improve.

(d) Support the individual with agreed follow-up action: training, coaching, specialist counselling and so on.

SIGNPOST

Workplace counselling, and the skills involved, is considered further in Chapter 11 as part of the related topic of employee welfare.

CHAPTER ROUNDUP

- Performance appraisal is the process whereby an individual's performance is reviewed against previously agreed goals, and where new goals are agreed which will develop the individual and improve performance over the forthcoming review period.

- Trends in appraisal include: the use of behavioural and results-oriented appraisal criteria; the use of multiple sources of feedback; and a problem-solving approach to interviewing.

- 360-degree feedback is designed to enable all the stakeholders in a person's performance to comment and give feedback.

- A **grievance** occurs when an individual feels that (s)he is being wrongly or unfairly treated by a colleague or supervisor: picked on, unfairly appraised, or discriminated against and so on.

- Performance management is a recent approach which emphasises *both* defining the knowledge, skills, behaviours and standards required to produce the desired results *and* the appraisal and comparison of performance against objectives for the purposes of on-going performance improvement. It is a forward-looking, ongoing and collaborative approach.

- Performance management interventions which may be required to address identified problems in an individual's performance include:

  - Disciplinary action, to address problems of behaviour or attitude: a model procedure is set out in the ACAS Code of Practice

  - Grievance procedures, to address workplace conflicts

  - Performance counselling, to investigate and collaboratively attempt to solve a range of performance problems

  - Training and development planning

QUICK QUIZ

1   What are the purposes of appraisal?

2   What bases or criteria of assessment might an appraisal system use?

3   What is 360-degree feedback?

4   What follow-up should there be after an appraisal?

5   Distinguish between motivational and developmental feedback.

6   What kinds of criticism might be levelled at appraisal schemes by a manager who thought they were a waste of time?

7   How can appraisal be made more positive and empowering to employees?

8   What is the difference between performance appraisal and performance management?

9   What are the four key performance management stages?

10 Distinguish between discipline and grievance.

ANSWERS TO QUICK QUIZ

1   Identifying performance levels, improvements needed and promotion prospects; deciding on rewards; assessing team work and encouraging communication between manager and employee.   (see Para 1.1)

2   Job analysis, job description, plans, targets and standards.   (Para 2.1)

3   Appraisal by all the stakeholders in a person's performance.   (Para 2.3)

4   Appraisees should be informed of the results, agreed activities should be undertaken, progress should be monitored and whatever resources or changes are needed should be provided or implemented.   (Para 2.5)

5   Motivational: used to reward and reinforce positive behaviour, increase confidence.

    Developmental: given in order to guide and motivate change and improvement, to increase competence.   (Para 2.6)

6   The manager may say that he or she has better things to do with his or her time, that appraisals have no relevance to the job and there is no reliable follow-up action, and that they involve too much paperwork.   (Para 3.1)

7   Ensure the scheme is relevant, fair, taken seriously and co-operative.   (Para 3.2)

8   Appraisal is a backward-looking performance review. Performance management is a forward-looking results-oriented scheme.   (Para 4.1)

9   Preparation of performance agreements or contracts, preparation of performance/development plans; ongoing management of performance; performance reviews.   (Para 4.3)

10 Discipline is the 'downward' process whereby a manager addresses the behaviours or performance of an employee which do not meet the firm's standards. Grievance is the 'upward' process by which employees can appeal to higher authority to address problems or conflicts affecting them.   (Sections 5 and 6)

ANSWERS TO ACTIVITIES

1   Disadvantages to the individual of not having an appraisal system include the following. The individual is not aware of progress or shortcomings, is unable to judge whether s/he would be considered for promotion, is unable to identify or correct weaknesses by training, and there is a lack of communication with the manager.

2   You will have come up with your own examples of criteria to assess some jobs but not others. You might have identified such things as:

    (a)   Numerical ability (applicable to accounts staff, say, more than to customer contact staff or other non-numerical functions)

    (b)   Ability to drive safely (essential for transport workers – not for desk-bound ones)

    (c)   Report-writing (not applicable to manual labour, say)

    (d)   Creativity and initiative (desirable in areas involving design and problem-solving not routine or repetitive jobs in mass production or bureaucratic organisations)

BPP
LEARNING MEDIA

3   Problems with upward appraisal include fear of reprisals or vindictiveness (or extra form-processing). Some bosses in strong positions might feel able to refuse to act on results, even if a consensus of staff suggested that they should change their ways.

4   Drawbacks to 360-degree appraisal include:

(a)   Respondents' reluctance to give negative feedback to a boss – or friend

(b)   The suspicion that management is passing the buck for negative feedback, getting people to 'rat' on their friends

(c)   The feeling that the appraisee is being picked on, if positive feedback is not carefully balanced with the negative

5   If follow-up action is not taken, employees will feel that appraisal is all talk and just a waste of time, and that improvement action on their side will not be appreciated or worthwhile.

6   The effects of appraisal on motivation are a tricky issue.

(a)   Feedback on performance is regarded as vital in motivation, because it enables an employee to make calculations about the amount of effort required in future to achieve objectives and rewards. Even negative feedback can have this effect – and is more likely to spur the employee on to post-appraisal action.

(b)   Agreement of challenging but attainable targets for performance or improvement also motivates employees by clarifying goals and the value (and 'cost' in terms of effort) of incentives offered.

(c)   A positive approach to appraisal allows employees to solve their work problems and apply creative thinking to their jobs.

However, people rarely react well to criticism – especially at work, where they may feel that their reward or even job security is on the line. In addition, much depends on the self-esteem of the appraisee. If (s)he has a high self-image, (s)he may be impervious to criticism. If (s)he has a low self-image, (s)he may be depressed rather than motivated by criticism.

7   Your own research.

8   Reasons for disciplinary action might include:

(a)   Breaking rules regarding rest periods and other time schedules, such as leaving work to go home early.

(b)   Improper personal appearance or dress.

(c)   Breaking safety rules, such as failing to observe fire regulations, failing to wear protective clothing and so on.

(d)   Other violations of rules, regulations and procedures, such as smoking in a non-smoking office, or abuse of expenses claims.

(e)   Open insubordination: refusal to carry out a legitimate order.

(f)   Fighting, sexual harassment, racial or religious abuse or other forms of unacceptable conduct towards others.

9   Assuming you did do something about your grievance, you probably found there were various stages of the procedure. Hopefully the first and second stages were sufficient to solve the problem, but you may have felt that the procedure was too cumbersome or long-winded.

Chapter 07

Exit rights and procedures

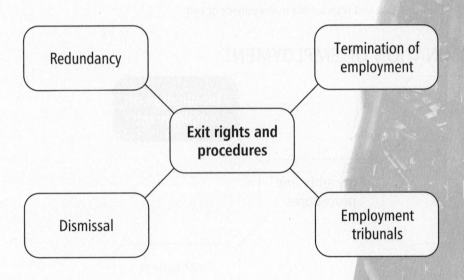

Redundancy

Termination of employment

Exit rights and procedures

Dismissal

Employment tribunals

Introduction

So far, this Course Book has covered some of the processes by which the human resource is managed as it moves into and through or within the organisation. In this chapter, we look at some of the ways in which it must be managed on its way *out* of the organisation.

The exit of employees from the organisation requires careful management because of the need for:

- Compliance with the legal framework on employment protection (particularly in regard to dismissal and redundancy)

- Sensitivity to the human issues involved (since the employment relationship, work and competence are so central to people's sense of their role and value in life)

- The organisation to gather feedback from voluntarily departing employees (resigners or early retirers) in order to identify retention problems.

We consider these aspects in the context of each type of exit.

As you encounter law and regulation on various employment-related issues, remember: 'The law is a floor'. It sets minimum standards below which no organisational practice may fall without penalties. It does not set out 'best practice'. HR managers should ask themselves 'What *must* we do?' (compliance) – but also 'What *should* we do?' (best practice) and 'What *could* we do to enhance business performance *and* employee satisfaction and commitment?'

Your objectives

In this chapter you will learn about the following.

- The role and operation of Employment Tribunals

- Various forms of termination of employment, including resignation, retirement and dismissal

- Wrongful, unfair and justified dismissal of employees

- The nature and procedures of redundancy

- Issues in the equitable and responsible management of exit

1 TERMINATION OF EMPLOYMENT

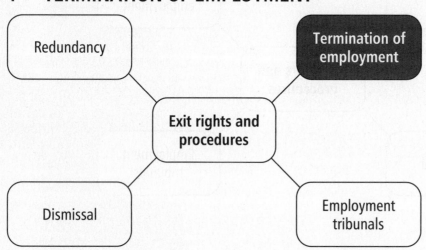

1.1 TERMINATION OF THE EMPLOYMENT CONTRACT

As we discussed in Chapter 4, the formation of a contract signals the beginning of an employment relationship. That relationship is finite: it comes to an end at some point.

Contracts of employment can be 'terminated' in the following ways.

(a) **By performance**

The employee does what (s)he was hired to do, and the employer gives the agreed payment or consideration: the contract is fulfilled. This is common in fixed-term contracts and contracts for specific services. (It may also be said to apply in the case of retirement, where there is an agreed age at which employment ends.)

(b) **By mutual agreement**

Both parties can agree that they are entitled to terminate the contract at any time, say in the event of 'irreconcilable differences'.

(c) **By notice**

One party can terminate the contract, but must give adequate notice or warning to the other. This happens in the case of:

(i) Resignation by the employee
(ii) Dismissal of the employee

There are strict rules on the periods of notice which must be given to protect both parties.

(d) **Breach of contract**

If one party 'breaks' or fails to fulfil key terms of the contract, the other party has the option of considering the contract to have been terminated. (In addition, (s)he may seek legal remedies to compensate for, or minimise the effects of, the breach.) Failure by the employer to pay the agreed wage, say, or gross misconduct by the employee, would constitute breach of contract.

(e) **Frustration**

A contract is 'frustrated' when it is prevented from being fulfilled – for example, because of the death, illness or imprisonment of one of the parties.

SIGNPOST

We now go on to examine at the HR department's role in managing the termination of employment contracts, looking, in particular, at the legislative and managerial frameworks that influence policy in this area. We start by considering the employee's reasons for leaving: retirement and resignation.

1.2 RETIREMENT

The average age of the working population has been steadily increasing, with higher standards of living and health care. The problems of older workers, and the difficulties of adjusting to retirement, are therefore commanding more attention. The time at which an individual will experience difficulties in obtaining or retaining jobs because of age will obviously vary according to the individual, his/her lifestyle and occupation, and the attitudes of his/her society (including diversity legislation, where relevant) and employers.

In the UK the compulsory retirement age has been phased out. The State Pension age is the earliest age at which someone can receive their State Pension. This is not the same as retirement age. Retirement age is when an employee chooses to retire, an employee can still work after State Pension age and receive their State Pension.

The current UK State Pension age for men and women is 65, but this is set to gradually increase to 68 by the middle of the century.

EXAMPLE   **DOCTORS STRIKE OVER PENSION REFORM**

Just 8% of doctors working for the NHS in England went on strike today, the Department of Health has claimed.

But despite only 11,500 doctors taking part in the action over the government's controversial pension reforms, patients will feel the impact after their appointments and operations were pushed back.

In some areas of England, 37% of GP surgeries would see only those patients in urgent need of care as doctors took action for the first time in almost four decades.

The numbers emerged after Andrew Lansley (Health Secretary) today attacked striking doctors, saying the pension deal they are fighting for would come at the expense of lower-paid NHS staff.

The comments followed his revelation last night that pension contributions for doctors have cost the taxpayer £67billion.

Doctors themselves, thousands of whom are expected to be on strike today over reforms to their pensions, have only paid £17billion towards their retirement, the Health Secretary said.

Mr Lansley revealed that the public were funding 80% of doctors' pensions, and the total cost of the pension pot of all working and retired doctors is a massive £83billion.

(*Daily Mail*, 2012)

ACTIVITY 1 (10 MINS)

Jon Andrews, head of the HR practice at PwC:

'The gradually rising state pension age raises big questions for employers. For instance, what impact will the ageing workforce have on opportunities for younger employees? How will companies have to adapt their organisation models and working practices? What changes do they need to make now to the benefits they offer their employees? This isn't some futuristic scenario – the state pension age is increasing steadily and firms need to start planning and adapting now.'

(Price Waterhouse Coopers, 2012)

Suggest three ways in which the HR department could help older employees.

1.3 RESIGNATION

DEFINITION

Resignation is the process by which an employee gives notice of his or her intention to terminate the employment contract.

Employees may resign for any number of reasons, personal or occupational. Some or all of these reasons may well be a reflection on the structure, management style, culture or HR policies of the organisation itself. Management should attempt to find the real reasons why an employee is leaving in an **exit interview**, which may provide helpful feedback on its policies and practices. Note, however, that there is no legal requirement for an employee to give reasons for leaving.

The principal aspect of any policy formulated to deal with resignations must be the length to which the organisation will go to try to dissuade a person from leaving. In some cases, the organisation may decide to simply let the person go, but when an employee has been trained at considerable cost to the firm, is particularly well qualified and experienced, or has knowledge of information and methods that should not fall into the hands of competitors, the organisation may try to keep him or her. Particular sources of employee dissatisfaction (eg salary) *may* sometimes be resolved, but there are dangers in setting precedents by giving special treatment.

FOR DISCUSSION

What issues are presented for an employer when a 'key talent' wants to leave the organisation? How can talent and knowledge be retained – or prevented from benefiting competitors?

Various arrangements have to be made when an employee decides to leave. There has to be co-operation and full exchange of information between the HR function and the leaver's immediate superior, so that procedures can begin when notice is given of an intended departure.

(a) If attempts to encourage the employee to stay have been unsuccessful, the exit interview has to be arranged.

(b) The period of notice required for the employee to leave should be set out in the contract of employment, but some leeway may be negotiated on this, for example if the employee wishes to take up another position immediately. The statutory minimum notice period (Employment Rights Act 1996) is one week.

(c) Details of the departure have to be notified to the wages clerk, pension fund officer, security officer etc, so that the appropriate paperwork and other procedures can be completed by the date of leaving. The organisation may have a departure checklist to ensure that all procedures are completed.

(d) The department head should complete a leaving report form: an overall assessment of the employee's performance in the organisation. This can then be used to provide references to his/her future employer(s).

It should be noted that during the notice period, all terms and conditions of the employment contract still apply: the employee still owes the employer duties of fidelity, obedience and care, while the employer still owes the employee duties of trust, care and provision of work. If there is any doubt that this relationship will not be possible during the notice period, due to the circumstances or feelings surrounding the resignation, it may be advisable to let the employee leave immediately with pay in lieu of notice. This may prevent loss of morale in the team from a disgruntled employee's behaviour and indeed possible sabotage of work or customer relations by the outgoing employee, including gathering of information for use by the new (competing) employer.

ACTIVITY 2   (30 MINS)

Brainstorm some notes on the following issues.

(a) Reasons for resigning from a job.
(b) Procedures that should be included on an Employee Departure Checklist.

SIGNPOST

Of course, not everybody leaves their organisation on a 'voluntary' basis. Where employees are required to leave employment, there is a clear need to protect their rights and livelihoods against injustice or exploitation by employers. After all, staff may be 'resources' and 'assets' – but they are also people. This is where employment protection legislation comes into force. We start by looking at the key bodies enforcing employee rights.

2   EMPLOYMENT TRIBUNALS

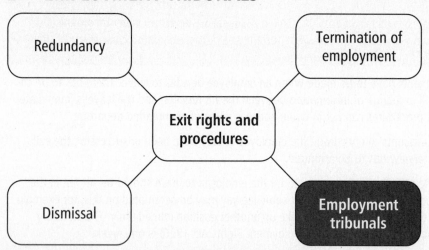

Redundancy

Termination of employment

Exit rights and procedures

Dismissal

Employment tribunals

DEFINITION

Employment tribunals are independent judicial bodies which arbitrate in employment matters including unfair dismissal, employment protection and claims in relation to sexual/racial discrimination and equal pay.

2.1   THE COMPOSITION OF TRIBUNALS

The composition of an employment tribunal is governed by the Employment Tribunals Act (ETA) 1996. A tribunal usually has three members.

- A legally-qualified chairperson (solicitor or barrister)
- An employer representative
- An employee representative (usually from a trade union)

2.2   THE POWERS OF TRIBUNALS

Tribunals have powers to hear disputes or claims, and to:

(a)   Order the disclosure and inspection of documents, or otherwise demand information relevant to the claim

(b)   Set timescales for compliance with information requests

(c)   Strike out applications and/or award costs, if a party does not comply with a directive order, or conducts proceedings in a disruptive or abusive fashion

(d)   Make legally binding decisions and orders (eg to reinstate an employee who has been unfairly dismissed) and award compensation payments, within the boundaries of employment legislation.

In effect, the tribunal is a court, with jurisdiction in a wide range of matters derived from relevant statutory provisions.

The **Employment Appeal Tribunal (EAT)** hears appeals on the decisions of employment tribunals, but only on matters of law – not disputed facts of the case.

2.3 TRIBUNAL PROCEDURES

A case is initiated when an employee presents an **application**, specifying the persons against whom relief is sought and the grounds on which it is sought.

The application is registered, and a copy is sent to the respondent in the case, and to ACAS. Either party to the case (or the tribunal itself) may then require that:

(a) The case proceeds through **mediation and/or arbitration** by ACAS. (Since April 2009, ACAS provides a free 'pre-claim' conciliation service for workplace disputes that cannot be resolved internally and are likely to become tribunal claims.)

(b) A **preliminary hearing** may be held to consider the merits of the case before proceeding to a full hearing.

(c) The other party provide further or better **particulars** relevant to the claim, so that both parties are clear in advance what the nature of the case is. The tribunal may enforce this with orders for the disclosure and inspection of documents.

If the case proceeds to a **full hearing**, both parties must gather witnesses and documentation to support their case. Employees may be represented by a lawyer, trade union representative or other person of their choice: if they do not have a representative, the tribunal will assist them as far as possible (without bias) to comply with proper procedure.

At the hearing, witnesses are heard, witness statements read out, cross-examination may take place and any questions by the tribunal addressed. Tribunal members then withdraw to consider their decision. If the employee is successful, further submissions may be made in regard to compensation or other forms of relief to be awarded.

WEBLINK

• CIPD (2009 Factsheet on Employment Tribunals)

▶▶ www.cipd.co.uk/hr-resources/factsheets/employment-tribunals.aspx

3 DISMISSAL

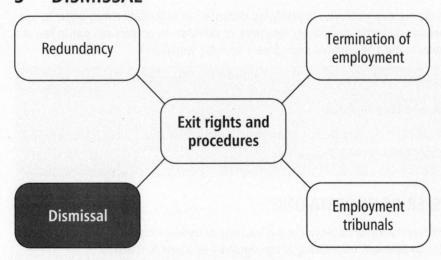

An individual can be legally dismissed in three ways.

• Employment is terminated with or without notice (eg summary dismissal for gross misconduct).

- Employment under a fixed-term contract comes to an end and is not renewed.

- The employee resigns (with or without notice) because of 'conduct [on the part of the employer] which is a significant breach of the contract of employment or which shows that the employer no longer intends to be bound by one or more of the essential terms of the contract'. This is known as 'constructive dismissal' because the employer's conduct is 'construed' or understood as constituting dismissal.

Dismissal with notice

In the UK, various Employment Rights Acts have set detailed requirements as to individual employee rights.

(a) The statutory minimum period of notice that must be given (depending on length of service and contract terms)

(b) Rights to waive notice periods, or accept payment in lieu

(c) Rights to explanation of reasons for dismissal

(d) Definitions of 'length of service' and 'continuous employment' (which qualify employees for many of the rights established by the Act) in regard to hours of work, periods of absence and transfer of the undertaking

Dismissal without notice

In most cases, the statutory and/or contractual minimum notice of dismissal *must* be given to the employee. However, rare circumstances may justify **'summary' dismissal** without notice. The law protecting employees from unfair dismissal (discussed below) requires that summary dismissal be limited to cases of serious breach of contract, such as:

(a) **Gross misconduct** by the employee: theft, violence, serious refusal to obey reasonable instruction, endangerment of other staff

(b) **Serious neglect of duties**, or absence from work without permission or good cause

(c) **Serious breaches of trust** or **conflicts of interest** affecting the organisation's business.

Even then, with the onus on employers to justify fair dismissal, an organisation may prefer to use temporary suspension and other disciplinary measures, or dismissal by notice (with pay in lieu of notice if the employee must be removed immediately from the workplace).

FOR DISCUSSION

Debate for and against the proposition:

'An employer should have the right to fire incompetent, incompatible and dishonest employees without costly restrictions and red tape.'

3.1 TRANSFER OF UNDERTAKING

A 'special case' of termination of employment is a business or undertaking, or part transferred to a new employer (eg by takeover, outsourcing or reassignment to a new contractor).

The Transfer of Undertakings (Protection of Employment) Regulations 2006 (a revision of 1981 TUPE Regulations) came into force in April 2006, to safeguard employees' rights to employment protection, terms and conditions, in such circumstances.

Essentially, employees employed when the undertaking is transferred or changes hands automatically become employees of the new employer, on the same terms and conditions. The new employers must take over all existing employment contracts, and all rights and obligations arising from them (including all prior collective agreements).

(a)   The new employer cannot dismiss employees because of the transfer, *unless* there is a sound economic, technical or organisational (ETO) reason to do so. In this case, dismissal would be defined as *redundancy* (see Section 4), and the usual rights and procedures would apply. Otherwise, the dismissal will be deemed unfair.

(b)   Representatives of any employees affected by the transfer (eg a recognised trade union) have a right to be informed about the transfer, and consulted about any proposed measures concerning the employees.

SIGNPOST

Dismissal is clearly somewhat of a political, legal and interpersonal minefield! Fortunately, there are two relatively clear definitions of circumstances in which an employee cannot legally be dismissed.

3.2 WRONGFUL DISMISSAL

A claim for wrongful dismissal is open to employees at common law, if they can show they were dismissed in **breach of contract** (for example, with less than the required notice) and that they thereby suffered loss. They may then be able to claim damages compensating for the amount lost: accrued wages, payment for an entitlement to notice, or the balance of wages due under a fixed-term contract. In practice, such claims are less common now that **unfair dismissal** provisions offer wider remedies, but the common law remedy is still useful for those who cannot claim unfair dismissal (for example, because they have not been continuously employed for long enough to qualify).

Wrongful dismissal claims are taken to Employment Tribunals if they are for less than £25,000, and to the County Court for larger sums.

SIGNPOST

Wrongful dismissal is compensated under common law – but only to the amount lost by the employee. Employment protection legislation has widened the scope of security and increased the range of remedies available. The concept of 'unfair dismissal' is an extremely important element of this legislation.

3.3 UNFAIR DISMISSAL

Employees have the right not to be unfairly dismissed. In most circumstances employees will need to qualify before they can make a complaint to an employment tribunal by being employed for:

•   At least one year's continuous service for employees in employment before 6 April 2012

•   Two years for employees starting employment on or after 6 April 2012

Dismissal will *automatically* be deemed either justified or unfair in the following cases.

Dismissal is justified where related to:	Dismissal is unfair where related to:
(a) **Redundancy** (provided that the selection for redundancy was fair)	(a) **Redundancy**, where the selection is deemed unfair
(b) **Legal impediment** – eg loss of driving licence or lack of work permit	(b) **Trade union membership** (actual or proposed) and activities, or refusal to join a trade union
(c) **Incapability** (including ill health) or lack of qualifications	(c) **Pregnancy**, maternity, dependant care or parental leave
(d) **Misconduct**, provided that minimum disciplinary procedures have been followed (Employment Act 2002)	(d) **Spent conviction** (Rehabilitation of Offenders Act 1974)
(e) Some other **'substantial' reason**: for example, the employee marries a competitor, or refuses to accept a reorganisation made in the interests of the business and with the agreement of other employees	(e) **Transfer of the undertaking** (unless economic, technical or organisational reasons justifying it)
	(f) **Assertion of a statutory right** (eg under Equal Pay or Working Time Regulations)
	(g) **Participation in official industrial action**, within the first 12 weeks (Employment Relations Act 2004)
	(h) **Refusal to work on a Sunday** (for shop or betting workers)
	(i) **Whistle-blowing**: disclosure of information believed to expose malpractice, injustice or health and safety dangers (Public Interest Disclosure Act 1998)
	(j) **Carrying out duties** as a safety representative or pension fund trustee
	(k) **Discrimination** (on the grounds of age, disability, gender reassignment, marriage and civil partnership, pregnancy and maternity, race, religion or belief, sex and sexual orientation)

3.4 REMEDIES FOR UNFAIR DISMISSAL

An employee who believes (s)he has been unfairly dismissed may present a complaint to an Employment Tribunal, within three months of dismissal.

Before a case comes to tribunal, ACAS will often try to help the parties reach a settlement, rather than proceed to a full tribunal hearing.

Defending a claim successfully relies on the employer being able to demonstrate that:

(a) The real or principal reason for the dismissal was one of the **justifiable reasons** listed above, or was otherwise a '**substantial reason** of a kind such as to justify the dismissal of an employee' (rather than some lesser action).

(b) It was '**reasonable**' to dismiss in all the circumstances of the case (including any mitigating circumstances on behalf of the employee).

ACTIVITY 3 (20 MINS)

All other criteria being met, would the following cases constitute fair or unfair dismissal?

(a) Bernie is a van-driver for a carrier firm. After a number of driving infringements in his own car and in his own time – ie not on the job – Bernie has lost his driving licence. The carrier firm dismisses him.

(b) Berenice is a shop manageress, but after a period when it has been observed that she leaves the shop dirty and untidy, fails to maintain cash registers and does not put stock away, the chain of shops dismisses her.

(c) Bernadette worked in telecommunications. The global economy and internet usage requires increased staffing at night, and the company proposes a change in its shift-working, which is accepted by the trade union following a vote. Bernadette refuses to work night shifts. She is dismissed.

(d) Benedict has noticed that he is not getting an itemised pay statement, and believes that he is entitled to one by law. The HR department is evasive. Benedict consults the union representatives, who press the question. The HR department stalls. Benedict starts putting up posters and holding meetings. He is told to stop 'being a trouble-maker'. He refuses, and continues lobbying his colleagues. He is dismissed for persistent trouble-making.

The Conciliation Officer or Employment Tribunal to whom a complaint of unfair dismissal is made may order various remedies.

(a) **Re-instatement** – giving the employee his old job back

(b) **Re-engagement** – giving him a job comparable to his old one

(c) **Compensation** – which may consist of:

(i) A **basic award** based on age and length of service. (If the employee is also entitled to redundancy pay, the lesser is set-off against the greater amount.)

(ii) A **compensatory award** (taking account of the basic award) for any additional loss (earnings, expenses, benefits) on common law principles of damages for breach of contract.

(iii) A **punitive additional award** if the employer does not comply with an order for re-instatement or re-engagement, and in cases of sex and race discrimination.

(iv) A **special award** in the case of health and safety, and trade union membership or activity.

In deciding whether to exercise its powers to order re-instatement or re-engagement, the Tribunal must take into account whether the complainant **wishes** to be reinstated; whether it is **practicable** for the employer to comply with such an order; and, if the complainant contributed to any extent to his or her dismissal, whether it would be **just** to make such an order. (Such orders are very infrequent!)

Compensation payments may also be reduced if the ex-employee is deemed to have contributed to his or her own dismissal or loss. So, for example, an employee may be found to have been unfairly dismissed on grounds of poor work performance because no warnings were given – but the poor performance will still be taken into account.

The Employment Relations Act 1999 provided that there should be *no* limit on compensation payouts for employees dismissed as 'whistleblowers', in order to protect the public interest.

3.5 DISMISSAL PROCEDURES

Procedures for dismissal should include the following.

(a) Ensuring that **standards** of performance and conduct are set, clearly defined and communicated to all employees.

(b) **Warning** employees where a gap is perceived between standard and performance, or where other legal impediments or 'substantial reasons' are foreseen to arise.

(c) Giving a clearly defined and reasonable **period for improvement** or adjustment – with help and training where necessary, and clear improvement targets.

(d) Ensuring that the company's **disciplinary procedures** (including appeal procedures, rights to representation and so on) are made clear and meticulously followed.

(e) Implementing fair and transparent procedures for **redundancy**, particularly in regard to selection (as discussed below).

(f) **Evaluating all decisions** and actions in the light of policy, legislation and the requirement to 'act reasonably' at all times.

SIGNPOST

One of the fair and justified reasons for dismissal (listed earlier) is 'redundancy' – provided that selection of employees for redundancy is fair. We now consider redundancy in some detail.

4 REDUNDANCY

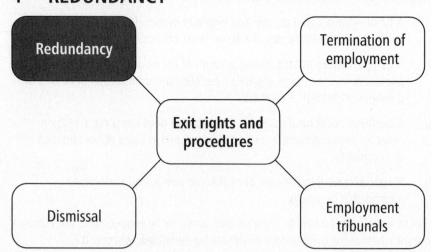

BPP
LEARNING MEDIA

DEFINITION

Redundancy is defined by the *Employment Rights Act* 1996 as dismissals for the following reasons.

(a)   The employer has ceased (or intends to cease) to carry on the business for the **purposes** of which the employee was employed

(b)   The employer has ceased (or intends to cease) to carry on the business in the **place** where the employee was employed

(c)   The **requirements** of the business for employees to carry out work of a particular kind have ceased or diminished, or are expected to

(d)   For reasons 'not related to the individual concerned.' (*The Trade Union Reform and Employment Rights Act 1993* says that all such dismissals shall be presumed to be for redundancy, for the purposes of statutory consultation with trade unions – though *not* for redundancy pay. This complies with the EU Directive on **collective redundancy**.)

4.1 CAUSES OF REDUNDANCY

In simple terms, 'redundancy occurs when the employer closes down completely, moves premises, requires fewer people for particular jobs or requires no people for particular jobs' (Gennard and Judge, 2003).

Over the past few decades, economic and business conditions have given rise to increasing levels of redundancy.

(a)   **Adverse trading conditions**, especially in recessionary phases of the economy. In recent years, though the UK economy has been perceived to be relatively strong and stable, there have been high-profile sector 'downturns' – such as the 'dot.com' collapse or the post-'9/11' downturn in air travel. The 2008/09 global recession has also hit UK jobs hard.

(b)   **Increased global competition** across business sectors. Many organisations have 'delayered' (eliminated excess layers of management and supervision), or 'downsized' (reduced their labour force) in order to reduce labour costs. Armstrong (2003) notes that productivity and added-value objectives have increased the use of indices such as added value per £ of employment cost to measure business performance.

(c)   The **introduction of information and communications (and manufacturing) technology** has reduced labour in unskilled and semi-skilled jobs. It has also permitted increased outsourcing of functions and replacement of customer service and other skilled jobs, notably through the development of e-commerce and 'virtual organisation' (linking dispersed employees and work units via the internet).

Redundancies are therefore a fact of life for HR practitioners, and are central to many **change management** projects in HRM.

FOR DISCUSSION

'Organisations are becoming mean as well as lean.'

(Armstrong, 2003)

Note that Armstong made this statement before the 2008 financial crisis!

How far is this true in your experience?

Why might an organisation wish to minimise redundancies – or minimise their impact on employees, beyond statutory requirements?

4.2 HR RESPONSIBILITIES IN REGARD TO REDUNDANCY

The HR function has the following responsibilities in regard to redundancy.

(a) Establish a redundancy policy which clarifies the psychological contract, balancing the organisation's commitment to maintain employment (on the one hand) with clear recognition of the need to ensure the economic viability of the business (on the other).

(b) Develop appropriate and socially responsible redundancy procedures.

(c) Conduct advance HR planning (see Chapter 2) in order to achieve downsizing, as far as possible, without involuntary redundancies.

(d) Advise on and/or implement other methods of avoiding or minimising involuntary redundancy.

(e) Advise on and/or take part in managing redundancy (in regard to consultation, outplacement, counselling, payment and other impact minimisation measures).

SIGNPOST

We look at some of these matters in turn.

ACTIVITY 4 (5 MINS)

(a) A's job is abolished, and A is transferred to B's job, and B is dismissed. Is this a case of redundancy?

(b) An employer wishes to alter employees' contract terms. It decides to do this by dismissing all employees and re-employing them all on new terms: no one effectively ceases to be employed, since everyone accepts the new terms. Has there been a redundancy?

4.3 MINIMISING INVOLUNTARY REDUNDANCIES

Unemployment can represent not only an economic threat to livelihood and lifestyle, but a source of stress, insecurity and loss of self-esteem. On grounds of social responsibility, therefore, as well as reduced cost and preserved morale, the organisation should attempt to minimise compulsory redundancy as far as possible. There are various ways by which this can be done.

(a) **Advance HR planning**, so that foreseen seasonal or other contractions in demand for labour taken into account, and natural wastage allowed to downsize the organisation.

(b) **Adjusting HR plans** to ban non-essential recruitment; reduce overtime working; develop job-sharing (people alternating or splitting days of work in the same job); encourage short-contract working; restrict the use of sub-contracted, temporary and casual staff; and, if necessary, implement temporary layoffs.

(c) Encouraging **voluntary redundancy**. People may be induced to volunteer to leave by the offer of financial incentives (above-statutory redundancy pay), the provision of outplacement training or counselling (to help them find work elsewhere) and so on.

(d) **Retraining and redeployment programmes**. This may be a solution where alternative jobs are available, employees have some of the skills (or at least aptitudes) required and retraining facilities are available. The organisation may use outplacement agencies, or liaison with other employers in the same industry, supply chain or area, with a view to securing redeployment within a network of organisations.

(e) Encouraging **early retirement**, or insisting on the retirement of employees over the normal retirement age. This may be felt to be fair, if careers are seen to 'wind down' in any case, but it may not be appropriate in a high loyalty/seniority culture such as that pertaining in Japan. It may also be a factor, in terms of social responsibility, that mature-aged employees will have greater difficulty in finding new employment if they wish to do so.

SIGNPOST

Most claims for unfair dismissal in respect of redundancy are for unfair selection and lack of consultation: we look at these two areas next.

4.4 SELECTION FOR COMPULSORY REDUNDANCY

There is no one fair method of selection, but the employer should seek to agree the criteria for selection with the representatives of the employees concerned.

Point score systems are favourably viewed by tribunals. These allow **retention by merit** – retaining good performers and dismissing less effective ones – while supporting the objectivity of the process.

(i) Clear criteria should be chosen, and agreed in advance with employee representatives. The main criteria may include:

- Experience
  - Skill
  - Knowledge

- Attendance

- Efficiency of the employee-performance and productivity

- Length of service, if it is established that it demonstrates business knowledge, otherwise there is a risk that the criteria constitutes discrimination

- Whatever the criteria chosen it must be fair and not constitute discrimination, such as requiring part-timers to be dismissed instead of full-time employees. The decision must be objectively based.

  A matrix of the above criteria may be the best approach.

(ii) Each employee is scored on each criteria to build up a points value.

(iii) Managers implementing the system should have clear definitions of criteria; points available for different degrees of fulfilment of each criterion; and weighting of criteria to reflect their relative importance and value to the organisation.

(iv) Once all scores have been calculated, employees with the lowest scores are selected for redundancy.

From the organisation's point of view, selection criteria should ensure that the skills needed for organisational survival and regrowth are not lost through redundancy and, if possible, that the best people are retained in the most value-adding jobs.

Employees who are employed on special projects or who have distinct skills required by the organisation may need to be removed from the pool prior to selection, or this should be provided for in the selection criteria.

4.5 EMPLOYEE RIGHTS AND REDUNDANCY PROCEDURES

Armstrong (2009) notes that redundancy procedures have three key aims, to:

(a) Treat employees as fairly as possible
(b) Reduce hardship as much as possible
(c) Protect management's ability to run the business effectively

In addition, of course, any procedure must take into account the employee's legal rights in redundancy situations. Many large organisations provide services and benefits well in excess of the statutory minimum with regard to consultation periods, terms, notice periods, counselling and aid with job search etc.

EXAMPLE   TOYOTA GB

Toyota GB's HR Director commented that.

'When I joined in January 2009, our priority was bringing down costs in line with revenue, but we were determined not to make redundancies'.

This attitude is rooted in Toyota's history and reflects the view that management is responsible for leading the company in a sustainable way for the benefit of all staff. So the last time Toyota was forced to make people redundant, in the harsh economic climate following the second world war, the entire executive management team, from the president down, resigned to show they knew they had failed.

While avoiding redundancies in 21st century Britain, the company did reduce staff by voluntary resignations and transfers to other Toyota businesses. But the main vehicle for reducing costs was the 'One Team' programme, which took the company's top 50 managers out of their functional silos and got them to work together to find efficiencies. This cross-functional approach proved so effective that the company continued to use One Team as a structured change management process in a variety of situations even after the desired savings were achieved.

Cuts were made in all sorts of areas, including pay and in 2009 no Toyota GB employee received a pay rise, merit payment or bonus, But these measures were taken in what is described as a team spirit, with everybody making a 'personal sacrifice to guarantee the stable employment of the collective'. That sacrifice began – and continues – at the top of the organisation, so while pay rises and bonuses for other parts of the workforce have gradually been restored, directors and senior management are still receiving very little or no bonus.

Individuals at all levels have also been expected to change jobs in response to business needs. Over the past two-and-a-half years, 44% of the company's 300 employees have either had a promotion or lateral rotation. The HR Director stresses that rotations were made not only to meet organisational needs, but with employees' long-term development very much in mind.

(*People Management*, 2011)

ACTIVITY 5 (90 MINS)

Use your research skills to find one or more further accounts (written or oral) of a redundancy situation: HR journals, quality press and acquaintances who have experienced redundancy are good sources. The **redundancy policy** of a business organisation, including selection criteria and ethical aims, will also be useful if you can gain access to one (or more).

Consultation

From a social responsibility point of view, it is obviously desirable to consult with employee representatives and to give warning of impending redundancies and methods of selection as early as possible. The legal requirements in the UK (based on the *Employment Protection Act 1975* and several subsequent amendments) are broadly as follows.

In the case of collective redundancies, affecting 20 or more employees, the employer must consult with '**appropriate representatives**'. If there is no recognised trade union in the workplace, employers are bound to make suitable arrangements for the fair election (by secret ballot) of employee representatives from among the affected workforce.

Consultation about proposed redundancies must begin 'at the earliest opportunity', as defined by the legislation:

(a) A minimum of 90 days before the first dismissal, if 100 or more employees are to be dismissed at any one establishment.

(b) A minimum of 30 days before the first dismissal of 20–99 employees.

These rules are applied to the total number involved and cannot be evaded by making essential dismissals in small instalments!

Prior to consultation, employees or their representatives must have been provided with information about: the reason for redundancies; numbers to be dismissed; proposed methods of selection for redundancy; timescale and methods of the redundancy programme; and method to be used in calculating redundancy pay (if not the statutory formula). The consultation period is not deemed to have started until sufficient information is provided on all these matters.

Consultation must be 'genuine', with the intention of reaching agreement with the employee representatives. It has to explore whether there are other options open to the business.

(a) Are there ways of avoiding dismissals altogether?

(b) Can the numbers to be dismissed be reduced?

(c) How can the impact of redundancy on those who must be dismissed be minimised?

Failure to comply with consultation requirements entitles the union to bring a complaint before an Employment Tribunal. If the complaint is upheld, the tribunal may postpone the dismissals and order consultation to take place, or may make a 'protective award' of pay to employees concerned, based on the number of redundancies and the period over which they are carried out.

Redundancies and transfers are also regarded as 'decisions likely to lead to **substantial changes** in work organisation or contracts' and are therefore subject to the **Information and Consultation of Employees (ICE)** regulations. ICE regulations give employees the right to be informed and consulted on these among other issues and are discussed further in the Human Resources Development and Employee Relations Course Book.

FOR DISCUSSION

'The obligation on the employer is only to consult before proposals become fixed decisions. The likely outcome of the consultation is that the employer's proposal will be implemented either unaltered or altered in a way that the employer finds acceptable.'

(Dalgarno & Davies, 2003)

What do you think is the purpose and importance of consultation?

Redundancy pay

Redundant employees are entitled to compensation, in the form of redundancy pay:

(a)   For loss of security

(b)   To encourage them to accept redundancy without damage to employee relations

The employee may not be entitled to redundancy pay if the employer has made an offer of 'suitable' alternative employment and the employee has 'unreasonably' rejected it.

The statutory minimum entitlement is half a week's pay for each year of employment under the age of 22; one week's pay for each year of employment between 22 and 40; and one-and-a-half weeks' pay for each year of employment above the age of 41. In practice, this is often supplemented by voluntary payments by the employer.

Other employee rights

Redundant employees also have:

(a)   The right to 'reasonable' time off with pay to look for another job or arrange training.

(b)   The right to accept alternative work offered by the employer for an agreed trial period, and to refuse that work (if unsuitable) at the end of the trial period without prejudice to the right of redundancy pay.

4.6 COMPASSIONATE EXIT MANAGEMENT

A number of measures may be taken to alleviate the consequences of redundancy for employees.

(a)   **Informing employees** who are to be dismissed of their selection should be managed with as much sensitivity as possible. This is generally done by what is called a **'release interview'**. The interview is generally conducted by a line manager, but an HR specialist may also be present, in order to explain the basis of selection, the employee's entitlements and organisational support services that will be offered. Managers should be given training and/or guidance in how to handle this difficult situation sensitively. They should also be given information about any special circumstances that might make the employee react particularly badly.

(b)   **Counselling** may be offered to employees, to aid their readjustment and job search. (Counselling is discussed in Chapter 11 of this Course Book.) The employee will be guided in reinforcing his or her sense of employability, redefining career objectives, devising strategies for job search, and working through personal issues (including anger and grief) around their job loss.

(c) **Outplacement services** may be offered, often through external consultancies, to help redundant employees find alternative work. The HR department or consultancy may offer services such as:

(i) Seeking specific job opportunities in the local area

(ii) Training employees in CV preparation, selection interview techniques and application filling

(iii) Helping employees to draw up skill or competence inventories, personal success/attainment inventories and other aids to applications

(iv) Carrying out psychometric assessments and helping employees to set career and job objectives

(v) Matching of employee details to advertised vacancies or network opportunities

(vi) Helping the employee to plan a focused job-search campaign

(d) **Information** on job, self-employment, retraining opportunities and funding should be made available. Individuals should also be made aware of the role and accessibility of Job Centre Plus facilities, and private sector services for careers counselling, recruitment, CV preparation and so on.

ACTIVITY 6 (30 MINS)

Conduct a web search and develop your own source list of organisations and websites that provide outplacement support.

Note that the impact of redundancy may also be felt by those who were *not* selected. '**Survivors**' may suffer guilt and anxiety, insecurity about their own jobs and a loss of loyalty to the organisation: they may tend to identify more closely with fellow workers and less with the organisation. Efforts have to be made to reinforce survivors' loyalty and morale by acknowledging their worth to the employer – particularly since, despite the concept underlying 'redundancy', remaining workers may, in fact, have to shoulder an increased workload!

DEFINITION

The term **survivor syndrome** has been coined for a psychological state which involves long-term anxiety about job loss, increased loyalty to co-workers and reduced loyalty to the employer.

'Survivor syndrome' can lead to increased labour turnover, deliberately restricted output, risk-averse behaviour (suppression of feedback, new ideas, innovation) and industrial conflict. In order to avoid these effects, management's motives and intentions must be transparent and true, and fairness (even generosity, if possible) demonstrated. Positive values around the redundancies (better chances of corporate survival and success, 'heroism' of the lean-mean workforce, the value of retained employees) must be promoted.

EXAMPLE

In an era when demand for corporate social responsibility is high, it is worth remembering the wider issues of social sustainability arising from redundancies ...

'Kilmarnock must secure a new future for itself rather than become simply a commuter base for Glasgow, East Ayrshire Council said yesterday.

'Pledging to work for the town's future after the closure of the Diageo plant, the council acknowledged that Kilmarnock may suffer the worst unemployment in Scotland, along with a £19 million clean-up bill.

'The council said that it was seeking substantial sums from Diageo to help with regeneration. The news came as the company continued consultations with employees and unions on plans for 700 redundancies among bottling and packaging workers at the Johnnie Walker plant.

'Fiona Lees, chief executive of the council, said the impact of job losses would be huge: "Unemployment here is just under 6%, fourth highest of any local authority in Scotland. This closure will push us up to about 7%, the highest."

'Asked if she feared that Kilmarnock would become a dormitory town for Glasgow, she said: "No, I don't. We have some well-placed businesses. We have a number of good food and drink firms – not on the scale of Johnnie Walker – but we hope to see them develop." She gave as an example Food Partnership Kilmarnock, a leading British sandwich-maker employing some 200 people. But she acknowledged that the town faces an uphill struggle. Consultants have estimated the lost wages from the plant alone will cost up to another 100 jobs, representing a loss of some £15.5 million to the local economy.

'The council has also been told the cost of making the Johnnie Walker site suitable for alternative use will be some £19 million. Miss Lees said public money from the Scottish government should be matched "pound for pound" by Diageo.

'There is growing cross-party local and national pressure on the company to repay a "debt of gratitude" to the town where Johnnie Walker has been bottled for 189 years.

'A Diageo spokesman said the company has a record of corporate responsibility, and assists communities where there have been closures, such as in West Dunbartonshire. He said: "We devote time and effort to ensure we are responsible and sustainable. We will work with political and community leaders in Kilmarnock to address the impact on the town."'

Jones (2009)

CHAPTER ROUNDUP

- Exit from employment takes several forms, voluntary and involuntary, including:

    - Retirement: termination of contract at a fixed, statutory or negotiated retirement age

    - Resignation: voluntary termination by notice on the part of the employee

    - Dismissal: termination, with or without notice, on the part of the employer, or (constructive dismissal) on the part of the employee where (s)he is entitled to assume that the employer has terminated the contract by breach

    - Redundancy: dismissal by reason of the ending of the work for which the employee was contracted

- Employment protection legislation and regulations set out employee rights with regard to:

    (a) Notice periods to be given for dismissal

    (b) Valid reasons for dismissal

    (c) Remedies in the event of dismissal being judged 'unfair'

    (d) Consultation with employee representatives over proposed redundancies

    (e) Redundancy pay

    (f) Time off to prepare for redundancy

    (g) Trial periods prior to acceptance of alternative employment

- In addition to statutory requirements, exit has ethical and employee relations implications. Attention is commonly given to:

    (a) Learning from resignations by means of exit interviews

    (b) Socially responsible polices surrounding progressive discipline, dismissal and redundancy

    (c) The motivation of 'surviving' employees

QUICK QUIZ

1   In what five basic ways may a contract (including a contract of employment) be terminated?

2   What is the current UK State Pension age for men and women?

3   What procedures should be carried out when an employee resigns from an organisation?

4   Who are the members of an Employment Tribunal?

5   What is the difference between wrongful dismissal and unfair dismissal?

6   What reasons may an employer rely on in seeking to show that a dismissal was fair?

7   When is dismissal called 'redundancy'?

8   What measures can be used to avoid compulsory redundancies?

9   When choosing criteria for redundancy selection, who should they be agreed with?

10 Explain the term 'survivor syndrome'.

ANSWERS TO QUICK QUIZ

1   Performance, mutual agreement, notice, breach or frustration.   (see Para 1.1)

2   65   (Para 1.2)

3   Persuade to stay (if appropriate); exit interview; negotiate notice period; notify key people; complete performance assessment.   (Para 1.3)

4   A legally-qualified chairperson, employer representative and employee representation.   (Para 2.1)

5   Wrongful dismissal is where there are insufficient reasons to justify dismissal, whereas unfair dismissal is where law and internal policies have been breached.   (Paras 3.3, 3.4)

6   Redundancy; legal impediment; non-capability; misconduct; some other substantial reason.   (Para 3.4)

7   Cessation of the business; cessation of the business in a particular location; cessation of the need for work of a particular kind.   (Para 4)

8   A full answer is provided in Paragraph 4.3.

9   The employee representatives   (Para 4.4)

10 A psychological state suffered by employees who have survived redundancy programmes, characterised by long-term anxiety, increased loyalty to co-workers and decreased commitment to the organisation.   (Para 4.6)

 ANSWERS TO ACTIVITIES

1   (a)   The burden of work in late years can be eased by shortening hours or a transfer to lighter duties.

    (b)   The final stage of employee training and development may take the form of courses, commonly run by local technical colleges, intended to prepare employees for the transition to retirement and non-work.

    (c)   The organisation may have, or may be able to put employees in touch with, social/leisure clubs and other facilities for easing the shock of retirement.

2   (a)   Reasons for leaving are many and various, but some of the ones you may have thought of are: relocation to another city/area; dissatisfaction with work conditions (or location, or workmates or scope for responsibility or any number of work-related factors); finding another (preferred) job; being head-hunted; change of career (or return to full-time education, or move to self-employment, or change of domestic circumstances/family responsibilities); clash of culture/values with the employer; ill-health; to pre-empt dismissal in order to save face.

    (b)   Procedures may include: return of keys, security passes and so on; handing of files to department head; completion or transfer of work-in-progress; removal of personal data/passwords from computer files; collection of final pay and leaving information; removal of personal effects.

3   (a)   Bernie was fairly dismissed by reason of legal impediment.

      (b)   Berenice was fairly dismissed by reason of lack of 'capability': she is clearly incompetent compared to the standard of performance required by the job.

      (c)   Bernadette was fairly dismissed: failure to accept necessary reorganisation is a 'substantial' reason.

      (d)   Benedict was unfairly dismissed, because he was trying to enforce his employment rights in a reasonable manner.

4   (a)   Yes – but it is **B** who has been made redundant.

      (b)   Yes – for the purposes of consultation with trade unions, since this fits the TURER '93 definition of collective redundancy (as mentioned in our definition of redundancy): the reasons for the proposed dismissal were not related to the individuals concerned. The employer was bound to consult – and to pay penalties if it had failed to do so. (This is based on an actual case brought before the EAT: *GMBV v Man Truck and Bus UK Ltd, 2000*.)

5   The answer is up to you!

6   A research activity. Find out more about outplacement – *and* the kind of information employees can be steered towards.

Part B

Human resource management (HRM) issues

Perspectives on HRM

```
                    ┌─────────────────┐                    ┌─────────────────┐
                    │ Soft and hard   │                    │ Storey's 'ideal │
                    │      HRM        │                    │ type' of HRM    │
                    └─────────────────┘                    └─────────────────┘
                              \                            /
                               \    ┌─────────────────┐   /
                                \───│ Perspectives on │──/
                                ┌───│      HRM        │──┐
                               /    └─────────────────┘   \
                              /                            \
                    ┌─────────────────┐                    ┌─────────────────┐
                    │ HRM and business│                    │ HRM as strategic│
                    │    success      │                    │   management    │
                    └─────────────────┘                    └─────────────────┘
```

Introduction

In this chapter, we explore further some of the themes already discussed in Chapters 1 and 2, highlighting the ambiguities and dualities in the role of Human Resource Management.

One of the key assumptions of HRM is that the employment relationship can be managed so that the needs of both organisation and employees are met, to mutual benefit. Ethical, people-friendly HR policies are intended to facilitate efficient and effective working as well as employee health, welfare and satisfaction. This dual emphasis is reflected in the following chapters as we look at some of the major issues facing HR managers in the 21st century workplace.

Your objectives

In this chapter you will learn about the following.

- Guest's model of the hard-soft, loose-tight dimensions of HRM
- Storey's model of the differences between HRM and personnel/industrial relations practices
- HRM from a strategic perspective, and its implications for the role of the line manager and employees
- How HRM impacts on the success of the business

1 SOFT AND HARD HRM

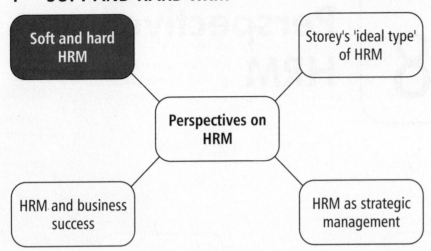

In Chapter 1, we defined HRM as 'a strategic approach to managing employment relations which emphasises that leveraging people's capabilities is critical to achieving sustainable competitive advantage'. (Bratton & Gold, 2007)

We have so far suggested that the role of HRM is twofold (leading to some ambiguity): both business-oriented (concerned with performance) and people-oriented (concerned with the motivation and quality of working life of employees). However, key writers on HRM (Storey, 1989; Legge, 1998; Guest, 1999) have identified two distinct versions of HRM, which they characterise as 'hard' and 'soft'.

1.1 HARD HRM

DEFINITION

Karen Legge (1998) defined the **'hard model'** of HRM as a process emphasising 'the close integration of human resource policies with business strategy which regards employees as a resource to be managed in the same rational way as any other resource being exploited for maximum return'.

The hard model of HRM may be summarised as follows.

(a) Its philosophy towards managing people is rational, quantitative and explicitly **business-oriented**: employees must be managed in such a way as to obtain value-adding performance, which will in turn give the organisation competitive advantage.

   The drive to adopt HRM is… based on the business case of a need to respond to an external threat from increasing competition. It is a philosophy that appeals to managements who are striving to increase competitive advantage and appreciate that to do this they must invest in human resources as well as new technology.

   (Guest, 1999)

(b) It regards employees as a resource of the organisation, to be managed (exploited) in as rational and strategic a manner as any other economic resource: **human capital** from which a return can be obtained by adding value, through judicious investment in performance management and employee development.

(c) It emphasises the interests, role and authority of **management** 'over' those of employees.

(d) It is essentially a **pluralist** viewpoint, which maintains that the interests of the owners and managers of a business are inherently different from those of the workers: organisations are therefore political systems, within which there is competition for scarce power and resources. Workers must be controlled in order to ensure that they perform in the organisation's interests.

Features of hard HRM include:

(a) A close matching or integration of the strategic objectives of the HR function with the **business strategy** of the organisation. 'Hard strategic HRM' will emphasise the yield to be obtained by investing in human resources in the interests of the business. (Storey, 1989)

(b) A focus on **quantitative, business-strategic objectives** and criteria for management.

(c) An emphasis on the need for **performance management** and other forms of managerial control.

ACTIVITY 1 (10 MINS)

What HRM techniques (covered so far) would you expect to be adopted as a result of a hard HRM approach?

1.2 SOFT HRM

DEFINITION

Legge defined the **'soft'** version of HRM as a process whereby employees are viewed as 'valued assets' and as a source of competitive advantage through their commitment, adaptability and high level of skills and performance.

The soft model of HRM may be summarised as follows.

(a) Its philosophy towards managing people is based in the human and neo-human relations schools of management thought, which emphasised the influence of **socio-psychological factors** (relationships, attitudes, motivation, leadership, communication) on work behaviour.

(b) It views employees as 'means rather than objects' (Guest, 1999): 'treating employees as **valued assets**, a source of competitive advantage through their commitment, adaptability and high quality (of skills, performance and so on)' (Storey, 1989).

(c) It focuses on **'mutuality'**, a unitarist viewpoint which assumes that the interests of management and employees can and should coincide in shared organisational goals, working as members of an integrated team. Employees are viewed as key stakeholders in the organisation.

The main **features of soft HRM** are:

(a) A complementary approach to strategic HRM, in relation to the business strategies of the organisation. Brewster (1999) argues that a **stakeholder perspective** and environmental constraints (such as EU legislation) mean that HR strategies cannot be entirely governed by business strategy. **'Soft strategic HRM'** will place greater emphasis on the human relations aspect of people management, stressing security of employment, continuous development, communication, involvement and the quality of working life.

(b) A focus on **socio-psychological and cultural objectives** and criteria for management.

(c) An emphasis on the need to gain the **trust and commitment** of employees – not merely compliance with control mechanisms.

ACTIVITY 2 (10 MINS)

What HRM techniques (covered so far) would you expect to be adopted as a result of a soft HRM approach?

SIGNPOST

We now look briefly at two early US models of HRM which reflect the roots of the soft and hard approaches respectively.

1.3 THE MICHIGAN MODEL

The **matching model** of HRM was developed by the Michigan School (Fombrun *et al*, 1984). It suggests that HR systems should be managed in such a way as to 'match', or be congruent with, the organisation's business strategy: an essentially hard orientation. The **human resource cycle** consists of four basic functions which are performed in all organisations to drive business performance.

(a) **Selection**: designed to match available human resources to jobs

(b) **Performance management/appraisal**: designed to match performance to objectives and standards

(c) **Rewards**: reinforcing short- and long-term achievements

(d) **Development**: matching the skill quality of the human resource to future requirements

Fombrun *et al* suggest that the HR function should be linked to line management by:

(a) Providing good HR databases

(b) Ensuring that senior mangers give HR issues as much attention as they give to other functions

(c) Measuring the contribution of the HR function at the strategic (long-term policies designed to encourage organisational 'fit' to its environment in the future), managerial (medium-term activities ensuring the acquisition, retaining and development of people) and operational (daily support of business activities) levels.

1.4 THE HARVARD FRAMEWORK

The Harvard Framework (Beer *et al*, 1984) was based on the belief that the problems of historical personnel management could only be solved:

When general managers develop a viewpoint of how they wish to see employees involved in and developed by the enterprise, and of what HRM policies and practices may achieve those goals…

BPP
LEARNING MEDIA

Today, many pressures are demanding... a longer-term perspective in managing people and consideration of people as potential assets rather than merely a variable cost.

The Harvard model was influential in emphasising the fact that:

(a) 'Human resource management involves **all management decisions** and actions that affect the nature of the relationship between the organisation and its employees.'

(b) Organisations involve a variety of **stakeholders** who have an interest in the practice and outcomes of HR policies: there is a 'trade-off' between the interests of owners, managers and employees, as well as other stakeholders, with a view to mutuality and commitment.

(c) Strategic HRM choices are influenced by a broad range of **contextual factors**, including both product-market and socio-cultural factors.

(d) Line managers are at the **interface** between competitive strategy and HR policies and must take more responsibility for their alignment.

The Harvard framework can be illustrated as follows (Beer *et al*, 1984): Figure 8.1.

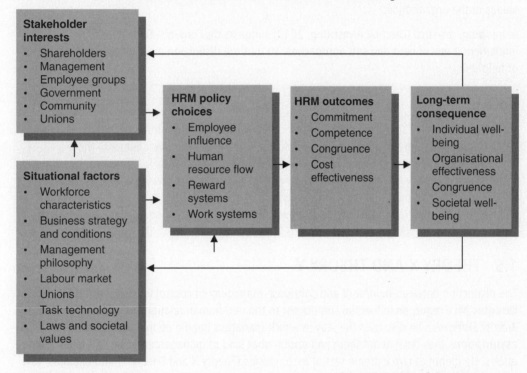

Figure 8.1: Map of the HRM territory

This is essentially a soft HRM model, composed of policies that promote **mutuality** – mutual goals, mutual influence, mutual respect, mutual rewards, mutual responsibility. The theory is that policies of mutuality will elicit commitment, which in turn will yield both **better economic performance** and **greater human development**.

(Walton, cited by Armstrong, 2003)

FOR DISCUSSION

How do you respond intuitively to the 'hard' and 'soft' versions of HRM? What words and phrases connected with each strike you as positively or negatively loaded: where do your perceptions come from? Are 'soft' and 'hard' perspectives really as different as contrasting descriptions make them seem? Does your experience of organisations suggest that they operate under *either* one *or* the other?

1.5 HARD OR SOFT?

In practice, there are likely to be times when a hard orientation (eg in the face of the need for organisational downsizing due to recessionary pressures) directly conflicts with the more developmental and paternal philosophy of the soft approach. Many organisations operate a mix of soft-hard, loose-tight systems. One way of formalising this is to segment the labour force into a 'core' of permanent employees managed via soft HRM policies, and a 'periphery' of short-contract labour used as an exploitable commodity. As Kramer, McGraw and Shuler (1997) note, 'whether an organisation leans more towards the hard or soft version of HRM depends very much on the values of the organisation.'

In addition, research (cited by Armstrong, 2012) suggests that organisations in practice implement a mix of hard and soft approaches, so that the distinction may not always be precise or helpful.

SIGNPOST

The broad 'achieve success through people' focus of HRM may therefore be approached from two different perspectives, which imply very different techniques of management. These techniques have been classified, according to the amount of control each orientation assumes to be necessary to obtain job performance from workers, as 'tight' and 'loose'. Before we discuss the characteristics of tight and loose HRM, we look at an early model of how managerial philosophy and assumptions set up the hard-soft, tight-loose continuum.

1.6 THEORY X AND THEORY Y

The distinction between hard/tight and soft/loose management control was suggested by **Douglas McGregor**, an influential contributor to the neo-human relations school. In *The Human Side of Enterprise*, he discusses the way in which managers handle people according to the **assumptions** they have about them and about what kind of management style will focus their efforts. He identifies two extreme sets of assumptions (Theory X and Theory Y) and explores how management style differs according to which set of assumptions is adopted (McGregor, 1987).

(a) **Theory X** holds that human beings have an inherent dislike of work and will avoid it if they can. People prefer to be directed, wishing to avoid responsibility. They have relatively little ambition and want security above all, resisting change. They are self-interested, and make little effort to identify with the organisation's goals. They must be coerced, controlled, directed, offered rewards or threatened with punishments in order to get them to put adequate effort into the achievement of organisation objectives: this is management's responsibility.

(b) According to **Theory Y**, however, the expenditure of physical and mental effort in work is as natural as play or rest. The ordinary person does not inherently dislike work: according to the conditions, it may be a source of satisfaction or deprivation. A person will exercise self-direction and self-control in the service of objectives to which (s)he is committed. Management's responsibility is to create conditions and methods that will enable individuals to integrate their own and the organisation's goals.

You will have your own viewpoints on the validity of Theory X and Theory Y. In fact, McGregor intentionally polarised his theories as the extremes of a continuum along which most managers' attitudes fall at some point. However, he also recognised that the assumptions are self-perpetuating, even where the 'types' of employee described do not really exist. If people are treated according to Theory X (or Theory Y) assumptions, they will begin to act accordingly – thus confirming management in its beliefs and practices. Essentially, Theory X embodies the 'hard-tight' **control theory of management**, while Theory Y embodies the 'soft-loose' **commitment theory of management**.

ACTIVITY 3 (45 MINS)

The following was sent to the letter page of *Personnel Management*.

> Hark, I think I detect the first cuckoo of a recessionary spring on your pages ('Making time for productivity', March). Come on, all you personnel folk. Off with your HR nomenclature; away with all this nonsense about the 'success culture', 'employee involvement', 'maximising people power', 'establishing the right climate' and 'sharing gains' (all drawn from the CIPD's current national priorities). Get out your sticks and stopwatches, 'precisely time' those tea breaks, slash that overtime, enforce 'bell-to-bell working', put in a few more controls and 'disincentives'… Surely employee involvement is not just an illusion created by the 1980s boom which we can ignore now times are tough?

What are the characteristics of the approach to HRM which the letter identifies? Why might economic recession lead managers to adopt such an approach?

1.7 TIGHT AND LOOSE HRM

The distinction between tight and loose HRM may be characterised as the difference between a system based on compliance and a system based on commitment.

DEFINITIONS

Compliance means performing according to set rules and standards, according to what you are expected and asked to do.

Commitment has been defined as 'the relative strength of an individual's identification with and involvement in a particular organisation. It is characterised by at least three factors:

(a) A strong belief in and acceptance of an organisation's goals and values
(b) A willingness to exert considerable effort on behalf of the organisation
(c) A strong desire to maintain membership of the organisation.'

(Mowdray *et al*, 1982)

Compliance-based systems of control reflect a low level of trust and challenge: performance is expected to be no less than the set standard – but also no *more*, since there is little room for creative or exceptional input or effort, which may militate against tight managerial control. Such systems may be effective and efficient: in a highly stable market environment; where the task is low-tech and low-discretion, with little need to differentiate skills or abilities and little difference between compliant and committed performance; and where the managerial prerogative of superiority and control continue to have meaning because of cultural values to do with respect and conformity (eg in Latino cultures and traditional family businesses).

Commitment-based systems of control reflect a high level of trust and mutuality, based on Theory Y assumptions that the work relationship can offer employees opportunities to meet their needs and aspirations as well as the organisation's needs. Such systems are effective in environments where customer demands and technologies are varied and changing, and employees are required to be flexible, creative and positive in contributing to the organisation's goals.

Guest (2001) set out the differences in HR policy in a compliance-based system of control and a commitment-based system of control, as follows.

Aspects of policy	Compliance	Commitment
Psychological contract of work	• 'Fair day's work for a fair day's pay'	• Mutual/reciprocal commitment
Behavioural references	• Norms, custom and practice	• Values/mission
Source of control over workers' behaviour	• External (rules, instructions)	• Internal (goals, values, willingness)
Employee relations	• Pluralist perspective ('Us' and 'Them') • Collective • Low trust	• Unitarist ('Us') • Individual • Trust
Organising principles/ organisational design	• Formal/defined roles • Top-down • Centralised control • Hierarchy • Division of labour • Managerial control	• Flexible roles • Bottom-up • Decentralised control (delegation, empowerment) • Flat structures • Teamwork/autonomy • Self-control
Policy goals	• Administrative/efficiency • Performance to standard • Minimising cost	• Adaptive/effectiveness • Constantly improving performance • Maximising utilisation for added value

Guest also identified these contrasting dimensions as distinguishing 'traditional industrial relations' and 'HRM' approaches.

ACTIVITY 4 (10 MINS)

Would you say you were compliant in your attitude to your studies, or committed? Think about how you approach the assignments set for you, the classes you attend and so on.

    (a)   What are (or would be) the benefits to you if you are/were committed rather than compliant?

    (b)   What are/would be the benefits to your trainers?

    (c)   What could (i) you and (ii) your trainers do to increase your commitment to your studies?

EXAMPLE

In 2010 Prudential UK and Europe (Financial Services company) ran an employee engagement survey.

'Being high performing and a great place to work is essentially what our people strategy is about' said Cathy Lewis, HR Director. 'We used the survey to provide the data to feed into improving our people strategy. It was an approach driven from the bottom-up'.

The survey actually showed a positive position for the company. However, rather than be satisfied with outcome the company wanted to further boost engagement and increase profitability. Pru UK took a number of initiatives.

The creation of an Engagement Board, consisting of senior staff from each part of the business.

The creation of an Engagement Forum, the purpose of this is to enable employees to propose improvements and changes.

When it realised that some line managers were not living up to the expectations of their role, the roles were clearly defined, with managers having greater autonomy and accountability. This new definition meant that some line managers were removed from post.

The benefits package was made more flexible to enable greater employee choice. But more importantly a communications programme was launched to educate employees about their rewards package, this resulted in a 13% increase in positive perception.

Senior members of management went out of their way to be more visible, and more communicative, for example by writing blogs.

The various office locations were also encouraged to take actions to make theirs a better place to work.

Reflecting on the achievements so far Lewis commented on the main lesson learnt is to:

'Keep asking, keep talking, because actually the answers are there… it's the people in the organisation who know what will make the difference'

(People Management, 2012)

2 STOREY'S 'IDEAL TYPE' OF HRM

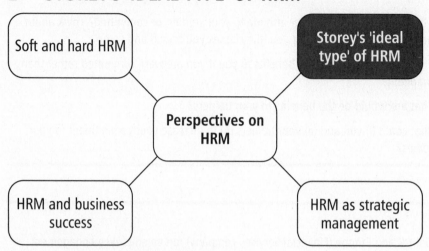

2.1 STOREY'S DEFINITIONS

Storey (1992) regarded HRM as a 'set of interrelated policies with an ideological and philosophical underpinning'. A meaningful version of HRM involves:

(a)   A particular cluster of beliefs and assumptions

(b)   A strategic focus to decision-making about people management

(c)   A central role for line managers in delivering HR outcomes

(d)   The use of 'levers' to shape the employment relationship, which can be distinguished from those used under traditional industrial relations systems

Storey put forward a theoretical 'ideal type' description of what a fully implemented model of HRM might look like, in contrast to a similarly abstracted description of the traditional personnel/industrial relations model. As you consider the table below, remember that this is an 'ideal': it is not meant to describe the current, typical state of affairs – since, as we have seen, the definition of HRM, and its application in practice, is by no means clear cut.

DIMENSION	PERSONNEL/IR APPROACH	HRM APPROACH
Beliefs and assumptions		
1 Contract	Careful delineation of written contracts	Aim to go 'beyond contract'
2 Rules	Importance of devising clear rules/mutuality	'Can do' outlook; impatience with 'rules'
3 Guide to management action	Procedures/consistency/control	'Business-need'/flexibility/commitment
4 Behaviour referent	Norms/custom and practice	Values/mission
5 Managerial task *vis-à-vis* labour	Monitoring	Nurturing
6 Nature of relations	Pluralist	Unitarist
7 Conflict	Institutionalised	De-emphasised

DIMENSION	PERSONNEL/IR APPROACH	HRM APPROACH
Beliefs and assumptions		
8 Standardisation	High (eg 'parity' an issue)	Low (eg 'parity' not seen as relevant)
Strategic aspects		
9 Key relations	Labour-management	Business-customer
10 Initiatives	Piecemeal	Integrated
11 Corporate plan	Marginal to	Central to
12 Speed of decision	Slow	Fast
Line management		
13 Management role	Transactional leadership	Transformational leadership
14 Key managers	Personnel/IR specialists	General/business/line managers
15 Communication	Indirect	Direct
16 Prized management skills	Negotiation	Facilitation
Key levers (strongly-featured issues and techniques)		
17 Foci of attention for interventions	Personnel procedures	Wide ranging cultural, structural and personnel strategies
18 Selection	Separate, marginal task	Integrated, key task
19 Pay	Job evaluation (fixed grades)	Performance-related
20 Job categories and grades	Many	Few
21 Conditions	Separately negotiated	Harmonisation
22 Labour management	Collective bargaining contracts	Towards individual contracts
23 Thrust of relations with union delegates	Regularised through facilities and training	Marginalised (with exception of some bargaining for change models)
24 Communication	Restricted flow	Increased flow
25 Job design	Division of labour	Teamwork
26 Conflict handling	Reach temporary truces	Manage climate and culture
27 Training and development	Controlled access to courses	Learning companies

Table 8.1: Twenty-seven points of difference

ACTIVITY 5 (10 MINS)

What kinds of HR policies and practices might:

   (a)   'Institutionalise' or 'de-emphasise' conflict (point 7)?
   (b)   'Restrict' or 'increase' the flow of communication (point 24)?

2.2 IMPLICATIONS FOR THE LINE MANAGER'S ROLE

Transactional and **transformational** leadership (referred to in Storey's model: point 13) were terms coined by Burns (1978) for two different styles of leadership.

- **Transactional leaders** see the relationship with their followers in terms of a trade: they give followers the rewards they want, in exchange for services, loyalty and compliance.

- **Transformational leaders** see their role as inspiring and motivating others to work at levels beyond mere compliance. Transformational leadership is achieved through role modelling, articulating powerful goals, team-building, high expectations, two-way communication, empowering and developing people and other such processes.

Transactional leadership can arguably be mediated via HR policies and practices. Transformational leadership is essentially an *interpersonal* process, underscoring the role of line managers and team leaders in delivering HRM.

2.3 IMPLICATIONS FOR THE WORKER'S ROLE

The HRM viewpoint, as outlined above, is explicitly unitarist (point 6). It implies that employees can be willingly co-opted to the business task of competition, quality enhancement and problem-solving. Tight managerial control over workers is replaced by a culture of trust: performance is assumed to be largely self-regulating within a guiding framework of inspirational leadership, shared cultural values and aspirations.

Instead of power being used from the top-down to **control** workers' performance, power is used to **support** workers' performance: performance (including quality, customer satisfaction, innovation and so on) becomes the guiding force of the organisation, not the wishes of senior management.

This has implications for the HR function, as illustrated in Figure 8.2.

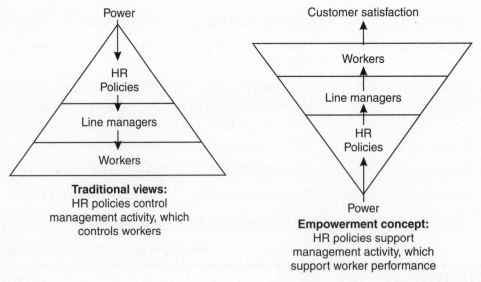

Figure 8.2: From control to empowerment

ACTIVITY 6 (10 MINS)

What might be the consequences of empowerment for HR policy in the areas of (a) recruitment and selection and (b) training?

2.4 IMPLICATIONS FOR HR RESPONSIBILITIES

One of the key features of HRM is that 'its performance and delivery are integrated into line management' (Storey, 1989).

According to Armstrong (2009) the hard HRM approach, in particular:

> is claimed to be a central, senior management-driven strategic activity that is developed, owned and delivered by management as a whole to promote the interests of the organisation that they serve. It purports to be an holistic approach concerned with the total interests of the organisation – the interests of the members of the organisation are recognised but subordinated to those of the enterprise. Hence the importance attached to strategic integration and strong cultures, which flow from top management's vision and leadership, and which require people who will be committed to the strategy, who will be adaptable to change, and who will fit the culture. By implication, as Guest (1991) says: 'HRM is too important to be left to personnel managers.'

Kramar, McGraw and Schuler (1997) note the ironic and paradoxical result:

> HRM has become more influential in company decision-making, yet has declined as a separate department within the organisation as HR tasks and decisions have been devolved to line managers. Many leading edge HR practitioners now see themselves more in an **internal consultancy capacity**, assisting line managers to devise and implement more sophisticated ways of managing people, rather than implementing and managing those systems themselves. Such HR managers would also claim to be working towards the eventual removal of their own positions within the organisation.

HR specialists, therefore, increasingly share responsibility for delivering HR policy outcomes with:

(a) **Top management**, who shape the aims, strategy and culture of the organisation supported by HR policies and consultancy. (We discussed the 'business partner' model, for example, in Chapter 1.)

(b) **Line managers**, who take on a day-to-day leadership-oriented responsibility for people management (supported by HR advice and services).

(c) **Employees themselves**. It is no longer uncommon for employees to appraise themselves (and their peers and superiors), write their own job descriptions, determine their own performance standards and improvement goals, and manage their own learning and career development.

SIGNPOST

We suggest in Chapter 1 that four key policy goals of an authentic HRM approach are: high commitment, flexibility, strategic integration and high quality. We discuss commitment (above), and will cover flexibility, in detail, in Chapter 9. Here, we look briefly at some models for the strategic integration of HRM, and then at HRM as a quality issue.

3 HRM AS STRATEGIC MANAGEMENT

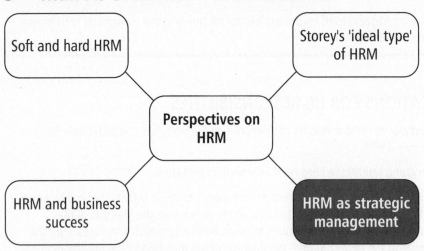

3.1 STRATEGIC HRM

The term 'strategic human resource management' emerged in the 1980s to describe a variety of models which attempt to explain how human resource policies can be **integrated with business strategy**.

> **DEFINITION**
>
> **Strategic management** 'denotes a specific pattern of decisions and actions undertaken by the upper echelon of an organisation in order to accomplish specific outcomes and/or performance goals'.
>
> **Strategic HRM** is 'the process of linking the human resource function with the strategic objectives of the organisation in order to improve performance'.
>
> (Bratton & Gold, 2007)

Bratton & Gold *(ibid)* note that the term 'strategic HRM' can be seen as:

- An **outcome**: 'organisational systems designed to achieve sustainable competitive advantage through people' (Snell *et al*)

- A **process**: 'the process by which organisations seek to link the human, social and intellectual capital of their members to the strategic needs of the firm' (Bamberger & Meshoulam).

Torrington *et al* (2002) note that strategic HRM may be achieved by the integration of HRM policy goals into business strategy and line management thinking, *or* by the involvement of the HR function in both organisational and HR strategy development. They argue that while there is a greater likelihood of involvement in strategy when the most senior HR person is a member of the Board of Directors, Board membership does not *guarantee* the involvement of specialists in strategy development – and is not necessarily *essential* to strategic involvement. In order to maximise opportunities to influence strategy, the HR function must:

(a) Use the business and financial language shared by corporate management (elements of 'hard' HR)

(b) Describe the rationale for HR activities in terms of business benefits, added value or competitive advantage (ie 'make a business case' for HRM)

(c)   Appoint line-experienced managers into the HR function (to enhance credibility and relevance)

(d)   Concentrate on the priorities defined by business strategy

(e)   Offer well-developed change-management skills

(f)   Demonstrate an ability to think strategically, having its own mission, strategy and integrative approach (involving line management in the development of HR strategy)

EXAMPLE

Harrods, the famous London store, found in 2010 that it needed to reconsider how HR was organised.

In 2007, Harrods had adopted a decentralised organisation structure with business units (food and restaurants, fashion, home etc) each supported by a dedicated HR team. In theory, the set-up was perfect for keeping HR in step with operational needs, but the reality had proved something of a let-down.

One problem was that senior HR staff, the HR Business Partners, were spending too much time in the trenches, instead of working strategically with directors to improve the store's management capabilities. At the same time, little inconsistencies were creeping in to how the divisions handled supposedly standard processes, such as staff transfers. At this time the HR Director decided to fully reorganise HR, preserving the benefits of embedding HR in the business but removing the inefficiencies.

The solution that was created was to keep the company's corporate specialists, eg recruitment, learning and development etc, and place day-to-day HR in a central services unit, leaving a core group of HR business partners in the business units focused purely on strategy.

(*People Management*, 2012)

SIGNPOST

We now examine some of the different approaches suggested for developing and integrating HR strategies.

According to Armstrong (2012):

The fundamental aim of strategic HRM is to generate organisational capability by ensuring that the organisation has the skilled, engaged, committed and well-motivated employees it needs to achieve sustained competitive advantage.

SHRM has three main objectives: first to achieve integration – the vertical alignment of HR strategies with business strategies and the horizontal integration of HR strategies. The second objective is to provide a sense of direction in an often turbulent environment so that the business needs of the organisation and the individual and collective needs of its employees can be met by the development and implementation of coherent and practical HR policies and programmes. The third objective is to contribute to the formulation of business strategy by drawing attention to ways in which the business can capitalise on the advantages provided by the strengths of its human resources.

3.2 STRATEGIC INTEGRATION OR FIT

The concept of strategic fit is central to strategic HRM. It suggests that to maximise competitive advantage, a firm must:

(a) Match its capabilities and resources to the opportunities and constraints of the **external environment (external fit)**

(b) Match the **macro features** of the organisation: its mission, strategy, structure, technology, products and services, culture and workforce (**internal fit**)

For Guest (1989), there are three aspects to strategic fit in HRM terms.

(a) Developing HR strategies that are integrated with the business strategy and support its achievement (**vertical integration or fit**)

(b) Developing integrated HR practices (resourcing, reward, development and so on) so that they complement and mutually reinforce one another (**horizontal integration or fit**), consistently encourage the quality, flexibility and commitment

(c) Encouraging line managers to **realise and internalise** the importance of human resources

As one of the key policy goals of HRM specified by Guest, strategic integration ensures that HRM 'is fully integrated into strategic planning so that HRM policies cohere both across policy areas and across hierarchies and HRM practices are used by line managers as part of their everyday work.'

3.3 APPROACHES TO DEVELOPING STRATEGIC HRM

Guest identified various types of fit, which reflect different approaches to developing HR strategies.

(a) **Fit as strategic integration**. HR strategies are congruent with, or aligned to, the thrust of business competitive strategies (for innovation, quality and cost-leadership); appropriate to the stage of the business lifecycle reached by the business (start-up, growth, maturity, decline); adapted to organisational dynamics and characteristics.

Employee expectations should also be aligned with strategic direction, by communication of the organisational vision, translating strategy into performance management, and developing a corresponding organisational culture.

(b) **Fit as an ideal set of practices**: ensuring that internal practices reflect 'best practice'. The best practice approach is based on the belief that adopting certain broadly-applicable HRM practices will lead to superior organisational performance.

Several sets of best practices, based on benchmarking, have been developed, including elements such as: employment security; sophisticated recruitment and selection processes; self-managed teams; high compensation contingent on performance; high-level participation processes; information sharing; coherent appraisal; skill flexibility; motivating job design (including responsibility, flexibility and development); ongoing training; use of quality improvement teams; and harmonised (single status) terms and conditions. (Armstrong, 2003)

Armstrong himself notes that while 'these could all be regarded as "good practice" … it is difficult to accept that they will universally constitute "best practice". What works well in one organisation will not necessarily work well in another.'

(c) **Fit as contingency**: ensuring that internal practices suit the particular (and changing) context of the firm, and its business strategy. The **'best fit' approach** (or contingency approach) is based on the belief that there is no 'one best way' or set of universal prescriptions for strategy: it all depends. Benchmarked 'good practices' must be selected and adapted to fit specific needs identified by analysis of the firm's context both external (opportunities, threats and constraints) and internal (culture, structure, technology and processes). Purcell *et al* (2003) note that the contingencies or variables in HR decision-making are so complex that it is impossible to isolate them all: the important thing is to be sensitive to changing needs and circumstances.

(d) **Fit as 'bundles'**: developing and implementing distinct **configurations** or 'bundles' of HR practices (such as quality management, performance management or competence frameworks) which can be used in multiple contexts to create coherence across a range of activities, ensuring that they complement and mutually reinforce each other.

In particular, practices designed to enhance employee **skills/competences** should be integrated with practices designed to enhance employee **motivation**, since both are essential to performance. So, for example, if the overall HR strategy is to improve performance, the sourcing strategies for competence-based *recruiting* will be integrated with development strategies for competence-based *training* and reward strategies to offer competence-related *pay*. Likewise, to increase motivation, strategies will need to integrate motivation-based selection criteria with development opportunities, job design and other intrinsic motivating factors.

ACTIVITY 7 (20 MINS)

What do you think might be the key HR policy issues and approaches of an organisation:

(a) Pursuing an innovation strategy?
(b) Pursuing a cost leadership strategy?
(c) In the growth stage of its life cycle?
(d) In the decline stage of its life cycle?

---

4 HRM AND BUSINESS SUCCESS

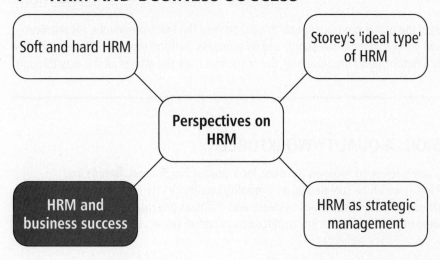

4.1 HOW DOES HRM IMPACT ON BUSINESS PERFORMANCE?

Key research carried out by the Work and Employment Research Centre, University of Bath (Purcell *et al*, 2003) attempted to look inside 'the black box' which previously obscured the process by which people inputs are transformed into performance outputs. The researchers developed a complex 'People and Performance Model', which is simplified in Figure 8.3. This is primarily a **behavioural model**.

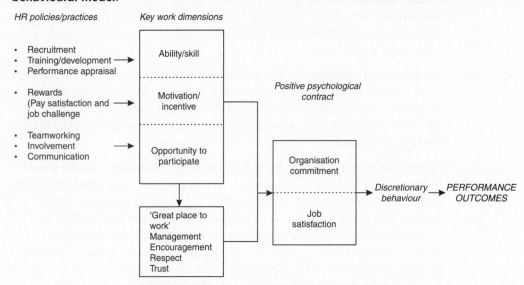

Figure 8.3: People and performance model (simplified and adapted by BPP)

A more **strategic model** was suggested by Guest *et al* (2000): Figure 8.4.

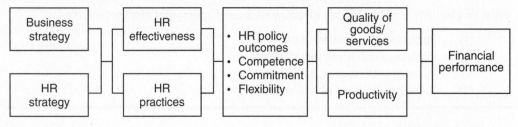

Figure 8.4: HRM and performance

ACTIVITY 8   (NO TIME LIMIT)

Using whichever of the above models appeals to you, analyse the link between the HR practices of an organisation you know (or know about) and its economic performance (or fulfilment of other outcomes, if it is a not-for-profit organisation). See if you can trace the effects all the way through the 'black box'.

4.2 HR VISION: A QUALITY WORKFORCE

Connock (1991) saw a renewed focus on the need for a 'productive, trained, flexible and innovative workforce', which he summed up as 'a **quality** workforce'. He argued that HR managers should use vision and strategies to create and maintain this quality workforce in support of business objectives, as HR's key contribution to added value.

Connock lists what he considers the **dimensions of quality** for employers.

(a) A customer services orientation
(b) Taking personal responsibility for quality output
(c) Well trained and developed staff to meet quality requirements
(d) Employee involvement in all aspects of quality
(e) Maintaining quality standards
(f) Communication and recognition programmes which reinforce quality
(g) Searching for continuous improvement
(h) Knowledge of and identification with quality from staff at all levels

4.3 HUMAN CAPITAL MANAGEMENT

'Human capital' consists of the combined intelligence, knowledge, skills, abilities and energies of the people employed by a given organisation. These attributes have **value** as an organisational resource, and can have **value added** to them by investment.

(a) *Organisations* invest in human capital (through recruitment, retention, training, development, organisation and motivation) in order to enlarge their skill base, increase levels of competence, and foster knowledge acquisition and sharing. This, in turn, should reap returns in the form of productivity, flexibility, innovation and performance.

(b) *Individuals* invest in human capital (through acquiring skills, knowledge and experience) and reap returns in terms of higher earnings, enhanced career (or employability) prospects, greater job satisfaction etc.

'Human resource accounting' (or **'human asset accounting'**) is an attempt to quantify the financial value of human capital to the firm, as part of its market worth and asset base.

Under recommendations published in 2003 by the (former) DTI's Accounting for People taskforce, employers are advised to report on human capital management (HCM) in their operating and financial reviews (FRs).

Following wide consultation with employers, investors and other stakeholders, the taskforce decided against a one-size-fits-all approach to HCM reporting. Instead, it advised that employers should report on the aspects of HCM they see as key to business performance and strategy, including training, recruitment, diversity and leadership. Employers should clearly show how these policies affect business strategy and performance.

EXAMPLE

The **Marks & Spencer** plc 'How Do We Do Business Report' (2012) states how well it is progressing against achieving its strategic objective (Plan A). Included in the whole range of measures are some relating to people:

- Provide one day's paid time off for all employees to participate in a Plan A initiative or charity event as part of an overall employee engagement programme.

- Achieve at least 90% of our Customer Assistants at the required levels of performance.

- Achieve a positive employee feedback score of at least 80% on M&S communications in our annual employee survey.

- Achieve a response rate of at least 85% in our annual employee survey with overall positive engagement and commitment scores, respectively, of at least 70%.

- Achieve a positive employee feedback score of at least 70% on 'intention to stay 12 months' in our annual employee survey.

- Report on an extended range of diversity measurements including senior management age, gender and ethnicity by 2010.

Check out the Annual Reports and Accounts (downloadable from corporate websites) of organisations that interest you, and look for the 'Our People' or 'Our employees' sections...

The *Accounting for People* recommendations highlighted four basic areas for Human Capital Reporting.

(a) The size and composition of the workforce – the numbers of people that the company relies on for its performance. This should include agency, contract staff and those on the payroll. Information should be produced in relation to age, gender and ethnicity.

(b) Employee motivation. As well as data on staff turnover and absentee rates, this should include information on arrangements for gathering employees' views.

(c) Staff training and development. This should include the match between the skills acquired and business objectives.

(d) Remuneration and fair employment – the organisation's approach to pay and incentives, and the means by which it satisfies itself that it does not discriminate unfairly.

WEBLINK

CIPD 2012 *Factsheet on Human Capital*

▶▶ www.cipd.co.uk/hr-resources/factsheets/human-capital.aspx

FOR DISCUSSION

'The amount of information in a company's annual report about its employees, and on how the ways in which they are managed and developed add value to the business, is pathetically inadequate. Maybe there's a bland statement on people being our most important asset, a few pictures, a dozen pages on executives' rewards and perhaps total numbers employed in the notes – but that's about it. Hardly a "true and fair" view in our knowledge-, information- and service-based economy.'

(Brown & Baron, 2003)

What benefits can you see for organisations, employees and other stakeholders (shareholders, potential investors, potential employees) in having more rigorous human capital reporting?

4.4 TALENT MANAGEMENT

DEFINITION

Talent management is 'the process of ensuring that the organisation has the talented people it needs to attain its business goals' (Armstrong, 2012). It refers to the overall process whereby an organisation systematically attracts skilled, high-quality recruits; integrates new workers into the organisation; systematically performance manages, trains and develops workers, in order to meet current and future competence requirements; and retains skilled workers within the organisation.

The concept of talent management addresses the flow of 'talent' (skills and abilities) into, and through, the organisation or team at all levels. It should be included in human resource planning at the strategic level, and implemented in day-to-day people management processes.

Key talent management processes include (Armstrong 2012):

- Talent planning – the process of establishing how many and what sort of talented people are needed now and in the future

- Resourcing – the outcomes of talent planning are programmes for obtaining people from within and outside the organisation

- Attraction and retention policies and programmes – these policies and programmes describe the approach to ensuring that the organisation gets and keeps the talent it needs

- Talent audit – identifies those with potential, often through a performance management assessment; it provides the basis for career planning and development

- Role development – ensuring the roles provide responsibility, challenge and autonomy required to create engagement and motivation; taking steps to ensure that people have the opportunity and are given the encouragement to learn and develop in their roles

- Talent relationship management – building effective relationships with people in their roles

- Performance management – these processes, including 360-degree feedback, provide ways of building relationships with people, identifying talent and potential, planning learning and development activities and making the most of the talent possessed by the organisation

- Learning and development – these policies and programmes are essential components in the process of talent management – ensuring people acquire and enhance the skills and competences they need

- Leadership and management development – these policies can include change management, people and performance management; decision-making and difficult conversations

- Management succession planning – to ensure that, as far as possible, the organisation has the managers it requires for future business needs

- Career management – the provision of opportunities for people to develop their abilities and their careers

CHAPTER ROUNDUP

- While HRM is about 'success through people', there are two different orientations of this view.

  - 'Hard' HRM emphasises the close integration of human resource policies with business strategy, and regards employees as a resource to be quantitatively measured and managed in the same rational way as any other resource being exploited for maximum returns.

  - 'Soft' HRM views employees as valued assets and as a source of competitive advantage through their commitment, adaptability and high level of skills and performance.

- The Michigan model stresses the matching of HR policy to business strategy (hard), while the Harvard model stresses development and neutrality (soft).

- HR policies may be categorised as tight or loose according to the extent of managerial control which they assume to be necessary to achieve performance goals. Guest identifies the contrast between (tight) systems of compliance and (loose) systems of commitment.

- Storey developed an ideal type model of HRM contrasted to the traditional personnel/industrial relations model of labour management. Twenty-seven points of difference (expressed as extremes) were identified in the areas of beliefs and assumptions, strategy, the line management role and key levers used to shape the employment relationship.

- Strategic HRM is the direction of HR policy in such a way as to achieve the strategic goals of the business. HR strategy may be developed using business strategy, 'best fit', 'best practice' or 'configuration/bundling' approaches.

- There is increasing emphasis on the need to report accurately on the value of human resources and their impact on business performance, with Human Capital Reporting requirements introduced in 2005. Various models have been devised to shed light on the 'black box' process whereby people inputs are transformed into performance outputs.

QUICK QUIZ

1   What are the features of hard HRM?

2   What are the philosophical underpinnings of soft HRM?

3   What levels of management should HR be involved in, according to the Michigan model?

4   List four key ideas of the Harvard Framework.

5   Distinguish between:

    (a)   Theory X and Theory Y
    (b)   Compliance and Commitment

6   What is the difference between a personnel/IR approach and an HRM approach in the dimensions of:

    (a)   The role of rules
    (b)   The nature of relations
    (c)   Prized managerial skills
    (d)   The focus of attention for interventions

7   What does 'strategic fit' involve as applied to HRM?

8   Distinguish between a 'best fit' and 'best practice' approach to HR strategy.

9   Draw Guest's model of HRM and performance.

10 What is human capital?

ANSWERS TO QUICK QUIZ

1   Matching of HR and business strategy; focus on yield on human resources; focus on quantitative measures of management effectiveness; emphasis on the need for performance management and managerial control.   (see Para 1.1)

2   Human relations school of management; socio-psychology; view of employees as assets/means rather than costs/objects; unitarist ideology; stakeholder perspective.
                                                                                        (Para 1.2)

3   Strategic (long-term, focus on future 'fit'), managerial (medium-term, focus on acquisition, retention and development), operational day-to-day, focus on supporting business activities.   (Para 1.3)

4   HRM involves all management decisions affecting the employment relationship. Organisations are made up of stakeholders and there is a trade-off between their interests. HRM is influenced by a range of contextual factors. Line managers take responsibility for aligning HR policy and competitive strategy.   (Para 1.4)

5   See Paragraphs 1.6 and 1.7 for a full account.

6   (a)   Importance of rules v 'can do' outlook creating impatience with rules
    (b)   Pluralist v unitarist
    (c)   Negotiation v facilitation
    (d)   Personnel procedures v wide-ranging cultural, structural and personnel strategies.
                                                                                        (Para 2.1)

7   HR strategies integrated with business strategy to support its achievement (vertical fit). HR practices developed to complement and mutually reinforce one another with consistent results (horizontal fit). Line managers internalising the importance of human resources.
                                                                                        (Para 3.2)

8   'Best practice' assumes there are universally effective HR practices; 'best fit' assumes that 'good practices' will need to be selected and adapted to fit the external and internal context of the organisation, and remain sensitive to change.   (Para 3.3)

9   See Paragraph 4.1, Figure 8.4.

10 The combined intelligence, knowledge, skills, abilities and energies of people employed by an organisation.   (Para 4.3)

ANSWERS TO ACTIVITIES

1   *Hard:* high levels of rules, procedures and instructions, and appropriate training; strong corporate culture/values for the purposes of selection, socialisation and 'weeding out'; selection on the basis of predetermined job criteria; close supervision and work inspection; administrative controls on time-keeping, absence, hours worked and so on; performance management focused on monitoring of performance against imposed standards and targets; job descriptions; job evaluation based on standard measures of performance; payment by results (narrowly defined); short-term cost-benefit evaluation of HR policies; centralised control over HR functions; adversarial mechanisms for dealing with discipline, grievance and relationships with trade unions; 'need to know' communication policies; welfare to minimise costs/lost production; managerial status symbols and tiered terms and conditions.

2   *Soft:* articulation of goals and values; strong corporate culture/values for the purposes of inspiration – especially quality; flexible working methods; emphasis on teamwork; self-managed time-keeping and attendance; consultation and agreement on work targets and criteria; values- and outputs-driven criteria; consultation and agreement on issues affecting the workforce; delegation and empowerment; HR fulfilling and enabling rather than controlling role; training for development, employability, flexibility; personal development and improvement plans; employee relations based on communication and involvement; welfare based on well-being and enabled performance; reward systems and performance management based on collaboratively agreed criteria; harmonised terms and conditions.

3   The writer is describing a Theory X, tight-control approach. In a recession, organisations are likely to be faced with pressures to cut costs and improve productivity in order to remain competitive: managers may be tempted to adopt this approach towards HR issues to achieve these goals. Remember that 'loose-tight' is a continuum. According to a contingency view of strategic 'fit', there is nothing inherently right or wrong about loose or tight control strategies: the chosen approach must suit the business needs of the organisation and respond to changes in its environment.

4   This answer will be highly individual to you and your situation (which may indicate why commitment is not easy to pin down or foster in practice). Benefits to *you* (analogous to the employee) may have included enjoyment, sense of purpose, possibly extra effort resulting in better results, which in turn may lead to further satisfaction and opportunities for development. Benefits for your *trainers* (analogous to employers) may have included the same, perhaps defined in different ways: better attendance and time-keeping, more creative ideas put forward to improve the course, encouragement to other students from your positive attitude, better results. Ways of *increasing commitment* may have included: clearer instructions, linking your studies to your goals in HRM, more enjoyable or challenging teaching methods and activities, and perhaps your willingness to put effort in now for rewards later.

5   Some examples you may have thought of:

(a)   *Institutionalise conflict* through strict procedures for disciplinary action, grievance handling, appeals mechanisms, conflict resolution, negotiation with union representatives. (These are all good and helpful in the event of conflict – but they do assume that conflict is going to occur…) *De-emphasise conflict:* interpersonal conflict resolution handled on a contingency basis by management; win-win approach (assuming mutuality of interests); emphasise and reward teamworking and co-operation.

(b)   *Restrict communication:* institutionalised communication avenues (eg house journal or bulletin); managerial control over in-house communication; hierarchical, functional channels of communication; 'need to know' policies; lack of training in communication skills; centralised information storage and retrieval; discouragement of social networking among employees (by job and work environment design). *Increase communication:* training in communication; cultural reinforcement of communication (management example, reward and appraisal on communication skills); encouragement of multi-functional teamworking and/or briefings; encouragement of informal networking; focus on quality/customer overriding procedure.

6   Empowerment might influence recruitment/selection in the following ways.

(a)   Empowered workers may wish to take over responsibility for recruiting new members of their teams.

(b)   Jobs (and therefore job descriptions and selection criteria) would need to reflect new ways of working such as multi-skilling, team-working etc.

(c)   Communication, leadership and facilitation skills would become key selection criteria for managers.

Empowerment might influence training as follows.

(a)   Training would be initiated and shaped by the job needs of empowered workers: relevant to the job, focused on areas such as responsibility, planning, teamworking and communication.

(b)   The trainer's role would be that of 'coach', reflecting the empowering/equipping philosophy towards training.

(c)   The manager may well take on the coaching/facilitating role: training would be seen to be a continuous on-the-job process and part of personal development by employees.

7   (a)   For innovation, the organisation will require creative behaviour, long-term thinking, collaborative working, willingness to take risks and tolerance of unpredictability. HR practices that may help foster these qualities include: teamworking, high communication flow, multi-skilling and flexible working; broader career/development paths allowing flexibility; longer-term, team-based performance appraisal; selection and reward for innovation values.

    (b)   For cost leadership, the organisation will need a focus on output quantity (with less concern for quality), a relatively short-term outlook, and controlled/low-risk performance. HR practices that may help foster these qualities include: narrow job design and explicit job descriptions; short-term, output-focused appraisal and reward; close monitoring of employee activities; little investment in training and development; focus on cost minimisation.

    (c)   In the growth stage, the organisation will require more progressive and sophisticated recruitment and selection (compared to start-up), training and development, performance management processes and reward systems, a focus on achieving high commitment and emphasis on developing stable employee relations.

    (d)   In decline, the organisation may have to shift to rationalisation, down-sizing by accelerated wastage or redundancy, curtailing of HR programmes (especially employee development) in order to cut costs, the attempt to marginalise or de-recognise trade unions.

8   This exercise is designed to help you build up case study material. It may also help you to realise how complex the relationships between all these variables are. In the 'People and Performance' model, Figure 8.3, for example, you might notice that the line management aspects (trust, respect) also *increase* the likelihood that HR policies (eg communication, teamworking, job satisfaction) will be successful. This underlines the key role of line managers in delivering HRM outcomes.

09 Flexibility

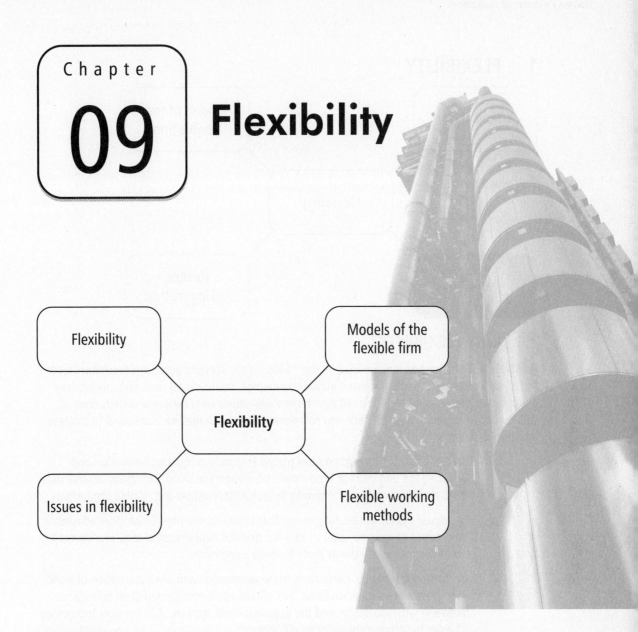

- Flexibility
- Models of the flexible firm
- **Flexibility**
- Issues in flexibility
- Flexible working methods

Introduction

In Chapters 2 and 3, we noted that sourcing labour requirements may be achieved from *within* the organisation as well as from the external labour market. The efficiency with which labour resources can be deployed and redeployed, at need, within the organisation depends on a measure of **flexibility**. Employees who are functionally versatile (or multi-skilled) and culturally flexible may be redeployed across the functional boundaries previously set by job descriptions and occupational demarcation zones. A numerically flexible workforce may be deployed at periods of peak workloads. Given the pace of change in technologies and marketplaces, and the 'ungluing' of traditional organisational structures to meet changing customer demands, flexibility is one of *the* Hot Topics in HRM!

Your objectives

In this chapter you will learn about the following.

- Labour market trends reinforcing the need for flexibility
- Models of the flexible firm
- Types of flexibility and flexible working methods
- The advantages and disadvantages of flexible working practices

1 FLEXIBILITY

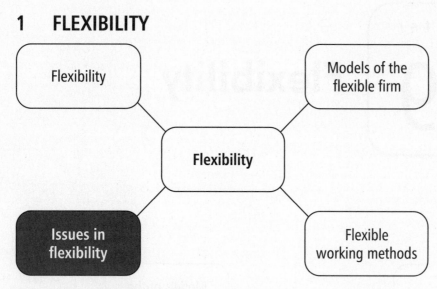

1.1 WHY FLEXIBILITY?

Flexibility first emerged as a major issue in the 1980s, as the Western European economies were forced to respond to change. Increased global competition, international recession, uncertainty about future markets and the effects of new technology undermined historical expectations of stable economic growth and the pace and complexity of such changes has continued to increase into the 21st century.

(a)   Increased global competition has placed emphasis on quality, innovation and reducing the unit costs of production. Job design and the organisation of work must both mobilise employees' energies for quality/innovation and reliable productivity.

(b)   Increased market uncertainty means that organisations need to be more adaptable to changes in demand: able to vary the size and deployment of their workforces to meet demand as effectively and efficiently as possible.

(c)   Technological change, particularly in the automation and computerisation of work processes and information flows, has eroded traditional demarcation boundaries between jobs: job design and the organisation of work must fit the new technology in order to secure its benefits for efficiency.

(d)   Demographic (and related labour market) changes have highlighted the need for flexible job and career designs, in order to meet the needs of dual income families, women and older workers for 'work-life balance'. (This is discussed in more detail below.)

The need for flexibility therefore underpins new working practices:

(a)   Increasing managerial ability to adapt the size and deployment of the workforce in line with changing demand and supply

(b)   Increasing scope for flexible working for individual employees

(c)   Raising the quality and/or quantity of workforce output.

1.2 LABOUR MARKET TRENDS AND FLEXIBILITY

In Chapter 2, we discussed how HR planners need to take account of demographic and other factors in the internal and external labour markets, in order to meet the organisation's demand for skills. Specific drivers of flexibility include the following.

(a) **Age structure**

Social Trends shows that the number of economically active people in the age group 16 – 24 is falling, while those aged 25 – 44 is rising. As well as the resourcing implications discussed in Chapter 2, this means that an increasing proportion of the workforce may have family and child-rearing responsibilities, or care of a dependent aged relative: focus on 'work-life balance' (Paragraph 1.3) has created the need for flexibility in working hours and place of work to support these workers.

(b) **Diversity**

The *Workplace Employee Relations Survey* data (WERS 2004) shows (Bratton & Gold, 2007) that in the UK:

- Women's share of total employment has continued to increase

- In some 44% of workplaces that employ part-time staff, women make up all of these part-time staff

- The majority of women workers are engaged in clerical, serving or cleaning work, but female participation has also increased in middle and senior management.

(The Workplace Employment Relations Study is a survey of employment relations in Britain that collects data from employers, employee representatives and employees in a representative sample of workplaces. It has been undertaken in 1980, 1984, 1990, 1998 and 2004. Fieldwork for the sixth WERS (WERS6) was completed in June 2012)

Gender diversity in the workplace, and the need to recruit and retain female workers (in order to meet both skill/labour shortages and equal opportunity requirements) has reinforced the focus on work-life balance. Organisations need to deploy labour flexibly in order to accommodate the demands made of working mothers (and fathers, given the related trend towards shared family responsibilities and dual career families) and the desire for career breaks and return after child-rearing.

(c) **The use of non-standard contracts**

The WERS 2004 data shows that the use of non-standard forms of employment has now become 'commonplace' in UK workplaces. 8.3% of workplaces employed part-time employees (less than 30 hours per week), up from 79% in 1998. Almost one-third of workplaces had employees on temporary contracts. There has also been an increase in the contracting out or outsourcing of services such as cleaning, transport, security – and HR and training.

(d) **Differences in particular labour markets**

Employers may compete for labour and skills in a number of different markets: local, national and international.

- Particular factors in the local labour market (people living in the 'travel to work area' or within reasonable commuting distance) may create pressure for flexibility. For example: geographical dispersion or lack of public transportation may require flexible starting hours, or work-from-home options.

- National/regional skill shortages and wage costs may encourage the outsourcing or 'off-shoring' of operations to low-cost labour countries, or the co-opting of overseas team-members through 'virtual' collaboration using ICT links.

- Different occupational structures and orientations (at local and national level) may also require different approaches to the employment relationship, career management and so on. Professionally and technically qualified staff, for example, may be treated differently (as 'core' employees) from lower-skilled and high-mobility workers (who may be more flexibly contracted).

(e) **Regulation of working hours**

The Working Time Regulations 1998 and subsequent amendments set (currently negotiable) limits on working hours per week and entitlement to rest breaks and days. In order to cover equivalent workloads, employers may have to implement job-sharing and other flexible work patterns. The EU Working Time Directive regulates minimum holidays, paid breaks, rest periods and night work and creates a right to work not more than 48 hours per week on average. Workers can opt out of the 48 hour maximum.

WEBLINK

The Workplace Employment Relations Survey (WERS) 2004

▶▶ www.wers2004.info/about/ourservices.php

ACTIVITY 1 (30 MINS)

To help develop your research skills see if you can locate the following information.

- The number of people in employment in the UK in the current year.
- The number of women in the UK labour force in the current year.
- The number of young unemployed people in the UK in the current year.

1.3 WORK-LIFE BALANCE

Work-life balance is a concept which recognises the need for employers to support workers in achieving a balance between the demands of their work and the demands of home and family responsibilities (including the care of children, older people and sick family members).

Flexible working policies, designed to give employees options in regard to their hours and/or locations of work, have been supported in recent years by equal opportunity and family-friendly rights law. These have provided a package of entitlements including: annual leave; maximum working hours; parental leave and time off for dependent care; maternity/paternity leave and adoption leave; equal rights for part-time workers and so on.

The *Employment Act 2002* provided for an additional package of rights in relation to flexible working.

(a) Any employee with 26 weeks' service, who is the parent or legal guardian of a child under six (or under 18 if the child is disabled) has the right to request flexible working arrangements: to change the total numbers of hours contracted to work; when those hours are worked; and/or where the work is done. The *Work and Families Act 2006* extended this rights to carers of adults, from April 2007.

(b) Requests must be written/e-mailed, and include details of the applicant's eligibility, the nature and timetable of the requested change, and consideration of the impact of the change on the business.

(c) The employer has 28 days to consider the request and approve – or at least meet with the applicant to discuss the application. Employees are entitled to be accompanied by a work colleague at any discussion.

(d) If the application is declined, the employee may appeal. Justified reasons for refusal include: the burden of extra costs; negative impact on productivity, quality or performance; inability to reorganise or redistribute work; or inability to recruit extra staff to make up lost hours.

(e) If the employer refuses to consider a request, or fails to follow the statutory procedure, the employee has three months to bring a complaint before an Employment Tribunal.

'For years, best-practice organisations have taken an informal approach to fielding flexible working requests, with local line managers making decisions that best fit an individual or department, by involving other team members in the matter. In many cases, this method will continue to be the most effective in driving a flexible work culture while avoiding red tape.' (Cartwright, 2003)

WEBLINK

For more information on work-life balance, you may like to check out the following websites.

►► www.tuc.org.uk/workplace/tuc-20603-f0.cfm

Parents at Work

►► www.workingfamilies.org.uk

EXAMPLE

'Putting part-time workers together in teams is the key to creating a happier flexible workforce, according to Kwik Fit Insurance (KFI).

'The company brings teams of part-time shift workers together under a scheme called "Morning Mums" and Elizabeth McVeigh, senior HR co-ordinator, [said] it had brought real benefits.

'McVeigh explained that the idea behind the teams is to give extra support to workers who have other commitments such as taking children to school, being adult carers or students. Shifts are organised to fit around these and allow a good work-life balance.

'Marie Stewart, KFI recruitment and induction training manager, and formerly a Morning Mum, said: "It makes the potential problem of juggling children and work much easier and brings with it a happier and more satisfied member of staff who in turn gives us a better performance."

'McVeigh added that happy workers tend to stay at the company longer. She said that the company also benefits because the shift pattern Morning Mums do coincide with one of the busiest times of day.

'The scheme is more practical than mixing full-time and part-time workers together, she added. "It's more difficult to set up meetings when part-time and full-time workers work together. When part-timers are all together and based in the same place it's easier to organise and maintain continuity," McVeigh said.

'Productivity has risen under the scheme and staff satisfaction rates were found to be high during the company's quarterly feedback survey. "We also found that staff scored flexibility within the organisation very highly and our part-timers felt very supported," McVeigh explained.'

(Churchard, 2009)

SIGNPOST

Flexibility is clearly in line with the HRM approach to making the most effective and efficient use of the human resource. As we saw in Chapter 8, however, there are two ways of looking at HR issues: from a 'hard' perspective and from a 'soft' perspective. What does flexibility look like from each of these.

1.4 HARD OR SOFT HRM?

There are two distinct orientations to flexibility, in accordance with the hard and soft views of HRM.

(a) Flexibility is a key goal of strategic HRM, with its hard emphasis on meeting business needs through **efficient deployment** of the labour resources. 'Hard' flexibility, in the words of Beardwell and Holden (1997), means 'the ability to adjust the size and mix of labour inputs in response to changes in product demand so that excess labour is not carried by the organisation'. This approach has been popularised as '**lean production**': minimising overhead labour costs by reducing jobs not directly contributing to production, and minimising the cost of directly productive labour by raising productivity.

(b) Flexibility is consistent with the soft HRM emphasis on **empowerment and involvement** of employees for increased commitment, motivation and development. 'Soft' flexibility means creating an adaptable workforce, by involving employees in decision-making, broadening their skills individually and through teamworking and creating a culture of continuous learning and improvement focused on quality outcomes rather than adherence to procedures.

1.5 MUTUAL BENEFITS

Depending on whether a hard or soft flexibility approach is used, flexibility may have benefits for the employing organisation and for employees. We discuss the advantages and disadvantages of specific flexible working practices, from both points of view, as we proceed through this chapter. In general, however, the intended benefits are as follows.

(a) For the **organisation**, it offers a cost-effective, efficient way of utilising the labour resource. Under competitive pressure, technological innovation and a variety of other changes, organisations need a flexible, 'lean' workforce for efficiency, control and predictability. The stability of the organisation in a volatile environment depends on its ability to adapt swiftly to meet changes, without incurring cost penalties or suffering waste. If employee flexibility can be achieved with the co-operation of the employees and their representatives, there may be an end to

BPP
LEARNING MEDIA

demarcation disputes, costly redundancy packages and other consequences of apparently rational organisation design.

(b)   From the point of view of the **employee**, the erosion of rigid specialisation, the micro-division of labour and the inflexible working week can also offer benefits. For example, a higher quality of working life; an accommodation with non-work interests and demands (work-life balance); greater job satisfaction, through variety of work; and perhaps job security and material benefits, since a versatile, mobile, flexible employee is likely to be more attractive to employers and have a higher value in the current labour market climate.

(c)   In addition, some flexible working practices, like 'tele-commuting' (or working from home) can support both organisations and individuals in reducing their 'carbon footprint' (in line with the UK's commitments under the Kyoto Protocol), by reducing greenhouse gas (GHG) emissions from commuting.

FOR DISCUSSION

Flexible working is the most valued benefit for UK employees, ahead of material perks such as bonuses, research revealed today.

In a PricewaterhouseCoopers (PwC) Managing Tomorrow's People survey of 1,167 workers, 47% rated flexible working arrangements as the most important benefit above performance-related bonuses, which came second (19%).

Flexible working was given fairly equal priority by men and women, with 41% and 54% respectively ranking this benefit the most valuable. Moreover, a better work-life balance was seen as more achievable in the long term by 42% respondents than vastly increased responsibility and salary (39%).

Michael Rendell, head of HR services at PwC, said two years of recession have changed people's attitude towards work.

'With companies mindful of taking on new employees, existing staff have been expected to do more with less,' he said. 'Our survey indicates that employees may be feeling the pressure, with large numbers hoping for a better work-life balance in the future, and half saying they would rather work for themselves.'

With bonuses unpredictable in uncertain economic conditions, employees are looking for broader benefits, Rendell added.

(*Personnel Today*, 2010)

How might work-life, family-friendly and flexible polices be undermined by corporate culture, management style and economic reality – particularly in the time of recession?

SIGNPOST

You may have noticed from the preceding paragraphs that there are a number of different types of flexibility, including not only the employer's ability to change the size of the workforce in response to demand, but the broadening of employees' skills and task variety, and the re-structuring of the working day or week. We now summarise the flexibility approaches.

1.6 TYPES OF FLEXIBILITY

There are a number of possible approaches to flexibility.

Type of flexibility	Responding to:	HRM approach
Numerical	Fluctuations in demand for staff numbers (seasonal, cyclical, task-related and so on)	Use of non-permanent, non-career labour: temporary staff, part-time staff, short-contract staff, consultants, sub-contractors
Temporal	Fluctuations in working patterns, over 24 hours/week/year: fluctuations in demand for labour at particular times; the need for work-life balance and support for equal opportunity	Use of 'flexi-time' and variations: overtime, shift-working, annualised hours
Functional (versatility)	Fluctuations in demand for particular skills – not necessarily related to staff numbers (since one person can be multi-skilled)	Deployment of staff across job/skill boundaries ('demarcation lines'): multi-skilling, multi-disciplinary teams, fewer or broader job descriptions
Financial	The need for functional/temporal staff to be rewarded flexibly and fairly – since 'the job' is no longer a fixed basis for reward. The need for choice (eg in incentive and benefit schemes) to raise value of rewards in a diverse workforce	Performance – and/or profit-related pay; individual pay negotiation; broad-band pay schemes; flexible benefits
Locational	Opportunities presented by information and communication technology (ICT) to reduce office costs and create 'virtual' (dispersed but interconnected) teams	Use of home-working, tele-working and networking; use of ICT to facilitate mobile working (eg for sales and service staff)
Cultural	The need for a change of traditional attitudes towards jobs, careers, occupational identify: the need for a culture which embraces flexibility, variety, change, entrepreneurship	Recruitment and reward systems geared to employ and advance culturally flexible and versatile people; communication of flexibility and work-life balance as key values; counselling to help overcome fear of change

ACTIVITY 2   (NO TIME LIMIT)

Observe staff at a local supermarket and talk to friends who might work for one of the big supermarket chains. What evidence of flexibility can you see within organisations such as these? Which 'type' of flexibility is suggested by each of your examples?

SIGNPOST

We now look in more detail at two key models for numerical flexibility.

2   MODELS OF THE FLEXIBLE FIRM

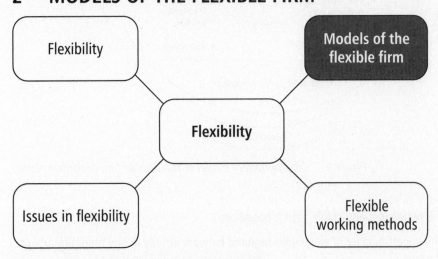

2.1   THE CORE/PERIPHERY MODEL

Fluctuations in the (numerical) demand for workers may be foreseeable: regular peaks due to daily, weekly or seasonal cycles (such as lunch and dinner times at an all-day restaurant, Saturdays at supermarkets, or Easter at a chocolate factory) or irregular peaks due to organisational activity (such as a product launch). Other fluctuations may be unforeseeable: industrial action affecting competitors; events or reports in the media which stimulate or 'kill' demand for the product/service and so on.

The organisation cannot afford to employ a full-time workforce based on the best-case scenario of greatest demand. Indeed, in times of pressure to downsize the workforce (or at least, not to expand it), organisations prefer to increase their proportion of non-permanent labour, to avoid redundancies and/or seasonal layoffs.

The **'flexible firm' or 'core periphery'** model (Atkinson, 1984; Atkinson & Meager, 1986) divides the workforce into 'core' and 'peripheral' groups: Figure 9.1.

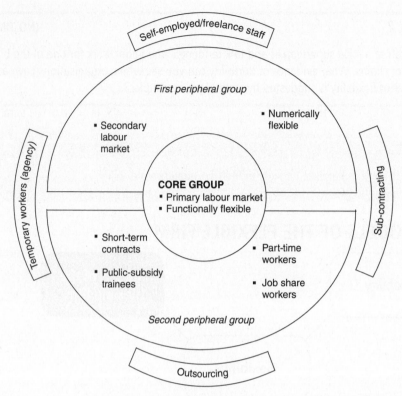

Figure 9.1: Core-periphery model of the flexible firm (Atkinson, 1984)

The core

The **core** group is permanent and stable, and is based on:

(a) The lowest number of employees required by work activity at any time throughout the year

(b) Core tasks which are specific to the firm and require firm-specific skills and experience.

The core group offers **functional** flexibility by virtue of re- or multi-skilling: training, retraining and redeployment within core tasks.

HR implications include:

(a) The need for training in core skills.

(b) The need to offer employment security/continuity in order to facilitate skill/experience build-up and in order to protect the firm's investment in core workers' training.

(c) The need for reward structures which reflect and support flexibility and multi-skilling by removing rigid grade or functional barriers.

(d) The need to secure the commitment of the core workforce: this would usually foster commitment-based 'soft' HRM policies.

The periphery

The **peripheral** group is designed to offer numerical flexibility: the ability to meet short-term fluctuations in demand for skills which are not distinctive of the firm. It includes:

(a) Full-time employees in areas where there is a high level of mobility and wastage/turnover (clerical/secretarial and so on), creating a relatively numerically flexible internal labour market: the *first peripheral group*.

(b)   Workers on non-standard contracts: the *second peripheral group*.

(c)   'Distance' workers not employed by the organisation, but contracted to supply services as required.

Core-periphery flexibility

By acting as a 'buffer' against the need to downsize the organisation in the face of fluctuating demand (Figure 9.2), the core-periphery model allows for relatively:

(a)   'Hard' HR policies aimed at reducing labour costs, and avoiding labour excesses and shortages, applied at the periphery.

(b)   'Soft' HR policies aimed at increasing productivity and commitment, providing employment security and organisational stability, applied at the core.

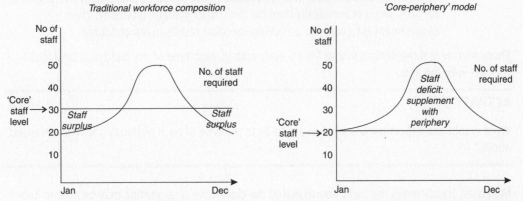

Figure 9.2: The flexible firm and HR planning

2.2   THE SHAMROCK ORGANISATION

Charles Handy (1989) put forward the idea of the shamrock (or clover-leaf) organisation, giving examples such as Rank Xerox and IBM.

Mullins (1999) represents this as follows: Figure 9.3.

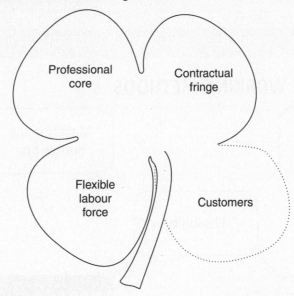

Figure 9.3: The Shamrock Organisation

(a)   The **professional core** are permanently-employed people who represent the distinctive knowledge and competences of the firm. They are qualified professionals, technicians and managers. Their commitment is focused on their work and career within the organisation.

(b)   The **flexible labour force** are temporary and part-time workers who can be brought in as and when needed – especially to meet peaks in the demand for services (since they have to be supplied in 'real time'). Their commitment is typically focused on the immediate job and work group, rather than career or the organisation. However, they are crucial in maintaining standards of service – so it is important for the firm not to treat them 'casually': they should receive fair and equitable treatment (now enshrined in employment law), adequate training and status.

(c)   The **contractual fringe** are external providers (freelancers, consultants and sub-contractors) who are able to undertake non-core activities and/or provide specialist services, more economically than the firm could manage internally. Their commitment is typically to achieving specified results in return for fees.

These represent three distinct labour forces, each with its own type of psychological (and legal) contract with the firm.

ACTIVITY 3   (5 MINS)

What would you expect the key HRM issues to be in the case of each of Handy's 'leaves' discussed above?

Moreover, Handy notes the 'lucky' fourth leaf of the clover: the organisation may be able to 'sub-contract' some sales, service and supply tasks – for free – to **customers**. Information and communication technology (ICT) has supported a wide range of 'self-service' applications such as: internet/phone banking and automated teller machines (ATMs); internet/telephone reservations and ticketing, in entertainment and travel; online information services etc – in addition to traditional self-service retail and catering outlets, self-assembly products and so on. This should allow labour savings in other 'leaves' of the organisation.

SIGNPOST

We now consider other approaches to numerical, locational, functional and temporal flexibility.

3   FLEXIBLE WORKING METHODS

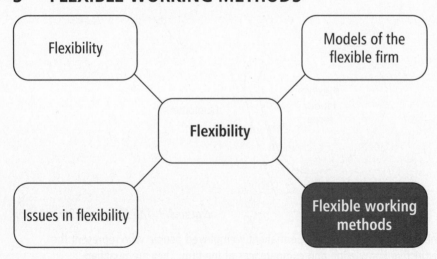

3.1 PART-TIME AND TEMPORARY WORKING

DEFINITION

Under the EU Directive on part-time work, a **part-time employee** is someone with a contract or employment relationship whose normal hours of work, averaged over a period of up to a year, are less than the normal hours of comparable full-timers.

ACTIVITY 4 (45 MINS)

Why do you think there has been an increase in part-time working?

Consider the employer and employee points of view.

The thrust of legislation and court decisions has been to protect 'peripheral' employees from exploitation by 'hard' flexibility policies.

EU Directives on part-time and temporary work were incorporated into UK law by regulations and a Code of Practice under the Employment Relations Act 1999. Part-time and temporary or fixed-contract employees are now entitled to the same employment and health and safety protection as permanent full-time staff: *Part-time Workers (Prevention of Less Favourable Treatment) Regulations 2000*, and *Fixed Term Employees (Prevention of Less Favourable Treatment) Regulations 2002*.

(a) Part-timers (who work eight hours or more per week) may not be treated less favourably because they work part-time. They are entitled to the same hourly rate of pay, sick pay, access to training, selection for promotion, protection from unfair dismissal, and so on. They also have the same entitlements to annual leave and maternity/paternity leave but on a *pro rata* basis.

(b) Obstacles to part-time work should be removed: there should be opportunities for part-time work at all levels, and for transfer between full-time, part-time and job-sharing arrangements: part-time (and temporary) workers should be informed of permanent full-time vacancies, for example.

(c) The *Working Time Regulations 1998* give equal rights to part-time and temporary workers in respect of night working, minimum rest periods and Health and Safety protection services, since they are held to be particularly at risk.

(d) Temporary and fixed-contract workers are also entitled to the same social security benefits as permanent employees.

(e) Individuals engaged under temporary contracts must be informed of the reasons for their being employed on a temporary rather than a permanent contract.

(f) Health and safety legislation applies equally to full-time, part-time and temporary workers.

FOR DISCUSSION

Does the protection and extension of part-time and temporary workers' rights defeat the object of the core-periphery model? What does it suggest about the perceived advantages of the model to employers and its perceived disadvantages to peripheral employees?

International comparisons

The USA has a comparatively free approach to part-time and temporary workers. Beardwell and Holden (1997) suggest that 'there are grounds for thinking that workers employed by temporary help agencies or contracting firms in the USA are denied the benefits of employment security, job progression and benefits such as pensions that go with internal labour markets.'

3.2 JOB-SHARING

Job-sharing is an approach to part-time job creation in which an existing full-time position is split in two, so that two people can share it, working part-time and paid pro-rata.

3.3 TELE-WORKING AND HOME-WORKING

DEFINITION

Tele-working describes the process of working from home, or from a satellite office close to home, with the aid of networked or internet-linked computers, fax machines and other ICT applications.

Tele-working offers:

(a) Savings on overheads, particularly premises costs, in view of rising rents in many of the major cities in the UK.

(b) The opportunity to bring into employment skilled and experienced people for whom traditional working practices have hitherto been impracticable: single parents, mothers, the disabled, carers and so on.

(c) Elimination of the need to commute – with consequent reductions in traffic congestion, fuel consumption, travel costs, pollution and greenhouse gas (GHG) emissions, commuter stress.

(d) Better work-life balance: less stress; more employment opportunities for those with family responsibilities.

Tele-working may take the form of:

(a) **Homeworking**: traditional outworkers such as home typists, market-research/ tele-sales workers etc

(b) **Freelancing**: working for a number of different clients from a home office, or in client offices

(c) **Mobile working**: using laptop computers, the internet and mobile phone technology to work 'on the road' (eg field sales staff)

(d) **Call-centre working**: working in specialist centres providing helpline services, telesales, data entry etc.

EXAMPLE

Being more efficient, improving recruitment and retention, and helping staff with their work-life balance: these were the motivations for the AA when they first piloted their virtual call centre in the Leeds area back in 1997.

All the AA's call centres are UK-based and the homeworking team are no different. In all, there are 250 home-based staff handling emergency breakdown calls, based around Newcastle, Manchester, Birmingham and Cardiff.

Kevin Horgan, the AA's Head of Emergency Breakdown Call Handling, is an enthusiast for the new way of working.

'We saw it as a way to expand the opportunities we were offering to our people. Like any call centre we're always exploring new avenues to help deal with attrition and retention. We consolidated our call centre operation in Leeds a number of years ago, and then ran a pilot for existing staff there to see if homeworking was a viable option.

The benefits were manifold. It provided the business with an opportunity to achieve productivity gains from people working split shifts and it gave our employees the opportunity to work in their own environment without the cost and inconvenience of commuting. It works from everyone's point of view. '

The AA expanded on the pilot, and now virtual call centre work has been mainstreamed. According to Kevin, there's been no reduction in the levels of service provided – quite the opposite in fact – thanks to increased staffing levels at drive time:

'It's enabled us to improve our management of peaks and troughs of demand throughout the day and we've reduced attrition. Our productivity has definitely increased with the quality of customer service always high on the agenda.'

(www.flexibility.co.uk – case study)

Barnes (1997) helpfully summarises how teleworking might be most effectively managed.

- Develop relationships of trust.

- Have policies covering operational issues such as insurance, confidentiality, taxation (possible capital gains tax liability arising from the use of domestic property for business purpose), security and health and safety.

- Use criteria when recruiting which enables the selection of those with self-discipline, good self-management skills and other attributes of effective teleworkers.

- Have formal and informal channels of communication (social isolation is the major disadvantage of teleworking as reported by the workers themselves) with visits by supervisors, regular meetings at the office, use of telephone, newsletters, informal gatherings etc.

(We might add video-conferencing, Skype, e-mail, texting and Twitter today!)

- Clearly define quantitative and qualitative targets to 'manage-by-results' and give thought to monitoring performance, making use of electronics whenever possible.

- Have performance appraisal, career management and training policies which meet the needs of teleworkers.

- Be open to part-time home and part-time office working and even 'occasional' teleworking if appropriate.

- Maintain the voluntary principle and have a 'revolving door' policy whereby as circumstances change workers can return to full-time office working.

- Evaluate outcomes against objective measures in productivity, quality of output, accommodation cost etc.

3.4 MULTISKILLING

Jobs are changing from simple, well-defined tasks (set out in job descriptions) to more flexible, multi-dimensional roles. Such a shift recognises that:

(a) Performing a whole meaningful job is more satisfying to a worker than performing only one of its component tasks (as in 'scientific' job design).

(b) Allowing workers to see the big picture enables and encourages them to contribute information and ideas for improvements, which might not otherwise have come to light.

(c) The focus on the task and overall objectives reduces the need for tight managerial control and supervision over work processes and practices.

DEFINITION

Multiskilling is functional versatility: the opposite of specialisation, with its tendency towards rigid job descriptions and demarcation lines between one job and another. It involves the development of versatility in the labour force, so that individuals can perform more than one task if required to do so: workers are being encouraged, trained and organised to work across the boundaries of traditional jobs and crafts.

Multiskilling has been difficult to achieve historically, because craft and occupational groups (such as trade unions) have supported demarcation in order to protect jobs and maintain special skills, standards and pay differentials. This situation is changing now that multi-skilled, flexible labour is highly prized in today's labour market.

EXAMPLE

An organisation with a large maintenance and engineering division, with four distinct and independent maintenance disciplines, had been through a process whereby there had been an enormous reduction in the number of skilled and authorised staff. Their skills base was to be replaced with the introduction of new equipment and through vendor support that was part of the supply contract.

Recruitment had already been minimal for a number of years and support services had been contracted out leading to fewer opportunities for rotation between support and operational assets.

However, having disbanded some of the functions and jobs, there was a delay before the new sophisticated equipment capability could be introduced, which meant that in the short term (one to three years) there was an expanding void of suitably trained/experienced maintenance engineers within the organisation. This meant that there was now a problem with the variation in the level of skills, knowledge and experience in staff between assets, groups and disciplines and a reduction in the overall depth of engineering required. However, some specialists were still required.

The approach taken was to use suitable, existing staff (by experience and skills) and provide them with a suitable training programme to train them to become multi-skilled in the different disciplines.

- Develop a master jobs matrix.

- Update the existing, competency matrix to determine suitable 'cross-over' tasks that would allow individuals to be trained outside their disciplines.

- Use the HR learning database to determine numbers (worldwide) of maintenance staff who had the skills and experience deemed suitable for the initial push towards multi-skilling.

- Design flexible training programmes that would:

  – Allow inter-disciplinary cross training

  – Realign the skills, knowledge and experience for selected personnel (all other personnel could then apply after initial 'bow wave' of compulsory training)

  – Cover all required functions/tasks (globally) to complete the competency matrix

  – Support the estimated future demands on the maintenance engineer requirement to be announced by strategic management

- Carry out a full training needs analysis for all tasks within current jobs.

Implementation

- Training delivered over a three-year period.

- Ongoing training needs analysis for future tasks based on emerging techniques and equipment. All new tasks would be matched to jobs and level of skills, knowledge and experience.

Results

- One-off 30% increase of maintenance engineers for tasking.

- Increase from 0.8 to 2.2 of maintenance engineers available for routine tasks.

- Increase of 0.5 to 1.3 of maintenance engineers available for specialist tasks.

- Four disciplines combined to one, thus realigning work allocation and ensuring equipment care was 'everybody's concern.

(*Tagus International*, 2012)

The benefits of multiskilling to the organisation are as follows.

(a) It is an efficient use of people resources.

(i) It smoothes out fluctuations in demand for different skills or categories of worker.

(ii) It may be possible to maintain a smaller staff, because specialists would not be needed in each skill area.

(b) It puts an end to potentially costly demarcation disputes, where one category of worker objects to others 'invading' their area of work, as defined by narrow job descriptions.

(c) On the other hand, it is less likely that a task will be left undone because it does not explicitly appear on anybody's job description.

ACTIVITY 5   (15 MINS)

What does multiskilling offer the employee?

3.5 FLEXIBLE WORKING GROUPS

The basic work units of organisations have traditionally been specialised functional departments. In recent decades, organisations have moved towards small, functionally flexible workgroups or teams. Teamworking allows work to be shared among a number of individuals, without the requirement for complex and lengthy co-ordination and communication mechanisms.

Teams may be:

(a) **Temporally flexible**: called together to achieve specific task objectives and then disbanded (eg in a project management approach).

(b) **Numerically flexible**: co-opting members and advisers as different skills, attributes and expertise are required.

(c) **Virtual**: consisting of individuals networking, data-sharing and collaborating as and when required, using ICT links.

In terms of functional flexibility, there are two basic types of flexible workgroups.

(a) **Multi-disciplinary teams**, which bring together individuals with different skills and specialisms, so that their skills, experience and knowledge can be pooled or exchanged (like different pieces making up a jigsaw puzzle).

This is regarded as a useful mechanism for organisational communication and co-ordination. It is particularly useful in problem-solving and creative ideas generation, since it fosters awareness of overall objectives, allows the airing of wide-ranging organisational issues, and accesses different ideas which can 'hitchhike' or 'leapfrog' on one another.

(b) **Multi-skilled teams**, which bring together a number of multi-skilled individuals who can each perform any of the group's tasks. These tasks can therefore be shared out in a more flexible way between group members, according to who is available and best placed to do a given job at the time it is required.

ACTIVITY 6   (45 MINS)

What may be the drawbacks to teamworking? (Your other studies in Organisations and Behaviour and Management should furnish some ideas …)

SIGNPOST

Finally, we look at approaches to temporal flexibility.

3.6 FLEXIBLE CONTRACTS

Forms of flexibly contracted hours of work include the following.

(a) **Overtime**: premium rates of pay for hours worked in excess of standard hours. A business may ask employees to work overtime to:

(i) Increase production to meet seasonal or *ad hoc* peaks in demand, without increasing the labour force

(ii) Maintain production (eg machine running) despite temporary shortages of labour. (Covering colleague absence is an example of this in the service sector.)

BPP
LEARNING MEDIA

Overtime can militate against efficiency where it is employee-driven, as a means of increasing outcome. Salaried workers are often not paid overtime, and some businesses negotiate higher basic pay rates for wage earners in lieu of overtime.

(b) **Zero hour contracts**: no guarantee of work (or pay) is given for the week. Staff may be called upon as and when required, on a full- or part-time basis, effectively imposing self-employed status. This is obviously highly flexible from the employer's point of view, but has been identified by the National Association of Citizens' Advice Bureaux (NACAB) as potentially abusive, since it creates financial insecurity and inability to plan commitments.

(c) **Annualised hours contracts**: agreeing a number of hours' work per year, rather than per week or month. Some or all of these hours may be committed to a rota schedule or roster while additional 'bank hours' may be held in reserve for unforeseen fluctuations (such as the need to cover for absences) plus 'reserve hours' designated for specific purposes other than normal working (such as training). Intensive hours can be called on during seasonal peaks in labour demand via longer working days or shifts, with time off in periods of low demand. This offers high flexibility for the employer, with employment security for the employee, although there is the danger of overwork during peak hours.

(d) **Term-time contracts**: similar to annualised-hours but allowing parents to maximise hours during school terms, so that family responsibilities can be met during holidays.

(e) **Compressed hours** permit staff to work the total hours required by their contracts but over fewer working days than would be usual. Typical examples would be the compression of a five-day week into four-and-a-half days or of a ten-day fortnight into nine days. Such schemes will often require a rota to ensure that there is cover for popular choices of time off, such as Mondays and Fridays.

3.7 FLEXI-TIME

There are many 'flexi-time' systems in operation, providing freedom from the restriction of a 'nine to five' work-hours routine. The concept of flexi-time is that predetermined fixed times of arrival and departure at work are replaced by a working day split into two different time zones.

(a) The main part of the day is called '*core time*' and is the only period when employees must be at their job (this is commonly 10.00 to 16.00 hours).

(b) The *flexible time* is at the beginning and the end of each day and during this time it is up to individuals to choose when they arrive, and leave. Arrival and departure times would be recorded by some form of 'clocking-in' system. The total working week or month for each employee must add up to the prescribed number of hours, though an individual may go into 'debit' or 'credit' for hours from day-to-day, in some systems.

This approach is also known as **staggered hours**.

ACTIVITY 7 (20 MINS)

Suggest three advantages to:

(a) The organisation

(b) The worker

of implementing a flexi-time system.

SIGNPOST

We have already covered some of the HR implications of flexible working on a method-by-method basis. Here, we draw together some of the threads.

4 ISSUES IN FLEXIBILITY

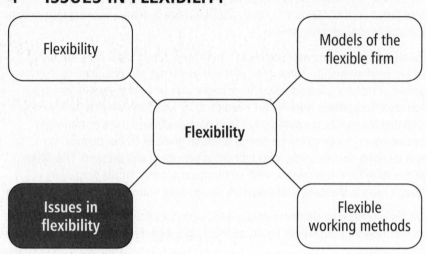

Flexibility

Models of the flexible firm

Flexibility

Issues in flexibility

Flexible working methods

4.1 HR ISSUES

Some of the HR policy choices to be considered are as follows.

(a) **Recruitment and selection**. Flexibility will need to be reinforced by selection criteria, both in terms of temperament (adaptability, willingness to adopt flexible working) and skills (trainability, existing multiple skills). In return, flexible working practices may act as a boost to the recruitment and retention of staff (especially women returners, say).

(b) **Training and development**. Performance management, training needs analysis and career planning will have to be tailored to flexible working in terms of: broadening skills, fostering flexible attitudes, teamworking (where relevant: criteria may be different for isolated homeworkers), opportunities for promotion (with equal access for part-time and temporary workers).

(c) **Supervision and control**. Flexibility militates against the supervisor's traditional role as monitor/controller of performance – especially where outworking and/or self-managing teams are used. The supervisor is increasingly becoming a coach/mentor/facilitator to empowered teams and/or a co-ordinator/facilitator ensuring that communication is maintained with distant or part-time workers. (This change in role may itself require HR interventions in training and counselling support.) Control mechanisms must be developed to retain cohesion without rigidity: performance management, communication of cultural values, commitment-based policies etc.

(d) **Motivation and reward**. Flexible payment structures will be required to reflect multiskilling and teamworking, while detailed administrative systems will have to support flexi-time and its variants. Attention will need to be given to employee morale and *esprit-de-corps*, particularly where people are only part-time or external members of the team: team-building will have to be broadened to include geographically separated 'virtual' teams.

(e) **Health and safety and other compliance aspects**. The employment environment is more highly regulated than ever before in terms of the protection of flexible workers. It places planning, administrative and employee relations duties on HR departments. In addition to compliance, there are the issues of social responsibility and employer branding/reputation, which dictate that 'soft' flexibility approaches may be more favourably regarded than 'hard' approaches such as zero hours contracting.

(f) **Cultural reinforcement**. HRM will have an important role in developing a culture which accepts and celebrates flexibility in general, through integrated systems for recruiting, rewarding, promoting, developing and facilitating flexibility, change, innovation and so on.

(g) **Problem-solving**. As we have seen, there are a number of drawbacks to flexibility from the point of view of the employee. HRM as a welfare function will have the task of minimising the impact of uncertainty, fluctuating earnings, isolation and so on, through supportive systems, compensations, safeguards and benefits. There may also be negative impacts on the firm's employer brand (and ability to attract and retain staff), if it is seen to abuse or exploit flexibility.

ACTIVITY 8 (2 HOURS)

Pick an organisation that you have worked for, or are familiar with, or can find out about. How flexible is the workforce in this organisation? Is it versatile, multi-skilled and happy to work unorthodox hours or without a strict job description? What does the human resource department in this organisation do to encourage, or to discourage, flexibility of labour? (Think about job descriptions, training and development, working hours and so on.)

4.2 NEW PSYCHOLOGICAL CONTRACTS

According to the concept of '**job shift**' (Bridges, 1995), the workforce is increasingly made up of 'skill vendors' who sell their services to a variety of clients on a project basis, and who take responsibility for their own *résumé* management: skill development, experience, self-marketing and so on.

This amounts to the rewriting of the traditional psychological contract of employment. Many organisations are making this explicit, by spelling out the new contract, in which concepts such as 'lifetime employment' or even a 'career' within a company are no longer valid. There are compelling reasons why an organisation may wish to repudiate responsibility for the job security and career development of its employees, even where it is offering 'permanent' employment.

(a) It may wish to discourage a culture of complacent performance based on job security and the fulfilment of job descriptions and, instead, encourage the perception that competitive, value-adding performance is required in order to keep one's position.

(b) It may genuinely be unable to guarantee long-term, secure employment: in making this explicit, it is being socially responsible in encouraging employees to take ownership of their careers.

(c) It may wish to establish an attractive employer brand as an honest, open and realistic employer, in a market where educated employees are cynical about unrealistic recruitment offers.

On the other hand, there are risks to such an approach.

(a) There may be some loss of morale and performance, as the effects of newly-articulated insecurity are felt.

(b) There may be some loss of skilled labour, where individuals are alienated by the implication that they are not doing enough, or made uncomfortable by the uncertainty and responsibility of having to manage their own careers.

(c) There may be some loss of skilled labour, where individuals embrace the 'skill vendor' approach and career mobility to the point where they leave the organisation in order to develop their career portfolio.

One concept arising from the de-jobbing of employment is '**employability**': a term which describes a portfolio of knowledge, skills and attributes that enhances an individual's marketability in the labour pool. Companies which have spelled out the new psychological contract may offer employability training in order to be socially responsible in facilitating employees' transition (if necessary) to other employment – while simultaneously benefiting from the resulting flexibility and versatility of employable individuals.

FOR DISCUSSION

The TUC when considering work-life balance argues that, without staff involvement and support, flexibility can mean management imposing forms of work organisation on employees who are given no opportunity to state their opinions or explain their needs. In contrast, "positive flexibility" gives people more autonomy and choice, with the employer investing in development and training and working in partnership with the workforce.

(Bond, 2003)

What do you think are the 'exploitative' and 'positive' aspects of flexibility?

EXAMPLE   PRICE WATER HOUSE COOPER'S APPROACH TO FLEXIBILITY

People are most successful when they have the everyday flexibility they need to meet the demands of their professional life and accomplish the things they identify as priorities outside of their career.

- Everyday flexibility
- Formal flexibility
- Perspectives on flexibility

In a truly flexible work environment, individuals and teams decide together how and where work gets done.

To do this, the firm offers several formal flexible work arrangements from telecommuting to a compressed workweek. Leaders and colleagues work collaboratively to assess these arrangements in the context of the needs of the individual, the team and the client.

The formal flexible work arrangements PwC offers include:

- **Reduced hours**: Reducing hours to less than a regular full-time week

- **Flextime**: Work hours move earlier or later than 'regular' business hours

- **PwC@Home**: Formal telecommuting, routinely working from home three or more days per week

- **PwC offsite**: Telecommuting, routinely working from home one or two days per week

- **Job-sharing**: Two people jointly fulfill the responsibilities of one full-time position

- **Compressed workweek**: Standard hours compressed into fewer than five work days

- **Seasonal employment**: Working a portion of the year on a special project or to fulfill a specific need

- **Sabbatical**: Leave of absence while maintaining benefits and a reduced salary rate

(PWC US website, 2012)

CHAPTER ROUNDUP

- Labour flexibility has been driven by demographic factors (notably the increased participation of women in the labour force) and the increasing focus on work-life balance. The rights of parents of small children to request flexible working arrangements have been enacted in law.

- Labour flexibility can be approached from a 'hard' HRM orientation (focused on reducing labour costs and unit costs of production and on minimising the organisation's exposure to 'excess' labour: an approach called 'lean production') or from a 'soft' HRM orientation (focused on enhancing the quality and adaptability of the labour resource through broadening skills and commitment).

- Flexibility may be numerical, temporal, locational and/or functional, and must be supported by cultural flexibility through integrated HRM systems. (A number of specific methods and techniques of flexibility are detailed.)

- Two broadly similar models have been put forward for the flexible firm: Atkinson's core-periphery model and Handy's Shamrock model.

- Flexibility poses key HR issues for recruitment and selection, training and development, control and the role of the supervisor, motivation and reward and compliance with legal requirements.

- 'Flexible working arrangements used positively can benefit employees as well as being in the interests of the business ... but abusing them could make it more difficult to recruit people and could damage competitiveness in the long run.' (CIPD)

- The nature of the 'job' and the psychological contract of employment have changed with the emphasis on flexible working.

QUICK QUIZ

1   What are the pressures that have led organisations to develop flexible working?

2   What kinds of flexible working arrangements are parents of small children entitled to request and what are the justified grounds for refusing such a request?

3   What are the five types of flexibility?

4   Outline (a) the core-periphery model and (b) the Shamrock organisation.

5   What are the rights of part-time workers under the Employment Relations Act 1999?

6   List three advantages of teleworking.

7   What are the two basic approaches to flexible group working?

8   List five methods of allowing flexibility in working hours.

9   How does flexibility affect the supervisor's role?

10   What is 'employability'?

ANSWERS TO QUICK QUIZ

1   Increased market uncertainty, increased competition, technological change, labour market demographics and the shift towards work-life balance.   (see Para 1.1)

2   See Paragraph 1.3 for a full answer.

3   Numerical, temporal, functional, financial, locational, cultural.   (Para 1.6)

4   For a full account, see Paragraphs 2.1 and 2.2.

5   Rights to equal treatment in respect to access to training, selection for promotion, protection from unfair dismissal (and other statutory requirements); proportional entitlement to benefits (paid holiday, sick pay, maternity pay); access to pension schemes and parental leave, protection under all health and safety legislation.   (Para 3.1)

6   Savings on overheads; employment access for home-bound workers; elimination of commuting; reduction in stress through better work/life balance.   (Para 3.3)

7   Multi-disciplinary teams, multi-skilled teams.   (Para 3.5)

8   Zero hours, annualised hours, overtime, flexi-time, term-time contracts.   (Para 3.6)

9   Shift from monitor/controller to coach/facilitator and/or co-ordinator.   (Para 4.1)

10 The development of a portfolio of knowledge, skills and experience that enhances a worker's marketability and mobility in the labour pool.   (Para 4.2)

ANSWERS TO ACTIVITIES

1   This is a research activity, designed to get you explaining sources of information on the labour market and labour market trends. You may only have been able to find forecasts relevant to the data requested – since the gathering and analysis of statistics takes time: this should remind you that HRM is a forward-looking activity!

Some suggested sources:

- www.ons.gov.uk/ons/rel/lms/labour-market-statistics/november-2012/video-summary.html

- www.tuc.org.uk/tucfiles/251.pdf

- www.parliament.uk/briefing-papers/sn05871.pdf

2   Examples of flexibility in a supermarket might include:

(a)   Extra staff employed for Christmas (numerical)

(b)   Adult staff with family responsibilities employed just during school term-times (numerical/temporal)

(c)   School-age staff employed just during school holidays (numerical/temporal)

(d)   Staff on zero hours contracts (only called in to work when needed) (numerical/temporal)

(e)   Staff paid according to their performance (financial)

(f)   All staff trained to use checkouts (functional)

(g)   Staff skilled enough to work in more than one department (functional)

3   *Professional core*: recruitment of high quality core people; retention, intrinsic rewards, career management; knowledge management. Possibly also delayering or downsizing: as the core is expensive, it makes sense to keep it as small as possible. This will take careful HR planning, to decide what core activities are and which people belong to the core group.

Flexible labour force: HR planning, management and control of work (to maintain standards), teambuilding, equitable treatment (while controlling costs), culture management and communication.

Contractual fringe: planned outsourcing, contracting (results and standard specification), relationship management, quality control, communication.

4   Connock (1991) gives seven main reasons for the increase in part-time working.

(a)   Employers can better match working hours to operational requirements.

(b)   The personal circumstances of key staff can be accommodated through part-time working. This will be particularly relevant to women returners.

(c)   The productivity of part-timers is generally higher than that of full-timers (hardly surprising, since work is undertaken in more concentrated time periods).

(d)   The absence levels of part-timers are generally lower: domestic requirements can more easily be fitted into the free periods in the part-time schedule.

(e)   A pool of trained employees is available for switching to full-time work, or extending working time temporarily.

(f)   Difficulties in recruiting full-time staff have prompted organisations to recruit and train part-time staff. Women returners are more likely to be attracted to an organisation if the hours of work are suitable, which will generally mean working part-time.

(g)   Part-time working can cut overtime costs, since it makes it possible to avoid paying premium rates.

You may have your own suggestions as to how the economic downturn has contributed to these!

5   The erosion of rigid specialisation and fragmented job design can offer:

(a)   A higher degree of job satisfaction, through variety of work and a greater understanding of its purpose and importance.

(b)   Job security and material benefits, since a versatile, flexible employee is likely to be more attractive to employers, and have a higher value in the current labour market.

(c)   Personal skill development.

6   (a)   Teamworking is not suitable for all jobs: it does not always lead to superior or faster decision-making or performance than individuals working alone.

(b)   Teams can delay decision-making in search of consensus (although consensus decisions do offer commitment and a rounded perspective).

(c)   Social relationships might be maintained at the expense of other aspects of performance.

(d)   Group norms may restrict individual personality and flair.

(e)   Group think, or self-maintaining consensus, may prevent consideration of alternatives or constructive criticism.

(f)   Personality clashes and political behaviour can get in the way of effective working.

7   Benefits to the organisation include: improved staff morale (because of flexibility); less stressed/distracted staff (because problems outside work can be solved without the guilt attached to lateness); less absenteeism (because of the 'I'm late for work: I'd better not go at all' syndrome).

Benefits to the workers include: less frustration in rush-hour commuting; less pressure over needs like the dentist or school sports days; time to shop, socialise etc in off-peak times; satisfaction of choice.

8   This allowed some space for your own research and reflection on your own experience. Plenty of sources of information: the HRM journals regularly report on flexibility initiatives, the currency of which is constantly renewed by fresh considerations like family-friendly policies for recruitment, EU Directives on worker rights and so on.

Equal
opportunities

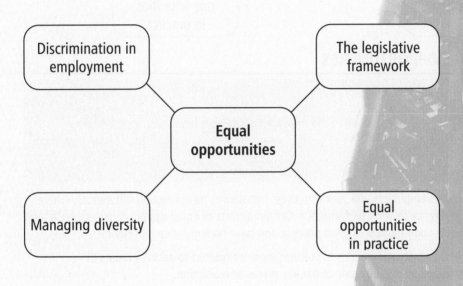

- Discrimination in employment
- The legislative framework
- **Equal opportunities**
- Managing diversity
- Equal opportunities in practice

Introduction

In this chapter, we study discrimination at work and the legal framework shaping HR policy in this area. As you read, be aware that while the law defines certain 'groups' against whom discrimination is illegal, discrimination can result from bias and prejudice of any kind. An ethical and cultural framework for justice, equality and diversity is as important as legislation and codes of practice: the 'management of diversity' concept is one development of this line of thought.

You may also note that discrimination can take subtle forms – classified as 'indirect' in current legislation: 'sexual harassment' is perhaps the most high-profile example of an issue which has emerged and been recognised as a form of discrimination.

Your objectives

In this chapter you will learn about the following.

- Forms of discrimination in employment
- The legislative framework on discrimination
- Equal opportunities practices and initiatives in the workplace
- The move from equal opportunity to managing diversity

1 DISCRIMINATION IN EMPLOYMENT

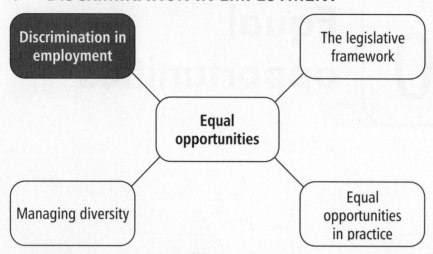

Discrimination in employment

The legislative framework

Equal opportunities

Managing diversity

Equal opportunities in practice

1.1 EQUAL OPPORTUNITIES

DEFINITION

Equal opportunities is an approach to the management of people at work based on equal access and fair treatment irrespective of gender, race, ethnicity, age, disability, sexual orientation or religious belief.

Equal opportunities employers will seek to redress imbalances based around differences, where they have no relevance to work performance. Certain aspects of equal opportunities are enshrined in law; others rely upon models of good practice and have no legislative foundation.

Prior to the 2010 Equality Act a series of statutes were introduced to address issues of discrimination. Listed below are some of the key pieces of legislation.

> The *Equal Pay Act 1970* was the first major attempt to tackle sexual discrimination. It was intended specifically 'to prevent discrimination as regards terms and conditions of employment between men and women'.

> The *Sex Discrimination Act 1975* (and amendments) outlawed certain types of discrimination on the grounds of sex, marital status, maternity or pregnancy.

> The *Race Relations Act 1976* (and subsequent amendments) outlawed certain types of discrimination on the grounds of colour, race, nationality, or ethnic or national origin.

> The **Disability Discrimination Act 1995**, previous legislation on disability focused narrowly on securing employment (on a Quota Scheme) for disabled people, without addressing the issue of discrimination.

Employment Equality Regulations 2003 (and **2007** amendments) outlawed discrimination on the basis of:

- Religion or belief

- Sexual orientation (also supported by the *Equality Act [Sexual Orientation] Regulations* 2007)

Employment Equality (Age) Regulations 2006 removed the age limit for unfair dismissal and redundancy rights (previously, age 65). Gave all employees the right to work **beyond** the age of 65 or the company's normal retirement age.

Due to membership of the European Union and inconsistency in the definitions within the existing law, in 2010, the Equality Act came into force, which consolidated the previous acts and brought consistency to the legislation.

SIGNPOST

We now look at some of the groups that have been subject to employment difficulties in recent history.

1.2 WOMEN IN EMPLOYMENT

Despite the fact that women have contributed directly to the national product since medieval times – on the land and in home-based industries such as textiles – the acceptance of women in paid employment has been a slow process, which is even now having to be enforced by law.

The distribution of women in the UK workforce today is still heavily concentrated in categories such as textiles, footwear, clothing and leather, hotel and catering, retail distribution and repairs, professional and scientific services, and miscellaneous services. A significant percentage of the women employed in these categories work part-time.

Only in recent decades has there been a widespread challenge to gender segregation in employment – the idea that there are 'men's jobs' and 'women's jobs', with only a few genuinely 'unisex' categories of work.

ACTIVITY 1   (30 MINS)

Why do you think women have been regarded as 'second-class citizens' in the workplace? Consider social values; educational influences; the changing nature of work; the historical composition of the workforce and so on.

Many assumptions about women's attitudes to work, and capabilities for various types of work, are being re-examined with the purpose of removing the barriers to women in employment.

Meanwhile, pay differentials between men and women have remained an issue, despite equal pay legislation. The *Annual Survey of Hours and Earnings* (2012) reported that the gender pay gap (ie the difference between men's and women's earnings as a percentage of men's earnings) based on median gross hourly earnings (excluding overtime) for full-time employees decreased to 9.6% from 10.5% in 2011. This is despite the original equal pay act being passed in 1970!

EXAMPLE

Research by the Higher Education Policy Institute shows that women now not only outnumber men overall at university, but they also outnumber them at every type of university. They are also more likely to get a 2:1 degree pass and are less likely to drop out. The institute's figures show 49.2% of women opt for higher education compared with just 37.2% of men. In the post-1992 universities (the former polytechnics), there are 23.8% of the women cohort and 18% of men.

Mary Curnock Cook, chief executive of the Universities and Colleges Admission Service said

'The gender pay gap may take another generation to close as the pay feeds through to the more senior workforce,' she said. The figures show that the gap between men and women's hourly pay is also closing among 18- to 21-year-olds and 30- to 39-year-olds.'

Last month, the Chartered Institute of Management reported that junior female managers are earning marginally more than their male peers for the first time, but that the pay gap stubbornly persists when averaged across all job and age levels. The institute warned that it would take a century before the average salary for female executives caught up with that of their male peers.

(The Independent, 2012)

However, pay is not the only challenge facing women. Pregnant workers still seem to be poorly treated. Research published in *People Management* (28 June 2007) reveals that they are frequently disadvantaged or bullied in ways ranging from being passed over for promotion or training, to not being given rest breaks, to being pressured to over-perform to make up for lost time – to being made redundant while on maternity leave.

Women's representation in top jobs also remains an issue.

EXAMPLE

In 2011, Viviane Reding, the European Union's justice commissioner, invited publicly listed firms to sign a pledge to increase the proportion of women on their boards to 30% by 2015 and 40% by 2020. In 2012 having seen little progress she was considering what action to take.

Only 13.7% of board members of large firms in the EU are women, up from 8.5% in 2003. Female presidents and chairwomen are even rarer: just 3.2% of the total now, compared with 1.6% in 2003. Women account for 60% of new graduates in the EU, and enter many occupations in roughly equal numbers with men. But with every step up the ladder more of them drop out, and near the top they almost disappear.

Plenty of research suggests that companies with lots of women in senior positions are more successful than those without (even if there is no proof of a causal relationship). So it seems to make sense to get more women on boards.

(The Economist, 2012)

1.3 ETHNIC MINORITIES IN EMPLOYMENT

In January 2010 the Public Policy Research looked at data from the Labour Force Survey – a quarterly sample of about 60,000 households. Within that, it examined the responses of 16- to 24-year-olds – a total of 7,200 in November 2009.

It said mixed ethnic groups had seen the biggest increases in youth unemployment since the recession began, rising from 21% to 35% in the period.

That trend echoed the recession in the early 1990s, it added, where unemployment among ethnic minorities rose by 10%, compared with a 6% increase overall.

In terms of individual groups, 48% of black people, 31% of Asians and 20% of whites reported that they were out of work.

While employment rates vary significantly between different minority groups, all have lower employment than the overall rate, people from ethnic minority backgrounds are one-and-a-half times more likely to be economically inactive than the overall working age population.

There is also ethnic segregation in the labour market, with a concentration of minority (male) employees in manufacturing, hotel, catering, repairs and distribution sectors.

The proportion of ethnic minority employees falls sharply at higher levels of the organisation (to only 1% of senior managers in FTSE 100 companies).

ACTIVITY 2 (5 MINS)

Have you ever felt discriminated against (at school, work or a training institution)? On what grounds: your sex, colour, age, social background/ beliefs/attitudes? What was the effect of the discrimination on your plans and attitudes?

Reasons cited for adopting positive action plans on racial equality include:

(a) Good HR practice, in attracting and retaining the best people (not just ethnic minority employees, but all those who care about discrimination).

(b) Compliance with the Codes of Practice which are used by Employment Tribunals.

(c) Widening the recruitment pool for access to more labour.

(d) Other potential benefits to the business, through its image as a socially responsible employer, and through greater identification with customers, particularly in geographical areas of significant ethnic diversity.

EXAMPLE WHY DIVERSITY MATTERS FOR THE BBC

There are around 60 million people in the UK – and we are all different by virtue of our own particular circumstances: from age and gender, disability and race, religion and sexual orientation, where we come from and where we choose to be – and other circumstances that form who we are and what our story is.

So, as a broadcaster, for the BBC the case for exploring diversity is simple:

Our audiences are becoming increasingly diverse and are ever-changing – both in make-up and in expectation. We must strive to stay relevant to all our audiences.

Our creativity – diversity is a creative opportunity for us to tell new and original stories, and to generate genuinely distinctive content.

Our funding – most UK households pay for the BBC through the licence fee, and should see themselves and their lives reflected through our services.

Legislation – the law (Equality Act 2010) is clear, and supports the advance of equality.

And as an employer and partner, the case is equally clear:

Our mission to deliver quality – efforts to provide quality and value for all audiences ensures diversity stays at the heart of our work.

Our values – a core organisational value is that 'we respect each other and celebrate our diversity so that everyone can give their best'. A workforce which fully reflects our society enables us to reflect our own diversity through our programmes and content.

(Extract from The BBC's Diversity Strategy, 2011–15)

1.4 DISABLED PEOPLE IN EMPLOYMENT

DEFINITION

Disability

The Equality Act 2010 replaced the previous Disability Discrimination Act 1995 definition of disability.

Under the Act, a person is disabled if they have a physical or mental impairment which has a substantial and long-term adverse effect on their ability to carry out normal day-to-day activities.

Disability covers a wide range of impairments, including mobility, manual dexterity, physical co-ordination, continence, lifting, carrying or otherwise moving everyday objects, concentration, vision, speech, learning/understanding and perception of danger. In 2005, 6.9 million people had a long-term health problem or disability which had a substantial adverse impact on their day-to-day activities and affects the work they can do. (Torrington *et al*, 2011). The choice of jobs for the disabled is often restricted, resulting in higher and longer unemployment rates than the general population. Jobs are concentrated in plant/ machine operative jobs, which tend to be low-paid: disabled people are under-represented in professional and managerial jobs.

Attitudes towards the disabled in the workplace have been extremely negative, tending to focus on generalised and stereotypical problems such as:

(a) Long periods off work for medical causes

(b) Accident-proneness

(c) Poor skill levels

(d) Difficulties of adjusting the work environment for wheelchair access and other disability needs

(e) Negative image to customers, who allegedly feel awkward in the presence of disabled people

(f) The 'positive' association of certain jobs with disabled workers (eg lift attendants, switchboard operators, simple assembly tasks), stereotyping disabled roles and capabilities.

1.5 AGE DIVERSITY IN EMPLOYMENT

Despite demographic and educational changes and associated skill shortages among the younger population, a certain amount of discrimination has continued to be directed at more mature workers.

The CIPD reported, in 2005, that age discrimination remained a significant problem in the workplace. Fifty-nine per cent of respondents reported that they had been disadvantaged by age discrimination at work.

ACTIVITY 3 (10 MINS)

List some reasons – perhaps based on your own experience or prejudices! – why organisations might practise age discrimination.

The fact is that older workers:

(a) Have developed experience and skills in the job that may counteract any age-related loss of performance.

(b) Tend to stay in the job, reducing turnover and associated costs, and have better attendance and disciplinary records.

(c) Do experience some loss of strength and stamina. However, this is unlikely to be relevant to performance in most modern jobs, and older workers typically understand and work within their physical limitations.

(d) Do experience some loss of mental functioning (short-term memory, for example) but retain – or even gain – in other cognitive functions.

(e) Are no more likely to be flexible or inflexible in relation to learning and change than younger employees.

(f) Do not necessarily cost the organisation more, as age-based reward systems are being replaced by performance-related ones.

International comparison

In the Far-East, great value is placed on 'the wisdom of age'. In Japan, age is equated with long service, the acquisition of skill and experience, and hence the quality of the worker.

1.6 OTHER FORMS OF DISCRIMINATION

As we noted in our introduction to this chapter, there are many potential differences that may be used as a point of discrimination.

(a) **Sexual orientation**. Gay, lesbian and bisexual people may experience discrimination in:

- The culture of the firm: behavioural norms and attitudes that may cause harassment, verbal abuse or isolation of 'outed' gay workers, or the need to hide sexual orientation for fear of discrimination.

- HR practices: discrimination in terms and benefits due to eligibility criteria which exclude same-sex partners, for example.

(b) **Religious belief**. Apart from direct religious (often related to ethnic) discrimination against adherents to particular faiths, there is indirect discrimination through work practices which affect some groups more than others. Dress codes, dietary laws, time off for religious holidays and available facilities to comply with prayer requirements, for example, have recently been highlighted as diversity issues.

EXAMPLE **STONEWALL EMPLOYER OF THE YEAR 2012 – ERNST & YOUNG**

One of the largest professional services firms in the world, EY put diversity and inclusiveness at the heart of everything they do. For 2011, one of their six global priorities was to 'lead in diversity and inclusiveness'. From employee policy to diversity training, and from monitoring and evaluation to community engagement, EY is able to demonstrate inspiring leadership in all areas of LGB-related diversity practice.

Responsibility for delivering a culture in which all people can excel at EY is driven at a senior level. On the UK & Ireland Leadership Team, Liz Bingham is the Managing Partner for People, defining and delivering EY's People Strategy.

Liz Bingham, said: 'To say we are thrilled and proud to be named Stonewall's 2012 Employer of the Year is truly an understatement. We believe that a strong commitment to diversity and inclusiveness is not only important for our people, but is also good business in an increasingly competitive and interconnected world.'

Liz is an openly gay woman and a member of EYGLES, the Ernst & Young employee network for lesbian, gay, bisexual and transgender staff.

FOR DISCUSSION

What aspects of religion or belief and sexual orientation are most clearly subject to discrimination, harassment or lack of understanding in your own work or study environment?

Is the discrimination systematic/procedural – or cultural/personal?

1.7 EQUAL PAY

The *Equal Pay Act 1970* was the first major attempt to tackle sexual discrimination. It was intended specifically 'to prevent discrimination as regards terms and conditions of employment between men and women'.

The *Equal (Amendment) Regulations 1984* established the right to equal pay for 'work of **equal value**', so that a woman would no longer have to compare her work with that of a man in the same or broadly similar work, but could establish that her work had equal value to that of a man in the same establishment. These provisions were discussed in Chapter 5.

Equal pay questionnaires were launched in 2003, giving employees the right to request the pay details of a named colleague (subject to their consent under the Data Protection Act) to support claims that they are being paid less because of their race or sex. HR commentators have noted that if pay systems are open, fair and transparent, such questionnaires are less likely to be submitted.

SIGNPOST

We now look at the laws passed to protect the rights of key disadvantaged groups, as well as some of the issues which are currently being worked out in European Courts and professional Codes of Practice.

2 THE LEGISLATIVE FRAMEWORK

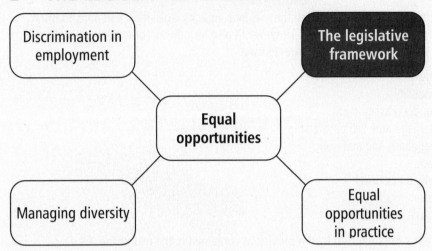

2.1 THE EQUALITY ACT 2010

The Government Equalities office summarises the changes implemented by the Equality Act as follows:

- The basic framework of protection against direct and indirect discrimination, harassment and victimisation in services and public functions; premises; work; education; associations, and transport.

- Changing the definition of gender reassignment, by removing the requirement for medical supervision.

- Levelling up protection for people discriminated against because they are perceived to have, or are associated with someone who has, a protected characteristic, so providing new protection for people like carers.

- Applying the European definition of indirect discrimination to all protected characteristics.

- Extending protection from indirect discrimination to disability.

- Introducing a new concept of 'discrimination arising from disability', to replace protection under previous legislation lost as a result of a legal judgement.

- Applying the detriment model to victimisation protection (aligning with the approach in employment law).

- Harmonising the thresholds for the duty to make reasonable adjustments for disabled people.

- Extending protection from third party harassment to all protected characteristics.

- Making it more difficult for disabled people to be unfairly screened out when applying for jobs, by restricting the circumstances in which employers can ask job applicants questions about disability or health.

- Allowing claims for direct gender pay discrimination where there is no actual comparator.

2.2 PROTECTED CHARACTERISTICS

The Equality Act effectively consolidates all the previous equality legislation and aims to bring consistency into the definitions and terms. However, it also introduces some new concepts, the most notable of these being 'protected characteristics':

- Age
- Disability
- Gender reassignment
- Marriage and civil partnership
- Pregnancy and maternity
- Race
- Religion or belief
- Sex
- Sexual orientation

These 'characteristics' are protected by the provisions contained in the rest of the Act.

Age

The legislation concerning age bans unjustified direct and indirect discrimination on the basis of age in recruitment. However, the Act does allow it a unique characteristic; it allows employers to justify direct discrimination if the employer can demonstrate that it is a proportionate means of meeting a legitimate aim.

Disability

Disability is subject to a new definition and other changes.

The Act does not give specific examples of what would be considered a disability. Under the Act, a person is disabled if they have a physical or mental impairment which has a substantial and long-term adverse affect on their ability to carry out normal day-to-day activities.

The meaning of 'impairment' here is where day-to-day activities are affected, for example, mobility, manual dexterity, physical co-ordination, continence, lifting, carrying or otherwise moving everyday objects, concentration, vision, speech, learning/understanding and perception of danger.

Gender reassignment

The Act provides protection for transsexual people and the term transsexual person is given new definition. A transsexual person is someone who proposes to, starts or has completed a process to change his or her gender. The Act also no longer has the requirement for the person to be under medical supervision to be protected.

Marriage and civil partnership

The legislation bans unjustified direct and indirect discrimination on the basis of marital status and civil partnership status.

Pregnancy and maternity

During any statutory maternity leave, a woman is protected against discrimination on the grounds of pregnancy and maternity. During this period, pregnancy and maternity discrimination cannot be treated as sex discrimination as it has been acknowledged that pregnancy is a unique condition.

In cases of direct discrimination because of pregnancy or maternity, the test is whether the treatment is unfavourable rather than less favourable.

Race

The legislation bans unjustified direct and indirect discrimination on the basis of race. 'Race' includes colour, nationality and ethnic or national origins.

Religion or belief

In the Equality Act, religion includes any religion. It also includes a lack of religion, in other words, employees or jobseekers are protected if they do not follow a certain religion or have no religion at all. Additionally, a religion must have a clear structure and belief system. Belief means any religious or philosophical belief or a lack of such belief.

Sex

The legislation bans unjustified direct and indirect discrimination on the basis of sex.

Sexual orientation

The legislation bans unjustified direct and indirect discrimination on the basis of sexual orientation.

2.3 POSITIVE ACTION

The new provision allows an employer to take positive action where they reasonably think that:

- People who share a protected characteristic suffer a disadvantage connected to that characteristic.

- People who share a protected characteristic have needs that are different from the needs of people who do not share it.

- Participation in an activity by people who share a protected characteristic is disproportionately low.

Employers may take action to achieve one of three legitimate aims, directly corresponding to the three situations described above:

- Enabling or encouraging people to overcome or minimise disadvantage
- Meeting different needs
- Enabling or encouraging participation

Positive action means providing training or support in development to enable the individual to overcome their disadvantage. The action that the employer takes should be proportionate to allow the individual to overcome that disadvantage or to encourage participation.

Positive action is not a requirement, the legislation simply says that it is not prohibited. Any employer using positive action will need to be able to demonstrate that there is good reason for the action, for example under-representation, and that their action is 'proportionate'.

The only exceptions to this are disability and age where discrimination can be justified in limited circumstances.

The steps an employer takes will be reasonable if there were no further reasonably practicable steps they could have taken.

Employees will be personally liable for unlawful acts which they commit during the course of employment where the employer is also liable. Employees may be liable for their actions even when their employer is able to rely successfully on the 'reasonable steps' defence.

2.4 RECRUITMENT AND PROMOTION

The Act allows positive discrimination in situations of recruitment and promotion purposes. They apply where two candidates are equally qualified for the role and the situation is balanced. In such circumstances the employer may prefer the candidate with the protected characteristic. This is not a requirement, however, the provision allows for the employer to take such action.

To recruit a less well-qualified candidate from an under-represented group will remain unlawful. The emphasis on this provision is that the candidates are as equally qualified as one another.

Liability of employers

An employer will be held liable for the actions of their employee during their employment, whether or not they knew the employee was engaged in the action. However, where the employer has taken all reasonable steps to prevent such acts, they will not be liable for unlawful acts committed by their employees.

2.5 DEFINITIONS

DEFINITIONS

Direct discrimination

Direct discrimination occurs when someone is treated less favourably than another person because of a protected characteristic they have or are thought to have, or because they associate with someone who has a protected characteristic.

This definition of direct discrimination applies to all protected characteristics. In relation to the protected characteristic of age, direct discrimination can be justified if it is a proportionate means of achieving a legitimate aim.

Discrimination arising from disability

The Act includes a new protection from 'discrimination arising from disability'. This states that it is discrimination to treat a disabled person unfavourably because of something connected with their disability (eg the need to take long breaks). In such cases the reason for the treatment does not matter, the question is whether the disabled person has been treated unfavourably because of something arising in consequence of their disability.

Unlike direct and indirect discrimination, discrimination arising from disability does not require the use of a comparator to establish unfavourable treatment. It is only necessary to demonstrate that the unfavourable treatment is because of the something arising as a consequence of their disability.

It is, however, possible to justify such treatment if it can be shown to be a proportionate means of achieving a legitimate aim. For this type of discrimination to occur, the employer or other person must know, or reasonably be expected to know, that the disabled person has a disability.

There is no change in the Act concerning the duty on the employer to make reasonable adjustments for staff to help them overcome any disadvantage of their disability. The protections of direct and indirect discrimination continue to apply.

Associative discrimination

This is direct discrimination against someone because they associate with another person who possesses a protected characteristic. Prior to the Act this already applied to race, religion or belief and sexual orientation. The Act extended this to cover age, disability, gender reassignment and sex. However, associative discrimination does not include marital status or civil partnership. This is because those protected characteristics are outside the scope of European discrimination legislation.

DEFINITIONS

Perceptive discrimination

This is direct discrimination against an individual because others think they possess a particular protected characteristic, even if they do not possess the characteristic.

Discrimination by perception was previously prohibited on grounds of sexual orientation, age, religion or belief or on racial grounds. However, this is now extended to include sex, gender reassignment and disability discrimination.

As with associative discrimination the protected characteristic of marital status or civil partnership is not covered.

Indirect discrimination

Indirect discrimination is where a provision, criterion or practice is applied to all employees and those with a particular protected characteristic are placed at a disadvantage. It is the phrase 'provision, criterion or practice' which is important here. It can be interpreted to mean any formal or informal policies, rules, customs and practices, arrangements, criteria, qualifications or provisions.

If the provision, criterion or practice cannot be justified as 'a proportionate means of achieving a legitimate aim', it will be unlawful. Being proportionate is interpreted as being fair and reasonable, including demonstrating the consideration of 'less discriminatory' alternatives to any decision being made.

It should be noted though that indirect discrimination does not include maternity or pregnancy. However, a pregnant woman who is adversely affected by a provision, criterion or practice may be able to bring a claim of indirect sex discrimination.

Harassment

The Equality Act identifies and prohibits three types of harassment.

(a) Involves unwanted conduct which is related to a relevant characteristic and has the purpose or effect of creating an intimidating, hostile, degrading, humiliating or offensive environment for the complainant or of violating the complainant's dignity.

(b) Sexual harassment which is unwanted conduct of a sexual nature where this has the same purpose or effect as the first type of harassment.

(c) Treating someone favourably because he or she has either submitted to or rejected sexual harassment, or harassment related to sex or gender reassignment.

Victimisation

Victimisation arises when the employer subjects the employee to a detriment because the employee has carried out a protected act or because the employer believes that the employee has done or may do a protected act in the future. 'Protected acts' in this context means supporting or raising a grievance under the Equality Act.

An example of **direct** discrimination would be failing to select or promote a woman because she is pregnant, or a person because they are of a particular nationality or race.

An example of **indirect** discrimination is changing shift patterns to include an early morning start, as women are more likely to be responsible for child care.

An example of **harassment** might be racial abuse, unwanted sexual advances – or even putting vital objects on a high shelf (as females are usually shorter).

An example of **victimisation** would be passing an employee over for promotion because (s)he had recently threatened to take the firm to an Employment Tribunal over discriminatory practices.

The obligation of non-discrimination generally applies to all aspects of employment, including advertisements, recruitment and selection programmes, access to training, promotion, disciplinary procedures, selection for redundancy, grounds for dismissal and retirement ages for men and women.

ACTIVITY 4 (15 MINS)

Suggest four examples that would constitute **indirect** discrimination on the grounds of sex.

2.6 COMPLAINTS OF DISCRIMINATION

Complaints of discrimination may be made to an Employment Tribunal within three months of the alleged offence. If conciliation is unsuccessful, the tribunal will hear the case, with the power to award:

(a) An order declaiming the rights of both parties

(b) A recommendation for action to redress discriminatory practices within a specified time

(c) An order requiring the discriminating employer to pay compensatory damages

2.7 THE EQUALITY AND HUMAN RIGHTS COMMISSION (EHRC)

The EHRC replaced the former Commission for Racial Equality, the Equal Opportunities Commission and the Disability Rights Commission. Launched on 1 October 2007, broadly, the EHRC:

(a) Promotes equal opportunities and anti-discrimination policy

(b) Keeps the legislation concerning discrimination under review, and advises the government on developing the law

(c) Works with employers, service providers and organisations to develop best practice

(d) Conducts enquiries into alleged discrimination

(e) Where necessary uses its powers to enforce the law

(f) Undertakes research and publishes advice and guidance

(g) Issues Codes of Practice

The EHRC will assist some applicants in Employment Tribunal proceedings with advice or legal representation. www.equalityhumanrights.com

FOR DISCUSSION

- 'We required an enthusiastic person, flexible enough to fit in with our dynamic organisation culture and in touch with the latest thinking.'

- 'How would you feel about managing older people?'

- 'Don't you think someone like you should be looking for something with a little more responsibility?'

Are these ageist comments? If so, why – and to whom?

WEBLINK

For more on equal opportunity and diversity:

CIPD (2011 Sex discrimination, sexual orientation, gender reassignment and employment)

▶▶ www.cipd.co.uk/hr-resources/factsheets/sex-discrimination-sexual-orientation-gender-reassignment-employment.aspx

CIPD (2012 Fact sheet on race, religion and employment)

▶▶ www.cipd.co.uk/hr-resources/factsheets/race-religion-employment.aspx

CIPD (2011 Fact sheet on harassment and bullying at work)

▶▶ www.cipd.co.uk/hr-resources/factsheets/harassment-bullying-at-work.aspx

3 EQUAL OPPORTUNITIES IN PRACTICE

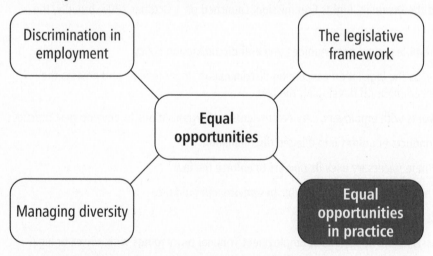

3.1 FORMULATING EFFECTIVE POLICIES

It is often suggested that many organisations make minimal efforts to avoid discrimination. They pay lip-service to the idea, to the extent of claiming 'We are an Equal Opportunities Employer' in advertising literature or (more recently) adding the words 'religion', 'sexual orientation' and 'age' to discrimination policies. A number of measures are necessary to establish equal opportunity in reality.

Ingham (2003) suggests the following key steps in implementing a **diversity policy**, taking into account all the equal opportunity requirements.

Step 1   **Analyse your business environment**

- Internally – does the diversity of the organisation reflect the population in its labour market?
- Externally – does the diversity of the workforce mirror that of the customer base?

Step 2   **Define diversity and its business benefits**

- Legal, moral and social benefits
- Business benefits: better understanding of market segments; positive employer brand; attraction and retention of talent
- Employee benefits: more representative workforce; value and respect for people; opportunity to contribute fully; enhanced creativity

Step 3   **Introduce diversity policy into corporate strategy**

- Weave diversity into corporate values and mission

Step 4   **Embed diversity into core HR processes and system**

- Review and refocus recruitment and selection, induction, reward and recognition, career management and training and development

Step 5   **Ensure leaders implement policy**

- Leaders and top management need to provide long-term commitment and resources
- Use diversity as a key factor in coaching, awareness training and development of managers

Step 6   **Involve staff at all levels**

- Educate the workforce through awareness training
- Create a 'diversity handbook'
- Set up diversity working parties and councils
- Establish mentoring schemes

Step 7   **Communicate, communicate, communicate**

- Communicate diversity policy and initiatives clearly
- Internally: updates, briefings, training, intranet pages
- Externally: to boost employer brand and recruitment

Step 8   **Understand your company's needs**

- Match resources to the size of the organisation and the scale of change required
- Consider using diversity consultants or best practice representatives to provide advice, support and training

Step 9   **Evaluate**

- Benchmark progress at regular intervals
- Internally: diversity score cards, employee climate surveys
- Externally: focus groups, customer/supplier surveys

Monitoring will be a particularly important part of the implementation process. The numbers of female, disabled, ethnic minority and mature-age staff can easily be monitored using workforce statistics and 'Equal Opportunity Monitoring Forms' filled out by employees on:

(a) Entering (and applying to enter) the organisation

(b) Leaving the organisation

(c) Applying for transfers, promotions or training schemes

Another area of particular sensitivity is recruitment and selection. There is always a risk that a disappointed job applicant, for example, will attribute his or her lack of success to discrimination, especially if the recruiting organisation's workforce is conspicuously lacking in representatives of the same ethnic minority, sex or age band.

ACTIVITY 5   (1½ HOURS)

Outline a set of anti-discrimination policy points for the recruitment manager, covering:

(a) Job advertising

(b) Use of recruitment agencies

(c) Job application forms

(d) Job interviews

(e) Selection tests

(f) Record-keeping

Bear in mind the need to avoid both *discrimination* and *allegations* of *discrimination*.

3.2 POSITIVE ACTION APPROACHES

In addition to responding to legislative provisions, some employers have begun voluntarily to address the underlying problems, by taking active steps to encourage the recruitment, training and promotion of previously under-represented groups. The following are just some of the positive action measures that might be used.

(a) Putting equal opportunities higher on the agenda by appointing Equal Opportunities Managers (and even Directors) reporting directly to the HR Director.

(b) Flexible hours, childcare vouchers, 'term-time' or annual hours contracts (to allow for school holidays), career break and return-to-work schemes to help women to combine careers with family responsibilities.

(c) Posting managerial vacancies internally, giving more opportunities for movement up the ladder for groups currently over-represented at lower levels of the organisation.

(d) Assertiveness training and business networking to support various groups in managing their career potential.

(e) Awareness training for managers and staff to encourage them to think about issues of discrimination, harassment and diversity.

(f) Positive action to encourage job and training applications from minority groups: using ethnic languages and pictures showing a racial/ethnic mix of people in advertisements, for example. Another example is pre-recruitment or pre-training instruction for minority groups: the Metropolitan Police piloted a scheme of such courses, covering literacy, numeracy, current affairs, physical fitness and interpersonal skills, to allow ethnic minority applicants to compete on an equal basis for training places.

(g) Alteration of premises to accommodate wheelchair users: supplying Braille or large-print versions of documentation; supplying computerised text-based telephones or interpreters for hearing impaired people.

We have illustrated other positive action approaches in our examples throughout this chapter.

SIGNPOST

Perhaps it is unfair to expect legislation to change deep-seated attitudes towards individual differences. Law may only change people's behaviour; to change how we feel and what we know (ie our attitudes) requires long-term education and actual experience of working with the affected groups. An alternative approach to the management of individual differences began in the USA and is now established in UK practice.

4 MANAGING DIVERSITY

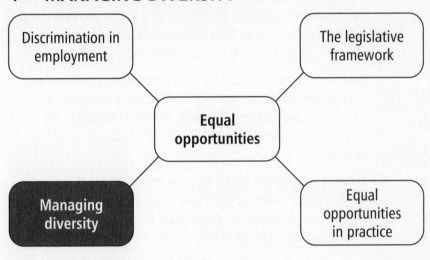

4.1 DIVERSITY

DEFINITION

Managing diversity is based on the belief that the individual differences we currently focus on under equal opportunities (gender, race, age etc) are crude and irrelevant classifications of the most obvious differences between people, and should be replaced by a genuine understanding of the ways in which individuals differ.

The ways in which people are *meaningfully* different in the workplace include personality, preferred working style and individual needs and drives. These things do not necessarily correlate with racial or gender differences in any way. For example, it would be a gross oversimplification to say that all women in your organisation require assertiveness training: it may be less appropriate for many women than for some men. Thus, effective managers seek to understand the job-relevant ways in which their staff differ and should seek to manage their performance in ways which recognise those differences as far as possible. Managers need to understand the unique contribution each person – not each 'category or person' – can make to the organisation.

A 'managing diversity' orientation implies the need to be proactive in managing the needs of a diverse workforce in areas (beyond equal opportunity and discrimination) such as:

(a) Tolerance of individual differences

(b) Communicating effectively with (and motivating) culturally diverse workforces. (We address this issue further in Chapter 12.)

(c) Managing workers with diverse family structures and responsibility

(d) Managing the adjustments to be made by the ageing workforce

(e) Managing diverse career aspirations and paths

(f) Confronting literacy, numeracy and qualifications issues in an international workforce

(g) Managing co-operative working in ethnically diverse teams

The other major difference is that having a diverse workforce is seen as being beneficial to an organisation in terms of its economic or service provision. Essentially, there are considered to be six key benefits:

Cost	Organisations have observed that, through employing a more diverse workforce, the productivity levels are high, attrition and absence rates lower. Certainly in the UK B&Q found attrition and absence were improved when employing an older workforce.
Resource acquisition	Organisations that develop a reputation for excelling in diversity management, will attract the best qualified employees from the minority groups. A diverse and highly capable organisation will become more successful, which will in turn attract even more applicants.
Marketing	A diverse organisation will be able to understand the needs of different market segments better than a less diverse organisation. Thus if computer games companies want to sell more games to women they would be sensible to employ female game designers.
Creativity	The argument suggests that a diverse organisation will be more creative and innovative. The more homogeneous the group, the more the norms and accepted thinking will limit the ability of the group to think creatively. Additionally, the group will not be coming into contact with new ideas and stimuli from a broader environment as they will typically sit within the same one.
Problem-solving	The greater and more diverse the pool of those trying to solve the problem, the more information and different perspectives available. Less diverse organisations will have fewer reference points and so will risk being stifled in their scope of thought.
Flexibility	A by-product of an organisation seeking to become more diverse, it must also become more flexible in order to accommodate the broad range of employees. The flexibility in turn becomes a strength as the flexible organisation is more effectively able to respond to its external environment.

This argument for a diverse workforce is especially powerful for customer-facing organisations, where a customer would expect to see the diversity of their environment reflected in the workforce.

The success of diversity management can often be linked to the culture of the organisation. Ideally, the culture of the organisation is one that sees all individuals as a valuable resource and as people who can be helped to achieve their potential. What needs to be recognised is that to help everyone achieve their potential is unlikely to be enrolling everyone through the same programmes or necessarily creating the same work environment.

The ways in which people are meaningfully different in the workplace include personality, preferred working style and individual needs and drives. These things do not necessarily correlate with racial or gender differences in any way. As stated earlier, it would be a gross oversimplification to say that all women in an organisation require assertiveness training: it may be less appropriate for many women than for some men. Thus, the organisation will be educating the managers to seek to understand the job-relevant ways in which employees differ and should seek to manage their performance in ways which recognise those differences as far as possible. Managers need to understand the unique contribution each person – not each 'category or person' – can make to the organisation.

It is recognised that during the initial phases of moving to a diverse environment that conflicts will occur. As with any group forming there will be a storming phase and this is the same for organisations. However, it has been found that after the conflict phase as the organisation becomes more accustomed to the diversity the value it can bring begins to emerge, and the organisation itself becomes multicultural.

During the recruitment the manner in which an organisation is operating with diversity at the heart of its operations will become apparent and applicants can be expected to pick this up.

EXAMPLE   BT'S APPROACH TO INCREASING GENDER DIVERSITY

BT recognises that it is crucial that its staff reflect the diversity of its customers and are able to meet their ever-changing needs. It has introduced a number of initiatives to ensure that more women are recruited and progress in their careers with the company.

Recruitment initiatives to improve diversity:

- From the recruitment stage of working with employment agencies, schools, universities, and college careers offices, representatives of BT's diversity networks attend careers fairs and promote BT as a place for women to work. These efforts are reflected in recruitment figures for the 2004 financial year: 32.8% of new recruits were women – including 42.2% of new graduates and 11.5% of modern apprentices compared with 22.7% of BT's total workforce.

- Career Space Consortium: To help address Europe's continuing shortage of people with good ICT skills, BT co-chairs the Career Space Consortium, a European Public Private Partnership that encourages people, particularly women, to acquire engineering and computer skills. Most of the graduate and skilled recruits are needed by the expanding IT, multimedia and e-commerce units. The general shortage of people with ICT skills presents an opportunity to attract more women.

- Equal Pay, Equal Value: BT recognises that benefits packages must be competitive if they are to recruit and retain the best people. Its approach to equal pay encompasses gender, ethnic origin and disability.

- Set Targets: BT has set targets for the recruitment and retention of ethnic minorities, disabled people and women.

- Diversity Champion: BT's commitment to diversity is demonstrated at strategic level. It has a diversity champion in the UK who chairs BT's Global Equality and Diversity Forum. The forum is composed of diversity champions, senior managers from each business unit. Senior managers also lead specific groups, which include race, gender, age, disability and sexual orientation. The company also demonstrates active involvement in many national and international networks that promote diversity in the workplace.

Retention initiatives to improve diversity

Attracting the best people is one thing, keeping them is another. For BT attaining its target for the representation of women employees (25%) is proving more difficult than for ethnic minorities and people with a disability. The figures show that retention rather than recruitment is the main barrier.

- Work-life Balance: The company has approximately 7,900 employees working from home and approximately 5,600 people working part-time.

  Using innovative communications technology many more BT people can work flexibly. For example, employees can mix home and office working, work long and short days and save blocks of non-working time to use during school holidays.

- To improve retention in 2003, BT undertook a review of maternity packages that led to the promotion of flexible working to address difficulties experienced by families with very young children.

- BT Women's Executive Network: Following the Tyson report commissioned by the UK government about increasing diversity on UK boards, BT Chairman Sir Christopher Bland, launched the BT Women's Executive Network. This was set up in 2003 to increase the proportion of women at senior management level.

The action plan includes tackling barriers to women's career progression, increasing role models and mentors and providing networking and support. In the 18 months to September 2003, of those promoted to management positions 43% were women and 12% from ethnic minorities.

The results of BT's commitment to increasing the diversity of its workforce are shown by BT's 'platinum' score in the recent Opportunity Now benchmarking exercise.

(DTI – Towards a Business case for Diversity, 2005)

4.2 EQUAL OPPORTUNITIES AND MANAGEMENT OF DIVERSITY

Torrington *et al* (2011) sum up the major differences between an 'equal opportunities' approach and a 'management of diversity' approach as follows.

	Equal opportunities	Managing diversity
Purpose	Reduce discrimination	Utilise employee potential to maximum advantage
Approach	Operational	Strategic
Case argued	Moral and ethical	Business objectives: improve profitability
Responsibility	HR/personnel function	All managers
Focuses on	Groups	Individuals
Perspective	Dealing with different needs of different groups	Integrated
Benefits for employees	Improved opportunities for disadvantaged employees, primarily through setting targets	Improved opportunities for all employees
Focus of management activity	Recruitment	Managing
Remedies	Changing systems and practices	Changing corporate culture
Monitoring success	Changed processes	Business outcomes

CHAPTER ROUNDUP

- Discrimination at work affects a number of different groups, including women, ethnic minorities, the disabled, gays and bisexuals, people of different religious beliefs and older workers – all are now protected under UK law.

- Discrimination can be either direct or indirect, or by implication. Victimisation and harassment should also be addressed by equal opportunities policies.

- Equal opportunities is not only concerned with access to employment but also the whole employment life cycle: training and development, appraisal, promotion, reward, employment protection and so on.

- Managing diversity means managing people in a way that respects their individuality and beliefs, instead of by crude stereotypes.

QUICK QUIZ

1   Identify two of the stereotypical reasons given for employers resisting employing disabled people.

2   List the nine 'protected characteristics' outlined in the Equality Act 2010.

3   A woman may lawfully be turned down for promotion if she is pregnant, and intends to take maternity leave. True or false?

4   During recruitment when is the employer allowed to positively discriminate?

5   What is meant by:

    (a)   Direct discrimination
    (b)   Indirect discrimination

6   What is sexual harassment?

7   What does EHRC stand for?

8   Outline a nine-step plan for implementing diversity policy.

9   What is managing diversity?

10 How is an 'equal opportunities' approach different from a 'managing diversity' approach?

ANSWERS TO QUICK QUIZ

1   Your answer could include long periods off work for medical causes, accident-proneness, poor skill levels, difficulties in adjusting to the work environment for wheelchair access and other disability needs, negative image to customers, who allegedly feel awkward in the presence of disabled people and the 'positive' association of certain jobs with disabled workers (eg lift attendants, switchboard operators, simple assembly tasks), stereotyping disabled roles and capabilities.   (see Para 1.7)

2   The nine protected characteristics are: Age, Disability, Gender reassignment, Marriage and civil partnership, Pregnancy and maternity, Race, Religion or belief, Sex and Sexual orientation.   (Para 2.2)

3   False. Pregnancy/maternity rights are protected regardless of circumstances.

(Para 2.2)

4   The Act allows positive discrimination in situations of recruitment and promotion purposes. They apply where two candidates are equally qualified for the role and the situation is balanced. In such circumstances the employer may prefer the candidate with the protected characteristic.   (Para 2.4)

5   Direct discrimination occurs when someone is treated less favourably than another person because of a protected characteristic they have or are thought to have, or because they associate with someone who has a protected characteristic.

Indirect discrimination is where a provision, criterion or practice is applied to all employees and those with a particular protected characteristic are placed at a disadvantage. It is the phrase 'provision, criterion or practice' which is important here. It can be interpreted to mean any formal or informal policies, rules, customs and practices, arrangements, criteria, qualifications or provisions.   (Para 2.5)

6   Sexual harassment is one of the three types of harassment defined under the Equality Act, it is unwanted conduct of a sexual nature where this has the same purpose or effect as the first type of harassment.   (Para 2.5)

7   The Equality and Human Rights Commission   (Para 2.7)

8   See Para 3.1 for a full answer.

9   It is an alternative to equal opportunities which seeks better performance from employees based on their individual differences in personality, style and needs, rather than cruder distinctions such as gender and ethnicity.   (Para 4.1)

10   See Para 4.2 for a full answer.

ANSWERS TO ACTIVITIES

1   Reasons for discrimination against women at work include the following.

(a)   Social pressures on the woman to bear and raise children, and on the man to make a lifetime commitment to paid work as the 'breadwinner'. Employers assumed – and sometimes still assume – that women's paid work would be short-term or interrupted, and that training and development was therefore hardly worthwhile.

(b)   The nature of earlier industrial work, which was physically heavy: legal restrictions were placed on women's employment in areas such as mines, night work in factories etc.

(c)   Lack of organisation of women at work and influence in trade unions (except in industries such as textiles), up until 1980s.

(d)   The reinforcing of segregation at home and at school: for example, lack of encouragement to girls to study mathematical and scientific subjects.

(e)   Career ladders which fail to fast-track women. Apprenticeships, for example, are rarely held by girls. A woman graduate starting as a secretary is less likely to advance than a male graduate who starts as a management trainee. In addition, organisations like banks, which have traditionally developed staff on the assumption of a lifetime career with the one employer, have tended to assume that women are unlikely to want a lifetime career. Commitments to geographical mobility are similarly assumed to be undesirable to women.

(f)   Child-bearing and family responsibilities. Part-time work has enabled many women to continue in paid employment, but tends to apply to jobs which carry little prospect for promotion.

2   This is personal to you. Note, however, how pervasive, subtle and influential discrimination can be.

3   Organisations offer a variety of excuses for doing this:

(a)   Cost (although performance-based pay systems are taking over from age-based ones in many companies).

(b)   Fear that the pay-back period on training will be too short.

(c)   A young customer base (on the supposition of an affinity between people of a common age).

(d)   A 'young' organisational culture.

(e)   In IT recruitment, lack of relevant experience among older workers.

(f)   Stereotypes about older workers' assumed resistance to change, inability to learn (and 'unlearn') skills and reduced motivation.

(g)   'Image' – if this is the right word! Middle managers will often favour very young glamorous secretaries, particularly if they are recruiting for themselves.

In addition, one of the principal reasons for discriminatory practices is that they have only recently been addressed in UK law.

4   (a)   Advertising a vacancy in a primarily male environment, where women would be less likely to see it.

(b)   Offering less favourable terms to part-time workers (given that most of them are women).

(c)   Specifying age limits which would tend to exclude women who had taken time out of work for child-rearing.

(d)   Asking in selection interviews about plans to have a family (since this might be to the detriment of a woman, but not a man).

5   (a)   **Advertising**

    (i)   Any wording that suggests preference for a particular group should be avoided (except for genuine occupational qualifications).

    (ii)   Employers must not indicate or imply any 'intention to discriminate'.

    (iii)   Recruitment literature should state that the organisation is an Equal Opportunities Employer.

    (iv)   The placing of advertisements only where the readership is predominantly of one race or sex is construed as indirect discrimination.

(b)   **Recruitment agencies**. Instructions to an agency should not suggest any preference.

(c)   **Application forms**. These should not include any questions which are not work-related (such as domestic details) and which only one group is asked to complete.

(d)   **Interviews**

    (i)   Any non-work-related question must be asked of all interviewees, if any. Even then, some types of question may be construed as discriminatory. (You cannot, for example, ask only women about plans to have a family or care of dependants, or ask – in the worst case – about 'the pill' or PMT.)

    (ii)   It may be advisable to have a witness at interviews, or at least to take detailed notes, in the event that a claim of discrimination is made.

(e)   **Selection tests**. These must be wholly relevant, and should not favour any particular group. (Even personality tests have shown to favour white male applicants.)

(f)   **Records**. Reasons for rejection, and interview notes, should be carefully recorded, so that in the event of investigation the details will be available.

Welfare, health and safety

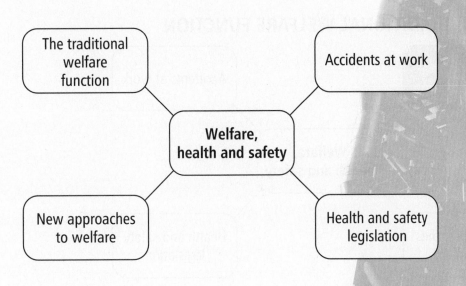

The traditional welfare function

Accidents at work

Welfare, health and safety

New approaches to welfare

Health and safety legislation

Introduction

Health, safety and well-being at work may be considered important for several reasons.

- Employees should be protected from needless pain and suffering (obvious – we hope!)

- Employers have legal obligations to take reasonable measures to protect the health and safety of their employees.

- Accidents, illness and other causes of employee absence and/or impaired performance cost the employer money.

- A business's employer brand and image in the marketplace may suffer if its health and safety record is bad.

This chapter looks at the law and best practice relating to health and safety at work, as well as broader welfare issues.

Your objectives

In this chapter you will learn about the following.

- The traditional welfare function

- Occupational health practices and policies

- The management of employee absence and absenteeism

- Accidents at work

- Health and safety legislation and the role of the Health and Safety Commission

- New approaches to welfare, ergonomics, substance abuse, stress, HIV/AIDS and workplace counselling

1 THE TRADITIONAL WELFARE FUNCTION

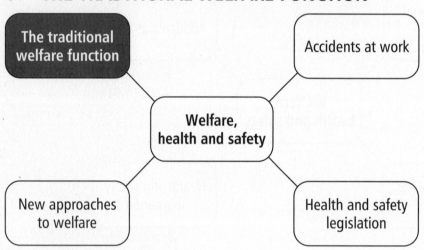

1.1 WHAT IS WELFARE?

DEFINITION

Welfare is 'a state of faring or doing well, freedom from calamity, enjoyment of health'. In HRM terms, this implies 'efforts to improve conditions of living for a group of employees or workers'.

In Chapter 1 of this Course Book, we described how the HR function grew out of industrial welfare work.

Employers might want to provide welfare:

(a) Because of a genuine sense of corporate social responsibility towards employees

(b) To improve the morale and loyalty of employees

(c) Because work (and non-work) problems impact on the 'steady state' performance of employees

(d) Because other companies and organisations are offering similar services/benefits, and they need to do the same in order to attract and retain the calibre of staff they require

FOR DISCUSSION

Staff spend at least half their waking time at work or in getting to it or leaving it. They know they contribute to the organisation when they are reasonably free from worry, and they feel, perhaps inarticulately, that when they are in trouble they are due to get something back from the organisation. People are entitled to be treated as full human beings with personal needs, hopes and anxieties; they are employed as people, they bring themselves to work, not just their hands, and they cannot readily leave their troubles at home.'

(Martin, 1967)

Is this a 'soft' or a 'hard' HRM view? Is it a convincing argument for welfare?

Note that a case be made *against* the provision of discretionary welfare.

(a)   Welfare is provided for by the state: why should other organisations duplicate services?

(b)   Welfare is irrelevant or even counter to the strategic objectives of the business (notably, profit maximisation).

(c)   Welfare services have not been shown to increase loyalty or motivation: they are largely taken for granted and, as such, are more likely to be a source of disappointment and dissatisfaction at any shortcomings than a source of satisfaction. Even gratitude/or appreciation is not a prime motivator. Any positive effects are hard to measure: the whole concept is relentlessly 'soft'.

(d)   The non-work affairs and interests of employees are not the business of employers. If this attitude prevails in some situations (so that if the employee commits an offence outside work, this is not sufficient grounds for dismissal) it should prevail in others.

(e)   Business organisations are not equipped to deal with welfare issues. Line managers are not trained to do so, and cannot devote sufficient time to follow-up. Centralising welfare responsibilities places a burden on HR specialists who are struggling to get away from the 'nursemaid' role and into strategic management.

Welfare may not demonstrably have a *positive* effect on morale and productivity – but anxiety, stress and distress invariably have a *negative* effect which should be alleviated where possible in the interests of effectiveness. In other words, welfare is a **hygiene factor**.

SIGNPOST

The more recent orientation of HRM towards welfare is that the health of the individual (in the broadest sense) represents the health of the organisation. If employees can be proactively helped not just to avoid accidents and illnesses, but to become more resilient to stress, healthier, physically fitter, mentally more flexible, emotionally more stable, they are more likely to perform at a consistent and high level on behalf of the organisation. We examine this orientation and its implications in Section 4 below. Here, we look at some of the concerns of traditional welfare.

1.2 OCCUPATIONAL HEALTH

Occupational health programmes are concerned largely with the effects of the working environment on workers. This may involve:

(a) Identifying substances, conditions or processes which are actually or potentially hazardous, and in what circumstances.

(b) Identifying the effect of methods and processes of work on the human body and mind.

(c) Exercising control over the working environment and substances used in the course of work, so as to minimise risk.

Thus, occupational health is concerned with toxic substances (such as lead oxide, chlorine, asbestos, and radiation) and with protective measures against all of these, as well as less obvious sources of ill health at work, including noise, fatigue and physical and mental stress (excessive demands on the body and mind). Increasingly, it is also concerned with personal substance abuse and other fitness and mental well-being factors that might have a direct or indirect effect on the workplace and work performance. We discuss these factors in Section 4 below.

ACTIVITY 1   (30 MINS)

Are there any aspects of your work or study environment that you would describe as a:

(a) Hindrance to your work?
(b) Source of stress or dissatisfaction?
(c) Hazard to your health?

Some of the key 'traditional' causes of ill-health at work, and the regulations applying to them, are as follows.

(a) **Noise**

Industrial hearing impairment has long been recognised as a problem for factory workers and machine operators, but the stressful and distracting effects of noise have more recently been identified. Continuous loud noise can be protected against by sound-proofing and personal ear protection. Sound-proofing (eg acoustic hoods over noisy office printers) and broadcast 'white noise' (soft, constant, featureless sound) are often used in office environments to reduce noise irritation. (*Noise at Work Regulations 1989*)

(b) **General environmental 'hygiene'**

The *Workplace (Health, Safety and Welfare) Regulations 1992* provides for health and hygiene in areas such as the following.

(i) **Ventilation**. Air should be fresh or purified.

(ii) **Temperature** levels must be 'reasonable' inside buildings during working hours: not less than 16°C where people are seated, or 13°C if moving about.

(iii) **Lighting** should be suitable and sufficient, and natural if practicable. Windows should be clear and unobstructed.

(iv) **Cleaning and decoration**. Premises must be kept clean.

(v) **Space**. Each person should have at least 11 cubic metres of space.

(vi)   **Sanitary conveniences and washing facilities** must be suitable and sufficient: properly ventilated and lit, properly cleaned, separate for men and women – and enough of them to avoid undue delay!

(vii)   **Drinking water** should be available in adequate supply, with suitable drinking vessels.

(viii)   **Rest facilities and eating facilities** must be provided unless the employees' work stations are suitable.

(ix)   **First aid** equipment should be provided, under the charge of a responsible person who should be trained in first aid.

(c)   **Hazardous substances and work-related diseases**

Procedures will need to be in place for: warning signs and labels identifying toxic or hazardous chemicals and other substances; training of staff in handling and storing substances and in first aid treatment and reporting mechanisms in the event of exposure; secure storage of substances; protective clothing and equipment for handling substances *(Control of Substances Hazardous to Health Regulations 1994 (COSHH))*. Hazards include not only burning, blinding, respiratory dysfunction, poisoning and other 'immediate' effects of substances, but also **work-related diseases**.

(d)   **Manual handling operations**

Back injuries due to the incorrect lifting and carrying of heavy objects accounts for more than a quarter of the accidents reported each year in the UK. Employers should, as far as is reasonably practical, avoid the need for employees to undertake risky manual handling activity. All remaining operations must be assessed, and steps taken to reduce risks to the lowest level reasonably practicable: providing properly maintained equipment and procedures (back braces, conveyer belts etc) and training in their use *(Manual Handling Operations Regulations 1992)*.

(e)   **Use of computer workstations**

The workstation has become one of the potentially toxic hazards of the workplace. If you have ever worked for a long period at a VDU you may personally have experienced some discomfort: back ache, stiffness, eye-strain and muscular disorders are common effects. Referred to collectively as **'Repetitive Strain Injury'** or RSI, such symptoms now account for more than half of all work-related injuries in the USA and have reached epidemic proportions in Australia. Problems are due both to the ergonomics of the workstation and to working practices: poor posture, insufficient breaks for movement and so on. The *Health and Safety (Display Screen Equipment) Regulations 1992* provide for the adaptation of computer workstations and equipment so that: VDU screens do not flicker, are free from glare and are able to swivel and tilt; radiation is reduced to negligible levels; and desk, chair and keyboard arrangement allows for forearm rest and adjustment for improved posture. Additional policies should emphasise education in posture, stretching exercises and the provision of regular work breaks or changes in activity for VDU users.

(f)   **Pregnancy/maternity**

Pregnant women, those who have recently given birth and those who are breastfeeding are traditionally recognised as a special at-risk group by occupational health regulation and policy. The EC Directive on pregnancy and maternity was incorporated into the *Management of Health and Safety at Work (Amendment) Regulations 1994.*

Provisions include: risk assessment; adjustment or offers of alternative work to reduce the risk; and suspension on full pay as a last resort.

ACTIVITY 2 (30 MINS)

Reassess your appraisal of the health of your workplace in answer to Activity 1 above, in the light of the specific issues and provisions discussed. Were any of the health hazards mentioned new to you – or easily overlooked in the course of work? If so, what does this say about the need for occupational health policies?

Occupational health policy

There will be several elements to occupational health policy in any given area.

(a) **Hazard minimisation**: removing hazards where possible. Assessing and reducing employees' exposure to risk.

(b) **Information about hazards**: education, warning signs and labels, consultation with employees and safety experts.

(c) **Equipment**: protective clothing, ergonomically-designed workstations, sound-proofing, safety equipment, maintenance.

(d) **Training in the use of equipment**: systems and procedures for safe and healthy working, compulsory use of safety/protective equipment and clothing.

(e) **Employee responsibilities**: to co-operate with health and safety policies, use systems responsibly, inform the employer of conditions placing them at risk, inform the employer or health and safety officer of identified hazards.

(f) **Monitoring of occupational health**: reporting of illness and injury, identification of emerging health issues.

SIGNPOST

'Ill-health' and 'injury' are obviously closely related, and occupational health policies would consider issues relating to both. We consider *accidents* as a particular workplace risk, in Section 2 of this chapter.

1.3 ABSENTEEISM AND EMPLOYEE ABSENCE

Employee absence

Ill-health and injury are major causes of long- and short-term employee absence from work. A 2010 (published in 2011) survey by the CBI/Pfizer suggested that such absences cost UK business more than £17 billion a year (and estimated that £2.7 billion is due to staff 'pulling sickies' rather than absence resulting from genuine ill-health!).

Other reasons for absence are covered by employment protection legislation, such as pregnancy, parental leave, redundancy preparation, trade union activities and (most recently) time off for jury service.

Various legislation in the UK provides for:

(a) **Maternity leave** of 52 weeks in total (Statutory Maternity Pay and Social Security Regulations 2006).

(b) **Paternity leave**, whereby employed fathers may take up to two weeks' leave within 56 days of their child's birth, and up to 26 weeks' Additional Paternity Leave (some of which could be paid), if the mother returns to work *(Work and Families Act 2006)*.

(c) **Right of return**, following maternity and paternity leave, to the same job on equivalent terms, provided that written notice of intention to return has been given prior to the absence.

(d) **Parental leave**, whereby parents, adoptive parents and legal guardians with one year's continuous service have the right to 13 weeks' unpaid leave during a child's first five years in order to care for that child. The time off in any one year is limited to four weeks, and leave has to be taken in blocks of at least one week.

(e) **'Reasonable' time off**, unpaid, to deal with 'family emergencies' involving a dependant, including sickness, accident, death or serious problems at a child's school.

As we noted in Chapter 10, many companies are now pursuing 'family friendly' policies over and above the statutory minimum, to support equality opportunity.

Absence procedure

An absence procedure should do the following.

(a) Require all employees to notify their manager as soon as possible on the first day of absence, giving as much information as possible about the nature and likely duration of the absence.

(b) Require all employees absent with prior consent to complete an absence form on their return to work.

(c) Require a medical certificate to be provided (where relevant) for absences of seven days or more. In the UK, the Statement of Fitness for work 'or FIT' note is a medical statement issued by GPs since April 2010 – replacing the sick note. It aims to focus on what an employee is able to do at work, rather than what they cannot do.

(d) Discuss absences with employees and keep in contact with them, alerting them to the possibility of disciplinary action where appropriate.

(e) Ensure access to medical information and check this is up-to-date, prior to any disciplinary action being considered.

(f) Require the employee to notify management in the event of infectious or dangerous illness (so that other staff can be checked or warned).

(g) Look for suitable alternative work within the organisation for employees no longer able to perform their duties, and consider requests for flexible working where this might help.

(h) Check employees' entitlements to relevant benefits.

EXAMPLE

An absence and health study conducted by the CBI/Pfizer found the following.

- The average rate of absence in 2010 was 6.5 days per employee, only a marginal change from the record low of 6.4 days reached in 2009.

- Viewed over the longer term, average annual employee absence levels have fallen by more than a quarter since the 1980s.

- Still more could be done to improve employee attendance levels: there is a widening gap between the best and worst performing organisations in terms of average absence levels, showing the scope to raise performance.

- Absence continues to be higher amongst manual employees than among non-manual staff but the gap is narrowing steadily.

- Average levels of absence climb with organisation size. While SMEs average under five days of absence per employee, larger employers average over seven days.

- While average absence levels remain higher in the public sector than in the private sector, 2010 saw the gap narrow.

Costs and causes of absence

- The median total cost for each absent employee in 2010 was £760 a year.

- Absence costs vary by size of organisation and sector, with costs per absent employee in the public sector averaging 46% more than in the private sector in 2010.

- The direct costs of absence alone amounted to over £17bn across the economy in 2010.

- Non-work related illness and injury is by far the most widespread driver of employee absence, followed by post-operative recovery time.

- Other factors contributing to absence include personal problems, caring responsibilities and misuse of sick pay provision by some employees.

- Health issues are seen as the most common factor causing employees to fail to perform to their potential capacity at work.

(CBI Absence and Workplace Health Survey, 2011)

SIGNPOST

'Absence' raises issues such as ill-health and injury and domestic problems. What might the organisation do to help its employees in such times?

1.4 WELFARE BENEFITS AND SERVICES

Some of the key issues (from the traditional welfare perspective) are as follows.

(a) **Pension schemes**

Many firms set up occupational pension schemes for their employees, with various levels of employer and employee contributions.

Tight controls have been placed over the operation of pension funds, particularly with regard to the accountability of trustees, fund managers, auditors and advisers (Social Security Act 1985; Pensions Act 1995). Employees in occupational schemes which are contracted-out of the State Earnings-Related Pension Scheme (SERPS) lose their future entitlements under the state scheme: occupational schemes are required to ensure that they provide adequate benefits, however, and are potentially much more generous than the state scheme.

Company schemes can be very advantageous in that the employer makes a significant contribution to the individual's retirement pension. In the case of final salary schemes, the size of this contribution is determined by the commitment to support a specific level of pension. Such schemes are now unpopular with employers because of the open-ended and potentially very large commitment and, to the extent that company schemes continue to be available, are being replaced with defined contribution schemes that pay only as much pension as can be funded by the retiree's accumulated pension fund.

In the UK during 2012 significant changes were introduced for pension schemes.

From 1 October 2012 new pension duties for employers were phased in. The very largest employers were first to be phased in, there continues to be some uncertainty as to the timescale for smaller employers but, for employers with 250 or more people the changes are as follows.

The key employers' duties:

- The right of a jobholder who is an active member of a 'qualifying scheme' to remain so.

- The automatic enrolment by employers of jobholders aged at least 22 (and below state pension age) earning over a set amount into 'an automatic enrolment scheme'.

- The automatic re-enrolment of certain jobholders into such schemes, generally at approximately three-yearly intervals.

Staging dates

These new duties do not generally apply to an employer until that particular employer's 'staging date'. For existing employers as at 1 April, the statutory staging dates are spread over a 4½ year period commencing on 1 October 2012.

An existing employer's staging date is generally determined by reference to the number of people in its PAYE scheme (so that those employers which have the most people in their PAYE schemes have their staging dates first).

Where an employer has at least 250 people, the staging dates are:

120,000 or more	1 October 2012
50,000-119,999	1 November 2012
30,000-49,999	1 January 2013
20,000-29,999	1 February 2013
10,000-19,999	1 March 2013
6,000-9,999	1 April 2013
4,100-5,999	1 May 2013
4,000-4,099	1 June 2013

3,000-3,999	1 July 2013	
2,000-2,999	1 August 2013	
1,250-1,999	1 September 2013	
800-1,249	1 October 2013	
500-799	1 November 2013	
350-499	1 January 2014	
250-349	1 February 2014	

There is a degree of flexibility around these dates:

- An employer may take steps so that the new duties apply sooner than the staging date as given in the table.

- An employer will be able to postpone an employee's automatic enrolment by up to three months from the staging date, by notice to the employee concerned.

For a money purchase scheme the employer's and jobholder's combined contributions must be at least 8%, of which the employer must pay at least 3%.

However, for the first five years there are transitional arrangements:

	1 October 2012 to 30 September 2017	1 October 2017 to 30 September 2018	From 1 October 2018
Employer's contributions	At least 1%	At least 2%	At least 3%
Total of employer's and jobholder's contributions	At least 2%	At least 5%	At least 8%

(b) **Sick pay**

Statutory Sick Pay provides a basic income to employees who are incapable of attending their normal place of work due to illness. Employers are responsible for the first four weeks of SSP, after which they can claim payments back from the State through reduced National Insurance contributions.

Employers may also wish to offer discretionary Occupational Sick Pay (OSP), for example by maintaining full salary payment for a defined period of time. In order to minimise abuse of OSP, HR practitioners and line managers will need to monitor absence rates and periods carefully.

For motivational reasons, claims of sickness might be taken on trust as far as possible (unless there is positive proof of malingering). An illness or diagnosis may be confirmed by referring the employee to a company-approved doctor – but disciplinary action cannot be taken against an employee who refuses to be examined (unless there is a contractual agreement).

Welfare calls and visits may also be made during prolonged absence, in order to identify financial or practical help that may be offered, alleviate anxiety, offer counselling and so on.

(c)   **Maternity**

Maternity leave and health and safety provisions for pregnant workers have already been discussed above.

Statutory maternity pay was extended in 2007 (under the *Work and Families Act 2006*) from 39 weeks to 52 weeks. Similar benefits are also offered for paternity and adoption.

(d)   **Domestic problems**

Situations such as marital breakdown or bereavement are essentially private, but their effects are likely to carry over into the workplace. The Employment Relations Act 1999 provides for what used to be called 'compassionate leave' (unpaid) to deal with 'family emergencies', but organisations may develop a policy on:

(i)   What constitutes 'reasonable' time off
(ii)   Whether time off will be paid to some degree
(iii)   Whether additional welfare interventions can be offered.

Welfare services may include: access to the firm's own counsellors or referral to other support organisations; help with financial, legal and funeral arrangements arising from bereavement; and so on.

(e)   **Retirement/redundancy**

As discussed in Chapter 7, retirement and redundancy may be regarded as major adjustment crises in the lives of employees, and a variety of counselling, training and other services may be offered.

(f)   **Annual leave**

People need holidays! All employees are currently entitled to a minimum of 28 days' annual holiday under the *Work and Families Act 2006*. Bank holidays can be counted towards this entitlement.

ACTIVITY 3   (45 MINS)

Does your college or workplace have provision for welfare services? What are they? How well publicised are they? Ask for information, if it is not available in the Student/Employee Handbook or on notice boards. List the issues highlighted by the counselling or welfare programme.

WEBLINK

CIPD (*2012 Factsheet on Absence Measurement and Management*)

► ► www.cipd.co.uk/hr-resources/factsheets/absence-measurement-management.aspx

SIGNPOST

We now look at a major health and safety issue: workplace accidents.

2 ACCIDENTS AT WORK

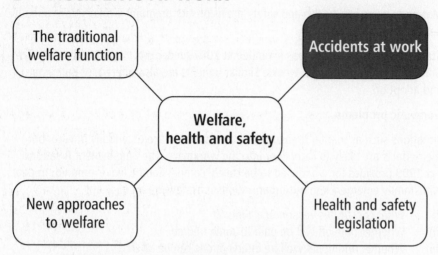

2.1 INCIDENCE OF INDUSTRIAL ACCIDENT

Newspapers frequently quote statistics showing large number of employee hours lost through accident and the associated cost to business. For example:

The head of micro-economics at Centre for Economics and Business Research (Cebr) said: 'Much research has been conducted into the cost of sick leave to the UK economy but this is the first time research … to examine the cost of long-term absence specifically. Cebr's estimates suggest that it is costing the UK private sector alone more than the government's annual rail budget.'

(*The Telegraph*, 2012)

However, it should be noted that:

(a) Accident rates vary substantially by industry, for example, a high proportion of deaths at work occur in the construction industry

(b) Small and large organisations have lower incidence rates than medium-sized organisations (perhaps because supervision is closer in small organisations and investment in safety/accident prevention staff and systems is greater in large ones).

(c) Working conditions (outdoor v indoor) and tools and technology (heavy machinery v PC) have the greatest impact on incident rates, followed by …

(d) Suggestions that some people are more prone to accidents than others (due to poor vision, stress, depression, alertness, immaturity and so on). However, 'accident proneness' is also related to the working patterns, responsibility and safety-awareness of individual employees: horseplay, practical jokes, cutting corners on safety measures and so on are frequent causes of accident.

ACTIVITY 4 (10 MINS)

A scene from everyday office life is shown below: Figure 11.1. Note down anything that strikes you as being dangerous about this working environment.

Figure 11.1: Unsafe work practices!

Apart from obviously dangerous equipment in factories, construction sites and even offices, there are many hazards to be found in the modern working environment. Many accidents could be avoided by the simple application of common sense and consideration by employer and employee, and by safety consciousness encouraged or enforced by a widely acceptable and well published **safety policy**.

2.2 COST OF ACCIDENTS

The **cost** of accidents to the employer consists of:

(a) Time lost by the injured employee

(b) Time lost by other employees whose work is interrupted by the accident

(c) Time lost by supervision, management and technical staff as a result of the accident

(d) A proportion of the cost of first aid materials, or even medical staff

(e) The cost of disruption to operations at work

(f) The cost of any damage and repairs and modification to the equipment

(g) The cost of any compensation payments or fines resulting from legal action

(h) The costs associated with increased insurance premiums

(i) Reduced output from the injured employee on return to work

(j) The cost of possible reduced morale, increased absenteeism, increased labour turnover among employees

(k) The cost of recruiting and training a replacement for the injured worker

An employer may also be liable to an employee in tort if the employee is injured as a result of either:

(a) The employer's failure to take reasonable care in providing safe premises and plant, a safe system of work and competent fellow employees.

(b) The employer's breach of a statutory duty – say, to fence dangerous machinery. Although the injured employee's damages may be reduced if the injury was partly a consequence of his/her own contributory negligence, due allowance is made for ordinary human failings, such as inattentiveness, tiredness and so on.

2.3 ACCIDENT PREVENTION

The prevention of accidents requires integrated HR-led policies and practices, including attention to workplace design, communication of health and safety rules and values, training etc. Some of the steps which might be taken to reduce the frequency and severity of accidents are as follows.

(a) Developing safety awareness among staff and workers and encouraging departmental pride in a good safety record.

(b) Developing effective consultative participation between management, workers and unions so that safety and health rules can be accepted and followed.

(c) Giving adequate instruction in safety rules and measures as part of the training of new and transferred workers, or where working methods or speeds of operation are changed.

(d) Minimising specific hazards. Materials handling, a major cause of accidents, should be minimised and designed as far as possible for safe working and operation.

(e) Building and equipment maintenance – apart from making sound job repairs, temporary expedients to keep production going should not prejudice safety.

(f) Safety inspections – carried out as a comprehensive audit, working through a checklist; or by using random spot checks or regular checks of particular risk points. Checklists used in the inspection process should identify corrective action to be taken, and allocate responsibility for that action.

(g) Compliance with legislation and industry/work environment codes of practice.

2.4 ACCIDENT REPORTING

An accident report is a management tool, designed to:

(a) Identify problems
(b) Indicate corrective action

Recurring accidents may suggest the need for special investigation, but only more serious incidents will have to be followed-up in depth. Follow-up should be clearly aimed at preventing recurrence – not placing blame.

The illustration below (Figure 11.2) shows the format of a **typical accident book** which should by law be kept by any organisation which employs more than ten people. (The one used by your organisation may be laid out differently, or it might consist of loose-leaf sheets.)

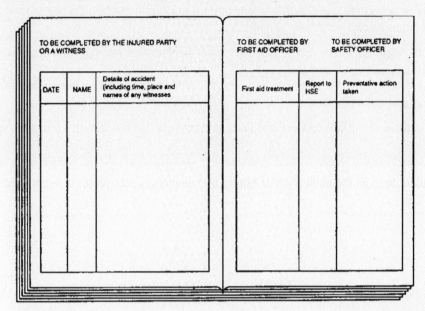

Figure 11.2: Accident Book

The **Reporting of Injuries, Diseases and Dangerous Occurrences Regulations 1995 (RIDDOR 95)** require employers to do the following.

(a)   Notify the environmental health authority or the Health and Safety Executive *immediately* if one of the following occurs.

   (i)   There is an accident connected with work and either an employee or self-employed person working on the premises is killed or suffers a major injury (including as a result of physical violence) or a member of the public is killed or taken to hospital.

   (ii)   There is a dangerous occurrence.

(b)   Send a completed **Accident report form** (see Figure 11.3) to do the following.

   (i)   Confirm within ten days a telephone report of an accident or dangerous occurrence (as described in (a) above).

   (ii)   Notify, within ten days of the accident, any injury which stops someone doing their normal job for more than three days.

   (iii)   Report certain work-related diseases.

DEFINITION

Major injuries include trauma like fractures other than to fingers, thumbs or toes, amputation, temporary or permanent loss of sight and any other injury which results in the person being admitted to hospital for more than 24 hours.

Dangerous occurrences are 'near misses' that might well have caused major injuries. They include the collapse of a load bearing part of a lift, electrical short circuit or overload causing fire or explosion, the malfunction of breathing apparatus while in use or during testing immediately before use, and many others.

Notifiable diseases include certain poisonings, occupational asthma, asbestos, hepatitis and many others.

The standard form for the notification of injuries and dangerous occurrences is reproduced at Figure 11.3.

HSE
Health & Safety
Executive

Health and Safety at Work etc Act 1974
The Reporting of Injuries, Diseases and Dangerous Occurrences Regulations 1995

Report of an injury or dangerous occurrence

Filling in this form
This form must be filled in by an employer or other responsible person.

Part A

About you

1 What is your full name?

2 What is your job title?

3 What is your telephone number?

About your organisation

4 What is the name of your organisation?

5 What is its address and postcode?

6 What type of work does your organisation do?

Part B

About the incident

1 On what date did the incident happen?

/ /

2 At what time did the incident happen?
(Please use the 24-hour clock eg 0600)

3 Did the incident happen at the above address?

Yes ☐ Go to question 4

No ☐ Where did the incident happen?

☐ elsewhere in your organisation - give the name, address and postcode

☐ at someone else's premises - give the name, address and postcode

☐ in a public place - give the details of where it happened

If you do not know the postcode, what is the name of the local authority?

4 In which department, or where on the premises, did the incident happen?

Part C

About the injured person

If you are reporting a dangerous occurrence, go to Part F.
If more than one person was injured in the same incident, please attach the details asked for in Part C and Part D for each injured person.

1 What is their full name?

2 What is their home address and postcode?

3 What is their home phone number?

4 How old are they?

5 Are they

☐ male?

☐ female?

6 What is their job title?

7 Was the injured person (tick only one box)

☐ one of your employees?

☐ on a training scheme? Give details:

☐ on work experience?

☐ employed by someone else? Give details of the employer:

☐ self-employed and at work?

☐ a member of the public?

Part D

About the injury

1 What was the injury? (eg fracture, laceration)

2 What part of the body was injured?

3 Was the injury (tick the one box that applies)

☐ a fatality?

☐ a major injury or condition? (see accompanying notes)

☐ an injury to an employee or self-employed person which prevented them doing their normal work for more than 3 days?

☐ an injury to a member of the public which meant they had to be taken from the scene of the accident to a hospital for treatment?

4 Did the injured person (tick all the boxes that apply)

☐ became unconscious?

☐ need resuscitation?

☐ remain in hospital for more than 24 hours?

☐ none of the above?

Part E

About the kind of accident
Please tick the one box that best describes what happened, then go to part G.

☐ Contact with moving machinery or material being machined

☐ Hit by a moving, flying or falling object

☐ Hit by a moving vehicle

☐ Hit by something fixed or stationary

☐ Injured while handling, lifting or carrying

☐ Slipped, tripped or fell on the same level

☐ Fell from a height
How high was the fall?

[_____] metres

☐ Trapped by something collapsing

☐ Drowned or asphyxiated

☐ Exposed to, or in contact with, a harmful substance

☐ Exposed to fire

☐ Exposed to an explosion

☐ Contact with electricity or an electrical discharge

☐ Injured by an animal

☐ Physically assaulted by a person

☐ Another kind of accident (describe it in part G)

Part F

Dangerous occurrences
Enter the number of the dangerous occurrence you are reporting. (The numbers are given in the Regulations and in the notes which accompany this form.)

[_____]

Part G

Describing what happened
Give as much detail as you can. For instance
• the name of any substance involved
• the name and type of any machinery involved
• the events that led to the incident
• the part played by any people.

If it was a personal injury, give details of what the person was doing. Describe any action that has since been taken to prevent a similar incident. Use a separate piece of paper if you need to.

[_____]

☐☐☐☐ [_____]

Part H

Your signature

[_____]

Date

[/   /   ]

Where to send the form
Please send it to the Enforcing Authority for the place where it happened. If you do not know the Enforcing Authority, send it to the nearest HSE office.

For official use
Client number [_____] Location number [_____] Event number [_____]   ☐ INV   REP ☐ Y ☐ N

Figure 11.3: RIDDOR Report Form

ACTIVITY 5 (30 MINS)

Invent (or carefully role-play) your own scenario for a typical (or unusual) workplace accident causing injury. Invent as many relevant details as you can. Now complete the specimen RIDDOR report reproduced in Figure 11.3.

SIGNPOST

We now consider at some of the main legislation on Health and Safety at work. Much of it is refreshingly practical, with lots of measures to be taken and procedures to be put in place: we only able to summarise. Like other legal provisions we have discussed in this Course Book, the 'law is a floor': remember that these are minimum standards – not 'best practice'! Best practice among employers is likely to be more:

- Scrupulous in enforcing safeguards

- Committed to providing consultation, information and training on health and safety

- Wide-ranging in its attempt to promote positive health and well-being and a culture of safety

3 HEALTH AND SAFETY LEGISLATION

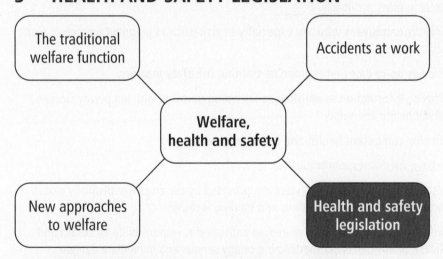

3.1 HEALTH AND SAFETY RESPONSIBILITIES

In the UK, the *Health and Safety at Work Act 1974* is the major piece of UK legislation on health and safety, together with Regulations and Codes of Practice implementing EU Directives. The 1974 Act provides for the introduction of a system of approved Codes of Practice, prepared in consultation with industry. Thus an employee, whatever his/her employment, should find that his/her work is covered by an appropriate code of practice.

Employers also have specific duties under the 1974 Act.

(a) All systems (work practices) must be safe.

(b) The work environment must be safe and healthy (well-lit, warm, ventilated and hygienic).

(c) All plant and equipment must be kept up to the necessary standard.

The **employee** also has a duty under the 1974 Act.

(a) To take reasonable care to avoid injury to himself/herself and others.

(b) To co-operate with his or her employers to help them comply with their legal obligations (including enforcing safety rules).

3.2 ONGOING RISK MANAGEMENT

Information, instruction, training and supervision should be directed towards safe working practices. Under the *Management of Health and Safety at Work Regulations 1992*, employers must:

(a) Carry out **risk assessment**, generally in writing, of all work hazards on a continuous basis.

(b) Introduce **controls** to reduce risks.

(c) Assess the **risks to anyone else** affected by their work activities (such as suppliers, customers, visitors).

(d) **Share hazard and risk information** with other employers, including those on adjoining premises, other site occupiers and all subcontractors coming onto the premises.

(e) **Revise safety policies** in the light of the above – or initiate safety policies if none were in place previously.

(f) Identify **employees who are especially at risk** (such as pregnant women or night shift workers).

(g) Provide up-to-date and appropriate **training in safety matters.**

(h) Provide **information to employees** (including part-time and temporary workers) about health and safety.

(i) Employ **competent health and safety advisers.**

Employees also have specific responsibilities to:

(a) Use all equipment, safety devices etc, provided by the employer **properly** and in accordance with the instructions and training received.

(b) **Inform** the employer, or an employee with specific responsibility for health and safety, of any perceived shortcoming or any serious and immediate dangers.

ACTIVITY 6 (NO TIME LIMIT)

Consider the health and safety programme at your place of work (or study).

(a) How well *aware* are you of any rules, procedures and information regarding health and safety? (Who is responsible for *making* you more aware of such matters?)

(b) How well do the organisation's rules, procedures and information comply with the requirements of the Regulations?

3.3 INFORMATION AND CONSULTATION

Under the *Health and Safety (Consultation with Employees) Regulations 1996*, employers must consult all of their employees on health and safety matters (such as the planning of health and

BPP
LEARNING MEDIA

safety training, any change in equipment or procedures which may substantially affect their health and safety at work or the health and safety consequences of introducing new technology). This involves giving information to employees *and* listening to and taking account of what they say before any health and safety decisions are taken.

FOR DISCUSSION

Safety flaws blamed as Pakistan factory fires kill more than 300

Factory fires in Pakistan's two biggest cities have killed more than 300 people – and been blamed on barred windows, shoddy building standards and the flouting of basic safety regulations. At least 289 died after becoming trapped in a blazing underwear factory in the coastal megalopolis of Karachi on Tuesday evening. That fire came just hours after a similar blaze in an illegally built shoe factory in Lahore, which killed at least 25.

The twin tragedies will focus attention on the weak workplace safety regime in a country that relies heavily on its low-cost garment and textile industries for vital export earnings.

(*The Guardian*, 2012)

What issues does this raise for HR practitioners participating in the outsourcing of organisational activities to overseas economies?

3.4 HEALTH AND SAFETY AUTHORITIES

The **Health and Safety Commission** was set up under the Health and Safety at Work Act 1974 to develop health and safety policies. It is made up of representatives of employers, employees, local government and relevant professional bodies. Responsibility for communicating, monitoring and enforcing the Commission's policies and relevant legislation falls to the Health and Safety Executive, which has powers of inspection and enforcement by:

(a) **Prohibition notice** requiring the shut down of hazardous processes until remedial action has been taken.

(b) **Improvement notice** requiring compliance with a statutory provision within a certain time (subject to appeal to an industrial tribunal).

(c) **Seizure** of hazardous articles for destruction or rendering harmless.

(d) **Prosecution** of offenders, liable to fine and even imprisonment in serious cases.

WEBLINK

The **Health & Safety Executive** has an extremely informative website, with an easy-to-use pull-down menu covering a wide range of 'health and safety topics'.

▶▶ http://www.hse.gov.uk

3.5 HEALTH AND SAFETY POLICY

There will be several elements to a health and safety policy, whatever the specific needs and hazards of a particular workplace.

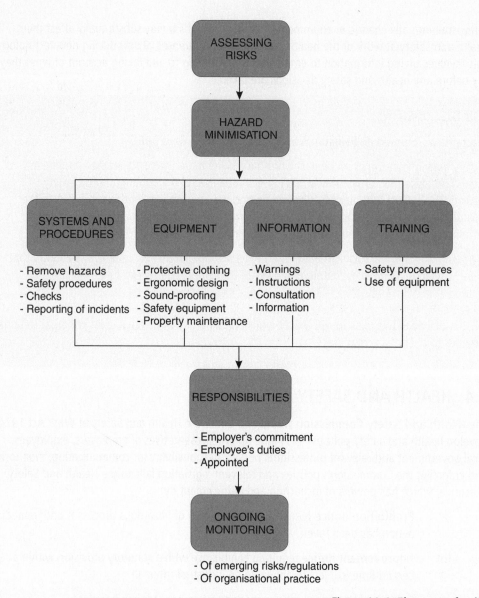

Figure 11.4: Elements of policy

The following is an **example of a Policy Statement** released by the former Department of Environment, Transport and the Regions (DETR), which used to have responsibility for the Health and Safety Commission (HSC) and the Health and Safety Executive (HSE). (In 2002, this responsibility was taken over by the Department for Work and Pensions.)

Health and Safety Policy Statement

This Health and Safety Policy Statement is to be observed by staff throughout the Department (including the Agencies and Government Offices). It reflects the importance I attach to the health, safety and welfare of all staff and others who may be affected by our activities. That includes contractors and visitors to our premises.

I expect all managers to give similar importance to these issues in their operational area and when determining local priorities, plans and resource allocation. I also recognise the valuable role played by Safety Representatives appointed by Trade Unions.

1   **Objectives**. The Department will meet all current and proposed legal requirements in the Health and Safety at Work Act 1974 and relevant subordinate legislation. This will be achieved through effective risk assessment and the implementation of appropriate

measures for the prevention or control of risks at work. The Department will promote continuous improvement in health and safety performance to become an exemplar of good practice. Regular feedback on progress will be provided.

2   **Systems**. The Department will put systems and procedures in place designed to ensure a safe system of work. As far as reasonably practicable, all equipment, vehicles, plant, premises, other work sites and work practices will be safe and free from any hazards to health and that employees, the public and others affected by our operations are not exposed to undue risk.

3   **Communication/Co-operation**. The policy will be brought to the attention of all employees and contractors. Legally all employees must co-operate in establishing and maintaining safe and healthy working conditions and avoid any actions which may adversely affect the health, safety and welfare of themselves, their colleagues, contractors or visitors. Consultation on Departmental health and safety issues will be undertaken...

4   **Monitoring and Auditing**. The Department will monitor and audit health and safety management systems and performance. An annual report on health and safety will be produced reflecting the Department's progress, forward plans and innovative initiatives.

5   **Review**. The policy will be continuously reviewed. A full review, including related management arrangements and performance, will be held in three years' time, or earlier, following any major change in health and safety legislation or our organisation.

This policy is fully endorsed by the Board and will be implemented by management throughout the Department. Roles and responsibilities will be clearly defined to ensure effective communication, provision of information, training, and systems for reporting to those with delegated responsibilities.

ACTIVITY 7   (5 MINS)

Underline or highlight the key words and phrases in the above example of a Policy Statement, which seem to you to reflect the most important aspects of health and safety policy, as described so far.

This will help you to know what to look for when you appraise the health and safety policies of your own organisation.

FOR DISCUSSION

Safety policy must be implemented in detailed practice (such as fire drills and equipment checking) but it is less likely to be consistently observed if senior managers fail to set a good example, to discipline breaches of policy, or to reward health and safety suggestions. The aim is to create a culture in which health and safety are key values.

What are the cultural values in your nation, local community and organisation that:

(a)   Promote health and safety?
(b)   Promote risk-taking and ill-health?

3.6 WORKING HOURS

You should be aware that working hours are also a health and safety issue, under the Working Time Regulations 1998 and subsequent amendments.

(a) Working hours are limited to 48 hours per week, averaged over a standard reference period of 17 weeks (or 26 weeks, where continuity of work is necessary, as in health or essential services, 24-hour production or seasonal work). This can be extended to a year by collective workplace agreement – to preserve annual hours schemes, for example.

(b) An employee may agree individually, in writing, to work more than 48 hours per week, and a record of hours should be retained in case the Health and Safety Commission requires it.

(c) All employees are entitled to a daily rest of 11 consecutive hours in every 24, and a 24-hour rest in every seven days (averaged over two weeks) – subject to adjustment by collective agreement.

(d) If the working day exceeds six hours, the employee is entitled to a minimum of 20 minutes' break.

ACTIVITY 8 (15 MINS)

Since you have broadened your awareness of what constitutes a threat to health and safety, take some time to think through HR policies. Suggest five other areas for consideration. (If you are currently employed, check your organisation's manual on health and safety: use the real-life resources available to you.)

SIGNPOST

Now let's look at the 'new' welfare role of HRM, and some of the hazards of the new workplace.

4 NEW APPROACHES TO WELFARE

BPP LEARNING MEDIA

4.1 A SHIFT IN PERSPECTIVE

HRM specialists have tried to distance themselves from the traditional welfare tag with its legalistic/reactive and paternalistic associations.

The new orientation to welfare activities is based on the recognition that healthy and focused individuals are likely to perform better at work, to be more flexible (physically, mentally and emotionally) and adaptable to change: in short, that it is possible to take a business-strategic view of employee health and well-being.

The new model of welfare is therefore:

(a) **Proactive** in its attempt to address potential health and safety issues, rather than reacting to regulation, complaint or crisis.

(b) **Positive** in its attempt to promote health and well-being rather than focusing solely on ill-health, injury and crisis.

(c) **Holistic** in its definition of health and well-being, including emotional and even spiritual factors.

(d) **Wide-ranging** in its attention to diverse issues, rather than being led by legislative agendas.

Goss (1994) summarised this new perspective as 'tough love': a hard-soft policy aimed at offering benefits and services which employees need and value, 'linked strategically with the needs of the organisation by enhancing performance'.

Issues in the new welfare model include:

(a) Work-life balance and the management of stress

(b) Ergonomics

(c) Promotion of positive health and fitness, and the management of substance abuse

(d) Confrontation of emerging health issues (such as HIV/AIDS or obesity) and other sources of distress

(e) Workplace counselling

(f) Employee Assistance Programmes (EAPs)

SIGNPOST

We discuss each of these issues, briefly, in turn.

4.2 WORK-LIFE BALANCE AND CONTROL OF STRESS

Overwork is frequently associated with poor diet, lack of exercise, inadequate relaxation, stress and relationship difficulties.

Despite the desire to increase productivity or enhance performance, many companies are realising that increasing workloads and working hours are in fact counter-productive, potentially encouraging absenteeism, ill-health, accidents and poor-quality work.

Elements in a work-life balance programme may include:

(a) In-house or consultant-led awareness training: clarification of values and priorities and so on.

(b)   In-house or consultant-led skills training: in time-management, delegation, work organisation, relaxation techniques.

(c)   Flexible working arrangements to allow time for family and social activities within the working week (as discussed in Chapter 9).

Stress and stress management

Stress is a term which is often loosely used to describe feelings of tension – usually associated with too much, or overly demanding, work. In fact, stress is the product of demands made on an individual's physical *and mental* energies: monotony and feelings of failure or insecurity are sources of stress, as much as the conventionally-considered factors of pressure, overwork and so on.

It is worth remembering, too, that demands on an individual's energies may be stimulating as well as harmful: many people, especially those suited to managerial jobs, work well under pressure, and even require some form of stress to bring out their best performance. (It is excessive stress that can be damaging: this may be called strain.) This is why we talk about the management of stress, not about its elimination: it is a question of keeping stress to helpful proportions and avenues.

Harmful stress can be identified in symptoms such as nervous tension, irritability, sensitivity, sleeplessness, withdrawal (reluctance to communicate, absenteeism), depression, substance abuse and a variety of physical symptoms (such as skin and digestive disorders, tension headaches). Some symptoms of stress – say, absenteeism – may or may not be correctly identified with stress: there are many other possible causes of such problems, both at work (lack of motivation) and outside (personal problems).

All these things can, however, adversely affect performance, which is why stress management has become a major workplace issue.

Stress can be caused or aggravated by:

(a)   Personality: competitive, sensitive and insecure people feel stress more acutely

(b)   Ambiguity or conflict in the demands made on an individual in their various roles

(c)   Insecurity, risk and change

(d)   Management style including:
    (i)   Unpredictability
    (ii)   Destruction of workers' self esteem
    (iii)   Setting up win/lose situations

ACTIVITY 9   (30 MINS)

What sources of stress are there in your own lifestyle? Are you aware of the symptoms of stress in yourself? What do you do (if anything) to control your stress?

Greater awareness of the nature and control of stress is a feature of the modern work environment. **Stress management techniques** are increasingly taught and encouraged by organisations, and include:

(a)   Counselling (to air and resolve conflicts)

(b)   Time off or regular rest breaks

(c)   Relaxation techniques (breathing exercises, meditation)

(d)   Physical exercise and creative self-expression (as a safety valve for tension)

(e)   Delegation and planning (to avoid work-load related stress)

(f)   Assertiveness (to control stress related to insecurity in interpersonal relations)

Ecological control can also be brought to bear on the problem of stress, creating conditions in which stress is less likely to be a problem: well designed jobs and environments, and an organisation culture built on meaningful work, mutual support, communication and teamwork.

EXAMPLE   **HARROGATE AND DISTRICT NHS FOUNDATION TRUST – NURSES CASE STUDY**

Harrogate and District NHS Foundation Trust cares for a population of approximately 200,000 in the Harrogate and Rural District and North East Leeds by providing essential hospital and community health services.

The Trust decided to tackle stress because they knew it was a big problem for the NHS in general based on various surveys, including figures from HSE. So a proactive approach was taken.

This included training for line managers and risk assessors; implementing a 'Managing Work Pressures Policy' in 2007 with Staff Side approval; conducting an annual Trust-wide generic risk assessment; carrying out individual risk assessments and involving the Trust's support functions.

The Trust's policy on stress follows HSE's Management Standards and they communicated it widely across the Trust via the intranet. It provides advice on how to recognise the signs of stress; identify and understand the causes; provide a risk rating; identify solutions and action plans and finally monitor and review those plans.

The training for managers and risk assessors raises awareness of work-related stress and equips both with the tools to identify causes of stress and manage them. Departmental risk assessments were carried out after this training and HR and Occupational Health monitored and reviewed the effectiveness of the stress policy.

Risk Assessment actions have included:

- Improved ways of working; departmental review of processes; streamlining to save time and duplication of effort.

- Improved working relationships through skills development and training, ie Managing Conflict and Breaking Bad News courses

- Changes to working patterns for work-life balance

- Delegation of tasks where appropriate

- Time management tools to cope with demands of the role and protected time for specific duties

- Short-term working to build confidence

- Mentorship and support

There were notable improvements: in the 2008 audit of the 'Managing Work Pressures policy', four cases of work-related stress were reported. This figure represents 0.2% of the total employee population and is a potential indicator that the Trust is proactively managing work pressures. The expected benefits include reducing working days lost, improving productivity levels and raising staff morale by reducing work pressures. All of which can impact on cost savings.

It's recognised that this project will add value to the patient experience by maintaining high quality of care; giving nurses more time to care; achieving higher levels of job satisfaction and going beyond patients expectations.

(HSE website – stress case studies, 2012)

International comparison

In extreme cases, stress is a killer. The Japanese, who work longer hours than people in the US and the UK, experience **karoshi** (death from overwork). This is a documented ailment in which people develop illnesses and die from high stress and the pressures of overtime. **Karoshi** was officially registered as a fatal illness in 1989.

Other causes of 'disease' at work

Workplace intimidation, harassment and physical violence have been the subject of recent studies, suggesting that **bullying** is every bit as prevalent – and painful – in the workplace as it is in the school playground! **'Cyber-bullying'**, in particular, is on the increase, involving abusive or detrimental e-mails, website posts and mobile phone text messages. Employers may be liable for these, as for other forms of harassment at work.

Policies should take into account victim-side factors (grievance procedures, confidentiality, counselling, transfer) and perpetrator-side factors (disciplinary procedures, counselling, transfer, cultural change).

WEBLINK

If you are interested in these areas, check out the Bully Online website:

▶▶ www.bullyonline.org

The HSEoutlines a 'good practice model' for reducing stress.

▶▶ www.hse.gov.uk/stress/index.htm

ACTIVITY 10   (15 MINS)

Brainstorm a list of behaviours you would consider 'bullying' in the workplace.

4.3 ERGONOMICS

DEFINITION

Ergonomics [(Greek: **ergos** (work) + **nomos** (natural laws)] is the scientific study of the relationship between people and their working environment. This sphere of scientific research explores the demands that can arise from a working environment and the capabilities of people to meet these demands.

Ergonomics supports the design of machines and working conditions which function well and are best suited to the capacities and health requirements of the human body. In old people's homes and hospitals, for example, switches are placed according to measurements of chair height and arm reach. In the same way, computer consoles and controls, office furniture, factory layout can be designed so that the individual expends minimal energy and experiences minimal physical strain in any given task.

More recently ergonomics has developed into a field that embraces the whole range of psychological factors that affect people at work. Apart from purely mechanical considerations – in what position should a worker be sitting in order to exert maximum force over a long period of time without physical strain or fatigue? – the ergonomist must now take into account the increasing problems of the worker as information processor. The perceptual limitations of the worker can also be measured, and systems designed which do not make unreasonable demands on the worker's attention span or capacity to absorb information – for example, the use of sound signals to attract attention to visual displays or equipment.

4.4 PROMOTING POSITIVE HEALTH AND FITNESS

Approaches to health promotion include the following.

(a) **Health monitoring and awareness campaigns**

Employees may be given regular health checks under occupational health regulations (hearing and eye tests, for example): this may be extended to checks for heart and cholesterol, general fitness, skin cancer and so on, as part of a campaign to increase health awareness. Campaigns may be run to educate employees on nutritional guidelines, smoking and substance abuse hazards, the need for exercise etc.

(b) **Nutritional support**

The link between motivation and health is well-documented. Employers can encourage healthy eating habits through education programmes and access to nutritionally balanced food in staff canteens, voucher schemes linked to health food outlets or products, sponsorship of weight-loss (or gain) programmes and so on.

(c) **Anti-smoking programmes**

In 2007, legislation in England and Wales placed an outright ban on smoking in enclosed public places including all workplaces. Organisations which had not done so already were encouraged (but not compelled) to take this further and adopt health-promoting thinking into their whole practice. Suggested supportive measures included consulting with staff in building smoke-free behaviour into health and safety policies and to support employees' or customers' attempts to quit smoking. For some organisations the benefits of being smoke-free – a fitter workforce, less downtime for cigarette breaks and the removal of the associated cleaning, ventilation and space – issues were outweighed by the detrimental effects to employee relations. On some premises a smoking culture has been enshrined in a 'smoking shelter' to continue the practice but within the terms of the law.

(d) **Fitness promotion**

Sedentary occupations erode physical strength, stamina and flexibility, interfere with sleep patterns and metabolic rate, reduce alertness and contribute to the long-term consequences of all the above in stress, heart disease and other serious ailments. Fitness promotion in the workplace may range from educating employees in basic stretching exercises during work breaks to extensive facilities, accessed via discounted membership at health clubs and sports centres. In radical cases (considered the norm in Japan), whole staff exercise may be held at the start of each day.

(e) **Sickness prevention**

General health and hygiene may be promoted in the workplace – particularly in industries in which employees are at risk of infection or other illnesses, or during seasons where illnesses (such as influenza) are prevalent.

EXAMPLE   FOSTERING EMPLOYEE WELL-BEING

- Almost nine out of ten organisations (89%) operate stress management policies

- Counselling and occupational health support are the most widely used arrangements, followed by flexible working

- Three-quarters of employers (74%) consider improving employee well-being to be a priority over the next year

- Approaches to improving employee well-being take many forms, the most widespread including some directly linked to health such as occupational health advice (74%) and others focused on day-to-day management actions, such as praise for a job well done (61%).

(CBI Absence and Workplace Health Survey, 2011)

4.5 SUBSTANCE ABUSE

Substance abuse has become a major workplace issue with up to 17 million working days lost annually in the UK as a result of alcohol-related absences, including accidents at work.

Most estimates place the numbers of drug users slightly below these levels, taking into account the sheer variety of prescription and non-prescription drugs used, and the difficulties of gathering user information (given the illegality of most drug use).

Alcohol policy

Alcohol may be part of the culture of the workplace. Studies have found that:

(a) Workers who suffer from job stress and organisational frustration frequently turn to alcohol as a tool for unwinding.

(b) Organisations continue to encourage social drinking, despite the known effects of physical/psychological dependency. Company celebrations frequently revolve around alcohol, and little concern is shown for the heavy drinker until his or her work is adversely affected, which may not be for some time after the onset of dependency.

ACTIVITY 11   (30 MINS)

What would you expect to be the symptoms of alcohol abuse that might alert a supervisor or manager to the problem?

Most alcohol policies embrace the following areas.

(a) **Positive aims and objectives** – including statistics on alcohol-related harm and affirmation of successful treatment.

(b) **Restrictions on alcohol possession or consumption** during working hours, in certain areas or for certain at-risk employees.

(c) **The links between the policy and disciplinary procedure.** This is a sensitive area, but random drunkenness and bad behaviour are usually treated under the heading of 'gross misconduct'.

(d) **Policy on testing**. Employers must be clear that the benefits of testing justify the privacy intrusion and tests should be restricted to jobs that pose safety risks, such as operating dangerous machinery.

(e) **Confidentiality** of all measures undertaken in relation to alcohol problems of individual employees.

(f) **Internal and external counselling services available**.

Drugs policy

Drug abuse policies are much more difficult to implement because:

(a) A significant number of workers may be legitimate short- or long-term users of prescription drugs and over the counter medicines which may impair performance in various ways (for example, by causing drowsiness).

(b) The illegality of the use of many drugs makes it difficult to gather information, and places drug use firmly within disciplinary as well as welfare policy frameworks.

(c) Harm minimisation approaches (restricted use, risk avoidance and so on) may be interpreted as condoning drug use, although they do address the major workplace issues of safety risk and impaired performance.

(d) It is difficult to distinguish fairly between 'acceptable' recreational drug use (of ecstasy or cannabis, say) and 'hard' drug use.

(e) Random drug testing is fraught with industrial relations and legal issues (for example, under the Human Rights Act 1998), particularly since there are major problems of test reliability and privacy.

Counselling, harm-minimisation (avoiding heavy machinery, driving and so on if affected) and voluntary supported rehabilitation programmes may be used judiciously as the basis of a policy. Entry into a company treatment programme should not be compulsory, where an employee can show that (s)he is undertaking independent treatment. The disciplinary issues will (as with alcohol) have to be worked out in detail.

FOR DISCUSSION

- Alcohol and drug use are a private matter.
- Zero tolerance is the only approach to stopping alcohol and drug abuse.

Debate these two propositions, from the perspective of HR policy.

SIGNPOST

We have already suggested 'counselling' as part of many welfare policies. We now go on to discuss counselling itself.

4.6 WORKPLACE COUNSELLING

DEFINITION

'**Counselling** can be defined as a purposeful relationship in which one person helps another to help himself. It is a way of relating and responding to another person so that that person is helped to explore his thoughts, feelings and behaviour with the aim of reaching a clearer understanding. The clearer understanding may be of himself or of a problem, or of the one in relation to the other.'

(Rees, 1996)

ACTIVITY 12 (10 MINS)

Suggest five situations, already mentioned in this Course Book, in which workplace counselling may be helpful.

The CIPD, in their document *Statement on Counselling in the Workplace,* make it clear that effective counselling is not merely a matter of pastoral care for individuals, but is very much in the organisation's interests.

(a) Appropriate use of counselling tools can prevent under-performance, reduce labour turnover and absenteeism and increase commitment from employees. Unhappy employees are far more likely to seek employment elsewhere.

(b) Effective counselling demonstrates an organisation's commitment to, and concern for, its employees and so is liable to improve loyalty and enthusiasm among the workforce.

(c) The development of employees is of value to the organisation, and counselling can give employees the confidence and encouragement necessary to take responsibility for self and career development.

(d) Workplace counselling recognises that the organisation may be contributing to the employees' problems and therefore it provides an opportunity to reassess organisational policy and practice.

The counselling process

Managers may be called on to use their expertise to help others make informed decisions or solve problems by:

(a) **Advising**: offering information and recommendations on the best course of action. This is a relatively *directive* role, and may be called for in areas where you can make a key contribution to the *quality* of the decision: advising an employee about the best available training methods, say, or about behaviours which are considered inappropriate in the workplace.

(b) **Counselling**: facilitating others through the process of defining and exploring their own problems and coming up with their own solutions. This is a relatively *non-directive* role, and may be called for in areas where you can make a key contribution to the *ownership* of the decision: helping employees to formulate learning goals, for example, or to cope with work (and sometimes non-work) problems.

The counselling process has three broad stages. (*Egan*, 1994)

Step 1   **Reviewing the current scenario**: helping people to identify, explore and clarify their problem situations and unused opportunities. This is achieved by listening, encouraging them to tell their 'story', and questioning/probing to help them to see things more clearly.

Step 2   **Developing the preferred scenario**: helping people identify what they want in terms of clear goals and objectives. This is undertaken by encouraging them to envisage their desired outcome, and what it will mean for them (in order to motivate them to make the necessary changes).

Step 3   **Determining how to get there**: helping people to develop action strategies for accomplishing goals, for getting what they want. This is undertaken by encouraging them to explore options and available resources, select the best option and plan their next steps.

Confidentiality is central to the counselling process. There will be situations when employees cannot be completely open unless they are sure that their comments will be treated confidentially. However, certain information, once obtained by the organisation (for example, about fraud, sexual harassment or criminal activity) calls for action. In spite of the drawbacks, therefore, CIPD guidelines are clear that employees must be made aware when their comments will be passed on to the relevant authority, and when they will be treated completely confidentially.

EXAMPLE   **HELP WITH STRESS CAN TAKE MANY FORMS**

There is a wide range of measures which organisations can use to help employees manage stress.

Counselling is the most widely used practice (86%), followed by access to occupational health support (81%). Flexible working (69%) is widely used to enable employees to work in ways which meet their particular needs and reduce stress caused by clashes of their home and work responsibilities, while just under half (44%) of employers say they have redesigned jobs or the organisation of work where possible to help employees reduce their levels of stress. Half of employers conduct regular risk assessments for stress (52%) and there are a number of sources of guidance available for employers concerned about the issue.

(CBI Absence and Workplace Health Survey, 2011)

4.7   EMPLOYEE ASSISTANCE PROGRAMMES (EAPS)

Recognising the difficulty of providing an effective counselling service in-house and also the special skills involved, a notable modern trend is to use outsiders for employee support.

Companies such as EAR, First Assist, and ICAS provide Employee Assistance Programmes (EAPs), offering a 24-hour telephone line with instant access to a trained counsellor. Meetings can be face-to-face if the employee wants, and their immediate families are also covered by the scheme. The providers offer thorough briefing on the scheme for all employees, and management information and consultancy for the employers.

An article in *People Management* (12 October, 2000) laid out how to get the best from an EAP.

What to look for in an EAP

- Effective promotion of services
- Easy access – normally through a round-the-clock operations centre

- Expert consultation and training for managers, HR and occupational health professionals
- Confidential, appropriate and timely assessment of problems
- 'Brief-focused' professional counselling
- Referrals to long-term treatment
- Follow-up and monitoring of employees who access clinical services
- Crisis support after critical incidents

Dos and don'ts for the HR manager

Do   Use the programme yourself

Press for a dedicated EAP account manager

Insist that complaints are fully investigated

Check take-up figures each year

Check the capabilities of the operations centre

Check up on clinical procedures, counsellors' qualifications and supervision processes

Intervene quickly during critical incidents and bigger crises

Encourage managers and supervisors to use the EAP

Don't Expect your EAP provider to be proactive on all of these issues

Imagine that your firm is receiving a high-quality EAP – verify it yourself.

CHAPTER ROUNDUP

- The traditional welfare function was legalistic/reactive or paternalist in its orientation, and regarded as entirely 'soft'. The new welfare model, while meeting its legal obligations (in traditional health and safety and welfare benefits and services) is more positive, proactive, holistic, flexible and strategic in aiming to improve employee performance.

- Occupational health and safety are key areas of legislation and regulation. The *Health and Safety at Work Act* and regulations implementing EU Directives cover many areas of policy and practice.

- The modern workplace contains many potential hazards and particular attention must be given to accident prevention and reporting.

- Issues in the new welfare model include: work-life balance and stress management; ergonomics; positive health promotion.

- Counselling in the workplace and Employee Assistance Programmes are two ways of accessing help.

QUICK QUIZ

1   Give reasons for the importance of health and safety at work.

2   What are the health risks associated with VDU use?

3   What is the cost of accidents to an employer?

4   What preventative action could be taken to reduce the possibility of illness or accidents at the workplace?

5   What are the duties placed on an employee by the *Health and Safety at Work Act 1974*?

6   What additional duties have been placed on employers by recent regulations?

7   What are the major work-related causes of stress?

8   What is ergonomics?

9   What were some of the benefits seen when the ban on smoking was introduced in the workplace?

10   What is an Employee Assistance Programme?

ANSWERS TO QUICK QUIZ

1   To protect employees from pain and suffering; legal obligations; the cost of workplace accidents; to improve the company's image.   (see Para 1.1)

2   Various manifestations of RSI.   (Para 1.2)

3   Time lost by employees and management; cost of first aid and staff; cost of disrupted work.   (Para 2.2)

4   Safety consciousness; consultation and participation; adequate instruction; minimal materials handling; safety devices on machines; good maintenance; codes of practice.
                                                                                           (Para 2.3)

5   To take reasonable care of self and others; to allow employers to carry out their duties.
                                                                                           (Para 3.1)

6   Risk assessment; risk control; information on risks and hazards; revise and initiate safety policies; identify 'at risk' employees; training; competence of advisers; consultation with employees.   (Para 3.2)

7   Job demands; role conflict; role ambiguity; role overload and underload; responsibility for others; lack of social support; non-participation in decision-making.   (Para 4.2)

8   The study of the relationship between people and their working environment.   (Para 4.3)

9   A fitter workforce, less downtime for cigarette breaks and the removal of the associated cleaning, ventilation and space.   (Para 4.3)

10 A contract for counselling services with an external service provider.   (Para 4.7)

ANSWERS TO ACTIVITIES

1 & 2   Your own environment and experience – but the text in paragraph 1.2 should give you some ideas. If you spot any hazards: make a report and submit it to the relevant person in authority!

3   Again, your own research: learn to use the real-life resources you have available to you!

4   You should have spotted the following hazards.

(a)   Heavy object on high shelf
(b)   Standing on swivel chair
(c)   Lifting heavy object incorrectly
(d)   Open drawers blocking passageway
(e)   Trailing wires
(f)   Electric bar fire
(g)   Smouldering cigarette unattended
(h)   Overfull waste bin
(i)   Overloaded socket
(j)   Carrying too many cups of hot liquid
(k)   Dangerous invoice 'spike'

If you can see others, you are probably right.

5   Up to you: have fun!

6   Your own research: do think the questions through, once you have gathered your data!

7   How about: risk assessment; feedback; systems and procedures; attention of all employees and contractors; monitor and audit; full review.

8   Some areas you might have thought of include:

(a)   Alcohol on the premises
(b)   Drug taking (including prescription drugs) on the premises
(c)   Horse play and practical jokes
(d)   Noise (or 'acoustic shock'), particularly from headset use
(e)   Workplace behaviour: running, throwing things, etc
(f)   Tiredness (dangerous objects, dust, slippery objects etc)

9   Your own experience. Be as honest as you can. If you aren't doing much to control your stress, consider doing some further research on the list of techniques following the activity.

10   Some suggestions are: shouting, swearing; persistent public criticism; ridicule and name-calling; threats; physical intimidation (use of threatening body language or actual violence); sexual harassment; racial vilification; victimisation in applying work rules; deliberately allocating difficult or unpleasant tasks to an individual; sabotaging the individual's work, complaining to other staff or supervisors about the individual; multiple grievance or disciplinary actions and so on.

11   Symptoms typically include: avoidance of supervisors and workmates; uncharacteristic aggression, mood swings and variations in work pace; sloppy appearance, signs of hangover; hand tremors, gastric upsets, insomnia; financial difficulties and relationship problems; bizarre excuses for work deficiencies; increased accidents and absences for ill health. (Similar symptoms apply to drug abuse, with the addition of: dilated or contracted pupils in the eyes; sudden 'nodding off'; slurred speech; uncontrolled laughter or tears; sloppy appearance and unsteady movements but without the smell of alcohol.)

12   The need for workplace counselling can arise in many different situations. Your answer should include five of the following.

(a)   During appraisal
(b)   In grievance or disciplinary situations
(c)   Following change, such as promotion or relocation
(d)   On redundancy or dismissal
(e)   As a result of domestic or personal difficulties, alcoholism, drug abuse, HIV/AIDS
(f)   In cases of sexual harassment or violence at work

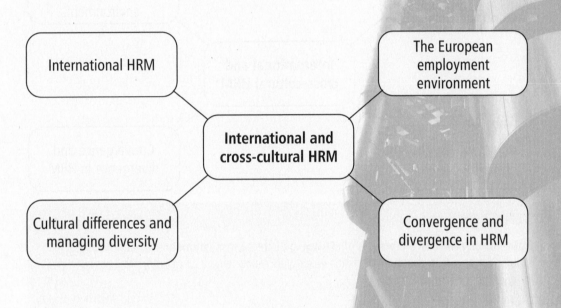

Chapter

12

International and cross-cultural HRM

International HRM

The European employment environment

International and cross-cultural HRM

Cultural differences and managing diversity

Convergence and divergence in HRM

Introduction

We have already made some international comparisons in the context of specific HR policies and practices, in earlier chapters with reference to employment development and employee relations. The key point, however, is that there are very many complex differences in the culture, law and practice relating to HRM from nation to nation.

In this chapter, we draw together the threads of an international perspective on HRM.

We begin by considering the implications of **cross-national transfer of people**: the impact of globalisation on the labour market and human resource planning, policy and practice.

We then go on to consider the implications of **cross-national transfer of HRM values and practices**: the extent to which there is (or should be) convergence or divergence.

Finally, we look at the ways in which **national cultures** differ, and the implications of this for the management of **diversity** in the workplace, following on from our discussion in Chapter 10.

This is clearly a vast area of study. We recommend that you use this brief overview to identify your own areas of interest and to guide you in follow-up reading (in the press, international HR journals and so on).

Your objectives

In this chapter you will learn about the following.

- The impact of globalisation on human resource planning and policy
- Areas of convergence and divergence in international HRM
- The impact of different national cultures on HRM values and practices
- Ways of managing a culturally diverse workforce

1 INTERNATIONAL HRM

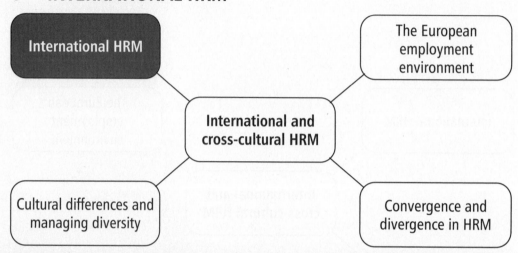

DEFINITION

International HRM is 'the process of managing people across international boundaries by multinational companies. It involves the worldwide management of people, not just the management of expatriates'.

(Armstrong, 2012)

1.1 THE GLOBAL EMPLOYMENT CONTEXT

People are increasingly likely to work in an organisation that has multinational or multiethnic elements, whether based in their own national culture, or in another culture at home or abroad. In some respects, a global labour market has developed in recent decades, because of such factors as:

- Domestic skill/education shortages, encouraging international recruitment – which in turn has been facilitated by social policy harmonisation (eg freedom of labour movement within the European Economic Area).

- The emergence, with political change, of new markets in areas such as Eastern Europe, South-East Asia and China.

- The development of integrated trading blocs such as NAFTA (North American Free Trade Agreement) and the European Union.

- The 'shrinking' of the world through Information and Communication Technology (ICT) developments and travel. There are now 'virtual organisations' scattered geographically around the globe, in which people work together via e-mail, the internet, web-conferencing and so on.

- The pressures of globalised competition. Under the ethos of globalisation, local markets are considered too small to justify the costs of developing and marketing new products. This has encouraged the growth of multinational corporations operating outside national boundaries, and an increase in international mergers, acquisitions, joint ventures and strategic alliances.

At the same time, however, geo-political 'chunking' (the separatist aspirations of political/ethnic/religious movements, as in the Balkan states) is creating new and more culturally complex markets.

ACTIVITY 1 (15 MINS)

What barriers to a common, global employment environment can you foresee? What, for example, might prevent a UK organisation from recruiting in China?

1.2 CHARACTERISTICS AND CHALLENGES OF CROSS-NATIONAL HRM

Torrington (1994) suggests that international personnel management has seven key characteristics.

1   **Cosmopolitan**. People who cope well with cross-national management tend to be culturally flexible, multilingual and geographically mobile.

2   **Culture**. Cross-national management faces major diversity in terms of cultural backgrounds and values.

3   **Compensation**. There are complex issues in the remuneration of people working outside their country of origin, and of ensuring a balance of equity and market rate across different national labour markets.

4   **Communication**. The flow of information and network of relationships must be maintained between geographically dispersed units of the business.

5   **Co-ordination**. Formal and informal methods must be used to ensure integration of the direction and effort.

6   **Competence**. Cross-national (and cross-cultural) working requires the definition, resourcing and development of a wider set of competences than intra-national working.

7   **Consultancy**. Where local requirements outstrip business competence in a given unit, there is a greater need to bring in expertise (from local partners or consultants, or from the parent company if the requirement is to transfer particular policies or practices from the 'home' nation).

Torrington proposes that international HRM is in many ways qualitatively similar to HRM within the borders of a single country – but on a wider scale, involving greater variety and complexity. However, Armstrong (2009) argues that international HRM is likely to be significantly more demanding than intra-national management for four reasons.

(a)   **The complexity of the workforce mix**. International organisations may include 'home' country nationals working in subsidiaries abroad, as well as foreign nationals working in the 'home' country or a third 'host' country (eg Europeans working for a UK-owned firm in the US). This particularly impacts on HRM because of the legal complexities of labour mobility.

(b)   **The management of diversity**. Different nations vary (as we see throughout this chapter) on a number of key dimensions, including cultural values and norms, social systems and legal requirements.

(c)   **The need for communication**. International co-ordination poses huge information and communication challenges. In the field of HRM, face-to-face communication is particularly important – and not easily substituted.

(d)   **Resourcing 'world-wide capabilities'**. International operations must recruit and retain people with the skills to deal with the complexities of cross-border and cross-cultural management.

1.3   HR AND INTERNATIONALISATION STRATEGY

HR issues will have a key influence on the strategic management of multinational organisations. The choice of a base of foreign operations, or the decision of whether to set up a foreign subsidiary or enter into a joint venture or strategic alliance with foreign partners, for example, might be influenced by a number of HR factors, including:

(a)   Labour costs

(b)   Skills available in the local or national labour market: government policy on education and training, available recruitment avenues and media and so on

(c)   Employment legislation, controlling the employment relationships (eg health and safety regulation, minimum wage)

(d)   Industrial relations culture, trade union power

(e)   Language, cultural and social differences that would make transfer of HR practices (and/or the use of expatriate staff) difficult to implement

1.4   HUMAN RESOURCING STRATEGY

Multinationals will have to develop specific human resourcing strategies about whether to use 'local' labour, or labour from the 'parent' (head office) country, especially in regard to:

(a)   Managerial staff, in order to transfer consistent HR (and business) culture and practices to the international operation

(b)   Technical and professional staff, since equivalent skills or qualifications may not be available in all nations in which the firm wishes to operate.

The range of strategies may be broadly summarised as follows.

Strategy	Advantages	Disadvantages
Key positions are filled with nationals of the 'parent' country. Eg: a US multinational transfers US employees to key positions in foreign subsidiaries.	Facilitates the transfer of the distinctive culture and practices of the parent company to the overseas subsidiary (or project), especially where straight-forward overseas expansion is involved.	• Expatriates find it difficult to adjust to the environment and culture of work/management in the foreign country. • May alienate local employees, because of reward disparity or lack of promotion opportunities.

Strategy	Advantages	Disadvantages
Key positions are filled by local nationals, although overall control is retained by senior management in the 'parent' country. Eg: a US multinational recruits within Italy to find managers for its Italian subsidiary.	Avoids difficulties of expatriate employment.	• May be cultural/ linguistic/priority barriers to co-operation between local and 'parent' country management. • Little genuine cross-cultural experience on either side.
Key positions are filled by the best available people, regardless of nationality. Eg: a US multinational recruits a German to manage a UK subsidiary.	Develops genuine cross-cultural experience.	• Difficult to implement, given 'protectionist' employment policies. • Requires strong corporate culture, communication and co-ordination.

'**Offshoring**' is a major trend of globalisation, whereby organisations in developed countries outsource functions to another group company or third-party provider overseas, in order to take advantage of large, low-cost and increasingly well-educated labour forces in countries such as India and China. This has been traditional in areas such as manufacturing and printing, but has more recently spread to financial services and other service industries: call centres, research and 'back-office' operations are extensively off-shored, using ICT developments such as the Internet to co-ordinate and control operations.

EXAMPLE

Manufacturers and consultancy firms are the most likely to uproot jobs abroad, with India and Eastern Europe being the most popular destinations, the survey by the Chartered Institute of Personnel and Development (CIPD) found.

The number of employers intending to offshore UK jobs to other parts of the world in the year to March 2013 has grown to 8%, up from 6% last year, the CIPD said.

In a further blow to the beleaguered British jobs market, 41% of employers planning to offshore roles said they would shift IT support roles, and 29% operations roles.

Finance, call-centre and HR roles were also popular jobs to be moved overseas, the survey showed.

However, the CIPD survey indicated some employers offshoring jobs might live to regret it, with more than a quarter of companies that have shifted jobs overseas now looking to relocate operations back to the UK.

Gerwyn Davies, policy adviser at the CIPD, said: 'The continuing pressure on employers to cut costs is highlighted by the increase in employer intentions to offshore UK jobs to other parts of the world.'

'Employers need to weigh up the wider impacts when considering offshoring decisions, such as the potential adverse impact on customer service or employer brand.'

(*The Telegraph*, 2012)

ACTIVITY 2 (10 MINS)

What are the HRM implications raised by the example given above?

1.5 HUMAN RESOURCE DEVELOPMENT

There may need to be strategies for developing required skills in overseas labour markets where they are currently underdeveloped, for example through the systematic education and training of employees, or the wider sponsorship of education and technical training in the community.

International HRM itself requires the organisation to recruit, retain and/or develop 'cognitively complex self-monitoring managers who have global perspectives and boundary spanning capabilities'. (Huczynski & Buchanan, 2001)

- **Cognitively complex**: able to use multiple-solution models rather than 'one best way' approaches.

- **Self-monitoring**: personally flexible, sensitive to verbal and non-verbal messages, and able to adjust their behaviour to the social demands of different cultures.

- **Global perspectives**: having an understanding of the interrelated and systemic nature of the global community and economy.

- **Boundary spanning capabilities**: able to act as interpreters between their own and other cultures.

Schneider and Barsoux (1997) suggest that individual background impacts on cross-cultural competence: exposure to different cultures at an early age (via multicultural environments, travel or media) develops flexibility. However, these skills can also be enhanced by human resource development strategies which:

(a) Offer diversified work experience in international or multicultural settings

(b) Offer relevant awareness and skills training (language learning, cultural briefings, cross-cultural interpersonal skills training)

(c) Encourage networking with professionals of other relevant cultures

(d) Encourage learning through all cross-cultural interactions in the workplace.

1.6 LABOUR MOBILITY ISSUES

Article 48 of the Treaty of Rome protects the free movement of 'workers' (including part-time and economically-active self-employed workers) within the European Economic Area. The general principle is that people coming to the UK for the purposes of employment (excluding short 'business visits') require a visa or work permit, but nationals from within the EEA have a right to work anywhere in the EEA without such a requirement.

Where an individual requires permission to work in the UK a five-tier points-based system is used to assess their suitability. However reflecting the political sensitivity of immigration the tiers are often subject to suspension or modification.

The points-based system

- The points-based system only covers migrants from outside the European Economic Area (EEA) and Switzerland.

- Migrants will need to pass a points-based assessment before they are given permission to enter or remain in the United Kingdom.

- The system consists of five tiers. Each tier has different points requirements.

The five tiers comprise:

- **Tier 1:** For highly skilled migrants, entrepreneurs, investors, and graduate students

- **Tier 2:** This is for skilled workers who have a job offer, most importantly for the employer, General (recruitment) and Intra-Company Transfers

- **Tier 3:** For a limited numbers of lower skilled workers to fill temporary shortages in the labour market

- **Tier 4:** Students

- **Tier 5:** For youth mobility and temporary workers, such as those entering the country under Working Holiday agreements with other countries

The role of the sponsor

Migrants applying under any tier except Tier 1 need to be sponsored in order for their application to be successful. If an employer wishes to recruit a migrant they will have to apply for a sponsor licence.

Employer sponsor licence

An employer is required to have a licence before they can sponsor skilled or temporary workers under the points-based system. To get a licence, they are required to have good human resources systems and compliance in place. This means:

- Monitoring immigration status and preventing illegal employment
- Maintaining migrant contact details
- Record-keeping
- Migrant tracking and monitoring
- Professional registrations and accreditations

The successful employer will be given an A or B rating and added to the UK Border Agency's published register of sponsors. The B rating is for sponsors who the Border Agency thinks could be a risk to immigration control or who do not have all the correct systems in place. They must follow a sponsorship action plan designed to help them become A-rated, or they risk losing their licence.

Certificates of sponsorship

Sponsors are responsible for assigning certificates of sponsorship to migrant workers in Tiers 2 and 5.

Once accredited as a sponsor the employer has an allocated number of certificates of sponsorship which empower them to bring sponsored workers into the country. The number will be first agreed with the Border Agency and based on the anticipated number required. Once these are allocated the employer is able to apply for a further allocation, however, this will need to be justified.

The worker will need the certificate of sponsorship when they apply for a visa to come to, or stay in, the UK and will also need to pass a points-based assessment.

Sponsorship duties

As a licensed sponsor, the employer is responsible for ensuring that migrants comply with their immigration conditions, by keeping records and reporting any changes (such as a failure to turn up for work) to the Border Agency. Failure to comply can result in a licence being downgraded or withdrawn.

FOR DISCUSSION

The UK Border Agency's decision to withdraw London Metropolitan University's licence to accept non-EU students has meant the suspension of study and threat of deportation for 2,000 international students, and financial crisis for the university. The agency's justification is London Met's 'systemic failure' to account for the immigration status of its international students.

What issues does this example raise for the immigration and employment of non-EU nationals for other employers in the UK?

2 THE EUROPEAN EMPLOYMENT ENVIRONMENT

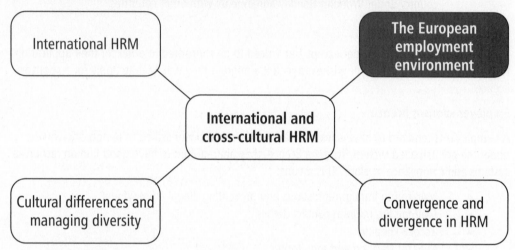

2.1 THE EUROPEAN LABOUR MARKET

Some of the key features of the European labour market are as follows.

(a) **General and vocational education**

About 23% of the EU's population is currently in full-time education (comparable to Japan, but slightly lower than in the USA) and 25% of people stay in education after the age of 19.

Vocational Education and Training (VET) varies widely in the extent of specialisation, financing, methods of testing competence and the status and role of VET in the national education system. VET begins at an earlier age in some nations than others, and in some EU countries, vocational qualifications obtained at school offer equal access to higher education as 'academic' qualifications.

Although the proportion of the UK workforce with higher skills (degree or equivalent and above) is similar to France and Germany, the UK compares less well by having a higher proportion of people with low skills and a low proportion with intermediate skills.

(b) **Age structure**

As in the UK, the EU workforce is ageing (and shrinking, due to accelerating retirements).

(c) **Non-permanent employment**

Some 15% of all EU workers are estimated to be on part-time contracts.

2.2 HR IMPLICATIONS OF EUROPEAN UNION

The implications for European HRM are still being worked out in detail, as EU directives are enacted in the law of member states, and other aspects of European social policy are still subject to negotiation and amendment. However, HR practitioners will need to be aware of the following issues.

(a) **Compliance with EU law** across a wide range of employment issues (as discussed in relevant chapters of this Course Book).

(b) **Differences in specific law and practice** in countries where the organisation may intend to recruit. The Posted Worker Directive provides that any employee posted to a foreign country for more than three months is entitled to the protection of the employment laws of the host country (minimum wage, working hours, notice periods and so on) rather than those of his or her home country, so that organisations cannot cut corners on employment protection by contracting labour from countries where the law is weaker.

(c) **The need for workers to be cross-educated in the languages and cultures of other states**: language is not an area amenable to harmonisation!

(d) **The mobility of labour within the EU**, allowing residence and permit-free working for full-time, part-time and economically active self-employed workers from all member states of the European Economic Area. The recognition and comparison of **qualifications** is a key related issue for recruitment, reward and development. Harmonised standards for Higher Educational Diplomas (HEDs) in specific professions and industry-based 'Certificates of Experience' are designed to facilitate mobility of qualified workers.

(e) **Implications of European Monetary Union**. Although the UK has not joined the EMU, the 'euro' has been the accepted currency of business in the EU since 1999, and national currencies have been phased out. This raises issues such as: the prospect of pan-European pay bargaining and settlements; the increased importance of European Works Councils for such pay bargaining; the need to reassess corporate structures in view of their potential for mergers and acquisitions, and opportunities for central payroll administrations.

(f) **Potential pan-European HRM**: cross-border head-hunting and recruitment advertising, choice of international education and training avenues, management of expatriate management and staff, training in relevant EU markets (and product standards and other differences), management of diversity, welfare for dislocated staff and families, pan-European reward harmonisation.

EXAMPLE

A feature in *People Management* (3 June 1999) described the Eurofighter programme, a four-nation exercise in political, technical, cultural and management integration between British Aerospace, Daimler Chrysler Aerospace (Dasa) of Germany, Alenia Aerospazio of Italy and Construcciones Aeronauticas of Spain, run by a German management company in Germany. Here are some soundbites on the HR issues (as identified by the German HR director) and the techniques used.

The project's official language is English, and all the teams are multinational, so fluency is essential. 'The southern Europeans feel disadvantaged... The Spanish especially will not admit that they haven't understood something – they simply agree. And you have to be sensitive to varying language skills.' Eurofighter has an open learning centre with language facilities...

But cultural differences go deeper. 'The decision-making process is different... The Latins need consensus and aren't empowered to make decisions. The Germans come closer to the Anglo-Saxon model of responsibility, but the Latins need more social contact, which develops trust. It's something we can learn from them'...

There is a handover period for new employees, who are coached by the previous incumbents. They are briefed on local law, including the formalities of registering with the town hall, their entitlement to state benefits, the availability of local services, and – vital to the British contingent, according to [the German HR director] – the fact that cycling drunk in Bavaria is an offence that could cost you your driving licence. Each partner company has a sponsor – a senior manager in Eurofighter – who looks after the welfare of its employees and their families while in Germany...

Managers need extra training to comply with German employment laws such as the rigid agreements on working hours and the role of the works council. 'You can't do overtime without authorisation.' Through the 'right of co-determination' legislation, works councils have the right to negotiate on all terms and conditions. Everyone has to comply, right up to the managing director. Yet it's not a confrontational relationship. 'This is a nightmare for British managers, who are used to the union system.'

'People here are very experienced. If the organisation is limiting them, they need to be given permission to act. We threw away all the terms of reference from the old days. Job descriptions, for example, were sometimes years old and did not reflect reality... Managers were given responsibility for designing their own jobs, and the works council backed the changes... Everyone now has a dynamic job description that is updated twice a year. It is job enlargement. This does frighten people, but we try to support them.'

Appraisals are a tradition familiar to BAE staff, but other people have had less experience of implementing them successfully. Dasa had an appraisal programme, but it had not provided effective feedback for junior staff. The Spanish had appraisals only for senior managers, while the Italians had no comparable system at all...'

2.3 HARMONISATION AND DIVERGENCE BETWEEN STATES

The intention of EU policy appears to be the convergence or harmonisation of employment law and practice in member states. However, the protection of common minimum standards and principles does not in itself create a 'pan-European' model for HRM. Member states still vary widely from each other (and from the UK) in:

(a) Their culture, which may dictate different approaches to motivation and reward, employee relations, discrimination issues.

(b) The extent of State intervention in employment practices, according to political ideology, and the extent to which regulation, prescription and bureaucratisation is accepted in national culture and systems.

(c) Their economic, technical and social development: standard of living, rates of unemployment, pressures on public sector expenditure, communication systems and other infrastructures, taxation incentives and disincentives to particular practices.

(d) The specific issues that affect their labour markets: for example, the extent of immigration from non-EU countries, trade agreements with other trading blocs.

(e) Their specific national laws and practices.

FOR DISCUSSION

'A French manager working in a subsidiary of an American corporation that insisted upon an open-door policy may well leave his office door open – thus adjusting to the behavioural requirements of the corporate culture – without any modification whatsoever to his basic concept of managerial authority.'

(Laurent, cited by Beardwell & Holden, 1997)

What does this suggest about the 'transferability' of HRM approaches? Do you think there is any possibility of a truly international model of HRM – or is the model too hard to pin down even within one country?

SIGNPOST

Having already mentioned harmonisation and differences in HR policy and practice within the European Union, we now go on to look more generally at issues of convergence and divergence in international HRM.

3 CONVERGENCE AND DIVERGENCE IN HRM

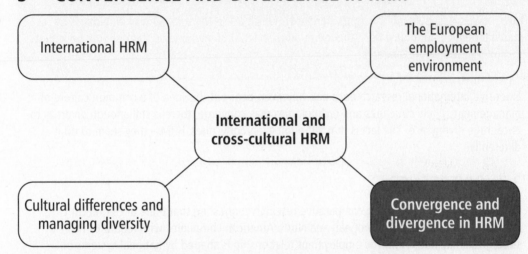

As we noted in relation to the European Union, there are attempts to 'harmonise' social and HRM policy for greater consistency and fairness across national borders, and to facilitate the free movement of labour: this process is known as **'convergence'**. However, there is also **'divergence'**: differentiation in response to local conditions and requirements.

Individual transnational organisations face the same pressures to standardise their HR policies as far as possible in the various countries in which they operate (in order to preserve their distinctive organisation culture, operating style and internal equity) while recognising the need for divergence in the face of environmental differences. The classic challenge is to **'think global, act local'**: to achieve consistency and equity in core activities and values, while allowing flexibility in non-core activities and values.

3.1 CONVERGENCE

It may be argued that the 'activities' of HRM – HR planning, recruitment and selection, appraisal and reward, training and development, welfare, discipline, employee exit and employee relations

– are common to organisations everywhere. The need to attract, retain, motivate and develop employees (the 'aims' of HRM) are universal.

The globalisation of business and communications has also encouraged:

- The exchange and sharing of certain technical terms, theories and practices: for example, the widespread adoption of Swedish-style autonomous working groups or Japanese-style quality circles.

- The standardisation of certain HR techniques, such as job evaluation and 360-degree appraisal.

- The subordination of national culture and national employment practices to corporate culture and HRM practices, which is a recognised tendency of international HRM.

In this sense, there seems to be a convergence of HR policy and practice. Schneider and Barsoux (1997) suggest that alongside the 'convergence myth' of the global village, there is a belief in the convergence of management practice and competence. According to this belief, 'management is management': principles and techniques (such as performance management) can be effective anywhere. With economic, technological and managerial development, business cultures worldwide will be brought into line.

FOR DISCUSSION

How 'universal' should human rights standards (which affect the treatment of employees by multinational corporations) be? What other areas of HRM (if any) do you think should be subject to globally consistent standards?

Extensive international research does not, however, bear out this idea of a common culture of management. While structures and technologies may converge, there is still enough diversity to encourage divergence. The fact is that although everybody 'does' HRM – they seem to do it differently!

3.2 DIVERGENCE

Bratton & Gold (2007) point to comparative research suggesting that there are significant differences between Asian, European and North American companies with regard to HR strategies. They note that: 'The employment relationship is shaped by national systems of employment legislation and the cultural contexts in which it operates. Thus, as the world of business is becoming more globalised, variations in national regulatory systems, labour markets and institutional and cultural contexts are likely to constrain or shape any tendency towards "convergence" or a "universal" model of best HRM practice.'

A number of factors contribute to divergence.

(a) **Cultural factors**, arising from the history, traditions, language, social development and values and religious beliefs of different countries and ethnic groups. Culture amounts to a national way of doing and perceiving things. Cultural factors influence management/worker models, career expectations, perceptions and attitudes to work, education and training needs, and are reflected in the culture of the organisation.

(b) **National legal frameworks**. Specific laws and regulations, and the systems by which they are derived, vary markedly from state to state. The extent of political/legal intervention in employment underscores the cultural dimension.

(c) **Structural factors**. Education and training systems influence the skills available in the labour pool, and therefore HRP, recruitment and development policies. Demographic factors likewise affect the structure of the labour market. Technological and communication infrastructures affect the way in which work is performed and structured, since work organisation and employment policies are different (as the UK experience has shown) in a fast-changing high-tech market than in a low-tech industrial market. Political factors also influence HRM via government intervention.

(d) **Employee relations traditions and ideologies**: the degree of state involvement in industrial conflict and regulation; government support for the unionisation or anti-unionisation of the workforce; collectivisation or individualisation of employment relationships; traditions of co-operation or conflict in industrial relations.

(e) **National economic development**: unemployment levels, rates of inflation, rate of economic growth, balance of trade: the extent of competition in the local product markets (encouraging HRM for competitive edge) and labour markets (encouraging HRM for attracting and retaining skills).

ACTIVITY 3 (30 MINS)

Brainstorm a number of cultural dimensions or values on which societies might differ. (Think about all aspects of life that might impact on attitudes in employment.) Suggest examples where possible.

WEBLINK

You might like to check out some HR professional bodies and journals around the world, for case studies and insights into HR law and practice in other cultures.

HR Magazine (USA) and the Society for HRM
▶▶ www.shrm.org/hrmagazine

HR Monthly (Australia) and the Australian HR Institute
▶▶ www.ahri.com.au

Japan Society for Human Resource Management
▶▶ www.jshrm.org (you may need to use a translator facility for this site)

Hong Kong Institute of HRM
▶▶ http://hkihrm.org

3.3 COMPARATIVE HRM

DEFINITION

Comparative HRM is 'a systematic method of investigation relating to two or more countries, which... seeks to explain the patterns and variations encountered in cross-national HRM.'
(Bratton & Gold, 2003)

SIGNPOST

We now examine in some detail national culture, as one of the key factors in comparative HRM and the management of diversity.

4   CULTURAL DIFFERENCES AND MANAGING DIVERSITY

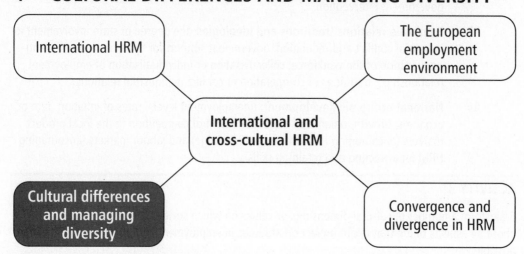

International HRM

The European employment environment

International and cross-cultural HRM

Cultural differences and managing diversity

Convergence and divergence in HRM

4.1   WHAT IS CULTURE?

Schein (1985) defined culture as 'a set of basic assumptions – shared solutions to universal problems of external adaptation (how to survive) and internal integration (how to stay together) – which have evolved over time and are handed down from one generation to the next'.

Manifestations of culture include:

(a)   **Behaviour**: norms of personal and interpersonal behaviour including forms of address, communication styles, expression of emotion and so on.

(b)   **Artefacts**: concrete expressions such as art and architecture, dress codes and symbols.

(c)   **Rituals**: patterns of collective behaviour which have customary or symbolic value, such as business formalities and social courtesies.

(d)   **Underlying values and beliefs**, which invest the behaviour, artefacts and rituals with meaning. For example, the size of a person's office may imply status and honour, or reflect the importance of privacy within a culture: it 'means' more than the surface suggests.

ACTIVITY 4   (30 MINS)

Select another culture with which you have had some contact (perhaps working or studying with someone from another culture).

What behaviours have you noticed that are different from the norms of your own culture?

What values do you think might underlie these behaviours?

How easy is it to interpret the cultural values underlying differences in behaviour?

4.2 GLOBALISATION AND CULTURAL DIFFERENCES

There is a prevailing sense that 'the world is getting smaller'. Travel, migration, multiculturalism and globalised communications and commerce (especially e-commerce) have eroded national distinctives in what societies wear and eat, what they buy, and how they view themselves in relation to the world. National boundaries are being broken down and global concerns (not just free trade, but social and economic justice and the environment) have gained increasing profile.

Does this mean that cultures are converging? Or, as Guirdham (1999) puts it: 'Are cultural differences disappearing so fast that it is unnecessary to allow for them?' If we look at people wearing jeans, drinking Coke, watching CNN and eating McDonalds in Moscow – or eating sushi in London – we may be tempted to think so. But these are essentially the surface expressions of culture, not the 'deep' culture of worldview and social organisation.

Ethnic separatist movements, ethnic clusters in multicultural cities (eg a 'Chinatown' or 'Little Italy') and anti-globalisation movements testify to the enduring power of cultural distinctives. Moreover, these cultural distinctives have been identified as a source of:

(a) Competitive advantage or disadvantage in domestic and international markets
(b) Friction in cross-cultural business relationships
(c) Success or failure in reaching cross-cultural markets

SIGNPOST

We look at two influential models of national cultural differences.

4.3 THE HOFSTEDE MODEL

Hofstede (1984, 1991) carried out cross-cultural research at 66 national offices of IBM and formulated one of the most influential models of work-related cultural differences.

The Hofstede model describes four primary dimensions of differences (predominant traits) between national cultures, which impact on all aspects of organisational behaviour: motivation, team working, leadership style, conflict management, HR practices and so on.

Power distance (PD): the extent to which unequal distribution of power is accepted.

High PD cultures accept greater centralisation, a top-down chain of command and closer supervision. Subordinates have little expectation of influencing decisions. White collar jobs are valued more than blue collar jobs.	*Low* PD cultures expect less centralisation and flatter organisational structures. Subordinates expect involvement and participation in decision-making. Clerical and manual jobs are equally valued.

Uncertainty avoidance (UA): the extent to which security, order and control are preferred to ambiguity, uncertainty and change.

High UA cultures respect control, certainty and ritual. They value task structure, written rules and regulations, specialists and experts, and standardisation. There is a strong need for consensus: deviance and dissent are not tolerated. The work ethic is strong. People are risk-averse and experience more stress.	*Low* UA cultures respect flexibility and creativity. They have less task structure and written rules; more generalists and greater variability. There is more tolerance of risk, dissent, conflict and deviance from norms. People take each day as it comes: there is less stress.

Individualism: the extent to which people prefer to live and work in individualist (focusing on the 'I' identity) or collectivist (focusing on the 'we' identity) ways.

High Individualism cultures emphasise autonomy and individual choice and responsibility. They prize individual initiative. The organisation is impersonal and tends to defend business interests: task achievement is more important than relationships. Management is seen in an individual context.

Low Individualism (or Collectivist) cultures interdependence, reciprocal obligation and social acceptability. The organisation is seen as a 'family' and tends to defend employees' interests: relationships are more important than task achievement. Management is seen in a team context.

Masculinity: the extent to which social gender roles are distinct. (Note that this is different from the usual sense in which the terms 'masculine' and 'feminine' are used.)

High Masculinity cultures clearly differentiate gender roles. Masculine values of assertiveness, competition, decisiveness and material success are dominant. Feminine values of modesty, tenderness, consensus, focus on relationships and quality of working life are secondary (and confined to women).

Low Masculinity (or Femininity) cultures minimise gender roles. Feminine values are dominant and both men and women are allowed to behave accordingly.

Each of these dimensions is a continuum. Hofstede placed various cultures on the continuum as follows.

Cultural group		Power distance	Uncertainty avoidance	Individualism	Masculinity
I	More developed Latin (Belgium, France, Italy, Argentina, Brazil, Spain)	High	High	Medium to high	Medium
II	Less developed Latin (Portugal, Mexico, Peru)	High	High	Low	Whole range
III	More developed Asian (Japan)	Medium	High	Medium	High
IV	Less developed Asian (India, Taiwan, Thailand)	High	Low to medium	Low	Medium
V	Near Eastern (Greece, Iran, Turkey)	High	High	Low	Medium

Cultural group	Power distance	Uncertainty avoidance	Individualism	Masculinity
VI Germanic (Germany, Austria, German Swiss)	Low	Medium to high	Medium	Medium to high
VII Anglo (UK, US, Australia, Canada)	Low to medium	Low to medium	High	High
VIII Nordic (Scandinavia, Netherlands)	Low	Low to medium	Medium to high	Low

ACTIVITY 5   (20 MINS)

According to the Hofstede model, what issues might arise in the following cases?

(a) A Swedish company sets up a subsidiary in Brazil under a Swedish general manager, who wishes to import Scandinavian decision-making styles.

(b) The newly appointed Spanish HR manager of a UK firm asks to see the Rules and Procedures Manual for the HR department.

(c) A US-trained HR manager attempts to implement a system of Management by Objectives in Thailand.

(d) A Dutch HR manager of a US subsidiary in the Netherlands is instructed to implement downsizing measures.

4.4 THE TROMPENAARS MODEL

Fons Trompenaars (1997) questioned 30,000 managers in 55 countries to identify cultural differences that may affect aspects of organisational behaviour. His findings suggest that certain cultures emphasise some values more than others, on seven key dimensions: cultures do not embody one value *or* another on each dimension, but differ in the amount of emphasis placed on each.

Universalism: behaviour is governed by the standards, rules and norms of the group Eg: North America, Switzerland, Scandinavia	**Particularism**: behaviour is governed by one's relationships with a particular individual Eg: Korea, China, Indonesia
Individualism: emphasis is on the individual and individual contribution, the 'I' identity and independence Eg: US, Eastern Europe, Denmark, Nigeria	**Collectivism**: emphasis is on the group/team contribution, the 'we' identity (firm, family) and interdependence Eg: Mexico, Indonesia, Japan, India

Affective: Issues are dealt with emotionally; emotions are openly expressed and displayed Eg: Middle East, Southern Europe	**Neutral**: issues are dealt with rationally and unemotionally, with a focus on goals Eg: Japan, Germany, UK, China, Korea
Specific: work and non-work roles and relationships are kept separate Eg: Netherlands, Sweden, US, UK	**Diffuse**: work and non-work roles and relationships are integrated and merged Eg: China, Singapore, Korea
Achievement: status is based on personal attainments and abilities Eg: North America, Norway, Austria	**Ascription**: status is based on attributes ascribed to age, gender, background etc Eg: Egypt, Indonesia, Korea, Spain, South America
Past/present: the future is seen as growing from the past, history and tradition Eg: France, Japan, UK	**Future**: the future is seen as created fresh from a 'zero base' Eg: US, Netherlands
Internal control: individuals are in control of their own lives: they shape events Eg: North America, UK, Israel, Austria	**External control**: nature and other external forces control much of life: individuals adapt Eg: Japan, Egypt, China

ACTIVITY 6 (NO TIME LIMIT)

Prepare (and if possible, give) a 'cultural briefing' to someone of another culture, explaining what you think are the important points about your culture in a work/business setting. (You may like to use either the Hofstede or Trompenaars model as a guide.) What are the top ten things a foreigner would need to know if doing business or working in your country? Describe it as you see it.

If possible, encourage the other person to give you a similar briefing and highlight the differences between his or her culture and your own. Consider any information that surprised you, or the other person: what does this say about cultural assumptions?

4.5 MANAGING CULTURAL DIFFERENCES

We have already discussed some of the specific HRM policies involved in managing diversity, in Chapter 10. However, it is worth noting that cultural diversity in the workplace also requires:

- **Cultural sensitivity:** the awareness of the potential differences in perception and behaviour that arise from diversity.

- **Cultural intentionality:** 'the ability to generate the thoughts, words and behaviours necessary to communicate and work effectively with a variety of diverse groups and individuals'. (Ivey *et al*, 1993)

'Rather than knowing *what* to do in country X, or whether national or functional cultures are more important in multicultural teams, what is necessary is to know *how to assess the potential impact* of culture, national or otherwise, on performance'. (Schneider and Barsoux, 1997)

Attention may have to be given to cultural values and norms around:

(a) **Teambuilding**

    (i) *Specificity/diffusion.* Forced camaraderie may violate the boundaries between work and non-work relationships.

    (ii) *Individualism/collectivism.* Teamworking and rewards may be more congenial to some cultures than to others.

(b) **Communication**

    (i) *Language.* Language dominance may create a power or contribution imbalance in a team or negotiation.

    (ii) *Communication patterns and styles.* Norms may have to be negotiated within a team or organisation in regard to: the balance of task and social communication; the style and pace of decision-making and negotiation; the nature of conflict and the style of conflict management; preferences for face-to-face or written media; the role of feedback and the style in which it is appropriately given.

    (iii) *Inclusive language.* Ensuring that barriers to intercultural communication are not created by phrases that exclude or give offence. Biased language may reflect inappropriate or demeaning attitudes or stereotypes.

    (iv) *Encouraging, integrating and balancing diverse contributions.* Making sure that all members are heard and that their views are properly considered.

    (v) *Different cultural values about interaction.* Some people may prefer to raise issues or ideas one-to-one rather than in a group; or in private rather than in public; or in social rather than formal settings.

(c) **Expectations of roles and relationships**

    (i) Roles and styles of leadership and team member contribution

    (ii) Appropriate degrees of formality and informality

    (iii) The role of women, younger people and other (traditionally non-dominant) groups in business contexts

Different expectations can be acknowledged by corporate 'diversity briefings' and awareness training. They should also be brought into the open and negotiated as part of a team 'contract' by line managers and team leaders.

The key aim is to avoid not only discrimination and harassment, but disempowerment of people from different cultures: to ensure that they are able to make a full contribution to the organisation.

CHAPTER ROUNDUP

- International HRM is the process of employing and developing people in international organisations. It means working across national boundaries to formulate and implement strategies, policies and practices which can be applied to an international workforce.

- Key challenges of international HRM include: the complexity of the workforce mix; the management of diversity; the need for communication; and the resourcing of 'worldwide capabilities'.

- Global HR issues will impact on the internationalisation, human resourcing and human resource development strategies of the organisation. Current practical issues affecting HR practitioners include: the trend towards offshoring and the legal ramifications of labour mobility.

- Issues in the European labour market relate to the mobility of labour, European Monetary Union, cultural and linguistic differences and continuing differences in national law and practice for companies exploring the possibilities of pan-European HRM.

- Despite some convergence in (or harmonisation of) the structure, technology and terminology of HRM across the 'global village', there is still enough diversity to support strategies of divergence. Certain aims and activities of HRM are international – but they are 'done' differently.

- Differences in policy and practice may arise from cultural factors, national law and regulation, structural factors (such as education, demographics, infrastructure, politics), employee relations traditions and ideologies, and economic and social development.

- Two influential models of the national cultural differences impacting on the workplace are the Hofstede model and the Trompenaars model.

- Managers need to exercise cultural sensitivity and intentionality, responding flexibly to cultural differences, in order to support organisational diversity policy.

QUICK QUIZ

1   What are the seven key characteristics (7 Cs) of international HR management?

2   What is 'offshoring'?

3   How can managers develop cross-cultural skills?

4   Outline the HR implications of European Union.

5   What aspects of HRM can be said to show 'convergence' across national boundaries?

6   What is 'comparative HRM'?

7   What are the manifestations of culture?

8   Explain the terms 'power distance, 'uncertainty avoidance', 'individualism' and 'masculinity' as they are used in the Hofstede model.

9   What are the seven dimensions on which Trompenaars distinguished national culture?

10   What is 'cultural intentionality'?

ANSWERS TO QUICK QUIZ

1   Cosmopolitan, culture, compensation, communication, co-ordination, competence, consultancy.   (see Para 1.2)

2   Organisations in developed countries outsourcing functions to another group company or third party overseas.   (Para 1.4)

3   Diversified work experience; awareness/skills training; networking; continuous learning through cross-cultural interactions.   (Para 1.5)

4   See Paragraph 2.2 for a full answer.

5   Basic HR activities (HRP, recruitment, selection, appraisal, training and so on); the broad aims of HRM (attract, retain, motivate, develop); technical terms and techniques (job evaluation, quality circles)   (Para 3.1)

6   A systematic method of investigation relating to two or more countries, which seeks to explain the patterns and variations encountered in cross-national HRM.   (Para 3.3)

7   Behaviour, artefacts, rituals, values and beliefs.   (Para 4.1)

8   See Paragraph 4.3 for a full answer.

9   Universalism-particularism; individualism-collectivism; affective-neutral; specific-diffuse; achievement-ascription; past-present; internal control-external control.   (Para 4.4)

10   The ability to generate the thoughts, words and behaviours necessary to communicate and work effectively with a variety of diverse groups and individuals.   (Para 4.5)

ANSWERS TO ACTIVITIES

1   Barriers to a global labour market include: language; culture (eg the fact that women are discouraged from certain jobs in some cultures); differences in employment law and practice; recognition/equivalency of education/training qualifications; market rates of pay in different currencies (and cost of currency dealings); different expectations of working conditions; personal attachment of workers to family/country of origin.

2   Some of the *positive* outcomes you may have identified for off-shoring include:

   (a)   Access to a highly motivated workforce.

   (b)   Access to specialised skills and infrastructure development (in cities or areas in which facilities such as IT and call-centre services are concentrated).

   (c)   Lower HR costs, due to lower costs of wages, benefits and welfare provision.

   (d)   Potential for greater productivity, due to workforce motivation, work culture, specialisation etc.

   (e)   Corporate Social Responsibility and sustainability: creating employment and income flow in developing economies; transfer of technology and management know-how to developing economies etc.

   Some of the *negative* issues you might have identified include:

   (a)   The requirement to consult with employee representatives on redundancies, together with other redundancy procedures and compensation.

   (b)   Likely trade union resistance to the loss of jobs.

(c)   Encouragement of trade union recruiting within the company, and potential loss of morale (because of the erosion of job security) in surviving employees.

(d)   Claims of unfair dismissal by redundant employees, if relocation cannot be shown to be a justifiable 'economic, technical or organisational' reason.

(e)   Impact on employer branding, given likely poor publicity, impacting on future recruitment.

(f)   Poor PR in general, since offshoring is a highly political issue.

3   Here are just some of the many dimensions you may have come up with.

(a)   Attitudes to the balance of work, leisure and family life ('work ethic': traditionally more pronounced in northern/protestant countries of Europe than in Mediterranean cultures).

(b)   The importance attached to the individual *vis-à-vis* the group or society as a whole (individualistic like the USA; family-oriented like Latino cultures; team/organisation-oriented like Japan).

(c)   Concepts of justice, fairness and ethical dealing (definitions of 'gifts' and 'bribes', for example are fluid in Eastern cultures).

(d)   The relative value of different forms of reward and incentive (money is high-value in the US: respect and belonging have high value in Asian cultures).

(e)   Attitudes towards gender roles (women in business are less accepted in Islamic and, to a lesser extent, Asian and 'macho' Latino cultures), age (the seniority culture of Asia or the youth culture of the US and Western Europe), diversity: attitude to disabled, ethnic minorities, sexual orientation, religious beliefs (including specific traditional conflicts, eg in Northern Ireland and Islamic states).

(f)   Valued personal attributes and attainments (status attached to education; different styles of education and training).

(g)   Perceptions of continuity/stability/security (Japanese 'commitment' system) v mobility/risk/change (Western 'flexibility' model).

(h)   Styles of interpersonal communication and decision-making (formality, reticence, consensus and hierarchy in Japan: informality, directness, authority in US: differences in eye contact and body language).

And so on...

4   Whichever specific behaviours you noted in your own experience, you may have found it difficult to interpret the values underpinning them. (Why is it more respectful in a Japanese business context to offer your business card with two hands rather than with one?) The behaviours you noted may have as much to do with the particular *individual's* personality or education or profession/occupation – or the *corporate* culture in which the behaviours were learned, as with his or her national culture.

The lesson is: beware making assumptions and interpretations. When attempting to manage a diverse workforce, it may be better to *ask* (respectfully) what people find helpful.

5   (a)   A low-PD manager is likely to attempt consultative joint decision-making: high PD workers will be inexperienced and uncomfortable with such styles, preferring authoritative instruction.

(b)   A high-UA manager, expecting to find detailed and generally adhered-to rules for everything, may be horrified by the adhocracy of a low-UA organisation: if (s)he attempts to impose a high-UA culture, there may be resistance from low-UA employees and management.

(c)   A high-individuality manager may implement MBO on the basis of individual performance targets, results and rewards: this may fail to motivate low-individuality workers, for whom group processes and performance is more important.

(d)   A low-masculinity manager may try to shelter the workforce from the effects of downsizing, taking time for consultation, retraining, voluntary measures and so on: this may seem unacceptably 'soft' to a high-masculinity parent firm.

6   Your own research.

Glossary

Benchmarking The 'establishment, through data gathering, of targets and comparators, that permit relative levels of performance (and particularly areas of underperformance) to be identified. Adoption of identified best practices should improve performance.

Centralisation and **decentralisation** The degree to which the authority to make decisions is held centrally by a particular group of people *or* delegated and spread to a number of individuals and groups within the organisation.

Commitment 'The relative strength of an individual's identification with, and involvement in, a particular organisation. It is characterised by at least three factors:

(a)   A strong belief in and acceptance of an organisation's goals and values
(b)   A willingness to exert considerable effort on behalf of the organisation
(c)   A strong desire to maintain membership of the organisation.'

Comparative HRM 'A systematic method of investigation relating to two or more countries, which... seeks to explain the patterns and variations encountered in cross-national HRM.'

Competence 'The set of behaviour patterns that the incumbent needs to bring to a position in order to perform its tasks and functions with competence'. (Woodruffe, 1992)

Compliance Performing according to set rules and standards, according to what you are expected and asked to do.

Cost-benefit analysis A comparison of the cost of an actual or proposed measure with an evaluation or estimate of the benefits gained from it. This will indicate whether the measure has been, or is likely to be, cost-effective – or 'worthwhile'.

Counselling A purposeful relationship in which one person helps another to help himself. It is a way of relating and responding to another person so that that person is helped to explore his thoughts, feelings and behaviour with the aim of reaching a clearer understanding. The clearer understanding may be of himself or of a problem, or of the one in relation to the other.

Dangerous occurrences 'Near misses' that might well have caused major injuries. They include the collapse of a load bearing part of a lift, electrical short circuit or overload causing fire or explosion, the malfunction of breathing apparatus while in use or during testing immediately before use, and many others.

Demography An analysis of statistics on birth and death rates, the age structure of populations, ethnic groups within communities, population movements and so on.

Direct discrimination One interested group is treated less favourably than another (except for exempted cases).

Disability 'A physical or mental impairment which has a substantial and long-term adverse effect on a person's ability to carry out normal day-to-day activities' (*Disability Discrimination Act 1995*).

Disabled person A person who has a physical or mental impairment that has a substantial and long-term (more than 12 months) adverse effect on his ability to carry out normal day to day activities. The effect includes mobility, manual dexterity, physical co-ordination, and lack of ability to lift or speak, hear, see, remember, concentrate, learn or understand or to perceive the risk of physical danger. Severe disfigurement is included, as are progressive conditions such as HIV even though the current effect may not be substantial.

Discipline 'A condition in an enterprise in which there is orderliness, in which the members of the enterprise behave sensibly and conduct themselves according to the standards of acceptable behaviour as related to the goals of the organisation'.

Emotional intelligence (EQ) Recognising our own feelings and those of others, for motivating ourselves, and for managing emotions well in ourselves and in our relationships.

Employment tribunals Independent judicial bodies which arbitrate in employment matters including unfair dismissal, employment protection and claims in relation to sexual/racial discrimination and equal pay.

Equal opportunities An approach to the management of people at work based on equal access and fair treatment irrespective of gender, race, ethnicity, age, disability, sexual orientation or religious belief.

Ergonomics The scientific study of the relationship between people and their working environment. This sphere of scientific research explores the demands that can arise from a working environment and the capabilities of people to meet these demands.

Grievance When an individual feels that (s)he is being wrongly or unfairly treated by a colleague or supervisor: picked on, unfairly appraised, discriminated against and so on.

Harassment An employee is subjected to conduct that violates his or her dignity, or creates an intimidating hostile, degrading, humiliating or offensive environment for him or her. (This now applies to conduct targeted at race, disability, sexual orientation, religious belief and – most recently – sex and gender reassignment, and age.)

'Hard model' of HRM A process emphasising 'the close integration of human resource policies with business strategy which regards employees as a resource to be managed in the same rational way as any other resource being exploited for maximum return'.

Human resource audit An investigation designed to:

(a)   Give a picture of the current structure, size and productivity of the organisation's labourforce.

(b)   Check that HR plans, systems, policies and procedures have been, and are being, carried out.

Human Resource Management (HRM) 'A strategic approach to managing employment relations which emphasises that leveraging people's capabilities is critical to achieving sustainable competitive advantage, this being achieved through a distinctive set of integrated employment policies, programmes and practices.'

Human resource planning 'A strategy for the acquisition, utilisation, improvement and retention of the human resources required by the enterprise in pursuit of its objectives.'

Indirect discrimination Recently redefined by the *Employment Equality (Sex Discrimination) Regulations 2005*. Basically, it occurs when an employer applies a provision, criterion or practice to men and women equally, but it has the effect of putting one sex at a particular disadvantage, without justification.

International HRM 'The process of employing and developing people in international organisations... It means working across national boundaries to formulate and implement... strategies, policies and practices which can be applied to an international workforce.'

Job analysis 'The determination of the essential characteristics of a job', the process of examining a job to identify its component parts and the circumstances in which it is performed (*British Standards Institute*).

Job description A broad description of a job or position at a given time (since jobs are dynamic, subject to change and variation). 'It is a written statement of those facts which are

important regarding the duties, responsibilities, and their organisational and operational interrelationships.'

Job evaluation The process of analysing and assessing the content, worth or size of jobs within an organisation, in order to rank and group them as a basis for an equitable remuneration system.

Job specification A detailed statement of the activities (mental and physical) involved in the job, and other relevant factors in the social and physical environment.

Labour market The sphere in which labour is 'bought' and 'sold', and in which market concepts such as supply, demand and price operate with regard to human resources.

Labour turnover The number of employees leaving an organisation and being replaced. The rate of turnover is often expressed as the number of people leaving, as a *percentage* of the average number of people employed, in a given period. The term *'natural wastage'* is used to describe a 'normal' flow of people out of an organisation through retirement, career or job change, relocation, illness and so on.

Major injuries Trauma like fractures other than to fingers, thumbs or toes, amputation, temporary or permanent loss of sight and any other injury which results in the person being admitted to hospital for more than 24 hours.

Managing diversity The belief that the individual differences we currently focus on under equal opportunities (gender, race, age etc) are crude and irrelevant classifications of the most obvious differences between people, and should be replaced by a genuine understanding of the ways in which individuals differ.

Multiskilling Functional versatility: the opposite of specialisation, with its tendency towards rigid job descriptions and demarcation lines between one job and another. It involves the development of versatility in the labour force, so that individuals can perform more than one task if required to do so: workers are being encouraged, trained and organised to work across the boundaries of traditional jobs and crafts.

Notifiable diseases Notifications of certain poisonings, occupational asthma, asbestos, hepatitis and many others.

Part-time employee Person with a contract or employment relationship whose normal hours of work, averaged over a period of up to a year, are less than the normal hours of comparable full-timers.

Performance appraisal The process whereby an individual's performance is reviewed against previously agreed goals, and whereby new goals are agreed which will develop the individual and improve performance over the forthcoming review period.

Performance management An approach in which there is a dual emphasis: on setting key accountabilities, objectives, measures, priorities and time scales for the following review period *and* monitoring, appraising and adjusting performance on an ongoing basis.

'Personnel management' Part of management concerned with people at work and with their relationships within an enterprise...'

Person specification Profile of the type of person the organisation should be trying to recruit for a given position: that is, the 'ideal' candidate.

Process A sequence of activities (often crossing functional and organisational boundaries) involved in achieving goals, delivering services or adding value.

Psychological contract The set of values that determines what an organisation expects of its employees, and what they expect of it, in the employment relationship.

Recruitment The part of the human resourcing process concerned with finding the applicants: it is a positive action by management, going into the labour market, communicating opportunities and information, and encouraging applications from suitable candidates.

Redundancy Defined by the *Employment Rights Act* 1996 as dismissals for the following reasons.

(a)   The employer has ceased (or intends to cease) to carry on the business for the **purposes** of which the employee was employed.

(b)   The employer has ceased (or intends to cease) to carry on the business in the **place** where the employee was employed.

(c)   The **requirements** of the business for employees to carry out work of a particular kind have ceased or diminished, or are expected to.

(d)   For reasons 'not related to the individual concerned.' (*The Trade Union Reform and Employment Rights Act 1993* says that all such dismissals shall be presumed to be for redundancy, for the purposes of statutory consultation with trade unions – though *not* for redundancy pay. This complies with the EU Directive on **collective redundancy**.)

Resignation The process by which an employee gives notice of his or her intention to terminate the employment contract.

Reward 'All of the monetary, non-monetary and psychological payments that an organisation provides for its employees in exchange for the work they perform.' (Bratton & Gold, 2007)

Reward system 'The mix of extrinsic and intrinsic rewards provided by the employer... [It] also consists of the integrated policies, processes, practices and administrative procedures for implementing the system within the framework of the human resources (HR) strategy and the total organisational system.'

Legge defined the **'soft'** version of HRM as a process whereby employees are viewed as 'valued assets' and as a source of competitive advantage through their commitment, adaptability and high level of skills and performance.

Strategic HRM 'The process of linking the human resource function with the strategic objectives of the organisation in order to improve performance'.

Strategic management 'Denotes a specific pattern of decisions and actions undertaken by the upper echelon of an organisation in order to accomplish specific outcomes and/or performance goals'.

Succession The act, process or right by which one person 'succeeds to' or takes over the office or post of another person. In a business organisation, there may be a policy whereby a 'successor' is developed to replace a more senior manager who retires or leaves.

Survivor syndrome A psychological state which involves long-term anxiety about job loss, increased loyalty to co-workers and reduced loyalty to the employer.

Talent management 'The process of ensuring that the organisation attracts, retains, motivates and develops the talented people it needs' (Armstrong, 2009). It refers to the overall process whereby an organisation systematically attracts skilled, high-quality recruits; integrates new workers into the organisation; systematically performance manages, trains and develops workers, in order to meet current and future competence requirements; and retains skilled workers within the organisation.

Tele-working The process of working from home, or from a satellite office close to home, with the aid of networked or internet-linked computers, fax machines and other ICT applications.

Victimisation An employer disadvantages workers because they have sought to exercise their legal rights or assisted others in doing so.

Welfare 'A state of faring or doing well, freedom from calamity, enjoyment of health'. In HRM terms, this implies 'efforts to improve conditions of living for a group of employees or workers'.

Work study methods Break down and measurement of the elements of a given task in order to define the standard number of staff hours per unit of output.

Bibliography

Adair, J and Allen, M (1999) *Time Management and Personal Development*. London: Hawksmere.

Adams, J S (1963) 'Toward an understanding of inequity'. *Journal of Abnormal and Social Psychology* 64/4.

Alberga, T, Tyson, S and Parsons, D (1997) 'An evaluation of the Investors in People Standard'. *Human Resource Management Journal* 7 (2).

Albrecht, K and Albrecht, S (1993) 'Added Value Negotiating'. *Training*, April pp 26-29.

Allen, A (2003) 'Out of the ordinary'. *People Management*, 4 December.

Armstrong, M (2000) *Strategic Human Resource Management: A Guide to Action*. (2nd edition). London: Kogan Page.

Armstrong, M (2003) *A Handbook of Human Resource Management Practice*. (9th edition). London: Kogan Page.

Armstrong, M (2009) *Armstong's Handbook of Human Resource Management Practice*. (11th edition). London: Kogan Page. Armstrong, M (2012) *Armstrong's Handbook of Human Resource Management Practice*. (12th edition). London: Kogan Page.

Arnold, J, Copper, C and Robertson, I (1995) *Work Psychology: Understanding Human Behaviour in the Workplace*. (2nd edition). London: Pitman.

Atkinson, J (1984) 'Manpower strategies for flexible organisations'. *Personnel Management*, August.

Atkinson, J and Meager, N (1986) *Changing patterns of Work*. London: IMS/OECD.

Barnes, P (1997) 'Teleworking'. *Chartered Secretary*, May.

Beardwell, I and Holden, L (1997) *Human Resource Management*. (2nd edition). London: Pitman.

Beer, M, Spector, B, Laurence, P, Quinn Mills, D and Walton, K (1984) *Managing Human Assets*. New York: Free Press.

Beer, M and Spector, B (1985) 'Corporate transformations in human resource management'. *HRM Trends and Challenges* (ed Walton and Lawrence). Boston, Mass: Harvard University Press.

Blyth, A (2003) 'The art of survival'. *People Management*, 1 May.

Blyton, P and Turnbull, P (1992) *Reassessing HRM*. London: Sage.

Bolton, T (1997) *Human Resource Management: An Introduction*. Oxford: Blackwell.

Bond, S (2003) 'How to effect changes in working hours'. *People Management*, 10 July.

Bottomley, C (1998) in *People Management*, 9 September.

Boxall, P F (1995) 'Building the theory of comparative HRM'. *HRM Journal*, 5 (5).

Boxall, P F and Purcell, J (2003) *Strategy and Human Resource Management*. Basingstoke: Palgrave Macmillan.

Bramley, P (1986) *Evaluation of Training: A practical guide*. London: BASIE.

Bratton, J and Gold, J (2007) *Human Resource Management: Theory and Practice*. (4th edition). Basingstoke: Palgrave Macmillan.

Brewster, C (1999) 'Strategic HRM: the value of different paradigms'. *Strategic Human Resource Management* (ed Schuler, Jackson). Oxford: Blackwell.

Bridges, W (1995) *Jobshift: How to Prosper in a Workplace Without Jobs*. London: Allen and Unwin.

Bronstein, M (2003) 'A life less ordinary'. *People Management*, 17 April.

Brown, D and Baron, A (2003) 'A capital idea'. *People Management*, 26 June.

Budhwar, P S and Mellahi, K (2006) *Managing Human Resources in the Middle East*. Abingdon, Oxon: Routledge.

Burgoyne, J (1999) *Developing Yourself, Your Career and Your Organisation*. London: Lemos and Crane.

Burns, J M (1978) *Leadership*. London: Harper and Row.

Cartright, A (2003) 'How to deal with requests for flexible working'. *People Management*, 6 November.

Chamberlain, N W and Kuhn, J (1965) *Collective Bargaining*. New York: McGraw Hill.

CIPD (1994) *Statement on Counselling in the Workplace*. London: CIPD.

Clague, I (2004) 'Soft touch strategies', posted at www.learningtechnologies.co/article on 02/03/04.

Clarke, K (2003) 'Show me the money'. *People Management*, 1 May.

Clegg, H (1976) *The System of Industrial Relations in Great Britain*. Oxford: Blackwell.

Clutterbuck, D (1991) *Everyone Needs a Mentor: How to Foster Talent Within the Organisation*. (2nd edition). London: IPM.

Connock, S (1991) *HR Vision: Managing a Quality Workforce*. London: IPM.

Constable, R and McCormick, R J (1987) *The Making of British Managers*. London: BIM.

Cooper, C (2003) 'Minority report'. *People Management*, 4 December.

Cornelius, H and Faire, S (1989) *Everyone Can Win: How to Resolve Conflict*. Sydney: Simon and Schuster Australia.

Critchley, R (1996) 'New paradigms for "sustainable employability"'. *HR Monthly*, April, pp22-23.

Cuming, M W (1993) *The Theory and Practice of Personnel Management*. London: Butterworth Heinemann.

Cushway, B and Lodge, D (1994) *Human Resource Management*. London: Kogan Page Ltd.

Dalgarno, D and Davies, P (2003) 'How to consult on collective redundancies'. *People Management*, 11 September.

Department for Education and Employment (1998) *The Learning Age: a renaissance for a new Britain*. Sheffield: DfEE.

Department for Education and Employment (1999) *Learning to Succeed: a new framework for post-16 education*. Sheffield: DfEE.

Department for Education and Employment (2000) *Labour Market and Skill Trends*. Sheffield: DfEE.

Dobler, D W, Burt D N and Lee, L (1990) *Purchasing and Materials Management*. (5th edition). New York: McGraw Hill.

Drucker, P (1955). *The Practice of Management*. London: Heinemann.

Equal Opportunities Commission (2000) *Good Practice Guide: Job evaluation schemes free of sex bias*. Manchester: EOC.

Evans, J (2003) 'DTI official hints at tougher law'. *People Management*, 10 July.

Fisher, R, Ury, W and Patton, B (1999) *Getting to Yes: Negotiating an Agreement Without Giving In*. (2nd edition). London: Random House.

Fombrun, C J, Tichy, N M and Devanno, M A (1984) *Strategic Human Resource Management*. New York: Wiley.

Fox, A (1975) *Industrial Relations and a Wider Society: Aspects of Interaction*. London: Faber and Faber.

Gardenswartz, L and Rowe, A (1993) *Managing Diversity: A Complete Desk Reference and Planning Guide*. Homewood, IL: Irwin.

Garvin, M (1993) 'Building a Learning Organisation'. *Harvard Business Review*, July-August.

Gennard, J and Judge, G (2002) *Employee Relations*. (3rd edition). London: CIPD.

Goldthorpe, J H, Lockwood, D C, Bechofer, F and Platt, J (1968) *The Affluent Worker: Industrial Attitudes and Behaviour*. Cambridge: CUP.

Goleman, D C (1998) Working with Emotional Intelligence. London: Bloomsbury.

Goss, D (1994) *Principles of Human Resource Management*. London: International Thomson Business Press.

Graham, H T and Bennett, R (1998) *Human Resources Management*. (9th edition). London: Pitman.

Gratton, L, Haily, V H, Stile, P and Truss, C (1999) *Strategic HRM*. Oxford: OUP.

Guest, D E (1989) 'Personnel and HRM: Can you tell the difference?'. *Personnel Management*, January pp 48-51.

Guest, D E (1991) 'Personnel management: the end of orthodoxy'. *British Journal of Industrial Relations* 29 (2).

Guest, D E (1999) 'Human Resource Management: the workers' verdict'. *Human Resource Management Journal* 9 (2).

Guest, D E (2001) 'Industrial relations and HRM'. *Human Resource Management: A Critical Text*. (2nd edition) (ed Storey). London: Thomson.

Guest, D E, Michie, J, Sheehan, M and Conway, N (2000) *Employment Relations, HRM and Business Performance*. London: CIPD.

Guirdham, M (1999) *Communicating Across Cultures*. Basingstoke: Palgrave.

Handy, C B (1989) *The Age of Unreason*. London: Business Books.

Handy, C B (1993) *Understanding Organisations*. Harmondsworth: Penguin.

Hargreaves, P and Jarvis, P (2000) *The Human Resource Development Handbook*. (revised edition). London: Kogan Page.

Hersey, P and Blanchard, K H (1988) *Management of Organisational Behaviour: Utilising Human Resources*. (5th edition). New Jersey: Prentice Hall.

Herzberg, F W (1966) *Work and the Nature of Man*. New York: Staples.

Higginbottom, K (2003 (a)) 'More than lip service'. *People Management*, 4 December.

Higginbottom, K (2003 (b)) 'HR in the spotlight'. *People Management*, 20 November.

Higginbottom, K (2003 (c)) 'Mind your own business'. *People Management*, 1 May.

Hofstede, G (1989) *Cultures Consequences*. Beverley Hills, CA: Sage.

Hofstede, G (1991) *Cultures and Organisations*. London: McGraw Hill.

Holmstrom, R (2003) 'Time well spent'. *People Management*, 28 August.

Honey, P and Mumford, A (1990) *The Opportunist Learner*. Maidenhead: Peter Honey.

Honey, P and Mumford, A (1992) *A Manual of Learning Styles*. (3rd edition). Maidenhead: Peter Honey.

Huczynski, A and Buchanan, D (2001) *Organisational Behaviour: An Introductory Text*. Harlow, Essex: FT Prentice Hall.

Hunt, J (1982) *Managing People in Organisations*. NY: McGraw Hill.

Huthwaite Inc (2000) *Behaviour of Successful Negotiators*. Percellville, VI: Huthwaite Inc.

Ingham, J (2003) 'How to implement a diversity policy'. *People Management*, 24 July.

Investors in People (2004) posted at www.investorsinpeople.co.uk/IIP/...CaseStudies, 12.02.04.

IPD (1998) *The IPD Guide to Outsourcing*. London: IPD.

IPM (1992) *Statement on Counselling in the Workplace*. London: IPM.

Ivey, A, Ivey, M and Simek Morgan, L (1993) *Counselling and Psychotherapy: a Multicultural Perspective*. (3rd edition). Boston, Mass: Allyn and Bacon.

Johns, E (1994) *Perfect Customer Care*. London: Random House.

Jones, B (1982) *Sleepers, Wake!: Technology and the Future of Work*. Oxford: OUP.

Kane, R and Stanton, S (1994) *Human Resource Planning in a Changing Environment*, in Nankervis, A R and Compton, R L (eds) *Readings in Strategic HRM*. Melbourne: Thomas Nelson Australia.

Katz, R (ed) *Career Issues in Human Resource Management*. New Jersey: Prentice Hall.

Kaufman, R and Keller, J M (1994) 'Levels of Evaluation: Beyond Kirkpatrick'. *HRP Quarterly* (5).

Kirkpatrick, D L (1998) *Evaluating Training Programmes: the Four Levels*. San Francisco: Berrett-Koehler.

Kohn, A (1993) 'Why incentive plans cannot work'. *Harvard Business Review*, Sep-Oct pp54-63.

Kolb, D (1984) *Experiential Learning*. New York: Prentice Hall.

Kramar, R, McGraw, P and Schuler, R (1997), *Human Resource Management in Australia*. (3rd edition). Melbourne: Addison Wesley Longman.

Lavelle, J (2007) *'On workforce architecture, employment relationships and lifecycles: expanding the purview of workforce planning and management'.* Public Personnel Management. Vol 36, No.4 pp371 – 84.

Leat, M (2007) Exploring Employee Relations. (2nd edition). Oxford: Butterworth-Heinemann.

Legge, K (1998) 'The morality of HRM'. *Experiencing HRM* (ed Mabey, Skinner and Clark). Cambridge.

Legge, K (1989) 'Human Resource Management: a critical analysis'. *New Perspectives in HRM* (ed Storey). London: Routledge.

Liff, S (2000) 'Manpower or HR planning: what's in a name?'. *Personnel Management*. (3rd edition) (eds Bach and Sisson). Oxford: Blackwell.

Livy, B (1988) *Corporate Personnel Management*. London: Pitman.

Lockett, J (1992) *Effective Performance Management*. Kogan Page.

LSC (2004 (a)), posted at www.lsc.gov.uk/National/media/News/Nationalemployersurvey on 02/02/04.

LSC (2004 (b)), posted at www.lsc.gov.uk/National/media/PressReleases/ASDAMA on 18.02.04.

Lupton, T (1974) *Wages and Salaries*. London: Penguin.

Maier, N (1958) *The Appraisal Interview*. New York: Wiley.

Manocha, R (2003) 'Catch 22'. *People Management*, 9 October.

Marchington, M, Goodman, J, Wilkinson, A and Ackers, P (1992) *New Developments in Employee Involvement*. London: HMSO.

Marchington, M, Wilkinson, A, Ackers, P and Dundon, A (2001) *Management Choice and Employee Voice*. London: CIPD.

Marchington, M and Wilkinson, A (2008) *Human Resource Management at Work*. (4th edition) London:CIPD Margolis, A (2003) 'Licenced to skill'. *People Management*, 26 June.

Martin, A O (1967) *Welfare at Work*. London: Batsford.

Maslow, A (1954) *Motivation and Personality*. New York: Harper and Row.

McClelland, D C (1987) *Human Motivation*. Cambrigde: Cambridge University Press.

McGregor, D (1987) *The Human Side of Enterprise*. London: Penguin.

Mowdray, R, Porter, L and Steers, R (1982) *Employee-Organisation Linkages* London: Academic Press.

Moxon, G R (1958) *Functions of a Personnel Department.* London: IPM.

Mullins, L (1985) 'The personnel function: a shared responsibility' *The Administrator*, May.

Mullins, L (1999) *Management and Organisational Behaviour.* (5th edition). Harlow, Essex: FT Prentice Hall.

Mullins, L (2007) *Management and Organisational Behaviour.* (8th edition). Harlow, Essex: Pearson.

Mumford, A (1994) *Management Development: Strategies for Action.* London: IPM.

Munro Fraser, J (1971) *Psychology: General, Industrial, Social.* London: Pitman.

National Skills Task Force (1998) *Towards a National Skills Agenda.* London: DfEE.

National Skills Task Force (2000) *Skills for All: research report from the NSTK.* London: DfEE.

Ouchi, W (1981) *Theory Z.* Reading, Mass: Addison Wesley.

Overman, S (2003) 'HR drives change at Levis'. *People Management*, 6 November.

Oxford Institute of International Finance (2002) *Managing Self Development.* London: OITF.

Parsloe, E and Wray, M (2000) *Coaching and Mentoring: Practical Methods to Improve Learning.* London: Kogan Page.

Pedler, M, Burgoyne, J and Boydell, T (1991) *The Learning Company.* Maidenhead: McGraw Hill.

Pedler, M, Burgoyne, J and Boydell, T (2001) *A Manager's Guide to Self Development.* (4th edition) Maidenhead: McGraw Hill.

Pedler, M, Brook, C and Burgoyne, J (2003) 'Motion Pictures'. *People Management*, 17 April.

Persaud, J (2003) 'Fitness First'. *People Management*, 11 September.

Personnel Standards Lead Body (1993) *A Perspective on Personnel.* London: PSLB.

Peters, T J and Waterman, R (1982) *In Search of Excellence.* New York: Harper and Row.

Peters, T J (1989) *Thriving on Chaos.* New York: Pan.

Peters, T J (1994) *Liberation Management.* New York: Pan.

Phillips, J (1997) *Return on Investment in Training and Performance Improvement Programs.* Houston, TX: Gulf.

Pickard, J (2003) 'Joint effort'. *People Management*, 24 July.

Plumbley, P (1991) *Recruitment and Selection.* (5th edition). Hyperion.

Prasad, R (2003) Connexions Special Supplement, *The Guardian*, January 29.

Purcell, J, Kinnie, N and Hutchinson, S (2003) 'Inside the black box'. *People Management*, 15 May.

Ream, B (1984) *Personnel Administration*. London: ICSA.

Rees, W D (1996) *The Skills of Management*. (4th edition). London: Thomson Business Press.

Redman, T and Wilkinson, A (2009) *Contemporary Human Resource Management*. Harlow Pearson.

Roberts, Z (2003 (a)) 'Barclays banks on older staff'. *People Management*, 29 May.

Roberts, Z (2003 (b)) 'BT drive for top women'. *People Management*, 11 September.

Roberts, Z (2003 (c)) 'Fast-track learning'. *People Management*, 10 July.

Rodger, A (1970) *The Seven Point Plan*. (3rd edition). London: NFER.

Roethlisberger, F J and Dickson, W J (1939) *Management and The Worker*. Harvard University Press, Cambridge, Massachusetts.

Rosenberg, M (2003) 'Best laid plans'. *People Management*, 3 April.

Schein, E H (1985) *Organisational Culture and Leadership*. San Francisco: Jossey Bass.

Schneider, S and Barsoux, J (1997) *Managing Across Cultures*. Harlow, Essex: FT Prentice Hall.

Schuler, R S (1995) *Managing Human Resources*. St Paul, Minn: West Publishing.

Senge, P (1990) *The Fifth Discipline: the Art and Practice of the Learning Organisation*. New York: Random Century.

Shepherd, C (2004) 'Assessing the ROI of training', www.fastrak-consulting.co.uk/tactix/features on 02/03/2004.

Sisson, K and Storey, J (2000) *The Realities of HRM: Managing the Employment Relationship*. Buckingham: OUP.

Sloman, M (2001) *The e-Learning Revolution*. London: CIPD.

Sloman, M (2003) 'Learning Curve'. *People Management*, 25 September.

Solomon, C M (2001) 'Managing Virtual Teams'. *Workforce*, June.

Stone, F M (1999) *Coaching, Counselling and Mentoring*. New York: AMACOM.

Storey, J (1989) 'From personnel management to human resource management', *New Perspective on HRM* (ed Storey). London: Routledge.

Storey, J (1992) *New Developments in the Management of Human Resources*. London: Routledge.

Taylor, F, (1911) *Shop Management*, Harper and Row and Project Gutenberg, http://www.gutenberg.org/dirs/etext04/shpmg10.txt, 19 August 2010.

Taylor, S (1998) *Employee Resourcing*. London: IPD.

Taylor, S (2010) *Resourcing and Talent Management*. London:CIPD. Torrington, D (1994) *International Personnel Management*. Englewood Cliffs, NJ: Prentice Hall.

Torrington, D and Hall, L (1991) *Personnel Management: A New Approach*. Englewood Cliffs, NJ: Prentice Hall.

Torrington, D, Hall, L, Taylor, S (2002) *Human Resource Management*. (5th edition). London: Pearson Education.

Torrington, D, Hall, L, Taylor, S, Atkinson, A (2011), *Human Resource Management.* (8th edition). Pearson Education Ltd, Harlow. Townsend, R (1985) *Further up the organisation.* London: Hodder and Stoughton.

Trades Union Congress (2000) *Qualifying for Racism.* London: TUC.

Trompenaars, F (1993) *Riding the Waves of Culture.* London: Nicholas Brealey.

Tulip, S (2003 (a)) 'Just rewards'. *People Management,* 25 September.

Tyson S (2006) *Essentials of Human Resource Management.* (5th Edition). Oxford: Butterworth-Heinemann.

Tyson, S and Fell, A (1986) *Evaluating the Personnel Function.* London: Hutchinson.

University for Industry (2003) 'Ufl/learndirect well placed to deliver Government's e-learning vision', posted at www.ufi.com/press/releases on 08/07/03.

Upton, R (2003) 'Star gazers'. *People Management,* 26 June.

Vroom, V (1964) *Work and motivation.* New York: Wiley.

Walsh, M (2004) 'Ill winds offshore'. *The Bulletin,* February 3.

Watkins, J (2003 (a)) 'Staff turnover hits four-year low'. *People Management,* 4 December.

Watkins, J (2003 (b)) 'Tests cut EA turnover'. *People Management,* 25 September.

Watkins, J (2003 (c)) 'Stress busters'. *People Management,* 25 September.

Watkins, J (2003 (d)) 'Serious turbulence'. *People Management,* 7 August.

Watkins, J and Staines, K (2003) 'Job firm risks discrimination'. *People Management,* 15 May.

Welch, J (2003) 'In the hiring line'. *People Management,* 26 June.

Whetten, D, and Cameron, K (2002) *Developing Management Skills.* (5th edition). New Jersey: Prentice Hall.

Whetten, D, Cameron, K and Woods, M (2000) *Developing Management Skills for Europe.* (2nd edition). Harlow, Essex: FT Prentice Hall.

Wild, A (2003) 'Pressure point'. *People Management,* 10 July.

Wood, R and Payne, T (1998) *Competency-based Recruitment and Selection.* Chichester: Wiley.

Woodruffe, C (1992) 'What is meant by a competency?' *Designing and Achieving Competency* (ed Boam and Sparrow). Maidenhead: McGraw Hill.

Woolnough, R (2003) 'Child benefits'. *People Management,* 4 December.

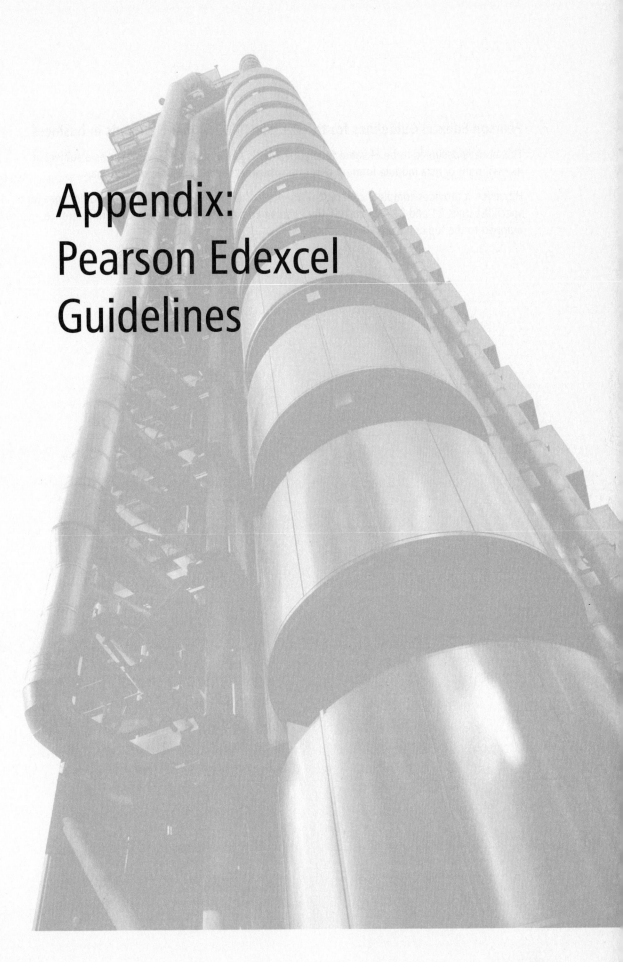

Appendix:
Pearson Edexcel
Guidelines

Pearson Edexcel Guidelines for the Pearson BTEC Higher Nationals in business

This book is designed to be of value to anyone who is studying finance, whether as a subject in its own right or as a module forming part of any business-related degree or diploma.

However, it provides complete coverage of the topics listed in the Pearson Edexcel Guidelines for specialist Units 21 and 22. We include the Pearson Edexcel Guidelines here for your reference, mapped to the topics covered in this book.

PEARSON EDEXCEL GUIDELINES

UNIT 21: HUMAN RESOURCE MANAGEMENT

Aim

This unit provides an introduction to the concepts and practices of human resource management within the United Kingdom and focuses on the management of recruitment, retention and employment cessation.

Unit abstract

Recruiting and retaining staff of the right calibre contributes to the achievement of organisational purposes. Staff must make a valued contribution to the work of the organisation. Eventually they will leave, more often than not because they find alternative employment or retire. Occasionally, however, employment has to be terminated. This unit considers how human resource management deals with these aspects of working. However, the focus of human resource management has moved beyond personnel management towards a more proactive approach that, in addition to the traditional roles associated with staff management, also considers how to get the best people and the best out of people so that they work in roles and ways that are closely aligned to organisational objectives. This often leads to the assertion by many senior managers that 'Our employees are our most valuable resource'.

Human resource management takes place against a background of organisational needs, policies and procedures that are themselves shaped by legal and regulatory requirements. The unit therefore gives consideration to the national and European legislation that has, for example, seen the introduction of a range of anti-discriminatory legislation, the significance of which can be seen regularly in high profile and often very expensive court cases. Organisations with effective human resource management policies, processes and practices will have committed, skilled employees who contribute effectively to the organisation. In competitive business contexts this is a significant contribution to maintaining a competitive advantage.

Learning outcomes

On successful completion of this unit a learner will:

1 Understand the difference between personnel management and human resource management

2 Understand how to recruit employees

3 Understand how to reward employees in order to motivate and retain them

4 Know the mechanisms for the cessation of employment.

Content	Covered in chapter(s)
1 Understand the difference between personnel management and human resources management	
Personnel management and human resource management: development of personnel management; change in contexts leading to human resource management	1, 8
Human resource management function: tasks (selection, recruitment, payroll administration, employee motivation, reward management, employment termination); training and development; performance management (planning, monitoring, recording, actioning); employee relations; working in partnership with functional areas; involvement of line managers (selection, recruitment, training, coaching, mentoring, appraisal, grievance, discipline, termination); ethical issues; equality of opportunity	1
Employment legislation: Sex Discrimination Act 1995/97; Race Relations Act 1992; Race Relations Amendment Act 2000; Equal Pay Act 1970; Disability Discrimination Acts 1995 and 2005; European Working Time Directive; Employment Act 2008; Employment Relations Act 2004; Work and Families Act 2006; national minimum wage; Data Protection Act 1998; employment tribunals	3 – 7
2 Understand how to recruit employees	
Human resource planning: definition, links (organisational purposes, organisational strategy, senior management); purpose (increased volume of business, changes to the required skills sets, employee turnover; labour cost control); time horizon (short term, medium term, long term); internal planning factors (organisational needs, demand for products and services, new products and services, new markets, technological change, location of production); workforce profiles (age, gender, ethnicity, ability, skills); external planning factors (supply and demand for labour (local, national international); government policy; labour market competition; changing nature of work; impact of technology	2
Recruitment and selection: recruitment policies, recruitment procedures, aims and objectives of the selection process; job analysis, job description (eg purpose, standard formats, responsibilities, scope of post, education and qualifications, experience); person specification (purpose, standard formats, job title, location in management line; essential and desirable attributes); recruitment methods (advertising vacancies, application methods including web-based methods, agencies, head hunters); interviews; assessment centres; tests (psychological, psychometric, aptitude, practical); resumés (CV); letters of application; references	3, 4

	Content	Covered in chapter(s)
3	**Understand how to reward employees in order to motivate and retain them**	
	Motivation: theories of motivation eg F Taylor, E Mayo, A Maslow, F Herzberg, D McGregor, D McClelland, V Vroom; relationship between motivation theories and reward; employee involvement techniques; membership of work groups board, works councils, quality circles, intra-organisational groups (transnational, national, site specific); devolved authority and responsibility; open communications; organisational culture (ethos, values, mission); national accreditation (Investors in People (IIP), Charter Mark, International Standards Organisation (ISO)	5, 6
	Monitoring: probation; appraisal, feedback; performance indicators (achievement against targets); goal theory; SMART (specific, measurable, achievable, realistic, time-constrained) targets (sales, growth, financial, waiting times, pass rates, punctuality, attendance); benchmarking	
	Reward management: job evaluation; factors determining pay, reward systems; pay; performance-related pay; pension schemes; profit sharing; employee share options; mortgage subsidies; relocation fees; bonuses; company vehicles; loans/advances; child care; school fees; corporate clothes; staff discounts; flexible working; leave; health care; extended parental leave, career breaks; cafeteria incentive schemes; salary sacrifice schemes; contracts of employment	
4	**Know the mechanisms for the cessation of employment**	
	Reasons: dismissal (wrongful, unfair, justified); termination of employment (resignation, retirement, termination of contract); redundancy; redeployment; retraining	7, 11
	Management of exit: procedures (retirement, resignation, dismissal, redundancy); legal and regulatory framework; counselling, training; employment tribunals (role, composition, powers and procedures)	

Learning outcomes and assessment criteria

Learning outcomes On successful completion of this unit a learner will:	Assessment criteria The learner can:
LO1 Understand the difference between personnel management and human resource management	1.1 distinguish between personnel management and human resource management
	1.2 assess the function of the human resource management in contributing to organisational purposes
	1.3 evaluate the role and responsibilities of line managers in human resource management
	1.4 analyse the impact of the legal and regulatory framework on human resource management
LO2 Understand how to recruit employees	2.1 analyse the reasons for human resource planning in organisations
	2.2 outline the stages involved in planning human resource requirements
	2.3 compare the recruitment and selection process in two organisations
	2.4 evaluate the effectiveness of the recruitment and selection techniques in two organisations
LO3 Understand how to reward employees in order to motivate and retain them	3.1 assess the link between motivational theory and reward
	3.2 evaluate the process of job evaluation and other factors determining pay
	3.3 assess the effectiveness of reward systems in different contexts
	3.4 examine the methods organisations use to monitor employee performance
LO4 Know the mechanisms for the cessation of employment	4.1 identify the reasons for cessation of employment with an organisation
	4.2 describe the employment exit procedures used by two organisations
	4.3 consider the impact of the legal and regulatory framework on employment cessation arrangements

PEARSON EDEXCEL GUIDELINES

UNIT 22: MANAGING HUMAN RESOURCE ISSUES

Aim

The aim of this unit is to develop an understanding of the theory and practice of human resource management focussing on current human resources practice and the impact of topical issues and legislation.

Unit abstract

This unit sets the scene by looking at the different theoretical perspectives of human resource management and exploring the differences in these approaches. A variety of changes in the labour market, and the increasing demand from employees for a more manageable work-life balance, has seen the development of much more flexible working practices. This has been the case in all sectors of the economy and in all organisations irrespective of their size or the nature of their business. Some workers have a statutory right to flexible hours and all workers can ask their employer to accommodate their needs in terms of a more flexible pattern of working. This unit examines a variety of flexible working models and looks at practical methods that have evolved in many organisations to meet the needs of employers and employees.

Some elements of the unit require an awareness of the legislative framework which determines the nature and scope of human resources policies and practices. However, the unit does not require detailed knowledge of health and safety or equal opportunities legislation. It examines the practical impact of this legislation on human resources policies and practices. New approaches are explored, including the implications for human resources management of the shift from equal opportunities to managing diversity in the workplace.

The unit explores the different methods of performance management. It examines issues that may affect performance at work, such as ill health and absenteeism and will develop learner understanding of counselling and human resources practices that support employee welfare in the workplace.

Learning outcomes

On successful completion of this unit a learner will:

1   Understand the different perspectives of human resource management

2   Understand ways of developing flexibility within the workplace

3   Understand the impact of equal opportunities in the workplace

4   Understand approaches to human resources practices in organisations.

	Content	Covered in chapter(s)
1	**Understand the different perspectives of human resource management**	
	The different perspectives of human resource management (HRM): 'soft' and 'hard' human resource management, 'loose' and 'tight' human resource management; differences between HRM and IR and personnel practices, eg use could be made of Storey's research, 1992 highlighting twenty seven points of difference; strategic approaches to HRM	8
2	**Understand ways of developing flexibility within the workplace**	
	Flexible working models: the core and periphery workforce model (Atkinson 1984); Handy's (1989) Shamrock Organisation	9
	Types of flexibility: eg numerical, functional, temporal, locational, financial	9
	Flexible working methods: eg employment of part-time and temporary staff, teleworking, homeworking, job sharing, zero hours contracts, annual hours, staggered hours, compressed hours	9
	Labour market and the need for flexibility: labour market demographics, employment statistics, local, regional and national labour markets and the growing recognition of the importance of work-life balance	9
3	**Understand the impact of equal opportunities within the workplace**	
	Discrimination in employment: forms of discrimination, eg gender, ethnicity, religion, disability, age, sexual orientation, education	10
	The legislative framework: direct and indirect discrimination; current legislation and proposed changes to the law, eg age	10
	Equal opportunities in employment: equal opportunities practices and initiatives in the workplace including initiatives such as Opportunity 2000 and positive action approaches, codes of practice, implementing policy, training within the law and monitoring; the move from equal opportunities to managing diversity	3, 10
4	**Understand the approaches to human resource practices in organisations**	
	Performance management: the role, purpose and types of appraisal, 360 degree feedback, the skills of carrying out appraisals and giving feedback, the link of appraisals to reward management	6
	Counselling and employee welfare: the traditional welfare function – occupational health practices and policies, the management of ill health at work, costs and absenteeism, accidents at work (statistics), ergonomics, alcohol and drug abuse, HIV and AIDS, stress and stress management, workplace counselling	11
	Health and safety legislation: Health and Safety at Work Act (1974) and the role of the Health and Safety Commission, European Community Directives, eg Working Time Regulations (1998), Parental Leave (2009)	11
	Other topical issues: e-recruitment, e-learning, flexible benefits, work-life balance, employee voice, changes to pension schemes	3, 5, 9–12

Learning outcomes and assessment criteria

Learning outcomes On successful completion of this unit a learner will:	Assessment criteria The learner can:
LO1 Understand the different perspectives of human resource management	1.1 explain Guest's model of HRM 1.2 compare the differences between Storey's definitions of HRM, personnel and IR practices 1.3 assess the implications for line managers and employees of developing a strategic approach to HRM
LO2 Understand ways of developing flexibility within the workplace	2.1 explain how a model of flexibility might be applied in practice 2.2 discuss the types of flexibility which may be developed by an organisation 2.3 assess the use of flexible working practices from both the employee and employer perspective 2.4 discuss the impact that changes in the labour market have had on flexible working practices
LO3 Understand the impact of equal opportunities within the workplace	3.1 explain the forms of discrimination that can take place in the workplace 3.2 discuss the practical implications of equal opportunities legislation for an organisation 3.3 compare the approaches to managing equal opportunities and managing diversity
LO4 Understand approaches to human resources practices in organisations	4.1 compare different methods of performance management 4.2 assess the approaches to the practice of managing employee welfare in a selected organisation 4.3 discuss the implications of health and safety legislation on human resources practices 4.4 evaluate the impact of one topical issue on human resources practices

Index

Notes

Notes

Notes

Notes

Review Form – Business Essentials – Human Resource Management (07/13)

BPP Learning Media always appreciates feedback from the students who use our books. We would be very grateful if you would take the time to complete this feedback form, and return it to the address below.

Name: _____   Address: _____

_____

_____

How have you used this Course Book?
(Tick one box only)

☐ Home study (book only)

☐ On a course: college _____

☐ Other _____

Why did you decide to purchase this Course Book? *(Tick one box only)*

☐ Have used BPP Learning Media Course Books in the past

☐ Recommendation by friend/colleague

☐ Recommendation by a lecturer at college

☐ Saw advertising

☐ Other _____

During the past six months do you recall seeing/receiving any of the following?
(Tick as many boxes as are relevant)

☐ Our advertisement

☐ Our brochure with a letter through the post

Your ratings, comments and suggestions would be appreciated on the following areas

	Very useful	Useful	Not useful
Introductory pages	☐	☐	☐
Topic coverage	☐	☐	☐
Summary diagrams	☐	☐	☐
Chapter roundups	☐	☐	☐
Quick quizzes	☐	☐	☐
Activities	☐	☐	☐
Discussion points	☐	☐	☐

	Excellent	Good	Adequate	Poor
Overall opinion of this Course book	☐	☐	☐	☐

Do you intend to continue using BPP Learning Media Business Essentials Course Books?   ☐ Yes   ☐ No

Please note any further comments and suggestions/errors on the reverse of this page.

The BPP author of this edition can be emailed at: pippariley@bpp.com

Please return this form to: Pippa Riley, BPP Learning Media Ltd, FREEPOST, London, W12 8AA

Review Form (continued)

Please note any further comments and suggestions/errors below